Corporate Bond Portfolio Management

Corporate Bond Portfolio Management

Leland E. Crabbe, Ph.D.

Frank J. Fabozzi, Ph.D., CFA

JOHN WILEY & SONS

Published by John Wiley & Sons, Inc.
Published simultaneously in Canada.

ISBN: 0-471-21827-8

Printed in the United States of America.

10 9 8 7 6 5 4 3 2 1

About the Authors

Leland E. Crabbe is a fixed income portfolio manager at Credit Suisse Asset Management in New York, and global head of emerging market debt. He received his Ph.D. in Economics from the University of California at Los Angeles in 1988. Subsequent to that, he worked for the Federal Reserve Board in Washington, DC as an economist in the capital market section, focusing on corporate bond and high yield research. From 1994 to 1998, he worked at Merrill Lynch in various capacities: in research as Merrill's Corporate Bond Strategist; in corporate bond syndicate as a developer of structured corporate bonds; and in emerging market bond trading.

Frank J. Fabozzi is editor of the *Journal of Portfolio Management* and an Adjunct Professor of Finance at Yale University's School of Management. He is a Chartered Financial Analyst and Certified Public Accountant. Dr. Fabozzi is on the board of directors of the Guardian Life family of funds and the BlackRock complex of funds. He earned a doctorate in economics from the City University of New York in 1972 and in 1994 received an honorary doctorate of Humane Letters from Nova Southeastern University. Dr. Fabozzi is a Fellow of the International Center for Finance at Yale University.

Preface

The purpose of this book is to present the essential elements of corporate bond portfolio management. We develop a framework to assess the key risks in the corporate bond market, such as credit risk, interest rate risk, and redemption risk. Also, along with covering the key features of corporate bonds, we discuss trading, yield curve, and sector strategies.

We have grouped the 18 chapters in this book into four major sections:

Section I: An Introduction to Corporate Bonds
Section II: Corporate Bond Valuation and Price Dynamics
Section III: Corporate Credit Risk
Section IV: Redemption Analysis

The material in those four sections gives portfolio managers the state-of-the-art analytical tools to enhance returns and control risk.

Several of the chapters in this book draw from research Leland Crabbe conducted while at the Federal Reserve Board in Washington D.C. in the early 1990s, next at Merrill Lynch in the mid-1990s, and more recently at Credit Suisse Asset Management. In particular, we would like to acknowledge permission granted by Merrill to use substantial portions of selected published research that he prepared when he was employed as an analyst at that firm. Specifically, the following material, all published and copyrighted by Merrill Lynch, Pierce, Fenner & Smith, was used in this book:

"Deferrable Bonds: An Analysis of Trust Preferreds and Related Securities" (January 2, 1997). Portions of this material appear in Chapter 14.

"An Introduction to Spread Curve Strategies" (November 7, 1996). This piece is the basis of Chapter 9.

"A Framework for Corporate Bond Strategy" (September 16, 1994). This piece is the core of Chapter 13.

"Corporate Yield Volatility — Part 1" (December 12, 1994). Portions of this material appear in Chapter 7.

"Corporate Yield Volatility — Part 2" (June 5, 1995). This material was used in the preparation of Chapter 17.

"The Putable Bond Market: Structure, Historical Experience, and Strategies" co-authored with Panos Nikoulis, former Analyst at Merrill Lynch (December 1997). A few sections of this material are used in Chapter 18.

We also wish to acknowledge that parts of Chapters 2 and 15 draw from material coauthored by Richard Wilson and Frank J. Fabozzi that was published in *Corporate Bonds: Structures & Analysis* (Frank J. Fabozzi Associates).

We thank Professor Edward Altman for allowing us to use some tables from his research on corporate bond defaults and recoveries and Standard & Poor's for allowing us to use the transition matrix in Chapter 11.

In addition, we are thankful for the discussions, comments, and encouragement from the following individuals: Michele Beach, Jane Brauer, Lea Carty, Dean Crowe, Jerry Fons, Marty Fridson, Rob Goldberg, Pat Hannon, Jean Helwege, Frank Jones, Bob Justich, Bill Kipp, Jerry Lucas, Phillip Mack, Bob Maddox, Steven Mann, Pamela Moulton, Lalit Narayan, Bryan Niggli, Joyce Payne, Peggy Pickering, Mitch Post, Scott Primrose, John Rea, Tony Rodriguez, Fred Roemer, Mary Rooney, Daniel Rossner, Steve Renehan, Tom Sowanick, Jeanne Sdroulas, Paul Stephenson, Joe Taylor, Chris Turner, Don Ullmann, Tom White, and Richard Wilson.

Finally, we are grateful to Jenny Sicat for careful reading and criticism, and to Megan Orem for editorial assistance.

Leland E. Crabbe
Frank J. Fabozzi

Table of Contents

Chapter 1

Introduction

The idea that investors demand higher returns for higher risks is the cornerstone of portfolio management. That idea is also a central tenet of corporate bond portfolio management, and it is a recurring theme in this book. Corporate bonds are exposed to a variety of risks, including interest rate risk, credit risk, liquidity risk, industry risk, cyclical risk, and company-specific event risk. As compensation for these and other risks, investors demand that corporate bond portfolios have higher expected returns than bond portfolios with lower risks.

The purpose of this book is to present the essential elements of corporate bond portfolio management. Before embarking on our analysis of the returns and risks of corporate bonds, we begin with a description of the bonds themselves. An important characteristic of a corporate bond is its credit rating. By convention, corporate bonds are rated investment-grade by the major rating agencies, while bonds rated below investment-grade are considered high-yield or "junk" bonds. In Chapter 2, we describe the key features of a corporate bond indenture, such as the bond's security, seniority, maturity, and coupon rate.

Modifications to the features of corporate bonds occur occasionally, as a result of tinkering by corporate borrowers and investment bankers. Most of the modifications have short lives, however, and most corporate bonds have standardized features. Nevertheless, the market has permanently adopted a few innovations that are highly desired by both investors and corporate borrowers. For example, as discussed in Chapter 3, medium-term notes and structured notes have greater flexibility than traditional corporate bonds, which makes them more attractive for issuers and investors. Structured notes, which have nontraditional coupon formulas, give investors the opportunity to obtain securities with desirable risk characteristics. Convertible bonds, which give investors the option to convert into common stock, also fill an important role in the financial markets. In Chapter 4, we analyze the features, valuation, and investment characteristics of convertible bonds.

A solid understanding of valuation and interest rate risk measurement is a prerequisite for making informed judgments about bond portfolio risks and returns. For option-free corporate bonds, valuation is fairly straightforward. In Chapter 5, we present the valuation framework, as well as various measures of corporate bond yields and spreads. The yield spread is defined as the difference between the corporate bond yield and the yield on a benchmark security, usually a Treasury bond with the same maturity. In a portfolio context, the portfolio's yield spread measures the portfolio's excess yield over a benchmark, such as a corporate bond index or an investment-grade aggregate index.

1

One of the first lessons in fixed income is the distinction between a bond's yield and its return: because markets fluctuate, yields can differ substantially from subsequent returns. The risk that yields will differ from returns is called interest rate risk. In Chapter 6, we review the most important measures of interest rate risk; namely, duration, convexity, yield curve risk, and spread duration. Interest rate risk exists because yields are volatile. By definition, volatility in corporate bond yields can be traced either to volatility in the yield spread or to volatility in the benchmark's yield. However, as discussed in Chapter 7, the conventional measure of yield volatility is defined in terms of the percentage change in yields, not as the absolute change in yields. As a consequence of that definition, corporate bond yield volatility is not the same as spread volatility, and corporate yields often exhibit less measured volatility than Treasury yields.

Just as the corporate yield consists of the benchmark yield plus the yield spread, the return on a corporate portfolio can likewise be separated into two categories: the return due to the Treasury or benchmark index, plus the excess return above the benchmark. In practice, most corporate bond portfolio managers monitor yield spreads and strive to earn high excess returns, as portfolio decisions about Treasury market yields and expected returns are farmed out to a Treasury portfolio manager.

Returns are difficult to forecast in all markets, including the corporate bond market. The process of estimating the expected excess return begins with the corporate bond yield spread. The realized excess return generally differs from the spread, however, as a consequence of spread volatility. In Chapter 8, we derive some useful formulas that reveal the relation between spreads and excess returns. For example, over a one-year horizon, the excess return is approximately equal to the spread minus the change in the spread times the end-of-period duration. In addition to anticipating the direction of corporate spreads, portfolio managers also evaluate the opportunities along the corporate bond yield curve. In Chapter 9, we present several strategies that allow investors to take a view on the slope of the corporate spread curve, such as box trades.

Understanding the fundamental factors that drive corporate spreads is at the heart of corporate bond portfolio management. At the macro level, the fundamentals of the corporate sector are usually closely linked to the fundamentals of the overall economy. In Chapter 10, we show that corporate spreads have exhibited a reasonably consistent pattern over past economic business cycles, reflecting the strong correlation between the economy and corporate profits. In addition to business cycle strategies, the chapter also discusses strategies for rotating across industry sectors.

Over long investment horizons, a corporate bond portfolio's excess return will usually be less than the portfolio's spread. Investors should expect the return to be less than the spread because the spread embodies several components that will subtract from returns. Exhibit 1 illustrates the major components of a portfolio's yield spread. The first component of the spread is credit risk. As explained in Chapter 11, credit risk is the risk of deterioration in a borrower's financial or operating condition. The most extreme form of credit risk is default, in which the borrower fails to make timely payments of interest or principal. For investment-grade corporate bonds, defaults occur infrequently. Nevertheless, as discussed in Chapter 12, credit risk remains the major concern for corporate bond portfolio managers because deteriorating fundamentals expose investors to increased risk of spread widening, along with downgrades of credit ratings. In Chapter 13, we present a framework for measuring expected excess returns based on credit rating transition probabilities. The analysis in that chapter shows that the migration of a portfolio's credit quality generally results in credit losses. As a consequence of those credit losses, some of the spread in a portfolio slips away, reducing the portfolio's return.

Seniority is another component of a portfolio's spread. Corporations frequently issue fixed-income obligations with different priorities in the corporate capital structure, such as bank loans, senior notes, subordinated notes, capital securities, and preferred stock. In the event of bankruptcy, investors who hold senior securities have first claim on the company's assets, while holders of subordinated securities have a weaker claim. Consequently, subordinated securities should trade with wider spreads to compensate for their risk of greater loss in the event of default. In Chapter 14, we present a method for valuing subordinated securities, with a particular focus on capital securities, which are deeply subordinated.

Exhibit 1: Components of the Corporate Portfolio Yield Spread

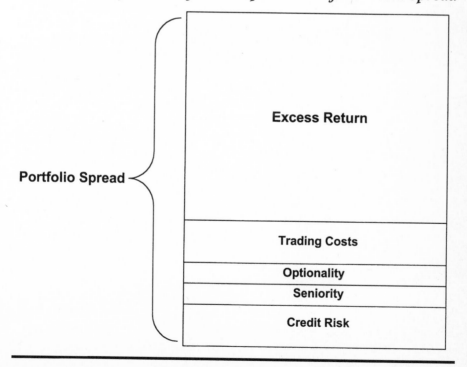

Optionality is a third component of the portfolio spread. As described in Chapter 15, corporate bonds often include embedded put, call, or sinking fund provisions that allow for early redemption before maturity. The value of those redemption options is reflected in the corporate spread. For example, a corporation's callable bonds will trade at wider spreads than its noncallable bonds at the same maturity because investors demand compensation for the risk of early redemption. As interest rates evolve over time, the value of redemption options will fluctuate, causing significant deviations between the portfolio spread and the subsequent excess return. Chapter 16 presents an analytical framework for valuing embedded options, and Chapter 17 examines how option values are affected by credit risk. In Chapter 18, we turn to the valuation of putable bonds, and we describe how putable bonds can be used in portfolio strategies.

Trading costs are another component of the corporate spread. Because trading is costly, the act of trading can eat into the portfolio spread and reduce the portfolio return. Of course, the goal of active trading is to improve portfolio returns, but that benefit of trading must be weighed against the cost. In Chapter 8, we show that trading costs depend on portfolio turnover, duration, and the bid-ask spread. We also discuss the mechanics of the secondary market, and we explore the factors that cause liquidity to vary over time and across different borrowers.

In summary, corporate bond portfolio management is a process of balancing risks and expected returns. The major risks center around the credit quality of the corporate borrower, the structure of the bonds, and the liquidity in the market. The objective of portfolio managers is not to avoid taking risk, for without risk there is little prospect of earning high returns. Rather, the job of portfolio managers is to determine whether they are being paid adequately to take risk, and to position their portfolios accordingly.

Section I

An Introduction to Corporate Bonds

Chapter 2

Features of Corporate Bonds

I n this chapter we describe the features of corporate bonds. Specifically, we look at the provisions contained in bond indentures, secured bonds and unsecured bonds, and interest payments. Another important feature of corporate bonds are provisions that may be available to issuers for allowing them to retire debt before maturity and provisions that may be available to bondholders granting them the right to alter the maturity of an issue. Understanding the nuances of these early redemption features is critical for corporate bond portfolio management. We review these features in the chapter but provide more detailed coverage in Chapter 16.

BOND INDENTURES

The buyer of a bond in a secondary market transaction becomes a party to the contract even though he or she was not, so to speak, present at its creation. Yet many investors are not too familiar with the terms and features of the obligations they purchase. They know the coupon rate and maturity, but they often are unaware of many of the issue's other terms, especially those that can affect the value of their investment. In most cases—and as long as the company stays out of trouble— much of this additional information may be unnecessary and thus considered superfluous by some. But this knowledge can become valuable during times of financial distress when the company is involved in merger or takeover activity. It is especially important when interest rates drop because the issue may be vulnerable to premature or unexpected redemption. Knowledge is power, and the informed corporate bond investor has a better chance of avoiding costly mistakes.

While prospectuses may provide most of the needed information, the *indenture* is the more important document. The indenture sets forth in great detail the promises of the issuer. Here we look at what indentures of corporate debt issues contain. For corporate debt securities to be publicly sold they must (with some permitted exceptions) be issued in conformity with the Trust Indenture Act of 1939. This act requires that debt issues subject to regulation by the Securities and Exchange Commission (SEC) have a trustee. Also, the trustee's duties and powers must be spelled out in the indenture.

Some corporate debt issues are issued under a *blanket* or *open-ended indenture*; for others a new indenture must be written each time a new series of debt is sold. A blanket indenture is often used by electric utility companies and other issuers of general mortgage bonds, but it is also found in unsecured debt.

7

The initial or basic indenture may have been entered into 30 or more years ago, but as each new series of debt is created, a supplemental indenture is written. For instance, the original indenture for Baltimore Gas and Electric Company is dated February 1, 1919, but it has been supplemented and amended many times since then due to new financings.

Another example of an open-ended industrial debenture issue is found in the Eastman Kodak Company debt prospectus dated March 23, 1988 and supplemented October 21, 1988, which says that "the Indenture does not limit the aggregate principal amount of debentures, notes or other evidences of indebtedness ('Debt Securities') which may be issued thereunder and provides that Debt Securities may be issued from time to time in one or more series."

While the promises of the issuer and the rights of the bondholders are set forth in great detail in the bond's indenture, bondholders would have great difficulty in determining from time to time whether the issuer was keeping all the promises made in the indenture. This problem is resolved for the most part by bringing in a *trustee* as a third party to the contract. The indenture is made out to the trustee as a representative of the interests of the bondholders; that is, a trustee acts in a fiduciary capacity for bondholders.

Covenants

As part of the indenture there are certain limitations and restrictions on the borrower's activities. These provisions are called *covenants*. Some covenants are common to all indentures, such as (1) to pay interest, principal, and premium, if any, on a timely basis; (2) to maintain an office or agency where the securities may be transferred or exchanged and where notices may be served upon the company with respect to the securities and the indenture; (3) to pay all taxes and other claims when due unless contested in good faith; (4) to maintain all properties used and useful in the borrower's business in good condition and working order; (5) to maintain adequate insurance on its properties (some indentures may not have insurance provisions since proper insurance is routine business practice); (6) to submit periodic certificates to the trustee stating whether the debtor is in compliance with the loan agreement; and (7) to maintain its corporate existence. These are often called *affirmative covenants* since they call upon the debtor to make promises to do certain things.

Negative covenants are those that require the borrower not to take certain actions. These are usually negotiated between the borrower and the lender or their agents. Setting the right balance between the two parties can be a rather difficult undertaking at times. In public debt transactions, the investing institutions normally leave the negotiating to the investment bankers, although they will often be asked their opinion on certain terms and features. Unfortunately, most public bond buyers are unaware of these covenants at the time of purchase and may never learn of them throughout the life of the debt. Borrowers want the least restrictive loan agreement available, while lenders should want the most restrictive, consistent with sound business practices. But lenders should not try to restrain borrowers from accepted business activities and conduct. A company might be willing to include additional restrictions (up to a point) if it can get a lower interest rate on the loan. When companies seek to weaken restrictions in their favor, they are often willing to pay more interest or give other consideration.

There is an infinite variety of restrictive covenants that can be placed on borrowers, depending on the type of debt issue, the economics of the industry and the nature of the business, and the lenders' desires. Some of the more common restrictive covenants include various limitations on the company's ability to incur debt, since unrestricted borrowing can lead a company and its debtholders to ruin. Thus, debt restrictions may include limits on the absolute dollar amount of debt that may be outstanding or may require a ratio test—for example, debt may be limited to no more than 60% of total capitalization or that it cannot exceed a certain percentage of net tangible assets. An example is Jim Walter Corporation's indenture for its 9½% Debentures due April 1, 2016. This indenture restricts senior indebtedness to no more than the sum of 80% of net installment notes receivable and 50% of the adjusted consolidated net tangible assets. The indenture for The May Department Stores Company 7.95% Debentures due 2002 prohibits the company from issuing senior-funded debt unless consolidated net tangible assets are at least 200% of such debt. More recent May Company indentures have dropped this provision.

There may be an *interest* or *fixed-charge coverage test*, of which there are two types. One, a *maintenance test*, requires the borrower's ratio of earnings available for interest or fixed charges to be at least a certain minimum figure on each required reporting date (such as quarterly or annually) for a certain preceding period. The other type, a *debt incurrence test*, only comes into play when the company wishes to do additional borrowing. In order to take on additional debt, the required interest or fixed-charge coverage figure adjusted for the new debt must be at a certain minimum level for the required period prior to the financing. Incurrence tests are generally considered less stringent than maintenance provisions. There could also be *cash flow tests* or requirements and *working capital maintenance provisions*. The prospectus for Federated Department Stores, Inc.'s debentures dated November 4, 1988, has a large section devoted to debt limitations. One of the provisions allows net new debt issuance if the consolidated coverage ratio of earnings before interest, taxes, and depreciation to interest expense (all as defined) is at least 1.35 to 1 through November 1, 1989, 1.45 to 1 through November 1, 1990, 1.50 to 1 through November 1, 1991, and at least 1.60 to 1 thereafter.

Some indentures may prohibit subsidiaries from borrowing from all other companies except the parent. Indentures often classify subsidiaries as restricted or unrestricted. Restricted subsidiaries are those considered to be consolidated for financial test purposes; unrestricted subsidiaries (often foreign and certain special-purpose companies) are those excluded from the covenants governing the parent. Often, subsidiaries are classified as unrestricted in order to allow them to finance themselves through outside sources of funds.

Limitations on dividend payments and stock repurchases may be included in indentures. Often, cash dividend payments will be limited to a certain percentage of net income earned after a specific date (often the issuance date of the debt and called the "peg date") plus a fixed amount. Sometimes the dividend formula might allow the inclusion of the net proceeds from the sale of common stock sold after the peg date. In other cases, the dividend restriction might be so worded as to prohibit the declaration and payment of cash dividends if tangible net worth (or other measures, such as consolidated quick assets) declines below a certain amount. There are usually no restrictions on the payment of stock dividends. In addition to dividend restrictions, there are often restrictions on a company's repurchase of its common stock if such purchase might cause a violation or deficiency in the dividend determination formulae. Some holding company indentures might limit the right of the company to pay dividends in the common stock of its subsidiaries.

A covenant may place restrictions on the disposition and the sale and lease-back of certain property. In some cases, the proceeds of asset sales totaling more than a certain amount must be used to repay debt. This is seldom found in indentures for unsecured debt, but at times some investors may have wished they had such a protective clause. At other times, a provision of this type might allow a company to retire high coupon debt in a lower interest rate environment, thus causing bondholders a loss of value. It might be better to have such a provision where the company would have the right to reinvest the proceeds of asset sales in new plant and equipment rather than retiring debt, or to at least give the debtholder the option of tendering bonds. Some indentures restrict the investments that a corporation may make in other companies, through either the purchase of stock or loans and advances.

Finally, there may be an absence of restrictive covenants. The shelf registration prospectus of TransAmerica Finance Corporation dated March 30, 1994, forthrightly says:

> The indentures do not contain any provision which will restrict the Company in any way from paying dividends or making other distribution on its capital stock or purchasing or redeeming any of its capital stock, or from incurring, assuming or becoming liable upon Senior Indebtedness or Subordinated Indebtedness or any other type of debt or other obligations. The indentures do not contain any financial ratios or specified levels of net worth or liquidity to which the Company must adhere. In addition, the Subordinated Indenture does not restrict the Company from creating liens on its property for any purpose. In addition, the Indentures do not contain any provisions which would require the Company to repurchase or redeem or otherwise modify the terms of any of its Debt Securities upon a change of control or other events involving the Company which may adversely effect the creditworthiness of the Debt Securities.

SECURED AND UNSECURED BONDS

A corporation can issue either *secured bonds* or *unsecured bonds*. We discuss each type as follows.

Secured Bonds

By a secured bond it is meant that there is some form of collateral that is pledged to ensure repayment of the issuer's obligation. The various types of secured bonds are described as follows.

Utility Mortgage Bonds

Debt secured by real property such as plant and equipment is called *mortgage debt*. The largest issuers of mortgage debt are the electric utility companies. Other utilities, such as telephone companies and gas pipeline and distribution firms, have also used mortgage debt as sources of capital but generally to a lesser extent than electrics.

Most electric utility bond indentures do not limit the total amount of bonds that may be issued. This is called an *open-ended mortgage*. The mortgage generally is a first lien on the company's real estate, fixed property, and franchises, subject to certain exceptions or permitted encumbrances owned at the time of the execution of the indenture or its supplement. The *after-acquired property clause* also subjects to the mortgage property acquired by the company after the filing of the original or supplemental indenture.

Property that is excepted from the lien of the mortgage may include nuclear fuel (it is often financed separately through other secured loans); cash, securities, and other similar items and current assets; automobiles, trucks, tractors, and other vehicles; inventories and fuel supplies; office furniture and leaseholds; property and merchandise held for resale in the normal course of business; receivables, contracts, leases, and operating agreements; and timber, minerals, mineral rights, and royalties. Permitted encumbrances might include liens for taxes and governmental assessments, judgments, easements and leases, certain prior liens, minor defects, irregularities and deficiencies in titles of properties, and rights-of-way that do not materially impair the use of the property.

To provide for proper maintenance of the property and replacement of worn-out plant, *maintenance fund, maintenance and replacement fund*, or *renewal and replacement fund provisions* are placed in indentures. These clauses stipulate that the issuer spend a certain amount of money for these purposes, usually as a percentage of operating revenues or based on a percentage of the depreciable property or amount of bonds outstanding. These requirements usually can be satisfied by certifying that the specified amount of expenditures has been made for maintenance and repairs to the property or by gross property additions. They can also be satisfied by depositing cash or outstanding mortgage bonds with the trustee; the deposited cash can be used for property additions, repairs, and maintenance or in some cases—to the concern of holders of high-coupon debt—the redemption of bonds.

Another provision for bondholder security is the *release and substitution of property clause*. If the company releases property from the mortgage lien (such as through a sale of a plant or other property that may have become obsolete or no longer necessary for use in the business, or through the state's power of eminent domain), it must substitute other property or cash and securities to be held by the trustee, usually in an amount equal to the released property's fair value. It may use the proceeds or cash held by the trustee to retire outstanding bonded debt. Certainly, a bondholder would not let go of the mortgaged property without substitution of satisfactory new collateral or adjustment in the amount of the debt because the bondholder should want to maintain the value of the security behind the bond. In some cases the company may waive the right to issue additional bonds.

Although the typical electric utility mortgage does not limit the total amount of bonds that may be issued, certain issuance tests or bases usually have to be satisfied before the company can sell more bonds. New bonds are often restricted to no more than 60% to 66% of the value of net bondable property. This generally is the lower of the fair value or cost of property additions, after adjustments and deductions for property that had previously been used for the authentication and issuance of previous bond issues, retirements of bondable property or the release of property, and any outstanding prior liens. Bonds may also be issued in exchange or substitution for outstanding bonds, previously retired bonds, and bonds otherwise acquired. Bonds may also be issued in an amount equal to the amount of cash deposited with the trustee.

A further earnings test found often in utility indentures requires interest charges to be covered by pretax income available for interest charges of at least two times. The Connecticut Light and Power Company prospectus for its 6⅛% First and Refunding Mortgage Bonds, Series B due February 1, 2004, states:

> . . . the Company may not issue additional bonds under the B Provisions unless its net earnings, as defined and as computed without deducting income taxes, for 12 consecutive calendar months during the period of 15 consecutive calendar months immediately preceding the first day of the month in which the application to the Trustee for authentication of additional bonds is made were at least twice the annual interest charges on all the Company's outstanding bonds, including the proposed additional bonds, and any outstanding prior lien obligations.

Mortgage bonds go by many different names. The most common of the senior lien issues are *first mortgage bonds*. Other names used are *first refunding mortgage bonds*, *first and refunding mortgage bonds*, and *first and general mortgage bonds*.

There are instances (excluding prior lien bonds as mentioned previously) when a company might have two or more layers of mortgage debt outstanding with different priorities. This situation usually occurs because the company cannot issue additional first mortgage debt (or the equivalent) under the existing indentures. Often this secondary debt level is called *general and refunding mortgage bonds* (G&R). In reality, this is mostly second mortgage debt.

As stated earlier, electric companies utilize mortgage debt more than other utilities. However, other utilities, such as telephone and gas companies, also have mortgage debt. Gas pipeline companies also use mortgage debt. Here, again, the issuance tests are similar to those for the electric issues, as are the mortgage liens. However, the pipeline companies may have an additional clause subjecting certain gas purchase and sale contracts to the mortgage lien.

Other Mortgage Bonds

Nonutility companies do not offer much mortgage debt nowadays; the preferred form of debt financing is unsecured. In the past, railroad operating companies were frequent issuers of mortgage debt. In many cases, a wide variety of secured debt might be found in a company's capitalization. One issue may have a first lien on a certain portion of the right of way and a second mortgage on another portion of the trackage, as well as a lien on the railroad's equipment, subject to the prior lien of existing equipment obligations. Certain railroad properties are not subject to such a lien. Railroad mortgages are often much more complex and confusing to bond investors than other types of mortgage debt.

In the broad classification of industrial companies, only a few have first mortgage bonds outstanding. While electric utility mortgage bonds generally have a lien on practically all of the company's property, industrial companies that issue mortgage debt have more limited liens. Mortgages may also contain maintenance and repair provisions, earnings tests for the issuance of additional debt, release and substitution of property clauses, and limited after-acquired property provisions. In some cases, shares of subsidiaries might also be pledged as part of the lien.

Some mortgage bonds are secured by a lien on a specific property rather than on most of a company's property, as in the case of an electric utility. For example, Humana Inc. sold a number of small issues of first mortgage bonds secured by liens on specific hospital properties. Although technically mortgage bonds, the basic security is centered on Humana's continued profitable operations. Because the security is specific rather than general, investors are apt to view these bonds as less worthy or of a somewhat lower ranking than fully secured or general lien issues. As the prospectuses say, the bonds are general obligations of Humana Inc. and also secured by the first mortgage.

Other Secured Bonds

Corporate bonds can be secured by many different assets. For example, an issue can be secured by a first priority lien on substantially all of the issuer's real property, machinery, and equipment, and by a second priority lien on its inventory, accounts receivables, and intangibles.

Collateral trust debentures, bonds, and notes are secured by financial assets such as cash, receivables, other notes, debentures or bonds, and not by real property. Collateral trust notes and debentures have been issued by companies engaged in vehicle leasing, such as RLC Corporation, Leaseway Transportation Corporation, and Ryder System, Inc. The proceeds from these offerings were advanced to various subsidiaries in exchange for their unsecured promissory notes, which, in turn, were pledged with the trustees as security for the parent company debt. These pledged notes may later become secured by liens or other claims on vehicles. Protective covenants for these collateralized issues may include limitations on the equipment debt of subsidiaries, on the consolidated debt of the issuer and its subsidiaries, on dividend payments by the issuer and the subsidiaries, and on the creation of liens and purchase money mortgages, among other things.

The eligible collateral is held by a trustee and periodically marked to market to ensure that the market value has a liquidation value in excess of the amount needed to repay the entire outstanding bonds and accrued interest. If the collateral is insufficient, the issuer must, within several days, bring the value of the collateral up to the required amount. If the issuer is unable to do so, the trustee would then sell collateral and redeem bonds. Another collateralized structure allows for the defeasance or "mandatory collateral substitution," which provides the bondholder assurance that the same interest payments will be received until maturity. Instead of redeeming the bonds with the proceeds of the collateral sale, the proceeds are used to purchase a portfolio of U.S. government securities in such an amount that the cash flow is sufficient to meet the principal and interest payments on the mortgage-backed bond. Because of the structure of these issues, the rating agencies have assigned triple-A ratings to them. The rating is based on the strength of the collateral and the issues' structure, not on the issuers' credit standing.

Equipment Trust Financing: Railroads

Railroads and airlines have financed much of their rolling stock and aircraft with secured debt. The securities go by various names such as *equipment trust certificates* (ETCs) in the case of railroads, and secured equipment certificates, guaranteed loan certificates, and loan certificates in the case of airlines. We look at railroad equipment trust financing first for two reasons: (1) the financing of railway equipment under the format in general public use today goes back to the late nineteenth century and (2) it has had a superb record of safety of principal and timely payment of interest, more traditionally known as dividends. Railroads probably constitute the largest and oldest group of issuers of secured equipment financing.

Probably the earliest instance in U.S. financial history in which a company bought equipment under a conditional sales agreement (CSA) was in 1845 when the Schuylkill Navigation Company purchased some barges. Over the years secured equipment financing proved to be an attractive way for railroads—both good and bad credits—to raise the capital necessary to finance rolling stock. Various types of instruments were devised—equipment bonds (known as the New York

Plan), conditional sales agreements (also known as the New York CSA), lease arrangements, and the Philadelphia Plan equipment trust certificate. The New York Plan equipment bond has not been used since the 1930s. The Philadelphia Plan ETC is the form used for most, if not all, public financings in today's market.

The ratings for ETCs are higher than on the same company's mortgage debt or other public debt securities. This is due primarily to the collateral value of the equipment, its superior standing in bankruptcy compared with other claims, and the instrument's generally self-liquidating nature. The railroad's actual credit worthiness may mean less for some equipment trust investors than for investors in other rail securities or, for that matter, other corporate paper. However, that is not to say that financial analysis of the issuer should be ignored.

Equipment trust certificates are issued under agreement that provides a trust for the benefit of the investors. Each certificate represents an interest in the trust equal to its principal amount and bears the railroad's unconditional guarantee of prompt payment, when due, of the principal and dividends (the term *dividends* is used because the payments represent income from a trust and not interest on a loan). The trustee holds the title to the equipment, which, when the certificates are retired, passes to, or vests in, the railroad. But the railroad has all other ownership rights. It can take the depreciation and can utilize any tax benefits on the subject equipment. The railroad agrees to pay the trustee sufficient rental for the principal payments and the dividends due on the certificates, together with expenses of the trust and certain other charges. The railroad uses the equipment in its normal operations and is required to maintain it in good operating order and repair (at its own expense). If the equipment is destroyed, lost, or becomes worn out or unsuitable for use (i.e., suffers a "casualty occurrence"), the company must substitute the fair market value of that equipment in the form of either cash or additional equipment. Cash may be used to acquire additional equipment unless the agreement states otherwise. The trust equipment is usually clearly marked that it is not the railroad's property.

Immediately after the issuance of an ETC, the railroad has an equity interest in the equipment that provides a margin of safety for the investor. Normally, the ETC investor finances no more than 80% of the cost of the equipment and the railroad the remaining 20%. Although modern equipment is longer-lived than that of many years ago, while there are exceptions, the ETC's length of maturity is still generally the standard 15 years.

The structure of the financing usually provides for periodic retirement of the outstanding certificates. The most common form of ETC is the serial variety. It is usually issued in 15 equal maturities, each one coming due annually in years 1 through 15.

The standing of railroad or common carrier equipment trust certificates in bankruptcy is of vital importance to the investor. Because the equipment is needed for operations, the bankrupt railroad's management will more than likely reaffirm the lease of the equipment because, without rolling stock, it is out of business. Cases of disaffirmation of equipment obligations are rare indeed. But if equipment debt were to be disaffirmed, the trustee could repossess and then try to release or sell the equipment to others. Any deficiency due the equipment debt-holders would still be an unsecured claim against the bankrupt railway company. Standard gauge, non-specialized equipment should not be difficult to release to another railroad.

The Bankruptcy Reform Act of 1978 provides specifically that railroads be reorganized, not liquidated, and subchapter IV of Chapter 11 grants them special treatment and protection. One important feature found in Section 77(j) of the preceding Bankruptcy Act was carried over to the new law. Section 1168 states that Section 362 (the automatic stay provision) and Section 363 (the use, sale, or lease of property section) are not applicable in railroad bankruptcies. It protects the rights of the equipment lenders while giving the trustee the chance to cure any defaults. Railroad bankruptcies usually do not occur overnight but creep up gradually as the result of steady deterioration over the years. New equipment financing capability becomes restrained. The outstanding equipment debt at the time of bankruptcy often is not substantial and usually has a good equity cushion built in. Equipment debt of noncommon carriers such as private car leasing lines does not enjoy this special protection under the Bankruptcy Act.

During the twentieth century, losses have been rare and delayed payments of dividends and principal only slightly less so.

Airline Equipment Debt

Airline equipment debt has some of the special status that is held by railroad equipment trust certificates. Of course, it is much more recent, having developed since the end of World War II. Many airlines have had to resort to secured equipment financing, especially since the early 1970s. Like railroad equipment obligations, certain equipment debt of certified airlines, under Section 1110 of the Bankruptcy Reform Act of 1978, is not subject to Sections 362 and 363 of the Act, namely the automatic stay and the power of the court to prohibit the repossession of the equipment. The creditor must be a lessor, a conditional vendor, or hold a purchase money security interest with respect to the aircraft and related equipment. The secured equipment must be new, not used. Of course, it gives the airline 60 days in which to decide to cancel the lease or debt and to return the equipment to the trustee. If the reorganization trustee decides to reaffirm the lease in order to continue using the equipment, it must perform or assume the debtor's obligations, which become due or payable after that date, and cure all existing defaults other than those resulting solely from the financial condition, bankruptcy, insolvency, or reorganization of the airline. Payments resume including those that were due during the delayed period. Thus, the creditor will get either the payments due according to the terms of the contract or the equipment.

The equipment is an important factor. If the airplanes are of recent vintage, well maintained, fuel efficient, and relatively economical to operate, it is more likely that a company in distress and seeking to reorganize would assume the equipment lease. On the other hand, if the outlook for reorganization appears dim from the outset and the airplanes are older and less economical, the airline could very well disaffirm the lease. In this case, releasing the aircraft or selling it at rents and prices sufficient to continue the original payments and terms to the security holders might be difficult. Of course, the resale market for aircraft is on a plane-by-plane basis and highly subject to supply and demand factors. Multimillion-dollar airplanes have a somewhat more limited market than do boxcars and hopper cars worth only $30,000.

In the event of a loss or destruction of the equipment, the company may substitute similar equipment of equal value and in as good operating condition and repair and as airworthy as that which was lost or destroyed. It also has the option to redeem the outstanding certificates with the insurance proceeds.

An important point to consider is the equity owner. If the airline runs into financial difficulty and fails to make the required payments, the owner may step in and make the rental payment in order to protect its investment. The carrier's failure to make a basic rental payment within the stipulated grace period is an act of default but is cured if the owner makes payment. Thus, a strong owner lends support to the financing, and a weak one little.

Do not be misled by the title of the issue just because the words *secured* or *equipment trust* appear. Investors should look at the collateral and its estimated value based on the studies of recognized appraisers compared with the amount of equipment debt outstanding. Is the equipment new or used? Do the creditors benefit from Section 1110 of the Bankruptcy Reform Act? As the equipment is a depreciable item and subject to wear, tear, and obsolescence, a sinking fund starting within several years of the initial offering date should be provided if the debt is not issued in serial form. Of course, the ownership of the aircraft is important as just noted. Obviously, one must review the obligor's financial statements because the investor's first line of defense depends on the airline's ability to service the lease rental payments.

Enhanced Equipment Trust Certificates (EETCs) also draw on the strength of Section 1100, as well as credit enhancements to reduce risk to investors. EETCs combine features of corporate bonds and asset-backed securities. Like corporate bonds and ETCs, the credit risk of EETCs is linked to the corporate borrower, namely, the airline. Like asset-backed securities, EETCs are issued in several tranches with different credit ratings and substantial overcollateralization. As a result of those structural enhancements, EETCs afford investors with a cushion of protection and liquidity support, which also results in tighter yield spreads and higher credit ratings than unsecured debt of the same airline.

Unsecured Bonds

We have discussed many of the features common to secured debt. Take away the collateral and we have unsecured debt. Unsecured debt, like secured debt, comes in several different layers or levels of claim against the corporation's assets. But in the case of unsecured debt, the nomenclature attached to the debt issues sounds less substantial. For example, "general and refunding mortgage bonds" may sound more important than "subordinated debentures," even though both are basically second claims on the corporate body.

Subordination of the debt instrument might not be apparent from the issue's name. This is often the case with bank and bank-related securities. Chase Manhattan Bank (National Association) had issues with the term "Capital Notes." It did not sound like a subordinated debt instrument to most inexperienced investors unfamiliar with the jargon of the debt world. Yet capital notes are junior securities. We analyze subordination in greater detail in Chapter 14.

Some debt issuers have other companies guarantee their loans. This is normally done when a subsidiary issues debt and the investors want the added protection of a third-party guarantee. The use of guarantees makes it easier and more convenient to finance special projects and affiliates, although guarantees are extended to operating company debt. There are also other types of third-party credit enhancements. Some captive finance subsidiaries of industrial companies enter into agreements requiring them to maintain fixed charge coverage at such a level so that the securities meet the eligibility standards for investment by insurance companies under New York State law. The required coverage levels are maintained by adjusting the prices at which the finance company buys its receivables from the parent company or through special payments from the parent company. These supplemental income maintenance agreements, while usually not part of indentures, are important considerations for bond buyers.

Another credit enhancing feature is the letter of credit (LOC) issued by a bank. An LOC requires the bank to make payments to the trustee when requested so that monies will be available for the bond issuer to meet its interest and principal payments when due. Thus the credit of the bank under the LOC is substituted for that of the debt issuer. Insurance companies also lend their credit standing to corporate debt, both new issues and outstanding secondary market issues.

While a guarantee or other type of credit enhancement may add some measure of protection to a bondholder, caution should not be thrown to the wind. In effect, one's job may even become more complex because an analysis of both the issuer and the guarantor should be performed. In many cases, only the latter is needed if the issuer is merely a financing conduit without any operations of its own. However, if both concerns are operating companies, it may very well be necessary to analyze both because the timely payment of principal and interest ultimately will depend on the stronger party. A downgrade of the enhancer's claims-paying ability reduces the value of the bonds.

Negative Pledge Clause

One of the important protective provisions for unsecured debtholders is the *negative pledge clause*. This provision, found in most senior unsecured debt issues and a few subordinated issues, prohibits a company from creating or assuming any lien to secure a debt issue without equally securing the subject debt issue(s) (with certain exceptions). Designed to prevent other creditors from obtaining a senior position at the expense of existing creditors, "it is not intended to prevent other creditors from sharing in the position of debenture holders." Again, it is not necessary to have such a clause unless the issuer runs into trouble. But like insurance, it is not needed until the time that no one wants arrives.

Negative pledge clauses are not just boiler plate material added to indentures and loan agreements to give lawyers extra work. They have provided additional security for debtholders when the prognosis for corporate survival was bleak. International Harvester Company and International Harvester Credit Company had negative pledge clauses that became operative when they secured sorely needed bank financing.

PAR VALUE

The *par value* of a bond is the amount that the issuer agrees to repay the bondholder by the maturity date. This amount is also referred to as the *principal, face value, redemption value*, and *maturity value*. Bonds can have any par value.

Because bonds can have a different par value, the practice is to quote the price of a bond as a percentage of its par value. A value of "100" means 100% of par value. So, for example, if a bond has a par value of $1,000 and the issue is selling for $900, this bond would be said to be selling at 90. If a bond with a par value of $5,000 is selling for $5,500, the bond is said to be selling for 110.

When computing the dollar price of a bond in the United States, the bond must first be converted into a price per US$1 of par value. Then the price per $1 of par value is multiplied by the par value to get the dollar price. Here are examples of what the dollar price of a bond is given the price quoted for the bond in the market and the par amount involved in the transaction:

Quoted price	Price per $ par value	Par value	Dollar price
90½	0.9050	$1,000	905.00
102¾	1.0275	$5,000	5,137.50
70⅝	0.7063	$10,000	7,062.50
113¹¹⁄₃₂	1.1334	$100,000	113,343.75

Notice that a bond may trade below or above its par value. When a bond trades below its par value, it is said to be *trading at discount*. When a bond trades above its par value, it is said to be *trading at a premium*. The reason why a bond sells above or below its par value is explained in Chapter 5.

INTEREST PAYMENTS

The *coupon rate*, also called the *nominal rate*, is the interest rate that the issuer agrees to pay each year. The annual amount of the interest payment made to bondholders during the term of the bond is called the coupon. The coupon is determined by multiplying the coupon rate by the par value of the bond. That is,

coupon = coupon rate × par value

For example, a bond with an 8% coupon rate and a par value of $1,000 will pay annual interest of $80 (= $1,000 × 0.08).

When describing a bond of an issuer, the coupon rate is indicated along with the maturity date. For example, the expression "6s of 12/1/2010" means a bond with a 6% coupon rate maturing on December 1, 2010.

In the United States, the usual practice for corporate bonds is for the issuer to pay the coupon in two semiannual installments. For corporate bonds issued in some markets outside the United States, coupon payments are made only once per year.

In addition to indicating the coupon payments that the investor can expect to receive over the term of the bond, the coupon rate also affects the bond's price sensitivity to changes in market interest rates. As illustrated in Chapter 6, all other factors being constant, the higher the coupon rate, the less the price will change in response to a change in market interest rates.

Zero-Coupon Bonds

Not all bonds make periodic coupon payments. Bonds that are not contracted to make periodic coupon payments are called *zero-coupon bonds*. The holder of a zero-coupon bond realizes interest by buying the bond substantially below its par value (i.e., buying the bond at a discount). Interest is then paid at the maturity date, with the interest being the difference between the par value and the price paid for the bond. So, for example, if an investor purchases a zero-coupon bond for 70, the interest is 30. This is the difference between the par value (100) and the price paid (70).

There is another type of fixed income security that does not pay interest until the maturity date. This type of zero-coupon bond has contractual coupon payments, but those payments are accrued and distributed along with the maturity value at the maturity date. These instruments are called *accrual bonds*. For example, an issuer may sell a 3-year bond with a par value of $1,000 and agree to pay 6% interest compounded semiannually at the bond's maturity. The accrued interest over this period of time would be $194.05. The issuer would then pay at maturity $1,000 plus the accrued interest of $194.05.

Step-Up Notes

There are corporate bonds and medium-term notes that have a coupon rate that increases over time. These securities are called *step-up notes* because the coupon rate "steps up" over time. For example, a 5-year step-up note might have a coupon rate that is 5% for the first 2 years and 6% for the last 3 years. Or, the step-up note could call for a 5% coupon rate for the first 2 years, 5.5% for the third and fourth years, and 6% for the fifth year. When there is only one change (or step up), as in our first example, the issue is referred to as a *single step-up note*. When there is more than one change, as in our second example, the issue is referred to as a *multiple step-up note*.

Deferred Coupon Bonds

Deferred coupon bonds combine the coupon features of standard bonds, zero coupon bonds, and step-up bonds. At the time of issuance, the coupon payments are deferred for a specific number of years. After that initial deferral period, the bonds typically pay a semiannual coupon until maturity. For example, a deferred coupon bond with a 10-year maturity may have a zero coupon for the first 5 years, and then a coupon of 9% for the final 5 years. As a result of the period of deferral, the bonds are priced at a substantial discount to par, but the discount is not as large as that of a zero-coupon bond, and deferred coupon bonds are typically structured with the expectation that the price will move near par at the end of the deferral period. Clearly, the period of deferral reduces the cash flow burden on the corporate issuer, and therefore mitigates the risk of financial distress. Deferred coupon bonds are issued frequently in the high-yield bond market, where issuers are willing to pay a yield premium to reduce their initial cash flow burden, but the structure also occasionally appears in the investment-grade market.

Payment-in-Kind Bonds

A variation of the deferred coupon bond is the *payment-in-kind* (PIK) bond. With PIKs, cash interest payments are deferred at the issuer's option until some future date. Instead of just accreting the interest as with zero-coupon bonds, the interest rate is paid out in smaller pieces of the same security, namely other pieces of the same paper. The option to pay cash or in-kind interest payments rests with the issuer, but in many cases the issuer has little choice because provisions of other debt instruments often prohibit cash interest payments until certain tests are satisfied. The bondholder just gets more pieces of paper, but these at least can be sold in the market without giving up one's original investment; zero-coupon bonds do not have provisions for the resale of the interest portion of the instrument.

Floating-Rate Securities

The coupon rate on a bond need not be fixed over the bond's life. *Floating-rate securities*, sometimes called variable-rate securities, have coupon payments that reset periodically according to some reference rate. The typical formula (called the *coupon formula*) for the coupon rate at the dates when the coupon rate is reset is as follows:

coupon rate = reference rate + quoted margin

The *quoted margin* is the additional amount that the issuer agrees to pay above the reference rate. For example, suppose that the reference rate is the 1-month London interbank offered rate (LIBOR). Suppose that the quoted margin is 120 basis points. Then the coupon formula is:

coupon rate = 1-month LIBOR + 120 basis points

So, if 1-month LIBOR on the coupon reset date is 5%, the coupon rate is reset for that period at 6.2% (5% plus 120 basis points).

The quoted margin need not be a positive value. The quoted margin could be subtracted from the reference rate. For example, the reference rate could be the yield on a 5-year Treasury security and the coupon rate could reset every 6 months based on the following coupon formula:

coupon rate = 5-year Treasury yield – 90 basis points

So, if the 5-year Treasury yield is 7% on the coupon reset date, the coupon rate is 6.1% (7% minus 90 basis points).

A *deleveraged floater* is a floater that has a coupon formula where the coupon rate is computed as a fraction of the reference rate plus a quoted margin. The general formula for a deleveraged floater is:

coupon rate = $b \times$ (reference rate) + quoted margin

where b is a value between zero and one.

Banker's Trust issued such a floater in April 1992 that matures in March 2003. This issue makes quarterly coupon payments according to the following formula:

$0.40 \times$ (10-year Constant Maturity Treasury rate) + 2.65%

with a minimum interest rate of 6%. For this issue b is 0.40 and the quoted margin is 2.65%.

It is important to understand the mechanics for the payment and the setting of the coupon rate. Suppose that a floater pays interest semiannually and further assume that the coupon reset date is today. Then, the coupon rate is determined via the coupon formula, and this is the interest rate that the issuer agrees to pay at the next coupon date 6 months from now. That is, the coupon rate is determined at the coupon reset date but paid in arrears.

Caps and Floors

A floater may have a restriction on the maximum coupon rate that will be paid at any reset date. The maximum coupon rate is called a *cap*. For example, suppose for a floater whose coupon formula is 3-month Treasury bill rate plus 50 basis points, there is a cap of 9%. If the 3-month Treasury bill rate is 9% at a coupon reset date, then the coupon formula would give a coupon rate of 9.5%. However, the cap restricts the coupon rate to 9%. Thus, for our hypothetical floater, once the 3-month Treasury bill rate exceeds 8.5%, the coupon rate is capped at 9%.

Because a cap restricts the coupon rate from increasing, a cap is an unattractive feature for the investor. In contrast, there could be a minimum coupon rate specified for a floater. The minimum coupon rate is called a *floor*. If the coupon formula produces a coupon rate that is below the floor, the floor rate is paid instead. An example of a floor would be the 6% minimum interest rate in the Bankers Trust deleveraged floater. Thus, a floor is an attractive feature for the investor. Caps and floors are effectively embedded options.

Some issues have declining floors. For example, for a Citicorp floater issue that was due September 1, 1998, the minimum rate was 7.50% through August 31, 1983, then 7.00% through August 31, 1988, and then 6.50% to maturity.

A floater can have both a cap and floor. This feature is referred to as a *collar*. There are some floaters, referred to as *drop-lock bonds*, which automatically change the floating coupon rate into a fixed coupon rate under certain circumstances.

Types of Coupon Formulas

There is a wide range of coupon formulas. Some of these formulas are discussed as follows. The reasons why issuers have been able to create floating-rate securities with offbeat coupon formulas is due to the use of derivative instruments in offering securities. These offbeat coupon formulas are typically found in structured notes.

Inverse Floaters Typically, the coupon formula for a floater is such that the coupon rate increases when the reference rate increases, and decreases when the reference rate decreases. There are issues whose coupon rate moves in the opposite direction from the change in the reference rate. Such issues are called *inverse floaters* or *reverse floaters*.

In the corporate markets, inverse floaters are created as structured notes. The coupon formula for an inverse floater is:

$$\text{coupon rate} = K - L \times (\text{reference rate})$$

where K and L are values specified in the prospectus for the issue.

For example, suppose that for a particular inverse floater K is 20% and L is 2. Then the coupon reset formula would be:

$$\text{coupon rate} = 20\% - 2 \times (\text{reference rate})$$

Suppose that the reference rate is the 3-month Treasury bill rate, then the coupon formula would be

$$\text{coupon rate} = 20\% - 2 \times (\text{3-month Treasury bill rate})$$

If at the coupon reset date the 3-month Treasury bill rate is 6%, the coupon rate for the next period is:

$$\text{coupon rate} = 20\% - 2 \times 6\% = 8\%$$

If at the next reset date the 3-month Treasury bill rate declines to 5%, the coupon rate increases to:

$$\text{coupon rate} = 20\% - 2 \times 5\% = 10\%$$

Notice that if the 3-month Treasury bill rate exceeds 10%, then the coupon formula would produce a negative coupon rate. To prevent this, there is also a floor imposed on the coupon rate. There is a cap on the inverse floater. This occurs if the 3-month Treasury bill rate is zero. In that unlikely event, the maximum coupon rate is 20% for our hypothetical inverse floater.

An example of an actual inverse floater is one issued by one of the Federal Home Loan Banks in April 1999. The issue matures in April 2002 and makes payments quarterly based on the following coupon formula:

$$\text{coupon formula} = 18\% - 2.5 \times (\text{3-month LIBOR})$$

Contractually, this inverse floater has a floor of 3% and a cap of 15.5%.

Dual-Indexed Floaters The coupon rate for a *dual-indexed floater* is typically a fixed percentage plus the difference between two reference rates. For example, the Federal Home Loan Bank System issued a floater in July 1993 (the issue matured in July 1996) whose coupon rate (reset quarterly) was as follows:

(10-year Constant Maturity Treasury rate)
− (3-month LIBOR) + 160 basis points

Range Notes There are floaters whose coupon rate is equal to the reference rate as long as the reference rate is within a certain range at the reset date. If the reference rate is outside of the range, the coupon rate is zero for that period. This floater is called a *range note* (or a *range bound floating-rate note*) and is another example of a structured note.

For example, a 3-year range note might specify that the reference rate is the 1-year Treasury rate and that the coupon rate resets every year. The coupon rate for the year is the Treasury rate as long as the Treasury rate at the coupon reset date falls within the range as specified below:

	Year 1	Year 2	Year 3
Lower limit of range	4.5%	5.25%	6.00%
Upper limit of range	5.5%	6.75%	7.50%

If the 1-year Treasury rate is outside of the range, the coupon rate is zero. For example, if in Year 1 the 1-year Treasury rate is 5% at the coupon reset date, the coupon rate for the year is 5%. However, if the 1-year Treasury rate is 6%, the coupon rate for the year is zero since the 1-year Treasury rate is greater than the upper limit for Year 1 of 5.5%.

Let's look at an actual range note. In August 1996 Sallie Mae issued one that matures in August 2003. This issue makes coupon payments quarterly. The investor earns 3-month LIBOR plus 155 basis points for every day during the quarter that 3-month LIBOR is between 3% and 9%. Interest will accrue at 0% for each day that 3-month LIBOR is outside this range. As a result, this range note has a floor of 0%.

Ratchet Bonds In 1998 a new adjustable-rate structure was brought to market by the Tennessee Valley Authority. This structure, referred to as a *ratchet bond*, has a coupon rate that adjusts periodically at a fixed margin over a reference rate. However, it can only adjust downward based on a coupon formula. Once the coupon rate is adjusted down, it cannot be readjusted up if the reference rate subsequently increases.

Stepped Spread Floaters Some issues provide for a change in the quoted margin at certain intervals over a floater's life. These issues are referred to as *stepped spread floaters* because the quoted margin could step to either a higher or lower level over the security's life. For example, consider Standard Chartered Bank's floater that matures in December 2006. From issuance until December 2001, the coupon formula is 3-month LIBOR plus 40 basis points. From December 2001 until maturity, the quoted margin "steps up" to 90 basis points, but the reference rate remains 3-month LIBOR over the life of the security.

Reset Margin Determined at Issuer Discretion There are floaters that require that the issuer reset the coupon rate so that the issue will trade at a prede-termined price (typically par or above par). These issues are called *extendible reset* bonds or *remarketed reset* notes. The coupon rate at the reset date may be the average of rates suggested by two investment banking firms. The new rate will then reflect: (1) the level of interest rates at the reset date, and (2) the margin required by the market at the reset date. The second element reflects economic conditions in the market.

Notice the difference between an extendible reset bond and a typical floater that resets based on a coupon formula. For a typical floater, the coupon rate resets based on a known margin (i.e., the quoted margin) over some reference rate. For example, suppose that the coupon formula is the 6-month Treasury rate plus 100 basis points. The 100 basis points is the quoted margin and does not change over the life of the floater. In contrast, the coupon rate on an extendible reset issue is reset based on the margin required by the market at the reset date (as determined by the issuer or suggested by several investment banking firms) for the security to trade at par value. For example, suppose that the coupon formula for an extendible reset bond is 6-month Treasury rate plus 100 basis points. At a coupon reset date suppose that investment bankers are contacted about what the price of the issue would be if the margin is 100 basis points. Assume that the investment bankers agreed that the price would be below par and that if the issue is to trade at par, the margin must be 125 basis points. Then at the coupon reset date, the coupon rate will be 6-month Treasury rate plus 125 basis points.

As a result of the coupon reset feature, an extendible bond with a long-dated maturity has the risk characteristics of a shorter-term security. In most long-dated securities, investors bear the risk of spread widening, but in an extendible bond, the risk is effectively transferred from the investor to the issuer. If the issuer's credit quality has deteriorated since the last reset date (e.g., a downgrade from single-A to double-B), the reset margin would have to increase substantially in order to make the bonds trade at par.

Noninterest Rate Indexes While the reference rate for most floaters is an interest rate or an interest rate index, a wide variety of reference rates appear in coupon formulas. This is particularly true for structured notes. The coupon for a floater could be indexed to movements in foreign exchange rates, the price of a commodity (e.g., crude oil), the return on an equity index (e.g., the S&P 500), or movements in a bond index. In fact, through financial engineering, issuers have been able to structure floaters with almost any reference rate.

The U.S. Department of the Treasury in January 1997 began issuing inflation-adjusted securities, referred to as Treasury Inflation Protection Securities (TIPS). The reference rate for the coupon formula is the rate of inflation as measured by the Consumer Price Index for All Urban Consumers (i.e., CPI-U). Corporations began to issue inflation-linked (or inflation-indexed) bonds shortly after the Treasury issuance. For example, in February 1997, J.P. Morgan & Company issued a 15-year bond that pays the CPI plus 400 basis points. In the same month, the Federal Home Loan Bank issued a 5-year bond with a coupon rate equal to the CPI plus 315 basis points and a 10-year bond with a coupon rate equal to the CPI plus 337 basis points.

Payment Frequency

Most fixed-rate corporate bond issues sold in the United States provide for the payment of interest twice a year at 6-month intervals. In the case of medium-term notes, interest is paid semiannually and at maturity if the maturity date does not coincide with the interest payment date; this is called a "short coupon." Another type of short coupon is found on some new issues where interest might accrue from the date the trade settles (i.e., the date payment is made by the purchaser to the underwriter). For example, if a new issue is sold with a settlement date of September 15 but with interest payment dates of March 1 and September 1, the price of the bond may not include interest from September 1. In this case, the first interest payment on March 1 will represent interest on the use of the money for 5½ months (i.e., from September 15). If the offering terms call for the purchaser to pay the offering price plus accrued interest (discussed later) from September 1 until the settlement date of the transaction, then the first interest payment due on March 1 will be a full coupon payment of 6 months.

Normally, interest payments (as well as principal payments) due on Sundays and holidays are paid on the next business day without additional interest for the extra period. Indentures might have a clause covering this in the covenant section of the indenture or in the miscellaneous provisions article of the indenture.

Since most corporate bonds are now in registered form, interest is paid to the holder by check on the interest payment date. The interest check is normally mailed on the business day preceding the interest payment date to the holder of record. The record date, usually 15 days prior to the payment date, is the date the trustee prepares the list of bondholders entitled to the approaching interest payment. There may be instances when corporations of shaky credit standing will not be able to make the interest payment on time. In such situations the regular interest record date is void and any purchaser of the bonds after that date may receive the interest when paid and if the new owner is a holder of record on the required date. When the company obtains the necessary funds, a new record date will be established for that interest payment.

Accrued Interest

The purchase of a coupon bond usually requires the payment of an amount equal to the agreed-upon sales price (including commission, if any) plus the interest that has accrued from the last interest payment date to the settlement date of the transaction. If the bond is in default (i.e., not currently paying interest) then there is no accrued interest and none will be paid. The bond is said to "trade flat" when it does not trade with accrued interest. The seller is entitled to accrued interest only if the bond is in good standing. If one sells a bond that settles after the interest record date and before the interest payment date (i.e., the seller is still a holder of record) the purchaser will have paid the seller accrued interest up to the date of settlement. Because the purchaser is entitled to the full interest payment on the payment date, the seller (or broker/dealer) will attach a due bill to the bonds that assigns the rights for the upcoming interest payment to the purchaser.

To determine the accrued interest, it is first necessary to determine the number of days in the accrued interest period. The number of days in the accrued interest period is determined as follows:

days in accrued interest period
= days in coupon period
— days between settlement and next coupon payment

The percentage of the next semiannual coupon payment that the seller has earned as accrued interest is found as follows:

days in accrued interest period
———————————————————
days in coupon period

The accrued interest is then:

accrued interest

$$= \text{semiannual coupon period} \times \frac{\text{days in accrued interest period}}{\text{days in coupon period}}$$

The practice for calculating the number of days between two dates depends on day count conventions used in the bond market. The convention differs by the type of security. Day count conventions are also used to calculate the number of days in accrued interest period and days in coupon period.

In calculating the number of days between two dates, the actual number of days is not always the same as the number of days that should be used in the accrued interest formula. The number of days used depends on the day count convention for the particular security. Specifically, there are different day count conventions for Treasury securities than for corporate bonds.

For coupon-bearing corporate bonds the day count convention is as follows. It is assumed that every month has 30 days, that any 6-month period has 180 days, and that there are 360 days in a year. This day count convention is referred to as "30/360." For example, consider a corporate bond purchased with a settlement date of July 17, the previous coupon payment on March 1, and the next coupon payment on September 1. The number of days until the next coupon payment is 44 days as shown below:

July 17 to July 31	13 days
August	30 days
September 1	1 day
	44 days

Note that the settlement date, July 17, is not counted. Since July is treated as having 30 days, there are 13 days (30 days minus the first 17 days in July). The number of days from March 1 to July 17 is 136, which is the number of days in the accrued interest period.

MATURITY

The term to maturity of a bond is the number of years over which the issuer has promised to meet the conditions of the obligation. The maturity date of a bond refers to the date that the debt will cease to exist, at which time the issuer will redeem the bond by paying the amount borrowed. The maturity date of a bond is always identified when describing a bond. For example, a description of a bond might state "due 12/1/2010."

The practice in the bond market is to refer to the "term to maturity" of a bond as simply its "maturity" or "term." As we explain later, there may be provisions in the indenture that allow either the issuer or bondholder to alter a bond's term to maturity.

Some market participants view bonds with a maturity between 1 and 5 years as "short-term." Bonds with a maturity between 5 and 12 years are viewed as "intermediate-term," and "long-term" bonds are those with a maturity of more than 12 years.

There are bonds of every maturity. Typically, the longest maturity is 30 years. However, Walt Disney Co. issued bonds in July 1993 with a maturity date of 7/15/2093, making them 100-year bonds at the time of issuance. In December 1993, the Tennessee Valley Authority issued bonds that mature on 12/15/2043, making them 50-year bonds at the time of issuance.

There are three reasons why the term to maturity of a bond is important. First, the term to maturity indicates the time period over which the bondholder can expect to receive interest payments and the number of years before the principal will be paid in full. Second, the yield offered on a bond depends on the term to maturity. The relationship between the yield on a bond and maturity is called the *yield curve* and discussed in Chapter 5. Finally, the price of a bond will fluctuate over its life as interest rates in the market change. The price volatility of a bond is a function of its maturity (among other variables). More specifically, as explained in Chapter 6, all other factors being constant, the longer the maturity of a bond, the greater the price volatility resulting from a change in interest rates.

PROVISIONS FOR PAYING OFF A BOND BEFORE MATURITY

A bond issue may have a provision granting either the issuer an option to retire all or part of the issue prior to the stated maturity date and/or the bondholder the right to force the issuer to purchase the bond. We discuss these provisions in more detail in Chapter 16. Here we review the basic elements of these provisions.

An issuer generally wants the right to retire a bond issue prior to the stated maturity date in order to take advantage of a decline in interest rates below the coupon rate of the issue. The right of the issuer to retire the issue prior to the stated maturity date is referred to as a *call provision*, and a bond that contains this provision is referred to as a *callable bond*. When a bond is issued, often there is a lockout period that restricts the issuer from calling the bond for a specified period of time.

A bond issue that is callable immediately is said to be a *currently callable bond*. Even if currently callable at issuance, a bond issue usually has restrictions against certain types of early redemption. The most common restriction is prohibiting the refunding of the bonds for a certain number of years or for the issue's life. By "refunding" it is meant that the issuer cannot call the issue using a cheaper source of funds than the issue.

An issuer may also be able to call a bond to satisfy any sinking fund requirements. We discuss these requirements in Chapter 16.

A call provision is an option granted to the issuer. A *put provision* gives the investor the option to either ask for repayment on a certain date(s) prior to the stated maturity or to hold the bond to either the next put date (if any) or maturity. This provision benefits the investor in a rising interest rate environment should the market rate rise above the issue's coupon rate.

Chapter 3

Medium-Term Notes and Structured Notes

Medium-term notes (MTNs) have emerged as a major source of funding for U.S. corporations. In deciding whether to finance with MTNs or with bonds, a corporate borrower weighs the interest cost, flexibility, and other advantages of each security. The growth of the MTN market indicates that MTNs offer advantages that bonds do not. However, most companies that raise funds in the MTN market have also continued to issue corporate bonds, suggesting that each form of debt has advantages under particular circumstances.

Borrowers with MTN programs have great flexibility in the types of securities they may issue, particularly with respect to coupon formula. An MTN with a nontraditional coupon formula is called a structured note. In this chapter, we discuss the features of MTNs and structured notes.

MEDIUM-TERM NOTES

Most MTNs are noncallable, unsecured, senior debt securities with fixed coupon rates and investment-grade credit ratings. In these features, MTNs are similar to investment-grade corporate bonds. However, they generally differ from bonds in their primary distribution process. MTNs have traditionally been sold on a best-efforts basis by investment banks and other broker-dealers acting as agents. In contrast to an underwriter in the conventional bond market, an agent in the MTN market has no obligation to underwrite MTNs for the issuer, and the issuer is not guaranteed funds. Also, unlike corporate bonds, which are typically sold in large, discrete offerings, MTNs are usually sold in relatively small amounts either on a continuous or on an intermittent basis.

As the market for MTNs evolved, issuers have taken advantage of this flexibility by issuing MTNs with less conventional features. Many MTNs are now issued with floating interest rates or with rates that are computed according to unusual formulas tied to equity or commodity prices. Also, many include calls, puts, and other options. Furthermore, maturities are not necessarily "medium term"—they have ranged from 9 months to 30 years and longer. Moreover, like corporate bonds, MTNs are now often sold on an underwritten basis, and offering amounts are occasionally as large as those of bonds. Indeed, rather than denoting a narrow security with an intermediate maturity, an MTN is more accurately defined as a highly flexible debt instrument that can easily be designed to respond to market opportunities and investor preferences.

Institutional Changes that
Fostered Development of the MTN Market

In the early 1980s, two institutional changes set the stage for rapid growth of the MTN market. First, in 1981 major investment banks acting as agents committed resources to assist in primary issuance and to provide secondary market liquidity. By 1984, the captive finance companies of the three large automakers had at least two agents for their MTN programs. The ongoing financing requirements of these companies and the competition among agents established a basis for the market to develop. Because investment banks stood ready to buy back MTNs in the secondary market, investors became more receptive to adding MTNs to their portfolio holdings. In turn, the improved liquidity and consequent reduction in the cost of issuance attracted new borrowers to the market.

Second, the adoption by the SEC of Rule 415 in March 1982 served as another important institutional change. Rule 415 permits delayed or continuous issuance of so-called shelf-registered corporate securities. Under shelf registrations, issuers register securities that may be sold for 2 years after the effective date of the registration without the requirement of another registration statement each time new offerings are made. Thus shelf registration enables issuers to take advantage of brief periods of low interest rates by selling previously registered securities on a moment's notice. In contrast, debt offerings that are not made from shelf registrations are subject to a delay of at least 48 hours between the filing with the SEC and the subsequent offering to the public.

The ability of borrowers to sell a variety of debt instruments with a broad range of coupons and maturities under a single prospectus supplement is another advantage of a shelf-registered MTN program. Indeed, a wide array of financing options have been included in MTN filings. For example, MTN programs commonly give the borrower the choice of issuing fixed- or floating-rate debt. Furthermore, several "global" programs allow for placements in the U.S. market or in the Euromarket. Other innovations that reflect the specific funding needs of issuers include MTNs collateralized by mortgages issued by thrift institutions, equipment trust certificates issued by railways, amortizing notes issued by leasing companies, and subordinated notes issued by bank holding companies. Another significant innovation has been the development of asset-backed MTNs, a form of asset securitization used predominantly to finance trade receivables and corporate loans. This flexibility in types of instruments that may be sold as MTNs, coupled with the market timing benefits of shelf registration, enables issuers to respond readily to changing market opportunities.

Exhibit 1: An Offering Rate Schedule for a Medium-Term Note Program

Medium-Term Notes		Yield Spread of	Treasury Securities	
Maturity Range	Yield (percent)	MTN over Treasury Securities (basis points)	Maturity	Yield (percent)
9 months to 12 months	*	*	9 months	3.35
12 months to 18 months	*	*	12 months	3.50
18 months to 2 years	*	*	18 months	3.80
2 years to 3 years	4.35	35	2 years	4.00
3 years to 4 years	5.05	55	3 years	4.50
4 years to 5 years	5.60	60	4 years	5.00
5 years to 6 years	6.05	60	5 years	5.45
6 years to 7 years	6.10	40	6 years	5.70
7 years to 8 years	6.30	40	7 years	5.90
8 years to 9 years	6.45	40	8 years	6.05
9 years to 10 years	6.60	40	9 years	6.20
10 years	6.70	40	10 years	6.30

* No rate posted

Mechanics of the Market

The process of raising funds in the public MTN market usually begins when a corporation files a shelf registration with the SEC. Once the SEC declares the registration statement effective, the borrower files a prospectus supplement that describes the MTN program. The amount of debt under the program generally ranges from $100 million to $1 billion. After establishing an MTN program, a borrower may enter the MTN market continuously or intermittently with large or relatively small offerings. Although underwritten corporate bonds may also be issued from shelf registrations, MTNs provide issuers with more flexibility than traditional underwritings in which the entire debt issue is made at one time, typically with a single coupon and a single maturity.

The registration filing usually includes a list of the investment banks with which the corporation has arranged to act as agents to distribute the notes to investors. Most MTN programs have two to four agents. Having multiple agents encourages competition among investment banks and thus lowers financing costs. The large New York–based investment banks dominate the distribution of MTNs.

Through its agents, an issuer of MTNs posts offering rates over a range of maturities: for example, 9 months to a year, a year to 18 months, 18 months to 2 years, and annually thereafter (see Exhibit 1). Many issuers post rates as a yield spread over a Treasury security of comparable maturity. The relatively attractive yield spreads posted at the maturities of 3, 4, and 5 years shown in Exhibit 1 indicate that the issuer desires to raise funds at these maturities. The investment banks disseminate this offering rate information to their investor clients.

When an investor expresses interest in an MTN offering, the agent contacts the issuer to obtain a confirmation of the terms of the transaction. Within a maturity range, the investor has the option of choosing the final maturity of the note sale, subject to agreement by the issuing company. The issuer will lower its posted rates once it raises the desired amount of funds at a given maturity. In the example in Exhibit 1, the issuer might lower its posted rate for MTNs with a 5-year maturity to 40 basis points over comparable Treasury securities after it sells the desired amount of debt at this maturity. Of course, issuers also change their offering rate scales in response to changing market conditions. Issuers may withdraw from the market by suspending sales or, alternatively, by posting narrow offering spreads at all maturity ranges. The proceeds from primary trades in the MTN market typically range from $1 million to $25 million, but the size of transactions varies considerably. After the amount of registered debt is sold, the issuer may "reload" its MTN program by filing a new registration with the SEC.

Although MTNs are generally offered on an agency basis, most programs permit other means of distribution. For example, MTN programs usually allow the agents to acquire notes for their own account and for resale at par or at prevailing market prices. MTNs may also be sold on an underwritten basis. In addition, many MTN programs permit the borrower to bypass financial intermediaries by selling debt directly to investors.

Reverse Inquiry in the MTN Market

With MTNs, investors often play an active role in the issuance process through the phenomenon known as *reverse inquiry*. For example, suppose an investor desires to purchase $15 million of A-rated finance company debt with a maturity of 6 years and 9 months. Such a security may not be available in the corporate bond market, but the investor may be able to obtain it in the MTN market through reverse inquiry. In this process, the investor relays the inquiry to an issuer of MTNs through the issuer's agent. If the issuer finds the terms of the reverse inquiry sufficiently attractive, it may agree to the transaction even if it was not posting rates at the maturity that the investor desires.

According to market participants, trades that stem from reverse inquiries account for a significant share of MTN transactions. Reverse inquiry not only benefits the issuer by reducing borrowing costs but also allows investors to use the flexibility of MTNs to their advantage. In response to investor preferences, MTNs issued under reverse inquiry often include embedded options and frequently pay interest according to unusual formulas.

STRUCTURED NOTES

Beginning in the 1990s, it has not been uncommon for corporations to issue debt with payments tied to a foreign exchange rate, a multiple of LIBOR, or a commodity price. Corporations issue nonstandard securities not because the securities are better suited for their needs, but rather because they can lower their cost of capital by combining the security with some type of swap (i.e., interest rate swap, currency swap, stock index swap, or commodity swap). These securities, in which the issuer sells a note and simultaneously enters into a swap or derivative transaction, are known as structured notes.

Structured notes have not only transformed the way that corporations raise capital, but they have also changed the way that institutions invest. When a structured note is created through reverse inquiry, the investor rather than the issuer plays a dominant role in determining the note's features. Each structured note is customized with unique features that match the preferences of the investor. For example, if an investor believes that the yield curve will flatten, a structured note would be designed with coupon payments that vary with the spread between short-term and long-term interest rates.

Structured notes are attractive to investors because the securities have risk/return characteristics that are hard to replicate with traditional securities. Consequently, compared with traditional securities, structured notes give investors greater flexibility in changing the risk profiles of their portfolios. Thus, from the investor's point of view, the difference between a structured note and a traditional note has been compared to the difference between buying a custom-made suit and buying a suit off the rack.

Characteristics of Structured Notes

In general, structured notes have three common elements that distinguish them from traditional notes and bonds. First, structured notes are designed to meet the needs of investors. When the securities are created, they are customized with features that reflect the investor's specific opinion on the course of interest rates or other financial variables. Thus, most structured notes have embedded options, such as caps, calls, and collars. In addition, many structured notes pay interest or principal according to precise formulas that reflect the investor's preferences for risk and return. For example, some structured notes have interest rate payments that vary inversely with market rates. Others have payments linked to forward interest rates, commodity prices, or the credit spreads on a basket of speculative-grade bonds.

A second characteristic of structured notes is that, at the time the note is issued, the issuer simultaneously enters into swap or other derivative transactions. The derivative allows the corporation issuing the note to eliminate its exposure to the customized terms of the note structure. By using derivatives, the corporate issuer may create a synthetic debt obligation that resembles a standard fixed-rate or floating-rate note.

Third, most structured notes are issued from MTN programs. As described earlier, a key feature of an MTN program is that it gives an issuer great flexibility in the timing and type of structured notes that may be sold under a single registration document. For example, most MTN programs allow for issuance of fixed- or floating-rate debt. MTNs also may be issued with a variety of options, such as puts, calls, collars, and floors. In addition, many programs allow for the debt to be indexed to foreign currencies, commodity prices, equity prices, or to financial and nonfinancial indices. Although MTNs remain the dominant issuance vehicle, other debt instruments also have been used to create structured notes. For example, CDs and commercial paper also account for a significant share of the structured note market.

The Security Design Process

Exhibit 2 gives a broad outline of the process of creating a structured note. The process begins when an investor has a market view about price or relative price movements, as shown by the first column of boxes. For example, an investor may have a market view about the direction of interest rates, the reshaping of the yield curve, or the path of foreign interest rates.

In the next stage of the process, the investor and an investment bank will design a security that reflects the market view of the investor. Together, they decide on the type of note structure that has the appropriate risk and return characteristics (the second column of boxes). For example, a floating-rate note would be appropriate for an investor who believes that interest rates will rise, and an inverse floater would be suitable for an investor who believes that rates will fall.

Exhibit 2: Security Design Process

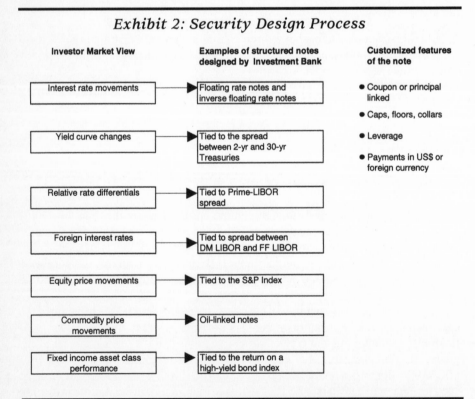

Next, to customize the note with desired risk characteristics, the investor may select additional features to include in the note. Consider, for example, an investor who believes that the yield curve will flatten (the second row of boxes). A security designed to reflect that view could have its coupon payments linked to the shape of the yield curve. Thus, the coupon on the note might be reset semiannually to a rate that depends on the yield spread between 30-year and 2-year Treasury notes. To gain more leverage, the interest payments might be set at four times the spread between 30-year and 2-year rates. In that case, the interest on the structured note would increase four basis points for every one basis point narrowing in the 30-year/2-year spread. In addition to the leverage factor, the investor may choose to tailor the riskiness of the note by embedding it with options, such as caps, floors, or collars. For the note linked to the 30-year/2-year spread, the investor might specify a minimum coupon rate of 1% and a maximum rate of 15%.

When the investment bank and the investor have decided on the specific security, the investment bank will approach an MTN issuer and propose a structured transaction. In the transaction, the issuer will sell the customized note to the investor and simultaneously enter into a derivative transaction.

Although structured transactions often originate with investors, investment banks frequently initiate such transactions. Most investment banks have specialists in derivative products who design securities to take advantage of temporary market opportunities. When an investment bank identifies an opportunity, it will inform investors and propose that they purchase a specialized security. If an investor tentatively agrees to the transaction, the MTN agents in the investment bank will contact an MTN issuer with the proposed structured transaction.

Examples of Structured Notes

Because the structured note market has expanded so rapidly, it would be difficult to catalogue all the note structures that have been created. New types of note structures are created in response to changing market conditions. Even with that great diversity, several types of note structures are issued with some regularity. These include inverse floating-rate notes, range notes, CMT indexed notes, and yield curve notes.[1]

We described the formula for an inverse floating-rate note (or inverse floater) in Chapter 2. The coupon formula is such that the coupon rate changes in the opposite direction to the change in the reference rate. An investor would purchase an inverse floater if he or she has a strong view that interest rates are poised to fall.

The determination of the coupon rate for a range note (or range bound floating-rate note) was described in Chapter 2. At issuance, for each period a range for the reference rate is specified. If the reference rate for the period is outside the range, there is no coupon payment made for that period. The reference

---

[1] For an illustration of each of these securities created using the derivatives market, see Leland E. Crabbe, "Medium-Term Notes and Structured Notes," Chapter 3 in Frank J. Fabozzi (ed.), *Handbook of Corporate Debt Instruments* (New Hope, PA: Frank J. Fabozzi Associates, 1998).

rate is typically a short-term interest rate such as LIBOR. The coupon rates in a range note are such that the investor profits if short-term interest rates rise, but in a gradual, predictable pattern. If interest rates rise as expected, the coupon payments on a range note will be greater than the payments on a standard floating-rate note. The interest premium compensates the investor for the risk that rates will rise outside of the prespecified range, in which case the interest will be lower than that received on a standard floating-rate note.[2]

A constant-maturity Treasury (CMT) indexed note is an example of a structured note whose coupon formula is linked to the yield on longer-term securities. (CMT yields are published by the Federal Reserve.) Investors will buy a CMT indexed note if they want to hedge their portfolios against rising interest rates or if they want their portfolio returns to be indexed to the yield on a particular Treasury. These notes differ from traditional floating-rate notes, in which coupon payments are usually linked to short-term interest rates, such as LIBOR, Treasury bills, or commercial paper.

For a yield curve note, the maturity value is tied to the spread between the yield on two points of the yield curve. Consequently, a yield curve note is appropriate for an investor who believes that the slope of the yield curve will change. For example, the investor may believe that the yield curve will flatten in coming months. To profit from that view, a note is designed in which the principal redemption value of the note is linked to the spread between 10-year and 2-year Treasury rates. Thus, the value of the note at maturity will be higher if the yield curve flattens and lower if the yield curve steepens.

The proliferation in the types of structured notes seems to suggest that a customized note could be designed to reflect any market view of an investor. However, practical considerations limit both the types of structured notes that are issued and the types of borrowers that issue structured notes. The most important limitations relate to the depth of the derivatives markets, the complexity of note structures and transaction costs, and the credit ratings of the issuers. In addition, regulatory restrictions on hybrid securities also discourage issuance of commodity-linked structured notes.

Why Do Investors Buy Structured Notes?

From the point of view of the investor, the key attraction of structured notes is that the notes can be customized with desirable risk characteristics. The risk features of structured notes allow investors to change the risk profiles of their portfolios. In many cases, a security with the risk features that the investor desires may not exist in the secondary market.

For example, a yield curve note effectively allows the investor to lock in a very specific view about forward bond yields. In contrast, with cash market instruments it is considerably more difficult to lock in forward rates. Moreover, structured notes allow investors to separate their appetite for duration from their

---

[2] Implicitly, the investor in the range bound floater is selling a series of interest-rate caps to the issuer.

appetite for credit risk. In the yield curve note, the investor's exposure to the credit risk of the issuer is limited to the 1-year maturity of the note. But the note could easily be designed to have the duration of a 10-year cash security.

The existence of the structured note market raises the fundamental question: why do investors buy structured notes instead of directly accessing the swap and derivative markets? In general, the cash flows from a structured note could be replicated by combining a traditional note with a derivative. Although many investors, of course, do use derivatives, there are several reasons why they may prefer to buy structured notes.

First, investors prefer structured notes for their administrative simplicity. Consider a money manager with 10 investment accounts. If the money manager buys a structured note, he can easily distribute the note among the 10 accounts. However, if the money manager uses swaps, he would not be permitted to allocate a single swap among his accounts. Rather, he would have to enter into 10 separate swap agreements, one for each of the accounts. Derivatives also involve significant administrative costs. The costs associated with interest rate futures, for example, include the cost of maintaining margins, the cost of rolling over contracts, legal costs, and other back office expenses.

Second, structured notes require less credit evaluation than swaps. With a structured note, the investor only evaluates the credit risk of the note issuer. In contrast, if the investor bought a standard note and a swap, he would evaluate the credit risk of both the note issuer and the derivative counterparty.

Third, structured notes can be easier to trade and transfer than swap contracts. Consider two investors, one that purchased a $50 million structured note, and another that purchased a $50 million swap contract. Now, suppose that both investors desire to reduce their positions to $20 million. The first investor could sell $30 million of the structured note to any dealer. The second investor, in contrast, will find it considerably more difficult to reduce his swap position. That difficulty arises because, in a swap contract, a swap counterparty has the right to approve any transfers. Moreover, whereas the structured note could be resold through any dealer, the swap transfer could potentially be limited to the dealer that originated the swap.

Finally, some investors face restrictions on using swaps and derivatives. Some mutual funds, for example, face restrictions on transacting in futures markets, and others have only recently changed their charters to permit transactions in the swap market. However, these investors generally do not face restrictions on investments in structured notes. Thus, an investor can eliminate institutional barriers to using derivatives by buying a structured note with payment characteristics that mimic those of a derivative contract.

Risks Associated with Investing in Structured Notes

Throughout this book we describe various types of risks associated with investing in corporate bonds. By design, the market risk characteristics of structured notes differ from those of standard notes. Some structured notes are designed to have durations that are much greater than standard notes, while others have short or negative durations.[3] Other structured notes are designed to be duration neutral, but highly sensitive to particular reshapings of the yield curve.

Structured notes exist because investors seek to profit from market risks. Market risks can be quantified with models of the term structure of interest rates, option pricing models, and measures of duration and convexity. However, in addition to market risk, structured notes have other types of risk that are important to recognize, even if they are more difficult to measure.

Liquidity Risk

For several reasons, an investor may want to sell a structured note before its maturity date. For example, the investor may have been correct in his or her view about the direction of interest rates, but may have been wrong about the timing of that view. Suppose that rates change earlier than anticipated. In that case, the investor may want to realize profits by selling the structured note before maturity. In other cases, the interest rates may move in a direction opposite to that expected when the investor purchased the structured note. For example, the investor may have purchased the note under the expectation that the yield curve would flatten. However, in response to unforeseen economic developments, the investor may later believe that the yield curve will steepen. Consequently, the investor may no longer desire to hold the structured note.

Structured notes are less liquid than traditional notes.[4] The difference in liquidity arises because structured notes are customized securities that have higher transaction costs than standardized securities. To value a structured note, an investor in the secondary market has to evaluate not only the credit risk of the note issuer but also the customized risk/return tradeoffs of the note structure. Of course, the cost of evaluating a structured note increases with the complexity of the note's features. This cost of valuing the security is a transaction cost that lowers the secondary market price of a structured note and reduces its liquidity.

Another factor that reduces the liquidity of structured notes is that the number of investors who are willing and able to buy notes in the secondary market is smaller than that for standard securities. Furthermore, even if an investor has the expertise to evaluate a structured note, he or she may not want to buy a structured note in the secondary market, simply because the note was designed to meet the needs of the original investor. Most investors would prefer to buy a new structured note and customize its features. In this sense, buying a structured note is like buying a custom-tailored suit. Rather than buying a suit that was customized to another individual's features, most people prefer to buy suits tailored to their own features.

These factors suggest that structured notes have less liquidity than standard notes. Investors need to be aware of liquidity risk because they might sell a structured note before maturity.

---

[3] We discuss duration in Chapter 6.

[4] We discuss liquidity risk in Chapter 8.

Systemic Risk

Another important risk in the structured note market is systemic risk. Systemic risk refers to the risk of a market disruption leading to a broader malfunctioning of the financial system. Structured notes are exposed to systemic risk because they are inextricably linked to the derivatives markets. Events that have been cited as capable of triggering systemic problems include the default of a major financial institution or disruptions in the clearing and settlement process such as the closing of a stock or commodity exchange. It is debatable whether the emergence of derivative markets, in itself, has increased the financial system's exposure to systemic risk. However, derivatives have clearly strengthened linkages between markets. As a result, derivatives may allow for the transference of disruptions across markets more quickly.

Unsophisticated Investors

Unsophisticated investors also pose a risk to the structured note market. The financial press has documented several instances in which unsophisticated investors have purchased complicated financial instruments without fully understanding their risks. Unsophisticated investors pose a risk to the structured note market because dealers could become lax in their restrictions. If unsophisticated investors become active in the structured note market, they may eventually suffer losses, which in turn will increase the probability of regulation on derivative markets, in general, and the structured note market, in particular.

Black Box Risk

While structured notes can be attractive instruments for investors who have well-defined views about the direction of financial markets, investors should not consider structured notes as a means to avoid developing an expertise in derivatives. Because structured notes are linked to derivatives, an investor must have some knowledge of derivative pricing in order to properly evaluate a structured note. Even if a structured note exactly matches the opinion of the investor, the note may be a bad investment if it is priced too high. Rather than treating the pricing as a black box, investors are advised to avail themselves of sophisticated models and to understand the assumptions those models make. Structure, in itself, should not blind investors to the fact that investment decisions ultimately boil down to decisions about price.

Chapter 4

Analysis of Convertible Bonds

A convertible bond is a bond that can be converted into common stock at the option of the bondholder. In this chapter we describe the features of convertible bonds, how they are valued, and their investment characteristics. Two valuation approaches are explained: traditional analysis and an option-based analysis.

BASIC FEATURES OF CONVERTIBLE BONDS

The conversion provision of a convertible bond grants the bondholder the right to convert the bond into a predetermined number of shares of common stock of the issuer. A convertible bond is therefore a bond with an embedded call option to buy the common stock of the issuer. An *exchangeable bond* grants the bondholder the right to exchange the issue for the common stock of a firm *other* than the issuer of the bond. Throughout this chapter we use the term *convertible bond* to refer to both convertible and exchangeable bonds.

In illustrating the calculation of the various concepts described as follows, we will use the General Signal Corporation (ticker symbol "GSX") 5¾% convertible issue due June 1, 2002. Information about the issue and the stock of this issuer is provided in Exhibit 1.

Conversion Ratio

The number of shares of common stock that the bondholder will receive from exercising the conversion option is called the *conversion ratio*. The conversion privilege may extend for all or only some portion of the issue's life, and the stated conversion ratio may change over time. It is always adjusted proportionately for stock splits and stock dividends. For the GSX convertible issue, the conversion ratio is 25.32 shares. This means that for each $1,000 of par value of this issue the bondholder exchanges for GSX common stock, he will receive 25.32 shares.

At the time of issuance of a convertible bond, the issuer effectively grants the bondholder the right to purchase the common stock at a price equal to:

$$\frac{\text{Par value of the convertible issue}}{\text{Conversion ratio}}$$

This price is referred to in the prospectus as the *stated conversion price*. Sometimes the issue price of a convertible bond may not be equal to par. In such cases, the stated conversion price at issuance is usually determined by the issue price.

Exhibit 1: Information About General Signal Corporation Convertible Bond 5¾% Due June 1, 2002 and Common Stock

Convertible bond
Market price (as of 10/7/93): $106.50
Issue proceeds: $100 million
Issue date: 6/1/92
Maturity date: 6/1/02
Noncall until 6/1/95

Call price schedule	
6/1/95	103.59
6/1/96	102.88
6/1/97	102.16
6/1/98	101.44
6/1/99	100.72
6/1/00	100.00
6/1/01	100.00

Coupon rate: 5¾%
Conversion ratio: 25.320 shares of GSX shares per $1,000 par value
Rating: A3/A−

GSX common stock
Expected volatility: 17%
Dividend per share: $0.90 per year
Dividend yield (as of 10/7/93): 2.727%
Stock price: $33

The conversion price for the GSX convertible issue is:

$$\text{Conversion price} = \frac{\$1,000}{25.32} = \$39.49$$

Call Provisions

Almost all convertible issues are callable by the issuer. Typically there is a noncall period (i.e., a time period from the time of issuance that the issue may not be called). The GSX convertible issue had a noncall period at issuance of 3 years. There are some issues that have a provisional call feature that allows the issuer to call the issue during the noncall period if the price of the stock reaches a certain price. For example, Whirlpool Corporation zero-coupon convertible bond due 5/14/11 could not be called before 5/14/93 unless the stock price reached $52.35, at which time the issuer had the right to call the issue. In the case of Eastman Kodak zero-coupon convertible bond due 10/15/11, the issuer could not call the issue before 10/15/93 unless the common stock traded at a price of at least $70.73 for at least 20/30 trading days.

The call price schedule of an issue is specified at the time of issuance. The call price schedule for the GSX convertible issue is shown in Exhibit 1. In the case of a zero-coupon convertible bond, the call price is based on an accreted value. For example, for the Whirlpool Corporation zero-coupon convertible, the call price on 5/14/93 was $28.983 and thereafter accretes daily at 7% per annum compounded semiannually. So, if the issue is called on 5/14/94, the call price would have been \$31.047 (\$28.983 times 1.035^2).

Putable Provision

A put provision grants the bondholder the right to require the issuer to redeem the issue at designated dates for a predetermined price. Some convertible bonds are putable. For example, Eastman Kodak zero-coupon convertible bond due 10/15/11 is putable. The put schedule is as follows: 32.35 if put on 10/15/94; 34.57 if put on 10/15/95; 36.943 if put on 10/15/96; 51.486 if put on 10/15/01; and, 71.753 if put on 10/15/06. The GSX convertible issue is not putable.

Put options can be classified as "hard" puts and "soft" puts. A hard put is one in which the convertible security must be redeemed by the issuer for cash. In the case of a soft put, the issuer has the option to redeem the convertible security for cash, common stock, subordinated notes, or a combination of the three.

TRADITIONAL ANALYSIS OF CONVERTIBLE SECURITIES

Minimum Value of a Convertible Security

The *conversion value* or *parity value* of a convertible bond is the value of the issue if it is converted immediately.[1] That is,

Conversion value = Market price of common stock × Conversion ratio

The minimum price of a convertible bond is the greater of (1) its conversion value and (2) its value as a bond without the conversion option. The latter value is based on the issue's cash flows if not converted (i.e., a plain vanilla bond). This value is called its *straight value* or *investment value*.

If the convertible security does not sell for the greater of these two values, arbitrage profits could be realized. For example, suppose the conversion value is greater than the straight value, and the issue trades at its straight value. An investor can buy the issue at the straight value and convert it. By doing so, the investor realizes a gain equal to the difference between the conversion value and the straight value. Suppose, instead, the straight value is greater than the conversion value, and the issue trades at its conversion value. By buying the convertible at the conversion value, the investor will realize a higher yield than a comparable straight security.

For the GSX convertible issue, the conversion value on 10/7/93 per \$1,000 of par value was equal to:

Conversion value = \$33 × 25.32 = \$835.56

Therefore, the conversion value per \$100 of par value was 83.556.

---

[1] Technically, the standard textbook definition of conversion value given here is theoretically incorrect because as bondholders convert, the price of the stock will decline. The theoretically correct definition for the conversion value is that it is the product of the conversion ratio and the stock price *after* conversion.

To simplify the analysis of the straight value of the bond, we will discount the cash flows to maturity by the yield on the 10-year on-the-run Treasury at the time, 5.32%, plus a credit spread of 70 basis points that appeared to be appropriate at that time. The straight value using a discount rate of 6.02%, and assuming same day settlement for theoretical purposes only, is 98.19. Actually, the straight value would be less than this because no recognition was given to the call feature. Since the minimum value of the GSX convertible issue is the greater of the conversion value and the straight value, the minimum value is 98.19.

Market Conversion Price

The price that an investor effectively pays for the common stock if the convertible bond is purchased and then converted into the common stock is called the *market conversion price* or *conversion parity price*. It is found as follows:

$$\text{Market conversion price} = \frac{\text{Market price of convertible bond}}{\text{Conversion ratio}}$$

The market conversion price is a useful benchmark because once the actual market price of the stock rises above the market conversion price, any further stock price increase is certain to increase the value of the convertible bond by at least the same percentage. Therefore, the market conversion price can be viewed as a breakeven price.

An investor who purchases a convertible bond rather than the underlying stock pays a premium over the current market price of the stock. This premium per share is equal to the difference between the market conversion price and the current market price of the common stock. That is,

Market conversion premium per share
= Market conversion price − Current market price

The market conversion premium per share is usually expressed as a percentage of the current market price as follows:

$$\text{Market conversion premium ratio} = \frac{\text{Market conversion premium per share}}{\text{Market price of common stock}}$$

Why would someone be willing to pay a premium to buy the stock? Recall that the minimum price of a convertible bond is the greater of its conversion value or its straight value. Thus, as the common stock price declines, the price of the convertible security will not fall below its straight value. The straight value therefore acts as a floor for a convertible bond's price.

Viewed in this context, the market conversion premium per share can be seen as the price of a call option. The buyer of a call option limits the downside risk to the option price. In the case of a convertible bond, for a premium the bondholder limits the downside risk to the bond's straight value. The difference between the buyer of a call option and the buyer of a convertible bond is that the former knows precisely the dollar amount of the downside risk, while the latter knows only that the most that can be lost is the difference between the convertible bond's price and the straight value. The straight value at some future date, however, is unknown; the value will change as market interest rates change or if the issuer's credit quality changes.

The calculation of the market conversion price, market conversion premium per share, and market conversion premium ratio for the GSX convertible issue based on market data as of 10/7/93 is shown below:

$$\text{Market conversion price} = \frac{\$1,065}{25.32} = \$42.06$$

$$\text{Market conversion premium per share} = \$42.06 - \$33 = \$9.06$$

$$\text{Market conversion premium ratio} = \frac{\$9.06}{\$33} = 0.275 = 27.5\%$$

Current Income of Convertible Security versus Common Stock

As an offset to the market conversion premium per share, investing in the convertible bond rather than buying the stock directly generally means that the investor realizes higher current income from the coupon interest paid than would be received from common stock dividends based on the number of shares equal to the conversion ratio. Analysts evaluating a convertible bond typically compute the time it takes to recover the premium per share by computing the *premium payback period* (which is also known as the *breakeven time*). This is computed as follows:

$$\text{Premium payback period} = \frac{\text{Market conversion premium per share}}{\text{Favorable income differential per share}}$$

where the favorable income differential per share is equal to:

$$\frac{\text{Coupon interest} - (\text{Conversion ratio} \times \text{Common stock dividend per share})}{\text{Conversion ratio}}$$

Notice that the premium payback period does *not* take into account the time value of money.

For the GSX convertible issue, the market conversion premium per share is $9.06. The favorable income differential per share is found as follows:

$$\text{Coupon interest from bond} = 0.0575 \times \$1,000 = \$57.50$$

$$\text{Conversion ratio} \times \text{Dividend per share} = 25.32 \times \$0.90 = \$22.79$$

Therefore,

$$\text{Favorable income differential per share} = \frac{\$57.50 - \$22.79}{25.32} = \$1.37$$

and

$$\text{Premium payback period} = \frac{\$9.06}{\$1.37} = 6.6 \text{ years}$$

Without considering the time value of money, the investor would recover the market conversion premium per share assuming unchanged dividends in about 6.6 years.

Downside Risk of a Convertible Bond

Investors usually use the straight value as a measure of the downside risk of a convertible bond because its price cannot fall below this value. Thus, the straight value acts as the *current* floor for the price of the convertible bond. The downside risk is measured as a percentage of the straight value and is computed as follows:

$$\text{Premium over straight value} = \frac{\text{Market price of convertible bond}}{\text{Straight value}} - 1$$

The higher the premium over straight value, all other factors being constant, the less attractive the convertible bond.

Despite its use in practice, this measure of downside risk is flawed because the straight value (the floor) changes as interest rates change. If interest rates rise (fall), the straight value falls (rises), making the floor fall (rise). Therefore, the downside risk changes as interest rates change.

For the GSX convertible issue, since its market price is 106.5 and the straight value is 98.19,

$$\text{Premium over straight value} = \frac{\$106.50}{\$98.19} - 1 = 0.085 = 8.5\%$$

The Upside Potential of a Convertible Bond

The evaluation of the upside potential of a convertible bond depends on the prospects for the underlying common stock. Thus, the techniques for analyzing common stocks discussed in books on equity analysis should be employed.

INVESTMENT CHARACTERISTICS OF A CONVERTIBLE BOND

The investment characteristics of a convertible bond depend on the common stock price. If the price is low, so that the straight value is considerably higher than the conversion value, the issue will trade much like a straight bond. The issue in such instances is referred to as a *fixed income equivalent* or a *busted convertible*.

When the price of the stock is such that the conversion value is considerably higher than the straight value, then the issue will trade as if it were an equity instrument; in this case it is said to be a *common stock equivalent* and the market conversion premium per share will be small.

Between these two cases, fixed income equivalent and common stock equivalent, the issue trades as a *hybrid security*, having the characteristics of both a fixed income security and a common stock instrument.

AN OPTION-BASED VALUATION APPROACH

In our discussion of convertible bonds, we did not address the following questions:

1. What is a fair value for the conversion premium per share?
2. How do we handle convertible bonds with call and/or put options?
3. How does a change in interest rates affect the stock price?

Consider first a noncallable/nonputable convertible security. The investor who purchases this bond would be effectively entering into two separate transactions: (1) buying a noncallable/nonputable straight bond and (2) buying a call option (or warrant) on the stock, where the number of shares that can be purchased with the call option is equal to the conversion ratio.

The question is: What is the fair value for the call option? The fair value depends on the factors that affect the theoretical value of a call option. The factors include the current price of the stock, the strike price, the time to expiration, the short-term rate, and the stock's expected price volatility. The higher the expected price volatility, the greater the value of the call option. The theoretical value of a call option can be estimated using an option-pricing model such as the Black-Scholes model.

As a first approximation to the value of a convertible bond, the relationship would be:

Convertible bond value = Straight value + Value of call option on stock

The value of the call option is added to the straight value because the investor has purchased a call option on the stock.

Now let's add in a common feature of a convertible security: the issuer's right to call the bond. The issuer can force conversion by calling the bond.[2] For example, suppose that the call price is 103 and the conversion value is 107. If the issuer calls the bond, the optimal strategy for the investor is to convert it and receive

---

[2] From the corporation's perspective, convertible bonds should be called when the conversion value exceeds the call price. In effect, a call of a convertible bond is a forced conversion because investors have the choice of converting into stock, rather than receiving the cash proceeds from a call. By forcing conversion, the corporate issuer eliminates the bondholders' premium or option value. Empirical studies of convertible bond calls suggest that corporations generally do call their bonds as soon as possible, except in instances where there are significant cash flow advantages for delaying calls. For more on convertible calls, see Paul Asquith, "Convertible Bonds Are Not Called Late," *Journal of Finance* (September 1995), pp. 1275–1289.

shares worth $107.[3] The investor, however, loses any premium over the conversion value that is reflected in the market price. Therefore, the analysis of convertible bonds must take into account the value of the issuer's right to call. This depends, in turn, on (1) future interest rate volatility and (2) economic factors that determine whether or not it is optimal for the issuer to call the bond. Stock option pricing models (such as the Black-Scholes option-pricing model) cannot handle this situation.

To link interest rates and stock prices together (the third question we raise earlier), statistical analysis of historical movements of these two variables must be estimated and incorporated into the model.

Valuation models based on an option-pricing approach have been suggested by several researchers.[4] These models can generally be classified as one-factor or multifactor models. By factor we mean the stochastic variables that are assumed to drive the value of a convertible bond. The obvious candidates for factors are the price movement of the underlying common stock and the movement of interest rates. The most widely used convertible bond valuation model has been the one-factor model, and the factor is the price movement of the underlying common stock.[5]

Specifically, the valuation model is based on the solution to a partial differential equation. The no arbitrage conditions that the convertible bond price must satisfy is:[6]

$$\frac{\delta V}{\delta t} + \frac{1}{2}\sigma^2 S^2 \frac{\delta^2 V}{\delta S^2} + rS\frac{\delta V}{\delta S} = rV$$

where

V = value of convertible bond = $V(S,t)$
S = price of the underlying stock
t = time
r = short rate
σ^2 = instantaneous variance of the stock price return

The characteristics of the issue such as the maturity, coupon rate, conversion ratio, call and put provisions, and changing conversion ratios and provisional call features are incorporated into the boundary conditions to solve the partial differential equation.

---

[3] Actually, the conversion value would be less than $107 because the per-share value after conversion would decline.

[4] See, for example: Michael Brennan and Eduardo Schwartz, "Convertible Bonds: Valuation and Optimal Strategies for Call and Conversion," *Journal of Finance* (December 1977), pp. 1699–1715; Jonathan Ingersoll, "A Contingent-Claims Valuation of Convertible Securities," *Journal of Financial Economics* (May 1977), pp. 289–322; Michael Brennan and Eduardo Schwartz, "Analyzing Convertible Bonds," *Journal of Financial and Quantitative Analysis* (November 1980), pp. 907–929; and, George Constantinides, "Warrant Exercise and Bond Conversion in Competitive Markets," *Journal of Financial Economics* (September 1984), pp. 371–398.

[5] Mihir Bhattacharya and Yu Zhu, "Valuation and Analysis of Convertible Securities," Chapter 42 in Frank J. Fabozzi (ed.), *The Handbook of Fixed Income Securities* (Chicago: Irwin Professional Publishing).

[6] Bhattacharya and Zhu, "Valuation and Analysis of Convertible Securities."

Exhibit 2: Motorola LYONs: Market Price versus Theoretical Value (9/7/89 — 3/26/93)

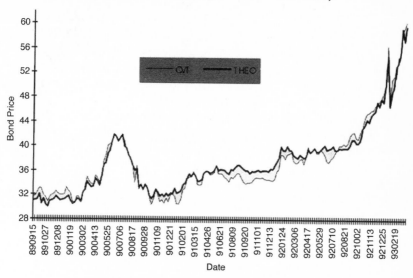

Source: Provided by Mihir Bhattacharya and Yu Zhu.

For the GSX convertible issue, the solution to the partial differential equation as of 10/7/93, assuming that the standard deviation of the stock price return is 17%, is 106.53. This value is equal to the actual market price at the time of 106.5, which suggests that the issue is fairly priced.

The difference between the value of the convertible bond as determined from the valuation model and the straight value (properly adjusted for the call option granted to the issuer and any put option) is the value of the embedded call option for the stock. That is,

Value of the embedded call option for underlying stock

= Theoretical value of convertible bond – Straight value

For the GSX convertible issue, since the theoretical value for the issue is 106.53 and the straight value is 98.19 (recall that this was not adjusted for the issuer's call option), the approximate value of the embedded call option for the underlying stock is 8.34.

The valuation model as applied to the GSX issue indicated that the issue was fairly priced. Exhibit 2 compares the theoretical value of Motorola's Liquid Yield Option Notes (LYONs)[7] to the actual market price of the convertible issue

---

[7] LYON is a Merrill Lynch trademark name for zero-coupon convertible bonds that are both callable and putable.

from the issue date (9/7/89) to 3/26/93. During this period, the price of Motorola's stock increased from $28¹⁄₁₆ to $65¼. In January 1991, the market conversion premium ratio reached a high of 44%. The exhibit indicates that the valuation appears to track the market price well.

Because the inputs into the valuation model are not known with certainty, it is important to test the sensitivity of the model. That is, there is modeling risk. As an example, the Merrill Lynch theoretical valuation model was used to value as of November 20, 1992 the Whirlpool Corporation zero-coupon bond due 5/14/11 (a LYON), assuming the following as a base case: a common stock price of $43⅝, volatility for the stock price of 25.21%, a constant dividend yield, a yield to maturity of 8.10%, and a yield to put of 6.98%. The theoretical value for the Whirlpool issue for this base case was $33.16.[8] The market price for this issue at the time was $33, so the issue appeared to be cheap relative to its theoretical value.

Tests of the sensitivity of the model to the base case inputs indicated the following for the theoretical value as of November 20, 1992 and also 1 year later by changing each input:

	Theoretical value (% change)			
	11/20/92		11/20/93	
Base case	$33.16		$33.33	
Stock volatility = 20%	32.67	−1.0%	33.07	0.2%
Stock price up 25%	39.52	19.8%	39.46	19.6%
Stock price down 25%	29.59	−10.3%	30.93	−6.3%
Interest rate down 100 bp	33.47	1.44%	33.66	1.9%
Interest rate up 100 bp	32.89	−0.3%	33.05	0.15%

The results for the stock volatility analysis indicate that if stock price volatility is 20% rather than the 25.21% assumed in the base case, the theoretical value as of November 20, 1992 would be less. This is expected since the value of a call option on a stock is lower the lower the expected stock price volatility. Thus, while the Whirlpool issue would be cheap relative to its market price of $33 if stock price volatility is 25.21%, it is expensive if stock price volatility is 20%.

THE RISK/RETURN PROFILE OF A CONVERTIBLE BOND

Let's use the GSX convertible issue and the valuation model to look at the risk/return profile by investing in a convertible issue or the underlying common stock.

Suppose on 10/7/93 an investor is considering the purchase of either the common stock of GSX or the 5¾% convertible issue due 6/1/02. The stock can be purchased in the market for $33. By buying the convertible bond, the investor is effectively purchasing the stock for $42.06 (the market conversion price per

---

[8] Preston M. Harrington II, Bernie Moriarty, and Hareesh Paranjape, *LYONs Review*, November/December 1992 Quarterly Update, Merrill Lynch, Pierce, Fenner & Smith, Inc., p. 104.

share). Exhibit 3 shows the total return for both alternatives 1 year later assuming (1) the stock price does not change, (2) it changes by ±10%, and (3) it changes by ±25%. The convertible's theoretical value is based on the Merrill Lynch valuation model.

If the GSX's stock price is unchanged, the stock position will underperform the convertible position although a premium was paid to purchase the stock by acquiring the convertible issue. The reason is that even though the convertible's theoretical value decreased, the income from coupon more than compensates for the capital loss. In the two scenarios where the price of GSX declines, the convertible position outperforms the stock position because the straight value provides a floor for the convertible. In contrast, the stock position outperforms the convertible position in the two cases where the stock rises in price because of the premium paid to acquire the stock via the convertible's acquisition.

One of the critical assumptions in this analysis is that the straight value does not change except for the passage of time. If interest rates rise, the straight value will decline. Even if interest rates do not rise, the perceived creditworthiness of the issuer may deteriorate, causing investors to demand a higher yield. The illustration clearly demonstrates that there are benefits and drawbacks of investing in convertible securities. The disadvantage is the upside potential giveup because a premium per share must be paid. An advantage is the reduction in downside risk (as determined by the straight value).

Exhibit 3: Comparison of 1-Year Return for GSX Stock and Convertible Issue for Assumed Changes in Stock Price

Beginning of horizon: 10/7/93
End of horizon: 10/07/94
Price of GSX stock on 10/7/93: $33.00
Assumed volatility of GSX stock return: 17%

Stock price change (%)	GSX stock return (%)	Convertible's theoretical value	Convertible's return (%)
−25	−22.24	100.47	−0.16
−10	−7.24	102.96	2.14
0	2.73	105.27	4.27
10	12.76	108.12	6.90
25	27.76	113.74	12.08

Section II

Corporate Bond Valuation
and
Price Dynamics

Chapter 5

General Principles of Corporate Bond Valuation and Yield Measures

T he valuation of option-free corporate bonds is fairly straightforward and is the subject of this chapter. We also explain in this chapter the various yield measures and yield spread measures. For corporate bonds with embedded options (e.g., putable bonds, callable bonds, and bonds with accelerated sinking fund provisions) and structured notes with a complex coupon formula (e.g., range notes and callable step-up notes), the valuation process is more complicated and is covered in the Chapter 16.

GENERAL PRINCIPLES OF VALUATION

Valuation is the process of determining the fair value of a financial asset. The fundamental principle of valuation is that the value of any financial asset is the present value of the expected cash flow. In this section, we explain the general principles of bond valuation. Based on these principles, the application to the valuation of option-free corporate bonds is straightforward.

Estimating the Cash Flow

Cash flow is simply the cash that is expected to be received each period from an investment. In the case of a bond, it does not make any difference whether the cash flow is interest income or repayment of principal.

The cash flow for any fixed-rate corporate bond in which neither the issuer nor the investor can alter the repayment of the principal before its contractual due date (i.e., an option-free bond) can easily be determined assuming that the issuer does not default. The cash flow is the coupon interest payments every 6 months up to the maturity date and the principal payment at the maturity date. So, for example, the cash flow per $100 of par value for a 7% 10-year corporate bond that is option free is $3.5 (7%/2/$100) every 6 months for the next 20 six-month periods and $100 20 six-month periods from now. Or, equivalently, the cash flow is $3.5 every 6 months for the next 19 six-month periods and $103.50 20 six-month periods from now.

The difficulty in determining the cash flow for a corporate bond arises under the following circumstances:

1. either the issuer or the investor has the option to change the contractual due date of the repayment of the principal;
2. the coupon payment is reset periodically based on some reference rate; or,
3. the investor has an option to convert the bond to common stock.

As explained in Chapter 2, a corporate bond issue may include a provision in the indenture that grants either the issuer or the bondholder the right to change the scheduled date or dates when the principal repayment is due. Assuming that the issuer does not default, the investor knows that the principal amount will be repaid, but does not know when that principal will be received. Because of this, the cash flow is not known with certainty.

A key factor determining whether either the issuer of the bond or the bondholder would exercise an embedded option is the level of interest rates in the future relative to the issue's coupon rate. Specifically, for a callable bond, if the prevailing market rate at which the issuer can refund an issue is sufficiently below the issue's coupon rate to justify the costs associated with refunding the issue, the issuer is likely to call the issue. For a putable bond, if the rate on comparable securities rises such that the value of the putable bond falls below the value at which it must be repurchased by the issuer, then the investor will put the issue.

What this means is that to estimate properly the cash flow of a bond it is necessary to incorporate into the analysis how interest rates can change in the future and how such changes affect the cash flow. As we will see later in this chapter, this is done in valuation models by introducing a parameter that reflects the expected volatility of interest rates.

Discounting the Cash Flow

Once the cash flow for a bond is estimated, the next step is to determine the appropriate interest rate to use to discount the cash flow. To determine the appropriate rate, the investor must address the following three questions:

1. What is the minimum interest rate the investor should require?
2. How much more than the minimum interest rate should the investor require for the specific corporate bond issue being valued?
3. Should the investor use the same interest rate for each estimated cash flow or a unique interest rate for each estimated cash flow?

The minimum interest rate that an investor should require is the yield available in the marketplace on a default-free cash flow. In the United States, this is the yield on a U.S. Treasury security, although as explained later, other benchmarks are being used. The premium over the yield on a Treasury security that the investor will require reflects the risks associated with realizing the estimated cash flow.

The traditional practice in valuation has been to discount every cash flow of a bond by the same interest rate (or discount rate). The fundamental flaw of this approach is that it views each security as the same package of cash flows. The proper way to view a bond is as a package of zero-coupon instruments. Each cash flow should be considered a zero-coupon instrument whose maturity value is the amount of the cash flow and whose maturity date is the date the cash flow will be received. The reason this is the proper way to value a bond is that it does not allow a market participant to realize an arbitrage profit. Hence this approach to valuation is referred to as the *arbitrage-free approach.*

By viewing any financial asset in this way, a consistent valuation framework can be developed. For example, under the traditional approach to the valuation of bonds, a 10-year zero-coupon corporate bond would be viewed as the same financial asset as a 10-year 8% coupon corporate bond. Viewing a financial asset as a package of zero-coupon instruments means that these two corporate bond issues would be viewed as different packages of zero-coupon instruments and valued accordingly.

To implement the arbitrage-free approach, it is necessary to determine the theoretical rate that the U.S. Treasury would have to pay to issue a zero-coupon instrument for each maturity. Another name used for the zero-coupon rate is the *spot rate*. As explained later, the spot rate can be estimated from the Treasury yield curve.

An investor can select a corporate benchmark to construct the theoretical spot rate curve. For example, Fannie Mae and Freddie Mac agency debentures have been suggested as a benchmark because of the reduction in the supply of Treasury securities caused by reduced issuance of long-term Treasury securities and the buy back of these securities by the U.S. Department of the Treasury. Funded investors have been using LIBOR as the benchmark because their funding costs are typically tied to LIBOR and they are concerned with the spread relative to LIBOR.

Spot Rates and their Role in Valuation

The key to the valuation of any security is the estimation of its cash flow and the discounting of each cash flow by an appropriate rate. The starting point for the determination of the appropriate rate is the theoretical spot rate on default-free securities. Since Treasury securities are viewed as default-free securities, the theoretical spot rates on these securities are the benchmark rates.

There are several ways that Treasury spot rates can be obtained from market prices and yields. Basically, the following three methodologies are used in practice for obtaining Treasury spot rates:

1. bootstrapping methodology based on the Treasury yield curve
2. statistical methodology based on Treasury yields
3. observing yields in the Treasury strip market

The Treasury yield curve is the graphical depiction of the relationship between the yield on Treasury securities of different maturities. The Treasury yield curve is constructed from on-the-run Treasury issues.[1] Treasury bills are

---

[1] Some dealers and vendors of analytical systems use on-the-run Treasury issues plus selected off-the-run Treasury issues.

zero-coupon securities. Treasury notes and bonds are coupon securities. Consequently, the Treasury yield curve is a combination of zero-coupon securities and coupon securities. In the valuation of securities what is needed is the rate on zero-coupon default-free securities or, equivalently, the rate on zero-coupon Treasury securities. However, there are no zero-coupon Treasury securities issued by the U.S. Department of the Treasury with a maturity greater than 1 year. The bootstrapping methodology is a methodology for constructing a theoretical rate that the U.S. government would have to offer if it issued zero-coupon securities with a maturity greater than 1 year. In the appendix to this chapter, we will demonstrate how to derive theoretical spot rates.

Using only on-the-run issues, even when extended to include a few off-the-run issues, fails to recognize the information embodied in Treasury prices that are not included in the bootstrapping methodology. Thus, it is argued that it is more appropriate to use all Treasury coupon securities and bills to construct the theoretical spot rate curve. When all coupon securities and bills are used,[2] statistical methodologies must be employed to construct the theoretical spot rate curve rather than bootstrapping since there may be more than one yield for each maturity. Several statistical methodologies have been proposed to estimate the spot rate curve. The most common methodology used is "exponential spline fitting."

There are zero-coupon Treasury securities with a maturity greater than 1 year that are created by government dealer firms. These securities are called *stripped Treasury securities*, or simply *Treasury strips*. Treasury strips are distinguished based on whether they are created from the coupon payments or the principal payments. The former are called *coupon strips* and the latter are called *principal strips*. It would seem logical that the observed yield on Treasury strips could be used to construct an actual spot rate curve rather than using the bootstrapping or statistical methodologies to obtain the spot rates. There are three problems with using the observed rates on strips. First, the liquidity of the strips market is not as great as that of the Treasury coupon market. Thus, the observed rates on strips reflect a premium for liquidity. Second, the tax treatment of Treasury strips is different from that of Treasury coupon securities.[3] Finally, there are maturity sectors where non-U.S. investors find it advantageous to trade off yield for tax advantages associated with a Treasury strip. Specifically, certain foreign tax authorities allow their citizens to treat the difference between the maturity value and the purchase price as a capital gain and tax this gain at a favorable tax rate. Some will grant this favorable treatment only when the strip is created from the principal rather than the coupon. For this reason, those who use Treasury strips to represent theoretical spot rates restrict the issues included to coupon strips.

---

[2] Some practitioners do not use callable Treasury bonds. Moreover, a common practice is to filter the Treasury securities universe to eliminate securities that are on special in the repo market.

[3] Specifically, the accrued interest on strips is taxed even though no cash is received by the investor. Thus they are negative cash flow securities to taxable entities, and, as a result, their yield reflects this tax disadvantage.

Exhibit 1: Determination of the Theoretical Price of an 8% 10-Year Treasury

Period	Years	Cash Flow ($)	Spot Rate (%)*	Present Value ($)**
1	0.5	4.00	3.0000	3.9409
2	1.0	4.00	3.3000	3.8712
3	1.5	4.00	3.5053	3.7968
4	2.0	4.00	3.9164	3.7014
5	2.5	4.00	4.4376	3.5843
6	3.0	4.00	4.7520	3.4743
7	3.5	4.00	4.9622	3.3694
8	4.0	4.00	5.0650	3.2747
9	4.5	4.00	5.1707	3.1791
10	5.0	4.00	5.2772	3.0828
11	5.5	4.00	5.3864	2.9861
12	6.0	4.00	5.4976	2.8889
13	6.5	4.00	5.6108	2.7916
14	7.0	4.00	5.6643	2.7055
15	7.5	4.00	5.7193	2.6205
16	8.0	4.00	5.7755	2.5365
17	8.5	4.00	5.8331	2.4536
18	9.0	4.00	5.9584	2.3581
19	9.5	4.00	6.0863	2.2631
20	10.0	104.00	6.2169	56.3828
				115.2619

* The spot rate is an annual discount rate. The convention to obtain a semiannual discount rate is to take one-half the annual discount rate. So, for period 6 (i.e., 3 years), the spot rate is 4.7520%. The semiannual discount rate is 2.376%.

** The present value for the cash flow is equal to:

$$\frac{\text{cash flow}}{(1 + \text{spot rate}/2)^{\text{period}}}$$

Applying the Spot Rates to Value a Treasury Coupon Security

To demonstrate how to use the spot rate curve, suppose that we want to price an 8% 10-year Treasury security. The price of this issue is the present value of the cash flow where each cash flow is discounted at the corresponding spot rate. This is illustrated in Exhibit 1. The fourth column shows the assumed Treasury spot rates. The third column shows the cash flow for each period. The sum of the present values is equal to $115.2619. This is the theoretical price or arbitrage-free value of this issue.

To value a corporate bond, an appropriate spread must be added to each of the Treasury spot rates or any benchmark that is selected. Before explaining how this is done, we must explain the various spread measures in the market. In turn, we must understand the various yield measures used by practitioners and their limitations. We now turn to this topic.

YIELD MEASURES AND THEIR LIMITATIONS

An investor who purchases a bond can expect to receive a dollar return from one or more of the following sources:

- coupon interest payments made by the issuer,
- any capital gain (or capital loss—negative dollar return) when the bond matures, is called, or is sold, and
- income from reinvestment of the coupon interest payments. This source of dollar return is referred to as *reinvestment income* or *interest on interest*.

Four yield measures are commonly cited by market participants: yield to maturity, yield to call, yield to put, and yield to worst. These yield measures are expressed as a percent return rather than a dollar return. However, the yield measure should consider each of the three potential sources of return cited above.

Yield to Maturity

The most popular measure of yield in the bond market is the *yield to maturity*. The yield to maturity is the interest rate that will make the present value of a bond's cash flow equal to its price plus accrued interest. The price plus accrued interest is called the *full price* or *dirty price*.[4] Calculation of the yield to maturity of a bond is the reverse process of calculating the price of a bond. To find the price of a bond we determine the cash flow and the required yield, then we calculate the present value of the cash flow to obtain the price. To find the yield to maturity, we first determine the cash flow. Then we search by trial and error for the interest rate that will make the present value of the cash flow equal to the full price.[5]

To illustrate, consider a 7% 20-year bond selling for $67.91. The cash flow for this bond is (1) 40 six-month payments of $3.5 and (2) $100 40 six-month periods from now. The present value using various discount (interest) rates is:

Interest rate	3.5%	4.0%	4.5%	5.0%	5.5%	6.0%	6.5%
Present value	$100.00	$90.10	$81.60	$74.26	$67.91	$62.38	$57.56

When a 5.5% interest rate is used, the present value of the cash flow is equal to $67.91, which is the price of the bond. Hence, 5.5% is the semiannual yield to maturity.

The market convention adopted is to double the semiannual interest rate and call that interest rate the yield to maturity. Thus, the yield to maturity for the above bond is 11% (2 times 5.5%). The yield to maturity computed using this convention—doubling the semiannual yield—is called a *bond-equivalent yield*.

The following relationships between the price of a bond, coupon rate, and yield to maturity hold:

---

[4] The price without accrued interest is called the *clean price*.
[5] In the illustrations presented in this chapter, we assume that the next coupon payment will be 6 months from now so that the full price is just the clean price.

Bond selling at a	Relationship
par	coupon rate = yield to maturity
discount	coupon rate < yield to maturity
premium	coupon rate > yield to maturity

The yield to maturity considers not only the coupon income but also any capital gain or loss that the investor will realize by *holding the bond to maturity*. The yield to maturity also considers the timing of the cash flow. It does consider reinvestment income; *however, it assumes that the coupon payments can be reinvested at an interest rate equal to the yield to maturity*. So, if the yield to maturity for a bond is 10%, for example, to earn that yield the coupon payments must be reinvested at an interest rate equal to 10%. The following illustration clearly demonstrates this.

Suppose an investor has $74.26 and places the funds in a certificate of deposit that pays 5% every 6 months for 20 years or 10% per year on a bond-equivalent basis. At the end of 20 years, the $74.26 investment will grow to $522.79. Instead, suppose an investor buys the following bond: a 7% 20-year bond selling for $74.26. The yield to maturity for this bond is 10%. The investor would expect that at the end of 20 years, the total dollars from the investment will be $522.79.

Let's look at what the investor will receive. There will be 40 semiannual interest payments of $3.50 which will total $140. When the bond matures, the investor will receive $100. Thus, the total dollars that the investor will receive is $240 if he held the bond to maturity. But this is less than the $522.79 necessary to produce a yield of 10% on a bond-equivalent basis. The shortfall is $282.79 ($522.79 − $240). How is this deficiency supposed to be made up? If the investor reinvests the coupon payments at a semiannual interest rate of 5% (or 10% annual rate on a bond-equivalent basis), then the interest earned by reinvesting the coupon payments will be $282.79. Consequently, of the $448.53 total dollar return ($522.79 − $74.26) necessary to produce a yield of 10%, about 63% ($282.79 ÷ $448.52) must be generated by reinvesting the coupon payments.

Clearly, the investor will only realize the yield to maturity that is stated at the time of purchase if (1) the coupon payments can be reinvested at the yield to maturity, and (2) the bond is held to maturity. With respect to the first assumption, the risk that an investor faces is that future reinvestment rates will be less than the yield to maturity at the time the bond is purchased. This risk is referred to as *reinvestment risk*. If the bond is not held to maturity, the bond may have to be sold for less than its purchase price, resulting in a return that is less than the yield to maturity. The risk that a bond will have to be sold at a loss is referred to as *interest rate risk.*

Two characteristics of a bond determine the degree of reinvestment risk. First, for a given yield to maturity and a given coupon rate, the longer the maturity the more the bond's total dollar return is dependent on reinvestment income to realize the yield to maturity at the time of purchase (i.e., the greater the reinvestment risk). The implication is that the yield to maturity measure for long-term coupon bonds tells little about the potential return that an investor may realize if the bond is held to maturity. For long-term bonds, in high interest rate environments the reinvestment income component may be as high as 80% of the bond's potential total dollar return.

The second characteristic that determines the degree of reinvestment risk is the coupon rate. For a given maturity and a given yield to maturity, the higher the coupon rate, the more dependent the bond's total dollar return will be on the reinvestment of the coupon payments in order to produce the yield to maturity at the time of purchase. This means that holding maturity and yield to maturity constant, premium bonds will be more dependent on reinvestment income than bonds selling at par. In contrast, discount bonds will be less dependent on reinvestment income than bonds selling at par. For zero-coupon bonds, none of the bond's total dollar return is dependent on reinvestment income. So, a zero-coupon bond has no zero reinvestment risk if held to maturity.

A bond's price moves in the opposite direction of the change in interest rates. As interest rates rise (fall), the price of a bond will fall (rise). For an investor who plans to hold a bond to maturity and need not mark to market a position, the change in the bond's price prior to maturity is of no concern; however, for an investor who may have to sell the bond prior to the maturity date, an increase in interest rates subsequent to the time the bond was purchased will mean the realization of a capital loss. Not all bonds have the same degree of interest rate risk. In Chapter 6 we explain the characteristics of a bond that determine its interest rate risk.

Given the assumptions underlying yield to maturity, we now can drive home with an illustration the key point that yield to maturity has limited value in assessing the relative performance of a bond. Suppose that an investor who has a 5-year investment horizon is considering the following four bonds:

Bond	Coupon	Maturity	Yield to Maturity
W	5%	3 years	9.0%
X	6%	20 years	8.6%
Y	11%	15 years	9.2%
Z	8%	5 years	8.0%

Assuming that all four bonds are of the same credit quality, which one is the most attractive to this investor? An investor who selects Bond Y because it offers the highest yield to maturity is failing to recognize that the bond must be sold after 5 years, the price of the bond depending on the yield required in the market for 10-year 11% coupon bonds at the time. Hence, there could be a capital gain or capital loss that will make the return higher or lower than the yield to maturity promised now. Moreover, the higher coupon on Bond Y relative to the other three bonds means that more of this bond's return will be dependent on the reinvestment of coupon interest payments.

Bond W offers the second highest yield to maturity. On the surface, it seems to be particularly attractive because it eliminates the problem faced by purchasing Bond Y of realizing a possible capital loss when the bond must be sold prior to the maturity date. In addition, the reinvestment risk seems to be less than for the other three bonds because the coupon rate is the lowest. However, the investor would not be eliminating the reinvestment risk since after 3 years he must reinvest the proceeds received at maturity for 2 more years. The yield that the investor will realize will depend on interest rates 3 years from now when the investor must reinvest the proceeds.

Which is the best bond? The yield to maturity doesn't seem to be helping us identify the best bond. The answer depends on the expectations of the investor. Specifically, it depends on the interest rate at which the coupon interest payments can be reinvested until the end of the investor's investment horizon. Also, for bonds with a maturity longer than the investment horizon, it depends on the investor's expectations about interest rates at the end of the investment horizon. Consequently, any of these bonds can be the best investment vehicle based on some assumed reinvestment rate and some future interest rate at the end of the investment horizon. The framework for assessing the performance of a bond over some investment horizon is the *total return*.

Yield to Call

When a bond is callable, the practice has been to calculate a yield to call as well as a yield to maturity. A callable bond may have a call schedule. The yield to call assumes that the issuer will call the bond at some assumed call date and the call price is then the call price specified in the call schedule. Typically, investors calculate a yield to first call or yield to next call, a yield to first par call, and yield to refunding. The *yield to first call* is computed for an issue that is not currently callable, while the *yield to next call* is computed for an issue that is currently callable. The *yield to refunding* is computed assuming the issue will be called on the first date the issue is refundable. (An issue may be callable, but there may be a period when the issue may not be called using a lower cost of funds than the issue itself, i.e., the issue is nonrefundable.)

The procedure for calculating the yield to call is the same as for any yield calculation: determine the interest rate that will make the present value of the expected cash flows equal to the price plus accrued interest. In the case of yield to first call, the expected cash flows are the coupon payments to the first call date and the call price. For the yield to first par call, the expected cash flows are the coupon payments to the first date at which the issuer can call the bond at par and the par value.

To illustrate the computation, consider a 7% 8-year bond with a maturity value of $100 selling for $106.36. Suppose that the first call date is 3 years from now and the call price is $103. The cash flows for this bond if it is called in 3 years are (1) six coupon payments of $3.50 and (2) $103 in six 6-month periods from now. The process for finding the yield to first call is the same as for finding the yield to maturity. The present value for several semiannual interest rates is shown as follows:

Annual interest rate	Semi-annual rate	Present value of 6 payments of $3.50	Present value of $103 6 periods from now	Present value of cash flows
5.0%	2.5%	$16.27	$91.83	$108.10
5.2	2.6	16.21	91.30	107.51
5.4	2.7	16.16	90.77	106.93
5.6	2.8	16.12	90.24	106.36

Since a semiannual interest rate of 2.8% makes the present value of the cash flows equal to the price, 2.8% is the yield to first call. Therefore, the yield to first call on a bond-equivalent basis is 5.6%.

Let's take a closer look at the yield to call as a measure of the potential return of a security. The yield to call does consider all three sources of potential return from owning a bond. However, as in the case of the yield to maturity, it assumes that each cash flow can be reinvested at the yield to call until the assumed call date. As we just demonstrated, this assumption may be inappropriate. Moreover, the yield to call assumes that (1) the investor will hold the bond to the assumed call date and (2) the issuer will call the bond on that date.

These assumptions underlying the yield to call are often unrealistic. They do not take into account how an investor will reinvest the proceeds if the issue is called. For example, consider two 5-year bonds, M and N. Suppose that the yield to maturity for bond M, a 5-year noncallable bond, is 8% while for bond N the yield to call assuming the bond will be called in 2 years is 8.5%. Which bond is better for an investor with a 5-year investment horizon? It's not possible to tell from the yields cited. If the investor intends to hold the bond for 5 years and the issuer calls the bond after 2 years, the total dollars that will be available at the end of 5 years will depend on the interest rate that can be earned from investing funds from the call date to the end of the investment horizon.

The total return framework takes these factors into account.

Yield to Put

When a bond is putable, the yield to the first put date is calculated. The *yield to put* is the interest rate that will make the present value of the cash flow to the first put date equal to the price plus accrued interest. As with all yield measures, yield to put assumes that any interim coupon payments can be reinvested at the yield calculated. Moreover, the yield to put assumes that the bond will be put on the first put date.

For example, suppose that a 6.2% coupon bond maturing in 8 years is putable at par in 3 years. The price of this bond is $102.19. The cash flows for this bond if it is put in 3 years are: (1) six coupon payments of $3.10 every 6 months and (2) the $100 put price in six 6-month periods from now. The semiannual interest rate that will make the present value of the cash flows equal to the price of $102.19 is 2.7%. Therefore, 2.7% is the semiannual yield to put and 5.4% is the yield to put on a bond-equivalent basis.

Yield to Worst

A yield can be calculated for every possible call date. In addition, a yield to maturity and, if applicable, a yield to put can be calculated. The lowest of all these possible yields is called the *yield to worst*. For example, suppose that there are only four possible call dates for a callable bond and that a yield to call assuming each possible call date is 6%, 6.2%, 5.8%, and 5.7%, and that the yield to maturity is 7.5%. Then the yield to worst is the minimum of these values, 5.7% in our example.

The yield to worst measure holds little meaning because of its underlying assumptions.

YIELD SPREAD MEASURES

Traditional analysis of the yield premium for a corporate bond involves calculating the difference between the bond's yield to maturity (or yield to call) and the yield to maturity of a comparable maturity Treasury coupon security. The latter is obtained from the Treasury yield curve. For example, consider the following 10-year bonds:

Issue	Coupon	Price	Yield to maturity
Treasury	6%	$100.00	6.00%
corporate	8%	$104.19	7.40%

The yield spread for these two bonds as traditionally computed is 140 basis points (7.4% minus 6%). We refer to this traditional yield spread as the *nominal spread*.

The drawbacks of the nominal spread are (1) for both bonds, the yield fails to take into consideration the term structure of the spot rates and (2) in the case of callable and/or putable bonds, expected interest rate volatility may alter the cash flow of the corporate bond. Here, we focus only on the first problem: failure to consider the spot rate curve. We deal with the second problem later in this chapter.

Zero-Volatility Spread

The *zero-volatility spread* is a measure of the spread that the investor would realize over the entire Treasury spot rate curve if (1) the bond is held to maturity and (2) the spot rates do not change. It is not a spread off one point on the Treasury yield curve, as is the nominal spread. The zero-volatility spread, also called the *static spread*, is calculated as the spread that will make the present value of the cash flow from the corporate bond, when discounted at the Treasury spot rate plus the spread, equal to the corporate bond's full price. A trial-and-error procedure is used to determine the zero-volatility spread.

To illustrate how this is done, let's use the corporate issue in our previous illustration (i.e., the 8% coupon 10-year issue) and the Treasury spot rates assumed in Exhibit 1. The Treasury spot rates are reproduced in the fourth column of Exhibit 2. The third column in the exhibit is the cash flow for the 8% 10-year corporate issue. The goal is to determine the spread that when added to all the Treasury spot rates will produce a present value for the cash flow of the corporate issue equal to its market price, $104.19.

Suppose we select a spread of 100 basis points. To each Treasury spot rate shown in the fourth column 100 basis points is added. So, for example, the 5-year (period 10) spot rate is 6.2772% (5.2772% plus 1%). The spot rate plus 100 basis points is then used to calculate the present value of $107.5414. Because the present value is not equal to the corporate issue's price ($104.19), the zero-volatility spread is not 100 basis points. If a spread of 125 basis points is tried, it can be seen from the next-to-the-last column of Exhibit 2 that the present value is $105.7165; again, because this is not equal to the corporate issue's price, 125 basis points is not the zero-volatility spread. The last column of Exhibit 2 shows the present value when a 146 basis point spread is tried. The present value is approximately equal to the corporate issue's price of 104.2. Therefore 146 basis points is the zero-volatility spread, compared to the nominal spread of 140 basis points.

Typically, for standard coupon paying bonds with a bullet maturity (i.e., a single payment of principal) the zero-volatility spread and the nominal spread will not differ significantly. In our example it is only 6 basis points (146 basis points versus 140 basis points). For short-term bullet issues, there is little divergence. The main factor causing any difference is the shape of the yield curve. The steeper the yield curve, the greater the difference.

The difference between the zero-volatility spread and the nominal spread is greater for issues in which the principal is repaid over time rather than only at maturity. Thus the difference between the nominal spread and the zero-volatility spread will be considerably greater for sinking fund bonds, mortgage-backed securities, and asset-backed securities in a steep yield curve environment.

Exhibit 2: Determination of the Zero-Volatility Spread for the 8%, 10-Year Corporate Issue Selling at 104.19 to Yield 7.4%

Period	Years	Cash Flow ($)	Spot Rate (%)	Present Value		
				Spread 100 bp ($)	Spread 125 bp ($)	Spread 146 bp ($)
1	0.5	4.00	3.0000	3.9216	3.9168	3.9127
2	1.0	4.00	3.3000	3.8334	3.8240	3.8162
3	1.5	4.00	3.5053	3.7414	3.7277	3.7163
4	2.0	4.00	3.9164	3.6297	3.6121	3.5973
5	2.5	4.00	4.4376	3.4979	3.4767	3.4590
6	3.0	4.00	4.7520	3.3742	3.3497	3.3293
7	3.5	4.00	4.9622	3.2565	3.2290	3.2061
8	4.0	4.00	5.0650	3.1497	3.1193	3.0940
9	4.5	4.00	5.1701	3.430	3.0100	2.9826
10	5.0	4.00	5.2772	2.9366	2.9013	2.8719
11	5.5	4.00	5.3864	2.8307	2.7933	2.7622
12	6.0	4.00	5.4976	2.7255	2.6862	2.6537
13	6.5	4.00	5.6108	2.6210	2.5801	2.5463
14	7.0	4.00	5.6643	2.5279	2.4855	2.4504
15	7.5	4.00	5.7193	2.4367	2.3929	2.3568
16	8.0	4.00	5.7755	2.3472	2.3023	2.2652
17	8.5	4.00	5.8331	2.2596	2.2137	2.1758
18	9.0	4.00	5.9584	2.1612	2.1148	2.0766
19	9.5	4.00	6.0863	2.0642	2.0174	1.9790
20	10.0	104.00	6.2169	51.1833	49.9638	48.9630
			Total	107.5414	105.7165	104.2145

The Term Structure of Credit Spreads

The Treasury spot rates can be used to value any default-free security. The failure of Treasury securities to be priced according to the Treasury spot rates creates the opportunity for arbitrage profits or enhanced returns.

For a corporate bond, the theoretical value is not as easy to determine. The value of a corporate bond must reflect not only the spot rate for default-free bonds but also a risk premium to reflect default risk and any options embedded in the issue.

It has been common in practice for the spot rate used to discount the cash flow of a corporate bond to be the Treasury spot rate plus a constant credit spread. For example, if the 6-month Treasury spot rate is 3%, and the 10-year Treasury spot rate is 6%, and a suitable credit spread is deemed to be 100 basis points, then a 4% spot rate is used to discount a 6-month cash flow of a corporate bond and a 7% discount rate to discount a 10-year cash flow.

The drawback of this approach is that there is no reason to expect the credit spread to be the same regardless of when the cash flow is expected to be received. Instead, it might be expected that the credit spread increases with the maturity of the bond. That is, there is a term structure for credit spreads.

In practice, the difficulty in estimating a term structure for credit spreads is that unlike Treasury securities in which there is a wide range of maturities from which to construct a Treasury spot rate curve, there are no issuers that offer a sufficiently wide range of corporate zero-coupon securities to construct a zero-coupon spread curve. Robert Litterman and Thomas Iben describe a procedure to construct a generic zero-coupon spread curve for corporate bonds by credit rating and industry using data provided from a trading desk.[6]

Typically, the credit spread increases with maturity. This is a typical shape for the term structure of credit spreads. In addition, the shape of the term structure is not the same for all credit ratings.[7] For investment-grade corporate bonds, the lower the credit rating, the steeper the term structure. One implication of an upward-sloping term structure for credit spreads is that it is inappropriate to discount the cash flow from a corporate bond at a constant spread to the Treasury spot rate curve. The short-term cash flows will be undervalued, and the long-term cash flows will be overvalued.

---

[6] Robert Litterman and Thomas Iben, "Corporate Bond Valuation and the Term Structure of Credit Spreads," *Journal of Portfolio Management* (Spring 1991), pp. 52–64.

[7] Theoretical reasons for this relationship are proffered in Robert C. Merton, "On the Pricing of Corporate Debt: The Risk Structure of Interest Rates," *Journal of Finance* (May 1974), pp. 449–470. For empirical evidence, see O. Sarig and Arthur D. Warga, "Bond Price Data and Bond Market Liquidity," *Journal of Financial and Quantitative Analysis* (September 1989), pp. 1351–1360; Jerome S. Fons, "Using Default Rates to Model the Term Structure of Credit Risk," *Financial Analysts Journal* (September/October 1994), pp. 25–32; and, Jean Helwege and Christopher M. Turner, "The Slope of the Credit Yield Curve for Speculative-Grade Issuers," *Journal of Finance* (October 1999), pp. 1869–1884.

Exhibit 3: Calculation of Value of a Hypothetical AAA Industrial 8% 10-Year Bond Using Benchmark Spot Rate Curve

Period	Years	Cash Flow ($)	Treasury Spot Rate (%)	Zero-coupon Credit Spread	Benchmark Spot Rate (%)	Present Value ($)
1	0.5	4.00	3.0000	0.20	3.2000	3.9370
2	1.0	4.00	3.3000	0.20	3.5000	3.8636
3	1.5	4.00	3.5053	0.25	3.7553	3.7829
4	2.0	4.00	3.9164	0.30	4.2164	3.6797
5	2.5	4.00	4.4376	0.35	4.7876	3.5538
6	3.0	4.00	4.7520	0.35	5.1020	3.4389
7	3.5	4.00	4.9622	0.40	5.3622	3.3237
8	4.0	4.00	5.0650	0.45	5.5150	3.2177
9	4.5	4.00	5.1701	0.45	5.6201	3.1170
10	5.0	4.00	5.2772	0.50	5.7772	3.0088
11	5.5	4.00	5.3864	0.55	5.9364	2.8995
12	6.0	4.00	5.4976	0.60	6.0976	2.7896
13	6.5	4.00	5.6108	0.65	6.2608	2.6794
14	7.0	4.00	5.6643	0.70	6.3643	2.5799
15	7.5	4.00	5.7193	0.75	6.4693	2.4813
16	8.0	4.00	5.7755	0.80	6.5755	2.3838
17	8.5	4.00	5.8331	0.85	6.6831	2.2876
18	9.0	4.00	5.9584	0.90	6.8684	2.1801
19	9.5	4.00	6.0863	0.95	7.0363	2.0737
20	10.0	104.00	6.2169	1.00	7.2169	51.1833
					Total	108.4615

Benchmark Spot Rate Curve

When the generic zero spreads for a given credit quality and in a given industry are added to the default-free spot rates, the resulting term structure is used to value bonds of issuers of the same credit quality in the industry sector. This term structure is referred to as the *benchmark spot rate curve* or *benchmark zero-coupon rate curve*.

For example, Exhibit 3 reproduces the default-free spot rate curve in Exhibit 2. Also shown in the exhibit is a hypothetical generic zero spread for AAA industrial bonds. The resulting benchmark spot rate curve is in the next-to-the-last column. This spot rate curve is used to value a AAA industrial bond. This is done in Exhibit 3 for a hypothetical 8% 10-year AAA industrial bond. The theoretical price is $108.4615.

In the same way that a zero-volatility spread relative to a default-free spot rate curve can be calculated, a zero-volatility spread to any benchmark spot rate curve can be calculated. To illustrate, suppose that a hypothetical AAA industrial bond with a coupon rate of 8% and a 10-year maturity is trading at $105.5423. The zero-volatility spread relative to the AAA industrial term structure is the spread that must be added to that term structure that will make the present value of the cash flow equal to the market price. In our illustration, the zero-volatility spread relative to this benchmark is 40 basis points.

Thus, when a zero-volatility spread is cited, it must be cited relative to some benchmark spot rate curve. This is necessary because it indicates the credit and sector risks that are being considered when the zero-volatility spread is calculated.

In the U.S. Treasury market, it is relatively easy to construct a spot rate curve using a bootstrap or spline method, because of the large number of liquid Treasury securities that span the maturity spectrum, from 3 months to 30 years. As the corporate bond market has matured, many corporations have nearly complete yield curves of liquid bonds across many maturities. In cases where the corporate curve is reasonably complete, the most rigorous approach to corporate bond valuation is to discount each cash flow at the appropriate spot rate for the corporate issuer. The appropriate spot rate can be derived by bootstrapping or splining the corporate yield curve. The difference between the corporate spot rate and the Treasury spot rate is the corporate spot spread. In turn, the curve of spot spreads can be used to construct an implied par coupon spread curve. Some investors measure relative value by comparing the implied coupon spread curve with spreads that are observed in the market. Moreover, this method of valuation is particularly useful for analyzing bonds with unusual structures, such as zero-to-full bonds and other step-up coupon bonds.

Swap Spreads

An extremely important spread measure that is cited by market participants is the *swap spread*. In an interest rate swap there are two parties (referred to as counterparties) who exchange payments based on some notional amount of principal. In the most common type of interest rate swap, one party pays a fixed interest rate and the other party pays a floating interest rate. The party that pays the fixed interest rate pays over the life of the swap an interest rate equal to a yield spread above the Treasury rate. More specifically, it is the yield spread above the on-the-run Treasury rate with the same maturity as the term of the swap. So, if the swap is a 5-year swap, the fixed-rate payer pays the 5-year Treasury rate plus a yield spread. The yield spread is called the *swap spread*. The fixed-rate payer receives a floating rate, typically the London Interbank Offered Rate (LIBOR).

LIBOR reflects the credit risk of international banks. So, if the swap is a 5-year swap and the swap spread is 80 basis points, this means that the fixed-rate payer pays the 5-year Treasury rate plus 80 basis points to receive LIBOR. The swap spread effectively reflects general corporate credit risk, as well as other factors. Historically, the swap spread has been highly correlated to the yield spread for corporate bonds. The point is that today when market participants discuss yield spreads they frequently refer to swap spreads. While swap spreads reflect several factors in addition to credit risk, they tend to be highly correlated with the yield spreads in certain sectors of the fixed-income market. Hence, they are used as a general gauge of credit spreads.

The other factors in addition to the general level of credit risk in the market that affect the size of the swap spread are (1) the supply of Treasury securities relative to the supply of credit spread products, (2) the liquidity premium demanded by the market, (3) market psychology toward spread products and the expected direction in interest rates, and (4) the risk appetite of dealer desks.[8]

Yield Spread Measures for Floating-Rate Securities

The coupon rate for a floating-rate security changes periodically according to a reference rate (such as LIBOR or a Treasury rate). Since the future value for the reference rate is unknown, it is not possible to determine the cash flows. This means that a yield to maturity cannot be calculated. Instead, there are several conventional measures used as margin or spread measures cited by market participants for floaters. These include *spread for life* (or *simple margin*), *adjusted simple margin*, *adjusted total margin*, and *discount margin*.

The most popular of these measures is discount margin, so we will discuss this measure and its limitations as follows.[9] This measure estimates the average margin over the reference rate that the investor can expect to earn over the life of the security. The procedure for calculating the discount margin is as follows:

Step 1. Determine the cash flows assuming that the reference rate does *not* change over the life of the security.

Step 2. Select a margin.

Step 3. Discount the cash flows found in Step 1 by the current value of the reference rate plus the margin selected in Step 2.

Step 4. Compare the present value of the cash flows as calculated in Step 3 to the price plus accrued interest. If the present value is equal to the security's price plus accrued interest, the discount margin is the margin assumed in Step 2. If the present value is not equal to the security's price plus accrued interest, go back to Step 2 and try a different margin.

For a security selling at par, the discount margin is simply the quoted margin in the coupon reset formula.

To illustrate the calculation, suppose that the coupon reset formula for a 6-year floating-rate security selling for $99.3098 is 6-month LIBOR plus 80 basis points. The coupon rate is reset every 6 months. Assume that the current value for the reference rate is 10%.

Exhibit 4 shows the calculation of the discount margin for this security. The second column shows the current value for 6-month LIBOR. The third column sets forth the cash flows for the security. The cash flows for the first 11 peri-

---

[8] These factors are explained in more detail in Richard Gordon, "The Truth About Swap Spreads," *Professional Perspectives on Fixed Income Portfolio Management: Volume 1* (New Hope, PA: Frank J. Fabozzi Associates, 2000).

[9] For a discussion of the other traditional measures, see Chapter 3 in Frank J. Fabozzi and Steven V. Mann, *Floating-Rate Securities* (New Hope, PA; Frank J. Fabozzi Associates, 2000).

ods are equal to one-half the current 6-month LIBOR (5%) plus the semiannual assumed margin of 40 basis points multiplied by $100. At the maturity date (i.e., period 12), the cash flow is $5.4 plus the maturity value of $100. The top row of the last five columns shows the assumed margin. The rows below the assumed margin show the present value of each cash flow. The last row gives the total present value of the cash flows.

For the five assumed margins, the present value is equal to the price of the floating-rate security ($99.3098) when the assumed margin is 96 basis points. Therefore, the discount margin is 96 basis points. Notice that the discount margin would be 80 basis points, the same as the quoted margin, when the security is selling at par.

There are two drawbacks of the discount margin as a measure of the potential return over the reference rate from investing in a floating-rate security. First, the measure assumes that the reference rate will not change over the life of the security. Second, if the floating-rate security has a cap or floor, or is callable or putable, this is not taken into consideration.

Exhibit 4: Calculation of the Discount Margin for a Floating-Rate Security

Floating rate security:

Maturity	= 6 years
Price	= 99.3098
Coupon formula	= LIBOR + 80 basis points
	Reset every six months

Period	LIBOR (%)	Cash flow ($)*	\multicolumn{5}{Present value ($) at assumed margin of**}
			80 bp	84 bp	88 bp	96 bp	100 bp
1	10	5.4	5.1233	5.1224	5.1214	5.1195	5.1185
2	10	5.4	4.8609	4.8590	4.8572	4.8535	4.8516
3	10	5.4	4.6118	4.6092	4.6066	4.6013	4.5987
4	10	5.4	4.3755	4.3722	4.3689	4.3623	4.3590
5	10	5.4	4.1514	4.1474	4.1435	4.1356	4.1317
6	10	5.4	3.9387	3.9342	3.9297	3.9208	3.9163
7	10	5.4	3.7369	3.7319	3.7270	3.7171	3.7122
8	10	5.4	3.5454	3.5401	3.5347	3.5240	3.5186
9	10	5.4	3.3638	3.3580	3.3523	3.3409	3.3352
10	10	5.4	3.1914	3.1854	3.1794	3.1673	3.1613
11	10	5.4	3.0279	3.0216	3.0153	3.0028	2.9965
12	10	105.4	56.0729	55.9454	55.8182	55.5647	55.4385
		Present value	100.0000	99.8269	99.6541	99.3098	99.1381

* For periods 1-11: cash flow = $100 (0.5) (LIBOR + assumed margin)
  For period 12: cash flow = $100 (0.5) (LIBOR + assumed margin) + $100
** The discount rate is found as follows. To LIBOR of 10%, the assumed margin is added. Thus, for an 88 basis point assumed margin, the discount rate is 10.88%. This is an annual discount rate on a bond-equivalent basis. The semiannual discount rate is then half this amount, 5.44%. This discount rate is used to compute the present value of the cash flows for an assumed margin of 88 basis points.

APPENDIX: DERIVING THE SPOT RATE CURVE

In this chapter several methodologies for deriving the Treasury spot rate curve were described. In this appendix we explain the bootstrapping method. This method begins with the on-the-run Treasury issues. These include the 1-month, 3-month, and 6-month Treasury bills and the 2-year, 5-year, and 10-year Treasury notes, and the 30-year Treasury bond.

There is an observed yield for each of the on-the-run issues. For the coupon issues, these yields are not the yields used in the analysis when the issue is not trading at par. Instead, for each on-the-run coupon issue, the estimated yield necessary to make the issue trade at par is used. The resulting on-the-run yield curve is called the *par yield curve*.

The goal is to construct a theoretical spot rate curve with 60 semiannual spot rates—6-month rate to 30-year rate. Excluding the 1-month and 3-month rates, there are only six maturity points available when only the on-the-run issues are used. The 54 missing maturity points are extrapolated from the surrounding maturity points on the par yield curve. The simplest extrapolation method, and the one most commonly used, is linear extrapolation. Specifically, given the yield on the par coupon curve at two maturity points, the following is calculated:

$$\frac{\text{Yield at higher maturity} - \text{Yield at lower maturity}}{\text{Number of semiannual periods between the two maturity points}}$$

Then, the yield for all intermediate semiannual maturity points is found by adding to the yield at the lower maturity the amount computed above.

For example, suppose that the yield from the par yield curve for the 2-year and 5-year on-the-run Treasuries is 6% and 6.3%, respectively. There are six semiannual periods. The extrapolated yield for the 2.5, 3.0, 3.5, 4.0, and 4.5 maturity points is found as follows. Calculate

$$\frac{6.3\% - 6.0\%}{6} = 0.05\%$$

Then,

2.5-year yield = 6.00% + 0.05% = 6.05%
3.0-year yield = 6.05% + 0.05% = 6.10%
3.5-year yield = 6.10% + 0.05% = 6.15%
4.0-year yield = 6.15% + 0.05% = 6.20%
4.5-year yield = 6.20% + 0.05% = 6.25%

There are two problems with using just the on-the-run issues. First, there is a large gap between some of the maturities points, which may result in misleading yields for those maturity points when estimated using the linear extrapolation method. Specifically, the concern is with the large gap between the 5-year and 10-year maturity points and the 10-year and 30-year maturity points. The second problem is that the yields for the on-the-run coupon issues themselves may be misleading because they may be on special in the repo market. This means that the true yield is greater than the quoted (observed) yield.

Now let's look at how the par yield curve is converted into the theoretical spot rate curve using the bootstrapping methodology. For simplicity, we will illustrate this methodology to calculate the theoretical spot rate curve for only 10 years. That is, 20 semiannual spot rates will be computed. Suppose that the par yield curve is the one shown in Exhibit A-1.[10] Our focus is on the first three columns of this exhibit. Our goal is to explain how the values in the last column of the exhibit are derived.

The basic principle to obtain the theoretical spot rates is that the value of a Treasury coupon security should be equal to the value of the package of zero-coupon instruments that duplicates the coupon security's cash flows. Consider the 6-month Treasury bill in Exhibit A-1. Since a Treasury bill is a zero-coupon instrument, its annualized yield of 3.00% is equal to the spot rate. Similarly, for the 1-year Treasury, the cited yield of 3.30% is the 1-year spot rate. Given these two spot rates, we can compute the spot rate for a theoretical 1.5-year zero-coupon Treasury. The price of a theoretical 1.5-year Treasury should equal the present value of the three cash flows from the 1.5-year coupon Treasury, where the yield used for discounting is the spot rate corresponding to the cash flow. Since all the coupon bonds are selling at par, the yield to maturity for each bond is the coupon rate. Using $100 as par, the cash flows for the 1.5-year coupon Treasury are:

Exhibit A-1: Par Yield Curve for 10 Years

Period	Years	Yield to maturity (%)	Spot rate (%)
1	0.5	3.00	3.0000
2	1.0	3.30	3.3000
3	1.5	3.50	3.5053
4	2.0	3.90	3.9164
5	2.5	4.40	4.4376
6	3.0	4.70	4.7520
7	3.5	4.90	4.9622
8	4.0	5.00	5.0650
9	4.5	5.10	5.1701
10	5.0	5.20	5.2772
11	5.5	5.30	5.3864
12	6.0	5.40	5.4976
13	6.5	5.50	5.6108
14	7.0	5.55	5.6643
15	7.5	5.60	5.7193
16	8.0	5.65	5.7755
17	8.5	5.70	5.8331
18	9.0	5.80	5.9584
19	9.5	5.90	6.0863
20	10.0	6.00	6.2169

[10] Note that the intermediate points in this illustration were not calculated using the linear extrapolation procedure.

$$
\begin{array}{lll}
0.5 \text{ year:} & 0.035 \times \$100 \times 0.5 & = \quad \$1.75 \\
1.0 \text{ year:} & 0.035 \times \$100 \times 0.5 & = \quad \$1.75 \\
1.5 \text{ year:} & 0.035 \times \$100 \times 0.5 + 100 & = \quad \$101.75
\end{array}
$$

The present value of the cash flow is then:

$$
\frac{1.75}{(1+z_1)^1} + \frac{1.75}{(1+z_2)^2} + \frac{101.75}{(1+z_3)^3}
$$

where

z_1 = one-half the 6-month theoretical spot rate,
z_2 = one-half the 1-year theoretical spot rate, and
z_3 = one-half the 1.5-year theoretical spot rate.

Since the 6-month spot rate and 1-year spot rate are 3.00% and 3.30%, respectively, we know that:

$$
z_1 = 0.0150 \text{ and } z_2 = 0.0165
$$

We can compute the present value of the 1.5-year coupon Treasury security as:

$$
\frac{1.75}{(1+z_1)^1} + \frac{1.75}{(1+z_2)^2} + \frac{101.75}{(1+z_3)^3} = \frac{1.75}{(1.015)^1} + \frac{1.75}{(1.0165)^2} + \frac{101.75}{(1+z_3)^3}
$$

Since the price of the 1.5-year coupon Treasury security is par, the following relationship must hold:

$$
\frac{1.75}{(1.015)^1} + \frac{1.75}{(1.0165)^2} + \frac{101.75}{(1+z_3)^3} = 100
$$

We can solve for the theoretical 1.5-year spot rate as follows:

$$
1.7241 + 1.6936 + \frac{101.75}{(1+z_3)^3} = 100
$$

$$
\frac{101.75}{(1+z_3)^3} = 96.5822
$$

$$
(1+z_3)^3 = \frac{101.75}{96.5822}
$$

$$
z_3 = 0.0175265 = 1.7527\%
$$

Doubling this yield we obtain the bond-equivalent yield of 3.5053%, which is the theoretical 1.5-year spot rate. That rate is the rate that the market would apply to a 1.5-year zero-coupon Treasury security if, in fact, such a security existed.

Given the theoretical 1.5-year spot rate, we can obtain the theoretical 2-year spot rate. The cash flows for the 2-year coupon Treasury in Exhibit A-1 are:

0.5 years: $0.039 \times \$100 \times 0.5$ = $1.95
1.0 years: $0.039 \times \$100 \times 0.5$ = $1.95
1.5 years: $0.039 \times \$100 \times 0.5$ = $1.95
2.0 years: $0.039 \times \$100 \times 0.5 + 100$ = $101.95

The present value of the cash flows is then:

$$\frac{1.95}{(1+z_1)^1} + \frac{1.95}{(1+z_2)^2} + \frac{1.95}{(1+z_3)^3} + \frac{101.95}{(1+z_4)^4}$$

where z_4 = one-half the 2-year theoretical spot rate.

Since the 6-month spot rate, 1-year spot rate, and 1.5-year spot rate are 3.00%, 3.30%, and 3.5053%, respectively, then:

$$z_1 = 0.0150, z_2 = 0.0165, \text{ and } z_3 = 0.017527$$

Therefore, the present value of the 2-year coupon Treasury security is:

$$\frac{1.95}{(1.0150)^1} + \frac{1.95}{(1.0165)^2} + \frac{1.95}{(1.017527)^3} + \frac{101.95}{(1+z_4)^4}$$

Since the price of the 2-year coupon Treasury security is par, the following relationship must hold:

$$\frac{1.95}{(1.0150)^1} + \frac{1.95}{(1.0165)^2} + \frac{1.95}{(1.017527)^3} + \frac{101.95}{(1+z_4)^4} = 100$$

We can solve for the theoretical 2-year spot rate as follows:

$$\frac{101.95}{(1+z_4)^4} = 94.3407$$

$$(1+z_4)^4 = \frac{101.95}{94.3407}$$

$$z_4 = 0.019582 = 1.9582\%$$

Doubling this yield, we obtain the theoretical 2-year spot rate bond-equivalent yield of 3.9164%.

The spot rates obtained are shown in the last column of Exhibit A-1 and agree with spot rates shown in Exhibit 1 in the text.

Chapter 6

Measuring Interest Rate Risk

A portfolio of corporate bonds is exposed to interest rate risk. More specifically, a portfolio of corporate bonds is exposed to both level risk and yield curve risk. *Level risk* refers to the effect on the portfolio's value due to shifts in the interest rate level, while *yield curve risk* refers to the effect on the portfolio's value due to changes in the shape of the yield curve. It is essential for a portfolio manager to be able to quantify the exposure to changes in interest rates in order to control that risk. In this chapter we discuss the measures used for quantifying level risk and yield curve risk of an individual corporate bond and a portfolio.

The two measures of level risk used by managers are duration and convexity. Duration is a first approximation as to how the value of an individual security or the value of a portfolio will change when interest rates change. Convexity measures the change in the value of a security or portfolio that is not explained by duration. The measure of yield curve risk that we discuss is key rate duration.

DURATION

The most obvious way to measure a bond's price sensitivity as a percentage of its current price to changes in interest rates is to change rates by a small number of basis points and calculate how its price will change. To do this, we introduce the following notation. Let

V_0 = initial value or price of the bond
Δy = change in the yield of the bond (in decimal)
V_- = the estimated value of the bond if the yield is decreased by Δy
V_+ = the estimated value of the bond if the yield is increased by Δy

There are two key points to keep in mind in the foregoing discussion. First, the change in yield referred to above is the same change in yield for all maturities. This assumption is commonly referred to as the *parallel yield curve shift assumption*. Thus, the foregoing discussion about the price sensitivity of a security to interest rate changes is limited to parallel shifts in the yield curve. At the end of this chapter we address the case where the yield curve shifts in a non-parallel manner.

Second, the notation refers to the estimated value of the bond. This value is obtained from a corporate bond valuation model, such as the one described in

Chapter 16. Consequently, *the resulting measure of the price sensitivity of a bond to interest rate changes is only as good as the valuation model employed to obtain the estimated value of the bond.*

Now let's focus on the measure of interest, namely duration. We are interested in the percentage change in the price of a bond when interest rates change. The percentage change in price per basis point change is found by dividing the percentage price change by the number of basis points (times 100). That is:

$$\frac{V_- - V_0}{V_0(\Delta y)100}$$

Similarly, the percentage change in price per basis point change for an increase in yield (times 100) is:

$$\frac{V_0 - V_+}{V_0(\Delta y)100}$$

The percentage price change for an increase and decrease in interest rates may not be the same. Consequently, the average percentage price change per basis point change in yield can be calculated. This is done by computing:

$$\frac{1}{2}\left[\frac{V_- - V_0}{V_0(\Delta y)100} + \frac{V_0 - V_+}{V_0(\Delta y)100}\right]$$

or equivalently,

$$\frac{V_- - V_+}{2V_0(\Delta y)100}$$

The approximate percentage price change for a 100 basis point change in yield is found by multiplying the previous formula by 100. The name popularly used to refer to the approximate percentage price change is *duration*. Thus,

$$\text{Duration} = \frac{V_- - V_+}{2V_0(\Delta y)} \tag{1}$$

To illustrate this formula, consider the following option-free bond: a 9% 20-year bond trading to yield 6%. The initial price or value (V_0) is 134.6722. Suppose the yield is changed by 20 basis points. If the yield is decreased to 5.8%, the value of this bond (V_-) would be 137.5888. If the yield is increased to 6.2%, the value of this bond (V_+) would be 131.8439. Thus, $\Delta y = 0.002$, $V_0 = 134.6722$, $V_- = 137.5888$, and $V_+ = 131.8439$. Substituting these values into the duration formula,

$$\text{Duration} = \frac{137.5888 - 131.8439}{2(134.6722)(0.002)} = 10.66$$

The duration of a security can be interpreted as the approximate percentage change in the price for a 100 basis point parallel shift in the yield curve. Thus a bond with a duration of 4.8 will change by approximately 4.8% for a 100 basis point parallel shift in the yield curve. For a 50 basis point parallel shift in the yield curve, the bond's price will change by approximately 2.4%; for a 25 basis point parallel shift in the yield curve, 1.2%, and so on.

A manager who anticipates a decline in interest rates will extend (i.e., increase) the portfolio's duration. Suppose that the manager increases the present portfolio duration of 4 to 6. This means that for a 100 basis point change in interest rates, the portfolio will change by about 2% more than if the portfolio duration was left unchanged.

Duration is related to percentage price change. However, for two bonds with the same duration, the dollar price change will not be the same. For example, consider two bonds, W and X. Suppose that both bonds have a duration of 5, but that W is trading at par while X is trading at 90. A 100 basis point change for both bonds will change the price by approximately 5%. This means a price change of $5 (5% times $100) for W and a price change of $4.5 (5% times $90) for X.

The dollar price volatility of a bond can be measured by multiplying duration by the full dollar price and the number of basis points (in decimal form). That is:

Dollar price change = Duration × Dollar price × Yield change (in decimal)

The dollar price volatility for a 100 basis point change in yield is:

Dollar price change = Duration × Dollar price × 0.01

or equivalently,

Dollar price change = Duration × Dollar price/100

The dollar price change calculated using the above formula is called *dollar duration*. In some contexts, dollar duration refers to the price change for a 100 basis point change in yield. The dollar duration for any number of basis points can be computed by scaling the dollar price change accordingly. For example, for a 50 basis point change in yields, the dollar price change or dollar duration is:

Dollar price change = Duration × Dollar price/200

For a 1 basis point change in rates, the dollar price change gives the price value of a basis point (also called the dollar value of an 01).

Modified Duration Versus Effective Duration

A popular form of duration that is used by practitioners is *modified duration*. Modified duration is the approximate percentage change in a bond's price for a 100 basis point parallel shift in the yield curve *assuming that the bond's cash flow does not change when the yield curve shifts.*[1] What this means is that in calculating the values of V_- and V_+ in equation (1), the same cash flow used to calculate V_0 is used. Therefore, the change in the bond's price when the yield curve is shifted by a small number of basis points is due solely to discounting at the new yield level.

The assumption that the cash flow will not change when the yield curve shifts in a parallel fashion makes sense for option-free bonds such as noncallable Treasury securities. This is because the payments made by the U.S. Department of the Treasury to holders of its obligations does not change when the yield curve changes. However, the same cannot be said for corporate bonds with embedded options. For these securities, a change in yield may alter the expected cash flow. We discuss this as follows for callable and putable corporate bonds.

The valuation model such as the binomial model described in Chapter 16 takes into account how shifts in the yield curve will affect the cash flow. Thus, when V_- and V_+ are the values produced from the valuation model, the resulting duration takes into account both the discounting at different interest rates and how the cash flow is expected to change. When duration is calculated in this manner, it is referred to as *effective duration* or *option-adjusted duration*. We will demonstrate in Chapter 16 how this is done.

Callable Corporate Bonds

The price/yield relationship for a callable corporate bond is shown in Exhibit 1. As yields in the market decline, the concern that yields will decline further so that the issue will benefit from refunding increases. The exact yield level at which investors begin to view the issue likely to be refunded may not be known, but we do know that there is some level. In Exhibit 1, at yield levels below y^*, the price/yield relationship for the callable corporate bond departs from the price/yield relationship for the option-free bond. If, for example, the market yield is such that an option-free bond would be selling for 115, but since the issue is callable at 105, investors would not pay 115. If they did and the issue is called, investors

---

[1] It is common in the literature to find the following formula for modified duration on a coupon anniversary date.

$$\frac{1}{(1 + \text{yield}/k)} \left[\frac{1\,\text{PVCF}_1 + 2\,\text{PVCF}_2 + 3\,\text{PVCF}_3 + \ldots + n\,\text{PVCF}_n}{k \times \text{Price}} \right]$$

where

k = number of payments per year
n = number of periods until maturity
yield = yield to maturity of the bond
PVCF_t = present value of the cash flow in period t discounted at the yield to maturity

The expression in the brackets of the formula is called *Macaulay duration*. Thus, modified duration is commonly expressed as:

$$\text{Modified duration} = \frac{\text{Macaulay duration}}{(1 + \text{yield}/k)}$$

The general formulation for duration as given by equation (1) provides a short-cut procedure for determining a bond's modified duration. Because it is easier to calculate the modified duration using the short-cut procedure, many vendors of analytical software will use equation (1) rather than the equation above to reduce computation time.

would receive 105 for a security they purchased for 115. Notice that for a range of yields below y^*, there is price compression—that is, there is limited price appreciation as yields decline. The portion of the callable corporate bond price/yield relationship below y^* is said to be *negatively convex*.

Negative convexity means that the price appreciation will be less than the price depreciation for a large change in yield of a given number of basis points. An option-free bond is said to exhibit *positive convexity*; that is, the price appreciation will be greater than the price depreciation for a large change in yield. The price changes resulting from bonds exhibiting positive convexity and negative convexity are summarized below:

Change in interest rates	Absolute value of percentage price change for:	
	Positive convexity	Negative convexity
−100 basis points	X%	less than Y%
+100 basis points	less than X%	Y%

Putable Corporate Bonds

Exhibit 2 shows the price/yield relationship for a corporate bond that is putable at some future date and an option-free bond. For yields above y^*, a putable bond's price diverges from that of an otherwise comparable option-free bond. Notice that as yields rise, the putable bond's price does not fall by as much as the option-free bond. That is, the putable bond has greater positive convexity than the option-free bond.

Exhibit 1: Price/Yield Relationship for an Option-Free Bond and a Callable Corporate Bond

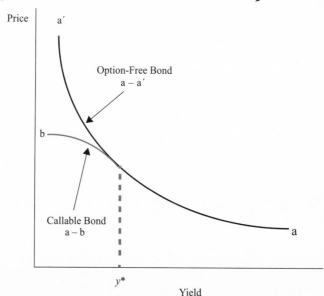

Exhibit 2: Price/Yield Relationship for an Option-Free Bond and a Putable Corporate Bond

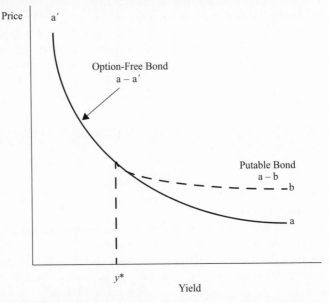

Spread Duration for Fixed-Rate Bonds

Duration is a measure of the change in the value of a bond for a parallel shift in interest rates. The interest rate that is assumed to shift is the Treasury rate. However, for corporates, the yield is equal to the Treasury yield plus a spread to the Treasury yield curve. A corporate's price can change even though Treasury yields are unchanged because the spread required by the market changes. A measure of how a corporate issue's price will change if the spread sought by the market changes is called *spread duration*.

In earlier applications of spread duration, the spread measure was the nominal spread.[2] Today, the spread measure used is the option-adjusted spread.[3] Thus, spread duration can be interpreted as the approximate percentage change in price of a corporate for a 100 basis point change in the option-adjusted spread (OAS), holding the Treasury rate constant. So, for example, if a corporate has a spread duration of 4, this means that if the OAS changes by 20 basis points, the price of the corporate will change by approximately 0.8% (0.04 times 0.002 × 100).

---

[2] Martin L. Leibowitz, William Krasker, and Ardavan Nozari, "Spread Duration: A New Tool for Bond Portfolio Management," in Frank J. Fabozzi (ed.), *Fixed Income Portfolio Strategies* (Chicago: Probus Publishing, 1989).

[3] Thomas E. Klaffky, Ardavan Nozari, and Michael Waldman, "New Duration Measures for Risk Management," Chapter 38 in Frank J. Fabozzi (ed.), *The Handbook of Fixed Income Securities, 5th ed.* (Burr Ridge, IL: Irwin Professional Publishing, 1997).

Later in this chapter we will see how to compute the spread duration for a portfolio.

Duration of a Floating-Rate Security

Our discussion of duration thus far has focused on fixed-rate securities. Now let's look at floating-rate securities (floaters). For a floater, the coupon rate is reset periodically based on a formula. In general the formula is as follows:

Reference rate + Spread

The spread is fixed over the floater's life. A floater will have a cap (i.e., a maximum coupon rate). Some floaters have a minimum coupon rate in addition to a cap.

The change in the price of a fixed-rate security when market rates change is because the security's coupon rate differs from the prevailing market rate. By contrast, for a floater, the coupon is reset periodically, reducing a floater's price sensitivity to changes in rates. A floater's price will change depending on three factors:

1. time remaining to the next coupon reset date.
2. whether or not the cap is reached.
3. whether the spread that the market wants changes.

The longer the time to the next coupon reset date, the greater a floater's potential price fluctuation. Conversely, the less time to the next coupon reset date, the smaller the floater's potential price fluctuation. For a floater whose coupon resets monthly, assuming the other two factors remain constant, the price will change by a minimal amount when rates change. That is, for such a floater, the duration is close to zero.

With respect to the cap, once the coupon rate as specified by the coupon reset formula rises above the cap, the floater then offers a below-market coupon rate, and its price will decline. Turning to the spread, at the initial offering of a floater, the spread is market determined so that the security will trade near par. If after the initial offering the market requires a higher spread, the floater's price will decline to reflect the higher spread. For example, consider a floater whose coupon reset formula is 1-month LIBOR plus a spread of 40 basis points. If market rates change such that investors want a spread of 50 basis points rather than 40 basis points, this floater would be offering a coupon rate that is 10 basis points below the market. As a result, the floater's price will decline.

Two measures have been developed to estimate the sensitivity of a floater to each component of the coupon reset formula. *Index duration* is a measure of the price sensitivity of a floater to changes in the reference rate (i.e., index) holding the spread constant. *Spread duration* measures a floater's price sensitivity to a change in the spread assuming that the reference rate is unchanged. As noted earlier, the term *spread duration* is also used to measure the sensitivity of the price of a fixed-rate corporate when the spread changes where the spread is measured in terms of OAS.

Portfolio Duration

A portfolio's (effective) duration can be obtained by calculating the weighted average of the duration of the securities in the portfolio. The weight is the proportion of the portfolio that a security comprises. Mathematically, a portfolio's duration can be calculated as follows:

$$W_1 D_1 + W_2 D_2 + W_3 D_3 + \ldots + W_K D_K$$

where

$\quad W_i$ = market value of security i/market value of the portfolio
$\quad D_i$ = effective duration of security i
$\quad K$ = number of securities in the portfolio

Similarly, the dollar duration of a portfolio can be obtained by calculating the weighted average of the dollar duration of the bonds in the portfolio.

To illustrate the calculation of a portfolio's duration, consider the following three-security corporate bond portfolio:

Security	Par amount owned	Market value
1	$4 million	$4,000,000
2	5 million	4,231,375
3	1 million	1,378,586

The market value for this portfolio is $9,609,961. The market price per $100 value of each bond, its yield, and its duration are given below:

Security	Price	Yield to Maturity	Duration
1	100.0000	10%	3.86
2	84.6275	10	8.05
3	137.8590	10	9.17

In this illustration, K is equal to 3 and:

$$W_1 = 4,000,000/9,609,961 = 0.416 \quad D_1 = 3.86$$

$$W_2 = 4,231,375/9,609,961 = 0.440 \quad D_2 = 8.05$$

$$W_3 = 1,378,586/9,609,961 = 0.144 \quad D_3 = 9.17$$

The portfolio's duration is:

$$0.416 \,(3.86) + 0.440 \,(8.05) + 0.144 \,(9.17) = 6.47$$

A portfolio duration of 6.47 means that for a 100 basis change in the yield for *all* three securities, the market value of the portfolio will change by approximately 6.47%. But keep in mind, the yield on all three bonds must change by 100 basis points for the duration measure to be useful. This is a critical assumption and its importance cannot be overemphasized. We return to this point later in this chapter when we discuss yield curve risk measures.

Similarly, the dollar duration of a portfolio can be obtained by calculating the weighted average of the dollar duration of the bonds in the portfolio.

An alternative procedure for calculating the duration of a portfolio is to calculate the dollar price change for a given number of basis points for each security in the portfolio and then adding up all the price changes. Dividing the total of the price changes by the initial market value of the portfolio produces a percentage price change that can be adjusted to obtain the portfolio's duration.

For example, consider the three-bond portfolio shown before. Suppose that we calculate the dollar price change for each bond in the portfolio based on its respective duration for a 50 basis point change in yield. We would then have:

Bond	Market value	Duration	Change in value for 50 bp yield change
10% 5-year	$4,000,000	3.861	$77,220
8% 15-year	4,231,375	8.047	170,249
14% 30-year	1,378,586	9.168	63,194
		Total	$310,663

Thus, a 50 basis point change in all rates changes the market value of the three-bond portfolio by $310,663. Since the market value of the portfolio is $9,609,961, a 50 basis point change produced a change in value of 3.23% ($310,663 divided by $9,609,961). Since duration is the approximate percentage change for a 100 basis point change in rates, this means that the portfolio duration is 6.46 (found by doubling 3.23). This is the same value for the portfolio's duration as found earlier.

Contribution to Portfolio Duration

Some portfolio managers look at their exposure to an issue or to a sector in terms of the percentage of that issue or sector in the portfolio. A better measure of exposure of an individual issue or sector to changes in interest rates is in terms of its *contribution to portfolio duration*. This is found by multiplying the percentage that the individual issue or sector is of the portfolio by the duration of the individual issue or sector. That is,

$$\text{contribution to portfolio duration}$$
$$= \frac{\text{market value of issue or sector}}{\text{market value of portfolio}} \times \text{duration of issue or sector}$$

The exposure can also be cast in terms of dollar exposure. To do this, the dollar duration of the issue or sector is used instead of the duration of the issue or sector.

A portfolio manager who wants to determine the contribution to portfolio duration of a sector relative to the contribution of the same sector in a broad-based market index can compute the difference between the two contributions.

Exhibit 3: Data for the Salomon Brothers' BIG Index as of May 1, 1998

Sector	Sector weight (%)	Effective duration	Spread duration
Treasury	41.38	5.19	0.00
Government sponsored	7.38	4.81	4.73
Mortgage	29.52	2.46	3.41
Corporate	21.72	5.99	5.89

Effective duration for index = 4.53
Spread duration for index = 2.63

Duration of a Market Index

As another example, let's look at how the duration of a broad-based bond market index is computed. Exhibit 3 shows for the four sectors of the Salomon Brothers' Broad-Investment Grade (BIG) Index the weights for each sector and the effective duration for each sector as of May 1, 1998. The effective duration for the index as reported by Salomon Brothers for that date was 4.53, calculated by multiplying the sector weights by the effective duration for the sector and summing. Using the notation above, the effective duration for the index is found as follows:

$$W_{Tre} D_{Tre} + W_{GS} D_{GS} + W_{Mort} D_{Mort} + W_{Corp} D_{Corp}$$

where the subscripts Tre, GS, $Mort$, and $Corp$ denote the Treasury, government sponsored, mortgage, and corporate sectors, respectively. Substituting the values reported in Exhibit 3 into the above equation we obtain the index's effective duration of 4.53:

$$0.4138 (5.19) + 0.0738 (4.81) + 0.2952 (2.46) + 0.2172 (5.99) = 4.53$$

The index's effective duration of 4.53 means that if the yield for all four sectors increased by 100 basis points and the OAS did not change, then the index's value will change by approximately 4.53%.

Portfolio Spread Duration

Earlier we discussed the spread duration for an individual fixed-rate corporate bond. The spread duration for a portfolio is found by computing a market weighted average of the spread duration for each sector. The same is true for a market index.

Let's use the data reported in Exhibit 3 for the Salomon Brothers' BIG Index on May 1, 1998 to illustrate this. The last column of the exhibit reports the spread duration for the credit sectors. The spread duration for the index is found as follows:

$$0.4138 (0) + 0.0738 (4.73) + 0.2952 (3.41) + 0.2172 (5.89) = 2.63$$

The computed value of 2.63 agrees with the value reported at the bottom of Exhibit 3. This value is interpreted as follows: if the OAS of all credit sectors changes by 100 basis points while Treasury yields do not change, then the index's value will change by approximately 2.63%.

Suppose that a portfolio manager wants to overweight the corporate sector in expectation of a narrowing of corporate spreads (i.e., OAS). Specifically, let's suppose the portfolio manager underweights exposure to the Treasury sector by investing only 29.38% in this sector rather than 41.38% and allocates the additional 12% to the corporate sector (i.e., increases exposure from 21.72% to 33.72%. The manager wants to maintain the same effective duration as the index. Thus, the proceeds allocated to the Treasury sector must be such that the duration for that sector produces a portfolio effective duration of 4.53. If the manager maintains an effective duration for the portfolio of 4.53 after the reallocation between the Treasury sector and the corporate sector, how much greater is the portfolio's spread duration than that of the index?

First let's look at how much the effective duration exposure of the Treasury sector must be. It is found by solving the previous equation for D_{Tre} given that in the portfolio that overweights the corporate sector and underweights the Treasury sector, $W_{Tre} = 0.2938$ and $W_{Corp} = 0.3372$:

$$0.2938\, D_{Tre} + 0.0738\,(4.81) + 0.2952\,(2.46) + 0.3372\,(5.99) = 4.53$$

Solving for D_{Tre} we get 4.87. Thus, in constructing the securities to be included in the Treasury sector, the manager must maintain a duration of 4.87 for that sector. The portfolio spread duration is then

$$0.3938\,(0) + 0.0738\,(4.73) + 0.2952\,(3.41) + 0.3371\,(5.89) = 3.34.$$

Thus, the exposure of the portfolio to changes in the OAS is 3.34 compared to 2.63 for the index.

Volatility Duration

In the binomial model, one important assumption that is made is the interest rate volatility. This assumption has an important impact on the theoretical value. More specifically, the higher the expected volatility, the higher the value of an option. The same is true for an option embedded in a bond. Correspondingly, this affects the value of the bond with an embedded option.

For example, for a callable bond, a higher interest rate volatility assumption means that the value of the embedded call option increases and, since the value of the option-free bond is not affected, the value of the callable bond must be lower. For a putable bond, higher interest rate volatility means that its value will be higher.

The impact of interest rate volatility on the price of a bond can be quantified. This involves changing the interest rate volatility assumption by changing the volatility and recomputing the price. The prices computed by shocking volatility up and down are the values used in equation (1). If the volatility used is a term structure of volatility, then the interest rate volatility for each maturity is shocked by the same amount. In computing the sensitivity of the bond to a change in volatility, the OAS is held constant.

Vendors have different names for this measure that capture the sensitivity of a bond to changes in volatility. Some vendors call it *volatility risk* or *vega*, the latter term being used in the options market to assess the sensitivity of an option to changes in volatility.

Duration of an Inverse Floater

The duration of an inverse floater will be a multiple of the duration of the fixed-rate bond from which it is effectively created. To see this, suppose that a 20-year fixed-rate bond with a market value of $100 million is split into a floater and an inverse floater with a market value of $80 million and $20 million, respectively. Assume also that the duration for the fixed-rate bond from which the floater/ inverse floater combination is created is 8. For a 100 basis point change in interest rates, the fixed-rate bond's value will change by approximately 8% or $8 million (8% times $100 million). This means that by splitting the fixed-rate bond's value, the combined change in value for a 100 basis point change in rates for the floater and inverse floater must be $8 million. If the duration of the floater is close to zero, this means that the entire $8 million change in value must come from the inverse floater. For this to occur, the duration of the inverse floater must be 40. That is, a duration of 40 will mean a 40% change in the value of the inverse floater for a 100 basis point change in interest rates and therefore a change in value of $8 million (40% times $20 million).[4]

Another way to understand the duration of the inverse floater is to look at the economics underlying the security. An investor who owns a fixed-rate bond effectively owns a floater and an inverse floater. Owning these securities means being long these securities. Thus:

long a fixed-rate bond = long a floater + long an inverse floater

Equivalently, this can be expressed as:

long an inverse floater = long a fixed-rate bond − long a floater

Now look at the position of an investor who is long (owns) an inverse floater. That investor has two positions. First, the investor owns a fixed-rate bond from which the floater/inverse floater combination was created. But owning a fixed-rate bond

---

[4] Notice from our illustration that the duration of the inverse floater is greater than the number of years to maturity of the fixed-rate bond used to create the inverse floater. That is, the maturity of the fixed-rate bond is 8 years and the duration of the inverse floater is 40. Portfolio managers who interpret duration in terms of years are confused that a security can have a duration greater than the fixed-rate bond from which it is created.

means that the investor has purchased this bond. In our example, this means the investor owns $100 million market value of the fixed-rate bond. But remember that the investor paid $20 million for the inverse floater but effectively owns $100 million market value of a fixed-rate bond. Where did the funds come from to finance the difference between the $100 million fixed-rate bond and the $20 million invested to acquire the inverse floater? It must have come from the investor somehow borrowing funds. That is what the minus sign in front of the position "Long a floater" means in the previous expression. The investor financed the $80 million to purchase the fixed-rate bond by borrowing on a floating-rate basis. Specifically, the investor borrowed $80 million and the funding rate is the coupon rate for the floater. Note also that the funding cost is capped by the cap on the floater.

Thus, one can describe the economic position of an investor in an inverse floater as a leveraged position in the fixed-rate bond. The investor has put up $20 million to buy $100 million of a fixed-rate bond and funded the balance ($80 million) on a floating-rate basis. This is why investors refer to an inverse floater as a security with *embedded leverage*. Consequently, the duration of the inverse floater will reflect the embedded leverage. In our example, the duration of the fixed-rate bond is 8. If an investor owns $20 million of this bond, the duration is 8. However, if the investor borrows $80 million to obtain the exposure to $100 million of the fixed-rate bond, the duration will be 5 times greater than the duration of $20 million of market value of the fixed-rate bond. That is, the duration is 40 (8×5). That is precisely what we found earlier for the duration of the inverse floater.

The duration will be less than the leveraged amount if the floater absorbs some of the change in value. Thus, recognition must be given to how the floater will change in value.

CONVEXITY

The duration measure indicates that regardless of whether the yield curve shifts up or down, the approximate percentage price change is the same. However, this does not agree with the properties of a bond's price volatility. Specifically, while for small changes in yield the percentage price change will be the same for an increase or decrease in yield, for large changes in yield this is not true. This suggests that duration is only a good approximation of the percentage price change for a small change in yield.

To see this, consider a 9% 20-year bond selling to yield 6% with a duration of 10.66. If yields increase instantaneously by 10 basis points (from 6% to 6.1%), then using duration the approximate percentage price change would be −1.066% (−10.66% divided by 10, remembering that duration is the percentage price change for a 100 basis point change in yield). The actual percentage price change is −1.07%. Similarly, if the yield decreases instantaneously by 10 basis points (from 6.00% to 5.90%), then the percentage change in price would be +1.066%. The actual percentage price change would be +1.07%. This example illustrates that for small changes in yield, duration does an excellent job of approximating the percentage price change.

Instead of a small change in yield, let's assume that yields increase by 200 basis points, from 6% to 8%. The approximate percentage price change is −21.32% (−10.66% times 2). The actual percentage change in price is only −18.40%. Moreover, if the yield decreases by 200 basis points from 6% to 4%, the approximate percentage price change based on duration would be +21.32%, compared to an actual percentage price change of +25.04%. Thus, the approximation is not as good for a 200 basis point change in yield.

Duration is in fact a first approximation for a small parallel shift in the yield curve. The approximation can be improved by using a second approximation. This approximation is referred to as *convexity*. The use of this term in the industry is unfortunate since the term *convexity* is also used to describe the shape or curvature of the price/yield relationship. The *convexity measure* of a security can be used to approximate the change in price that is not explained by duration.

Convexity Measure

The convexity measure of any security can be approximated using the following formula:

$$\text{Convexity measure} = \frac{V_+ + V_- - 2V_0}{2V_0(\Delta y)^2} \tag{2}$$

where the notation is the same as used earlier for duration [equation (1)].

For our hypothetical 9% 20-year bond selling to yield 6%, we know that for a 20 basis point change in yield $\Delta y = 0.002$, $V_0 = 134.6722$, $V_- = 137.5888$, and $V_+ = 131.8439$. Substituting these values into the convexity measure formula,

$$\text{Convexity measure} = \frac{137.5888 + 131.8439 - 2(134.6722)}{2(134.6722)(0.002)^2} = 81.96$$

Convexity Adjustment to Percentage Price Change

Given the convexity measure, the approximate percentage price change adjustment due to the security's convexity (i.e., the percentage price change not explained by duration) is:

$$\text{Convexity measure} \times (\Delta y)^2$$

For example, for the 9% coupon bond maturing in 20 years, the convexity adjustment to the percentage price change if the yield increases from 6% to 8% is

$$81.96 \times (0.02)^2 = 0.0328 = 3.28\%$$

If the yield decreases from 6% to 4%, the convexity adjustment to the approximate percentage price change would also be 3.28%.

The approximate percentage price change based on duration and the convexity adjustment is found by simply adding the two estimates. So, for example, if yields change from 6% to 8%, the estimated percentage price change would be:

Estimated change approximated by duration	=	−21.32%
Estimated adjustment for convexity	=	+3.28%
Total estimated percentage price change	=	−18.04%

The actual percentage price change is −18.40%.

For a decrease of 200 basis points, from 6% to 4%, the approximate percentage price change would be as follows:

Estimated change approximated by duration	=	+21.32%
Estimated adjustment for convexity	=	+3.28%
Total estimated percentage price change	=	+24.60%

The actual percentage price change is +25.04%. Thus, duration, with the convexity adjustment, does a good job of estimating the sensitivity of a security's price change to large changes in yield.

Notice that when the convexity measure is positive, we have the situation described earlier that the gain is greater than loss for a given large change in rates. We can see this in the example above. However, if the convexity measure is negative, we have the situation where the loss will be greater than the gain. For example, suppose that a callable corporate bond has an effective duration of 4 and a convexity measure of −30. This means that the approximate percentage price change for a 200 basis point change is 8%. The convexity adjustment for a 200 basis point change in rates is then

$$-30 \times (0.02)^2 = -0.012 = -1.2\%$$

Therefore, the approximate percentage price change after adjusting for convexity is:

Estimated change approximated by duration	=	−8.0%
Estimated adjustment for convexity	=	−1.2%
Total estimated percentage price change	=	−9.2%

For a decrease of 200 basis points, the approximate percentage price change would be as follows:

Estimated change approximated by duration	=	+8.0%
Estimated adjustment for convexity	=	−1.2%
Total estimated percentage price change	=	+6.8%

Notice that the loss is greater than the gain—a property called *negative convexity* that we discussed earlier.

Scaling the Convexity Measure

The convexity measure as given by equation (2) means nothing in isolation. It is the substitution of the computed convexity measure into equation (3) that provides the estimated adjustment for convexity. Therefore, it is possible to scale the convexity measure in any way and obtain the same convexity adjustment.

For example, in some books the convexity measure is defined as follows:

$$\text{convexity measure} = \frac{V_+ + V_- - 2V_0}{V_0(\Delta y)^2} \qquad (3)$$

Equation (4) differs from equation (2) since it does not include 2 in the denominator. Thus, the convexity measure computed using equation (4) will be double the convexity measure using equation (2). So, for our earlier illustration, since the convexity measure using equation (2) is 81.96, the convexity measure using equation (4) would be 163.92.

Which is correct, 81.96 or 163.92? Both. Because the corresponding equation for computing the convexity adjustment would not be given by equation (3) if the convexity measure is obtained from equation (4). Instead, the corresponding convexity adjustment formula would be:

convexity adjustment to percentage price change
$$= (\text{convexity measure}/2) \times (\Delta y)^2 \times 100 \qquad (4)$$

Equation (5) differs from equation (3) in that the convexity measure is divided by 2. Thus, the convexity adjustment will be the same whether one uses equation (2) to get the convexity measure and equation (3) to get the convexity adjustment or one uses equation (5) to compute the convexity measure and equation (5) to determine the convexity adjustment.

Some dealers and vendors scale in a different way. One can also compute the convexity measure as follows:

$$\text{convexity measure} = \frac{V_+ + V_- - 2V_0}{2V_0(\Delta y)^2(100)} \qquad (5)$$

Equation (6) differs from equation (2) by the inclusion of 100 in the denominator. In our illustration, the convexity measure would be 0.8196 rather than 81.96 using equation (2). The convexity adjustment formula corresponding to the convexity measure given by equation (6) is then

convexity adjustment to percentage price change
$$= \text{convexity measure} \times (\Delta y)^2 \times 10{,}000 \qquad (6)$$

Similarly, one can express the convexity measure as shown in equation (8):

$$\text{convexity measure} = \frac{V_+ + V_- - 2V_0}{V_0(\Delta y)^2(100)} \qquad (7)$$

For the bond we have been using in our illustrations, the convexity measure is 1.6392. The corresponding convexity adjustment is:

convexity adjustment to percentage price change
$$= (\text{convexity measure}/2) \times (\Delta y)^2 \times 10{,}000 \qquad\qquad (8)$$

Consequently, the convexity measures (or just simply convexity, as it is referred to by some market participants) that could be reported for this option-free bond are 81.96, 163.92, 0.8196, or 1.6392. All of these values are correct, but they mean nothing in isolation. To use them to obtain the convexity adjustment requires knowing how they are computed so that the correct convexity adjustment formula is used.

It is also important to understand this when comparing the convexity measures reported by dealers and vendors. For example, if one dealer shows a manager Bond A with a duration of 4 and a convexity measure of 50, and a second dealer shows the manager Bond B with a duration of 4 and a convexity measure of 80, which bond has the greater percentage price change response to changes in interest rates? Since the duration of the two bonds is identical, the bond with the larger convexity measure will change more when rates decline. However, not knowing how the two dealers computed the convexity measure means that the manager does not know which bond will have the greater convexity adjustment. If the first dealer used equation (2) while the second dealer used equation (4), then the convexity measures must be adjusted in terms of either equation. For example, using equation (2), the convexity measure of 80 computed using equation (4) is equal to a convexity measure of 40 based on equation (2).

Modified Convexity and Effective Convexity

The prices used in equation (2) to calculate convexity can be obtained by either assuming that when the yield curve shifts in a parallel way the expected cash flow does not change or it does change. In the former case, the resulting convexity is referred to as *modified convexity*. (Actually, in the industry, convexity is not qualified by the adjective modified.) Effective convexity, in contrast, assumes that the cash flow does change when yields change. This is the same distinction made for duration.

As with duration, for corporate bonds with embedded options there can be quite a difference between the calculated modified convexity and effective convexity. In fact, for all option-free bonds, either convexity measure will have a positive value. For corporate bonds with embedded options, the calculated effective convexity can be negative when the calculated modified convexity gives a positive value.

YIELD CURVE RISK

As noted earlier, duration is an approximation of the percentage price change for a parallel shift in the yield curve. This measure of interest rate risk assumes that all interest rates change by the same number of basis points. The same applies to the convexity measure.

Exhibit 4: Three Hypothetical Bonds to Illustrate the Limitations of Duration and Convexity

Bond	Coupon rate (%)	Price ($)	Yield to maturity (%)	Maturity (Years)
A	6.500	100	6.500	5
B	8.000	100	8.000	20
C	7.500	100	7.500	10

Calculation of duration: Change yield up and down by 10 basis points

Bond	V_+ ($)	V_- ($)	Duration	Convexity
A	99.5799	100.4222	4.21122	10.67912
B	99.0177	100.9970	9.89681	73.63737
C	99.3083	100.6979	6.94821	31.09724

Two portfolios with the same duration may perform quite differently if the yield curve does not shift in a parallel fashion. To illustrate this point, consider the three bonds shown in Exhibit 4. Bond A is the short-term bond, bond B is the long-term bond, and bond C is the intermediate-term bond. Each bond is selling at par, and it is assumed the next coupon payment is 6 months from now. The duration and convexity for each bond are calculated from the information in the second panel of the exhibit. Since the bonds are trading at par value, the duration and convexities are then the dollar duration and dollar convexity.

Suppose that the following two portfolios are constructed. The first portfolio consists of only bond C, a 10-year bond, and shall be referred to as the "bullet portfolio." The second portfolio consists of 51.86% of bond A and 48.14% of bond B, and this portfolio shall be referred to as the "barbell portfolio."

The dollar duration of the bullet portfolio is 6.49821. Recall that dollar duration is a measure of the dollar price sensitivity of a bond or a portfolio. The dollar duration of the barbell is the weighted average of the dollar duration of the two bonds and is computed below:

$$0.5186 (4.21122) + 0.4814 (9.89681) = 6.49821$$

The dollar duration of the barbell is equal to the dollar duration of the bullet. In fact, the barbell portfolio was designed to produce this result.

Duration is just a first approximation of the change in price resulting from a change in interest rates. The convexity measure provides a second approximation. The dollar convexity measure of the two portfolios is not equal. The dollar convexity measure of the bullet portfolio is 31.09724. The dollar convexity measure of the barbell is a weighted average of the dollar convexity measure of the two bonds. That is,

$$0.5186 (10.67912) + 0.4814 (73.63737) = 40.98658$$

Thus, the bullet has a dollar convexity measure that is less than that of the barbell portfolio.

Exhibit 5: Comparison of Yield, Dollar Duration, and Dollar Convexity of Bullet and Barbell Portfolios

	Portfolio	
Parameter	Bullet	Barbell
Yield	7.50%	7.22%
Dollar duration	6.49821	6.49821
Dollar convexity	31.09724	40.98658

The "yield" for the two portfolios is not the same. The yield for the bullet is simply the yield to maturity of bond C, 7.50%. The traditional yield calculation for the barbell portfolio, which is found by taking a weighted average of the yield to maturity of the two bonds included in the portfolio, is 7.22%. This would suggest that the "yield" of the bullet portfolio is 28 basis points greater than the barbell portfolio. Thus, both portfolios have the same dollar duration, but the yield of the bullet portfolio is greater than the yield of the barbell portfolio. However, the dollar convexity of the barbell portfolio is greater than that of the bullet portfolio. The difference in the two yields is sometimes referred to as the "cost of convexity." This is summarized in Exhibit 5.

Which is the better portfolio in which to invest? The answer depends on the portfolio manager's investment objectives and investment horizon. Let's assume a 6-month investment horizon. The last column of Exhibit 6 shows the difference in the total return over a 6-month investment horizon for the two portfolios, assuming that the yield curve shifts in a "parallel" fashion.[5] By parallel it is meant that the yield for the short-term bond (A), the intermediate-term bond (C), and the long-term bond (B) change by the same number of basis points, shown in the first column of the exhibit. The total return reported in column (4) of Exhibit 6 is:

bullet portfolio's total return − barbell portfolio's total return

Thus a positive value in column (4) means that the bullet portfolio outperformed the barbell portfolio, while a negative sign means that the barbell portfolio outperformed the bullet portfolio.

Which portfolio is the better investment alternative if the yield curve shifts in a parallel fashion *and* the investment horizon is 6 months? The answer depends on the amount by which yields change. Notice in the last column that if yields change by less than 100 basis points, the bullet portfolio will outperform the barbell portfolio. The reverse is true if yields change by more than 100 basis points.

Now let's look at what happens if the yield curve does not shift in a parallel fashion. Exhibit 6 also shows the relative performance of the two portfolios

---

[5] Note that no assumption is needed for the reinvestment rate since the three bonds shown in Exhibit 4 are assumed to be trading right after a coupon payment has been made and therefore there is no accrued interest.

for a nonparallel shift of the yield curve. Specifically, in columns (5), (6), and (7) it is assumed that if the yield on bond C (the intermediate-term bond) changes by the amount shown in column (1), bond A (the short-term bond) will change by the same amount plus 30 basis points, whereas bond B (the long-term bond) will change by the same amount shown in column (1) less 30 basis points. That is, the nonparallel shift assumed is a flattening of the yield curve. For this yield curve shift, the barbell will outperform the bullet for the yield changes assumed in column (1). While not shown in the exhibit, for changes greater than 300 basis points for bond C, the opposite would be true.

In columns (8), (9), and (10), the nonparallel shift assumes that for a change in bond C's yield, the yield on bond A will change by the same amount less 30 basis points, whereas that on bond B will change by the same amount plus 30 points. That is, it assumes that the yield curve will steepen. In this case, the bullet portfolio would outperform the barbell portfolio for all but a change in yield greater than 250 basis points for bond C.

Exhibit 6: Difference in Total Return Between Barbell and Bullet for Different Yield Curve Shifts

Yield change (bp)	Total Return (%)								
	Parallel shift[1]			Flattening[2]			Steepening[3]		
	Bullet	Barbell	Diff.[4]	Bullet	Barbell	Diff.[4]	Bullet	Barbell	Diff.[4]
(1)	(2)	(3)	(4)	(5)	(6)	(7)	(8)	(9)	(10)
−300	53.47	55.79	−2.32	53.47	58.98	−5.51	53.47	52.82	0.65
−250	44.95	46.38	−1.43	44.95	49.26	−4.31	44.95	43.70	1.24
−200	36.79	37.55	−0.76	36.79	40.15	−3.36	36.79	35.14	1.65
−150	28.99	29.26	−0.27	28.99	31.60	−2.62	28.99	27.09	1.89
−100	21.51	21.47	0.05	21.51	23.58	−2.06	21.51	19.52	1.99
−50	14.35	14.13	0.22	14.35	16.03	−1.67	14.35	12.39	1.97
−25	10.89	10.63	0.26	10.89	12.42	−1.53	10.89	8.98	1.91
0	7.50	7.22	0.28	7.50	8.92	−1.42	7.50	5.66	1.84
25	4.18	3.92	0.27	4.18	5.53	−1.35	4.18	2.44	1.74
50	0.93	0.70	0.23	0.93	2.23	−1.30	0.93	−0.69	1.63
100	−5.36	−5.45	0.09	−5.36	−4.09	−1.27	−5.36	−6.70	1.34
150	−11.39	−11.28	−0.11	−11.39	−10.06	−1.33	−11.39	−12.38	0.99
200	−17.17	−16.79	−0.38	−17.17	−15.70	−1.47	−17.17	−17.77	0.60
250	−22.71	−22.01	−0.70	−22.71	−21.04	−1.67	−22.71	−22.88	0.17
300	−28.03	−26.96	−1.06	−28.03	−26.11	−1.92	−28.03	−27.73	−0.30

[1] Assumptions:
   The change in the yield for all three bonds is the same as in column (1).
[2] Assumptions:
   Change in yield of bond C (column 1) results in a change in the yield of bond A plus 30 basis points.
   Change in yield of bond C (column 1) results in a change in the yield of bond B minus 30 basis points.
[3] Assumptions:
   Change in yield of bond C (column 1) results in a change in the yield of bond A minus 30 basis points.
   Change in yield of bond C (column 1) results in a change in the yield of bond B plus 30 basis points.
[4] A positive sign indicates that the bullet portfolio outperformed the barbell portfolio; a negative sign indicates that the barbell portfolio outperformed the bullet portfolio.

Exhibit 7: Three Hypothetical Bonds to Illustrate the Lack of Tradeoff Between Yield and Convexity

Bond	Coupon rate (%)	Price ($)	Yield to maturity (%)	Maturity (years)
X	7.900	100	7.900	2
Y	8.800	100	8.800	7
Z	8.200	100	8.200	4

Bullet portfolio: Bond Z
Barbell portfolio: Bonds X and Y as follows
    Bond X: 53.86%   Bond Y: 46.14%

Parameters

Parameter	Portfolio	
	Bullet	Barbell
Yield	8.20%	8.32%
Dollar duration	3.35253	3.35253
Dollar convexity	6.90699	8.89010

The key point here is that looking at measures such as yield (yield-to-maturity or some type of portfolio yield measure), duration, or convexity tells us little about performance over some investment horizon because performance depends on the magnitude of the change in yields (what we referred to as "level" shift) and how the yield curve shifts.

The statement made earlier that there is a tradeoff between convexity and yield does not necessarily arise in the market. This should not be surprising since as argued in earlier chapters, the yield measure is not a good indicator of the potential return. To illustrate this, consider the three hypothetical bonds shown in Exhibit 7. A barbell portfolio with the same dollar duration as the bullet portfolio was constructed. At the bottom of the exhibit is the yield, dollar duration, and dollar convexity. Notice that the average yield and the dollar convexity are greater for the barbell portfolio than the bullet portfolio.

Thus, it would seem that the barbell portfolio in our illustration would perform better than the bullet portfolio over a 6-month investment horizon. This is, in fact, the case for a parallel shift in the yield, as can be seen in columns (2), (3), and (4) in Exhibit 8. However, this is not the case for a nonparallel yield curve shift. From columns (5), (6), and (7) in Exhibit 8 it can be seen that if the yield curve steepens as assumed in the exhibit, the bullet outperforms the barbell over the 6-month investment horizon.

Key Rate Duration

From our illustrations we can see that a measure to supplement duration is needed to help a manager identify a portfolio's exposure to a nonparallel shift in the yield curve (i.e., to measure yield curve risk). Several measures have been suggested for measuring yield curve risk. The measure we discuss is *key rate duration*.

Exhibit 8: Performance of Bullet and Barbell Portfolios Over a 6-Month Horizon

Yield change (bp)	Total Return (%)					
	Parallel shift[1]			Steepening [2]		
	Bullet	Barbell	Diff.[3]	Bullet	Barbell	Diff.[3]
(1)	(2)	(3)	(4)	(5)	(6)	(7)
−300	27.18	27.75	−0.57	7.18	26.62	0.56
−250	23.86	24.30	−0.43	23.86	23.21	0.65
−200	20.61	20.93	−0.32	20.61	19.89	0.72
−150	17.42	17.66	−0.23	17.42	16.65	0.77
−100	14.29	14.46	−0.17	14.29	13.50	0.79
−50	11.22	11.35	−0.13	11.22	10.43	0.79
−25	9.70	9.82	−0.12	9.70	8.92	0.78
0	8.20	8.32	−0.12	8.20	7.43	0.77
25	6.71	6.83	−0.12	6.71	5.96	0.75
50	5.24	5.36	−0.12	5.24	4.51	0.73
100	2.33	2.47	−0.14	2.33	1.66	0.67
150	−0.53	−0.34	−0.19	−0.53	−1.12	0.60
200	−3.33	−3.08	−0.25	−3.33	−3.83	0.50
250	−6.08	−5.76	−0.32	−6.08	−6.48	0.40
300	−8.79	−8.37	−0.41	−8.79	−9.06	0.28

[1] *Assumptions:*
The change in the yield for all three bonds is the same as in column (1).
[2] *Assumption:*
Change in yield of bond Z (column 1) results in a change in the yield of bond X minus 30 basis points.
Change in yield of bond Z (column 1) results in a change in the yield of bond Y plus 30 basis points.
[3] A positive sign indicates that the bullet portfolio outperformed the barbell portfolio; a negative sign indicates that the barbell portfolio outperformed the bullet portfolio.

The key rate duration approach for measuring yield curve risk is to change the spot rate for a particular maturity and determine the sensitivity of a security or portfolio to this change holding all other spot rates constant. The sensitivity of the change in value to a particular spot rate change is called *rate duration*. There is a rate duration for every point on the spot rate curve. Consequently, there is not one rate duration, but a vector of durations representing each maturity on the spot rate curve. The total change in value if all rates change by the same number of basis points is simply the duration of a security or portfolio to a parallel shift in rates.

This approach was first suggested by Donald Chambers and Willard Carleton in 1988, who called it "duration vectors."[6] Robert Reitano suggested a similar approach in a series of papers and referred to these durations as "partial durations."[7]

---

[6] Donald Chambers and Willard Carleton, "A Generalized Approach to Duration," *Research in Finance* 7 (1988).
[7] See, for example, Robert R. Reitano, "Non-Parallel Yield Curve Shifts and Durational Leverage," *Journal of Portfolio Management* (Summer 1990), pp. 62–67, and "A Multivariate Approach to Duration Analysis," *ARCH* 2 (1989).

The most popular version of this approach is that developed by Thomas Ho in 1992.[8]

Ho's approach focuses on 11 key maturities of the spot rate curve. These rate durations are called *key rate durations*. The specific maturities on the spot rate curve for which a key rate duration is measured are 3 months, 1 year, 2 years, 3 years, 5 years, 7 years, 10 years, 15 years, 20 years, 25 years, and 30 years. Changes in rates between any two key rates are calculated using a linear approximation.

The impact of any type of yield curve shift can be quantified using key rate durations. A level shift can be quantified by changing all key rates by the same number of basis points and determining, based on the corresponding key rate durations, the effect on the value of a portfolio. The impact of a steepening of the yield curve can be found by (1) decreasing the key rates at the short end of the yield curve and determining the change in the portfolio's value using the corresponding key rate durations, and (2) increasing the key rates at the long end of the yield curve and determining the change in the portfolio's value using the corresponding key rate durations.

To illustrate the key rate duration methodology, suppose that instead of a set of 11 key rates, there are only three key rates: 2 years, 16 years, and 30 years.[9] The duration of a zero-coupon security is approximately the number of years to maturity. Thus, the three key rate durations are 2, 16, and 30. Consider the following two $100 portfolios comprised of 2-year, 16-year, and 30-year issues:

Portfolio	2-year issue	16-year issue	30-year issue
I	$50	$0	$50
II	$0	$100	$0

To simplify the illustration, we use only three points on the curve, and the key rate durations for these three points are denoted by $D(1)$, $D(2)$, and $D(3)$ and defined as follows:

$D(1)$ = key rate duration for the 2-year part of the curve
$D(2)$ = key rate duration for the 16-year part of the curve
$D(3)$ = key rate duration for the 30-year part of the curve

The key rate durations for the three issues and the duration are as follows:

Issue	$D(1)$	$D(2)$	$D(3)$	Duration
2-year	2	0	0	2
16-year	0	16	0	16
30-year	0	0	30	30

A portfolio's key rate duration is the weighted average of the key rate durations of the securities in the portfolio. The key rate duration and the duration for each portfolio are calculated below:

---

[8] Thomas S.Y. Ho, "Key Rate Durations: Measures of Interest Rate Risk," *The Journal of Fixed Income* (September 1992), pp. 29–44.
[9] This is the numerical example used by Ho, "Key Rate Durations," p. 33.

Portfolio I

$D(1) = (50/100) \times 2 + (0/100) \times 0 + (50/100) \times 0 = 1$
$D(2) = (50/100) \times 0 + (0/100) \times 16 + (50/100) \times 0 = 0$
$D(3) = (50/100) \times 0 + (0/100) \times 0 + (50/100) \times 30 = 15$

effective duration $= (50/100) \times 2 + (0/100) \times 16 + (50/100) \times 30 = 16$

Portfolio II

$D(1) = (0/100) \times 2 + (100/100) \times 0 + (0/100) \times 0 = 0$
$D(2) = (0/100) \times 0 + (100/100) \times 16 + (0/100) \times 0 = 16$
$D(3) = (0/100) \times 0 + (100/100) \times 0 + (0/100) \times 30 = 0$

effective duration $= (0/100) \times 2 + (100/100) \times 16 + (0/100) \times 30 = 16$

Thus, the key rate durations differ for the two portfolios. However, the effective duration for each portfolio is the same. Despite the same duration, the performance of the two portfolios will not be the same for a nonparallel shift in the spot rates. Consider the following three scenarios:

Scenario 1: All spot rates shift down 10 basis points.
Scenario 2: The 2-year key rate shifts up 10 basis points and the 30-year rate shifts down 10 basis points.
Scenario 3: The 2-year key rate shifts down 10 basis points and the 30-year rate shifts up 10 basis points.

Let's illustrate how to compute the estimated total return based on the key rate durations for Portfolio I in scenario 2. The 2-year key rate duration [D(1)] for Portfolio I is 1. For a 100 basis point increase in the 2-year key rate, the portfolio's value will decrease by approximately 1%. For a 10 basis point increase (as assumed in scenario 2), the portfolio's value will decrease by approximately 0.1%. Now let's look at the change in the 30-year key rate in scenario 1. The 30-year key rate duration [D(3)] is 15. For a 100 basis point decrease in the 30-year key rate, the portfolio's value will increase by approximately 15%. For a 10 basis point decrease (as assumed in scenario 2), the increase in the portfolio's value will be approximately 1.5%. Consequently, for Portfolio I in scenario 2 we have:

change in portfolio's value due to 2-year key rate change	−0.1%
change in portfolio's value due to 30-year key rate change	+1.5%
change in portfolio value	+1.4%

In the same way, the total return for both portfolios can be estimated for the three scenarios. The estimated total returns are shown below:

Portfolio	Scenario 1	Scenario 2	Scenario 3
I	1.6%	1.4%	−1.4%
II	1.6%	0%	0%

Thus, only for the parallel yield curve shift (scenario 1) do the two portfolios have identical performance based on their durations.

The key rate durations can be computed for an individual security and for a portfolio. As an illustration, let's look at the sample corporate bond portfolio shown in Exhibit 9. There are 25 issues in the portfolio, each with a par value of $5 million. The information is based on market values on May 4, 1998.

Look at the first issue—AT&T 7.5s of 9/1/2009. The effective duration for this issue is 2.36. Look at the 5-year key rate duration. The value is 0.46. This means that if the 5-year rate changes by 100 basis points while all other rates along the yield curve remain the same, this issue's value will change by approximately 0.46%. Adding up the 11 key rate durations gives the effective duration of 2.36.

The last line of Exhibit 9 shows the key rate duration for the portfolio. It is found by multiplying the key rate duration for a given key rate for each issue by its market weight in the portfolio and summing over all the issues. The key rate durations tell us that the major exposure of this portfolio is to changes in rates in the 3-year to 15-year range.

NEED TO RECOGNIZE YIELD VOLATILITY

A limitation of any duration measure as a stand-alone measure of price sensitivity is that it does not recognize the volatility of yields. This is critical because the total potential price sensitivity of a portfolio depends not only on the duration but also the volatility of the yield that affects that bond. For example, the duration of a Treasury bond will be greater than that of a high-yield (or "junk") bond with the same maturity and issued at the same time. There are two reasons for this. First, the coupon rate is lower on the Treasury security and second, it trades at a lower yield level. Does this mean that a Treasury security has a greater price volatility exposure? Not necessarily. It also depends on the relative volatility of yields of Treasury securities compared to high-yield bonds. It is the combination of the duration and yield volatility that affects the price volatility of a bond and a portfolio. Recall that the value-at-risk measure described in the previous chapter recognizes the price sensitivity of a bond position or a portfolio to rate changes and the expected yield volatility.

SUMMARY

It is critical for a portfolio manager to be able to measure the sensitivity of an individual security and a portfolio to changes in interest rates. In this chapter, we describe various measures that seek to capture that sensitivity. Duration is a first approximation of the change in the value of a security to a change in rates. More specifically, it is the approximate percentage change in the value of a bond or a portfolio to a 100 basis point change in rates.

Exhibit 9: Key Rate Duration Profile for a 25-Issue Corporate Portfolio

Issuer	Coupon (%)	Maturity Date	Market Value ($)	Percent of Market Value	Effective Duration	Key Rate Duration for										
						3-Mos	1-Year	2-Year	3-Year	5-Year	7-Year	10-Year	15-Year	20-Year	25-Year	30-Year
AT&T Corp	7.50	09/01/09	5,027,300	3.89	2.36	0.05	0.22	0.31	0.42	0.46	0.38	0.44	0.07	0.0	0.00	0.00
Aetna Services	8.00	01/15/17	4,973,600	3.85	5.77	0.03	0.12	0.27	0.50	0.67	0.78	1.01	1.27	1.12	0.00	0.00
Tenet Healthcare	9.50	11/15/01	5,156,600	3.99	2.02	0.05	0.25	0.30	1.11	0.32	0.00	0.00	0.00	0.00	0.00	0.00
Bank of New York	7.00	03/15/11	4,666,900	3.61	5.97	0.02	0.06	0.27	0.48	0.71	0.83	2.00	1.60	0.00	0.00	0.00
CMS Energy Corp	8.00	06/15/04	4,750,400	3.68	4.02	0.02	0.07	0.30	0.53	1.66	1.43	0.00	0.00	0.00	0.00	0.00
Caterpillar Fin	7.68	04/15/99	5,048,900	3.91	0.87	0.11	0.76	0.00	0.00	0.00	0.00	0.00	0.00	0.00	0.00	0.00
Chase Manhattan	9.05	02/01/02	5,124,100	3.97	0.76	0.11	0.19	-0.02	0.31	0.16	0.0	0.00	0.00	0.00	0.00	0.00
Citicorp	7.50	06/17/12	4,793,100	3.71	5.53	0.02	0.07	0.38	0.51	0.67	0.77	1.29	1.83	0.00	0.00	0.00
Coca-Cola Enter	8.50	02/01/12	5,447,300	4.22	8.11	0.02	0.07	0.13	0.30	0.52	0.80	2.47	3.80	0.00	0.00	0.00
Delta Airlines	10.00	05/17/09	6,018,400	4.66	6.75	0.01	0.07	0.14	0.31	0.55	0.84	3.97	0.85	0.00	0.00	0.00
Walt Disney Com	7.50	06/27/11	4,793,800	3.71	5.40	0.02	0.06	0.38	0.58	0.66	0.75	1.59	1.35	0.00	0.00	0.00
Dow Chemical	7.75	09/15/20	5,038,900	3.90	10.34	0.02	0.06	0.13	0.29	0.51	0.79	1.41	1.75	3.40	1.99	0.00
Eastman Kodak	9.75	10/01/04	5,628,300	4.36	4.83	0.02	0.07	0.15	0.33	1.59	2.67	0.00	0.00	0.00	0.00	0.00
GMAC	7.50	05/02/03	5,032,300	3.90	4.11	0.02	0.06	0.12	0.29	3.62	0.00	0.00	0.00	0.00	0.00	0.00
GTE South Inc	9.38	04/01/00	5,077,500	3.93	0.01	-0.03	0.01	0.02	0.00	0.00	0.00	0.00	0.00	0.00	0.00	0.00
Dow Chemical	9.00	05/15/10	5,800,700	4.49	6.07	0.01	0.07	0.18	0.45	0.76	1.05	2.51	1.03	0.00	0.00	0.00
Equitable of IO	9.30	06/01/98	5,012,800	3.88	0.08	0.08	0.00	0.00	0.00	0.00	0.00	0.00	0.00	0.00	0.00	0.00
Federal Realty	8.75	05/15/10	5,122,500	3.97	0.03	-0.06	0.00	0.00	0.00	0.00	0.21	-0.11	0.00	0.00	0.00	0.00
First Chicago	9.88	08/15/00	5,358,600	4.15	2.01	0.02	0.08	1.39	0.52	0.00	0.00	0.00	0.00	0.00	0.00	0.00
Firemans Fund	8.88	10/15/01	5,140,500	3.98	2.95	0.02	0.07	0.04	2.04	0.58	0.00	0.00	0.00	0.00	0.00	0.00
First Brands Co	9.12	04/01/99	5,061,800	3.92	0.08	0.08	0.00	0.00	0.00	0.00	0.00	0.00	0.00	0.00	0.00	0.00
Wells Fargo	9.38	11/15/98	5,272,500	4.08	0.50	0.31	0.18	0.00	0.00	0.00	0.00	0.00	0.00	0.00	0.00	0.00
Fleet Financial	8.62	01/15/07	5,423,300	4.20	6.04	0.02	0.07	0.13	0.30	0.53	2.50	2.50	0.00	0.00	0.00	0.00
Goldman Sachs	8.12	02/01/99	5,132,900	3.97	0.71	0.25	0.46	0.00	0.00	0.00	0.00	0.00	0.00	0.00	0.00	0.00
Honeywell Inc.	9.38	06/15/09	5,252,400	4.07	0.33	-0.13	0.00	0.00	0.34	0.00	0.05	0.09	-0.02	0.00	0.00	0.08
Total Portfolio			$129,155,400		3.45	0.04	0.12	0.19	0.39	0.56	0.57	0.80	0.54	018	0.08	0.00

For each issue, $5 million of par value is purchased.

There are two types of duration—modified and effective. Modified duration assumes that when rates change, the expected cash flows do not change. It is not a good measure for securities with an embedded option (such as callable and putable bonds) since a change in rates may change the expected cash flows. Effective duration takes into consideration that when rates change, the expected cash flows may change. The calculation of duration of a corporate bond requires the use of a valuation model. In this chapter we have shown how the binomial model can be used to calculate the duration of a corporate bond with an embedded option.

For fixed-rate corporates, it is possible to measure the impact of a change in rates due to a change in Treasury rates and a change in the spread to Treasuries at which the security trades. The change in the spread is not the change in the nominal spread for a corporate bond with an embedded option, but a change in the OAS. The price sensitivity of a corporate bond to a change in the spread to Treasuries is called *spread duration*. That is, spread duration indicates the approximate percentage change in the value of a corporate bond if Treasury rates are unchanged but the OAS changes by 100 basis points.

For floating-rate corporates, the price will change depending on the time remaining to the next coupon reset date, if the cap is reached, and/or if the spread the market requires changes. For a floating-rate corporate bond, two duration measures are computed: index duration and spread duration. The former is a measure of how the price will change assuming that the spread is unchanged but the index changes. Spread duration for a floating-rate corporate bond is a measure of how the price will change when the spread the market requires changes but the index does not change.

The duration measure can be improved by using the convexity measure. As with duration, an effective convexity and a (modified) convexity can be computed. A security with positive convexity is one in which when rates decline there is a greater gain than there is a loss if rates rise by the same number of basis points. If a security exhibits negative convexity, the loss is greater than the gain for a given change in rates.

A limitation of duration is that it measures price sensitivity to a parallel shift in the yield curve. There have been several measures used to estimate the sensitivity to a nonparallel shift in the yield curve. One of the more popular measures is key rate duration. A key rate duration is the sensitivity of the price of a security or portfolio to a change in a particular rate holding all other rates along the yield curve constant.

Chapter 7

Yield Volatility, Spread Volatility, and Corporate Yield Ratios

D o corporate bonds have greater yield volatility than Treasuries? Do low-rated corporate bonds have greater yield volatility than high-rated bonds? These questions are important because yield volatility is a key input for option-pricing models. At first glance, intuition suggests that corporate volatility should be greater than Treasury volatility because corporates have an element of spread volatility that is not present in Treasuries. That same intuition would suggest that AAA bonds should have lower volatility than BBB bonds, which have greater spread volatility.

However, yield volatility for corporate bonds has generally been lower than the volatility of comparable Treasuries. Exhibit 1 displays volatility statistics for selected intermediate-term corporate and Treasury bonds during 1994 and 2000, two years of significant volatility in the fixed-income market. Volatility is expressed on an annualized basis, measured with daily yield data over the trailing year. Most of the corporates in the exhibit had lower yield volatility than comparable Treasuries. Indeed, corporate volatility was high only for those issuers that experienced unusually wide swings in their spreads, such as Telecommunication Inc. and Long Island Lighting in 1994, and JC Penney and Southern Cal Edison in 2000. But spread volatility does not always give rise to greater yield volatility. In 1994, Philip Morris' spreads moved significantly, but its bonds had lower yield volatility than Treasuries. Similarly, in 2000, Ford and AT&T bond spreads fluctuated markedly, but their yields were less volatile than Treasuries.

How can the low-yield volatilities of corporates be reconciled with our intuition about spread volatility? In this chapter, we show that the low corporate volatilities arise because volatility is measured as the *percentage change* in yields. As a result, when corporate and Treasury yields move by 10 basis points, Treasury yields will record a greater *percentage change* than will corporate yields, simply because corporate yields are higher than Treasuries. Corporate yield volatility is typically lower than Treasury volatility, except in situations when yield spreads are unusually volatile.

Exhibit 1: Historical Yield Volatility for Selected Corporate and Treasury Bonds
Period: 1994

Security	Rating	Yield Vol
U.S. Treasury 5¾% 2003		16.63%
Ford 5.95% 2003	A2/A	14.86%
Norwest 6⅛% 2003	Aa3/AA−	15.23%
Southern Company 6⅛% 2003	A2/A	15.41%
Coca-Cola 6% 2003	Aa3/AA	15.64%
Citicorp 8% 2003	A3/A−	15.83%
Wells Fargo 6⅛% 2003	A3/BBB+	15.94%
Philip Morris 7¼% 2003	A2/A	16.17%
Telecommunications Inc. 8¼% 2003	Baa3/BBB−	16.88%
Long Island Lighting 7.05% 2003	Ba1/BB+	19.07%

Period: 2000

Security	Rating	Yield Vol
US Treasury 6% 2009		13.36%
Ford 7⅜% 2009	A2/A	8.98%
Chase 7% 2009	A1/A+	10.35%
Duke Energy 7½% 2009	A3/A	9.56%
Coca-Cola 5¾% 2009	Aa3/A+	11.72%
Citicorp 6.2% 2009	Aa2/AA−	9.52%
AT&T 6% 2009	A2/A	9.40%
Safeway 7½% 2009	Baa2/BBB	10.78%
JC Penney 7⅜% 2008	Baa3/BBB−	37.96%
Southern Cal Edison 7⅝% 2010	Baa3/BBB−*	146.20%

All the bonds are bullet bonds. Volatility is measured with daily data.
* Subsequently downgraded to Caa2/CC.

THE ARITHMETIC OF CORPORATE YIELD VOLATILITY

In measuring yield volatility, it is customary to assume that percentage changes in yields are log normally distributed. The skew associated with the log distribution prevents yields from falling below zero. In this framework, the continuously compounded percentage yield change can be expressed as:

$$\log (C_t /C_{t-1}) = \text{percentage yield change} \tag{1}$$

where

C_t = yield on the corporate bond at time t

The Yield Ratio Formulation
To understand corporate yield volatility, it is convenient to focus on the *ratio* of corporate yields to Treasury yields, rather than the spread between corporate and

Treasury yields. The corporate yield can be defined as the Treasury yield times a ratio:

$$C_t = G_t \times R_t \tag{2}$$

where

G_t = yield on a comparable maturity Treasury bond at time t
R_t = C_t/G_t = ratio of corporate yield to Treasury yield at time t

Because corporate bonds have less liquidity and an element of default risk, the yield ratio will be greater than one ($R_t > 1$). Notice that the yield ratio, R_t, can vary over time. For example, the ratio may widen and narrow over the business cycle, just as yield spreads widen in recessions and narrow in expansions. As we will see, variation in the yield ratio plays a key role in determining whether corporate yield volatility is greater or less than Treasury yield volatility.

By substituting the definition of the corporate yield (2) into equation (1), we can show that the percentage change in the corporate yield equals the percentage change in the Treasury yield plus the percentage change in the yield ratio:

$$\log(C_t/C_{t-1}) = \log(G_t \times R_t/G_{t-1} \times R_{t-1}) \tag{3}$$

or, using a logarithm rule,

$$\log(C_t/C_{t-1}) = \log(G_t/G_{t-1}) + \log(R_t/R_{t-1}) \tag{4}$$

or, to simplify the notation,

$$\text{Corp} = \text{Treas} + \text{Ratio} \tag{5}$$

where

Corp = $\log(C_t/C_{t-1})$ = percentage change in the corporate yield
Treas = $\log(G_t/G_{t-1})$ = percentage change in the Treasury yield
Ratio = $\log(R_t/R_{t-1})$ = percentage change in the yield ratio

Yield Volatility Defined

Yield volatility is usually measured by the standard deviation of the percentage change in the yield. For example, under continuous compounding, corporate yield volatility is simply the standard deviation of the log ratio:

$$\text{vol (Corp)} = \text{standard deviation of } \log(C_t/C_{t-1}) \tag{6}$$

Yield volatility is usually quoted on an annualized basis. For example, suppose that we gather a sample of daily data on corporate bond yields and calculate that the standard deviation of the percentage change in yields is 0.7%. If there are 250 trading days per year, then the annualized yield volatility is[1]

$$\text{Annualized Yield Volatility} = 0.7\% \times \sqrt{250} = 11.07\%$$

CORPORATE AND TREASURY YIELD VOLATILITY

We are mainly concerned with the relationship between corporate yield volatility and Treasury yield volatility. This relationship can be seen directly by taking the variance of equation (5):[2]

$$\text{var(Corp)} = \text{var(Treas)} + \text{var(Ratio)} + 2\,\rho\,\text{vol(Treas)} \times \text{vol(Ratio)} \tag{7}$$

Because the variance is the square of volatility (i.e., $\text{var(Corp)} = \text{vol(Corp)}^2$), it is convenient to make a substitution and rewrite equation (7) as:

$$\text{vol(Corp)}^2 - \text{vol(Treas)}^2 = \text{vol(Ratio)}^2 + 2\,\rho\,\text{vol(Treas)} \times \text{vol(Ratio)} \tag{8}$$

This equation is useful because it tells us under what conditions corporate vol will be greater than Treasury vol. The equation shows that corporate yield vol depends critically on the correlation between movements in Treasury yields and movements in the yield ratio. That correlation is measured by the coefficient ρ. Clearly, if ρ is greater than zero, corporate vol will be greater than Treasury vol, because both terms on the righthand side of (8) would be positive.

Taking another look at equation (8), we see that

$$\text{vol (Corp)} < \text{vol (Treas)} \tag{9}$$

if

$$\text{vol (Ratio)} + 2\,\rho\,\text{vol (Treas)} < 0 \tag{10}$$

Equations (9) and (10) show that corporate yield vol could be less than Treasury vol if ρ is negative. However, ρ has to be sufficiently negative to offset the volatility in the yield ratio, which cannot be negative. It is possible, therefore, for corporate yields to be less volatile than Treasuries, provided that ρ is sufficiently negative *and* that vol(Treas) is large relative to vol(Ratio).

---

[1] Yield volatility is not the same as price volatility. Bonds with short durations often exhibit greater yield volatility than bonds with long durations, but as a consequence of duration, the price volatility of short-duration bonds is generally lower. The relation between yield volatility (the percentage change in yields) and price volatility (the percentage change in price) can be approximated by the following formula:

  Yield Volatility = (Price Volatility) × [1/(Yield × Duration)] × 100

[2] The formula for the variance of a sum is:

  $\text{var}(X + Y) = \text{var}(X) + \text{var}(Y) + 2\,\rho\sigma(X)\sigma(Y)$

where $\sigma(X)$ and $\sigma(Y)$ are the standard deviations of X and Y, respectively, and ρ is the correlation coefficient for X and Y.

Exhibit 2: Example of Corporate Yield Spreads and Yield Ratios when ρ < 0

ρ = −0.82

Treasury Yield (%)	Treasury Yield Change (log difference)	Corporate Yield (%)	Corporate Yield Change (log difference)	Yield Ratio	Yield Ratio Change (log difference)	Spread (%)	Spread Change (log difference)
5.00		6.00		1.20		1.00	0.00
5.50	0.095	6.55	0.088	1.19	−0.008	1.05	0.05
6.00	0.087	7.12	0.083	1.19	−0.004	1.12	0.07
6.50	0.080	7.67	0.074	1.18	−0.006	1.17	0.04
7.00	0.074	8.25	0.073	1.18	−0.001	1.25	0.07
7.50	0.069	8.85	0.070	1.18	0.001	1.35	0.08
8.00	0.065	9.40	0.060	1.18	−0.004	1.40	0.04
7.50	−0.065	8.87	−0.058	1.18	0.007	1.37	−0.02
7.00	−0.069	8.30	−0.066	1.19	0.003	1.30	−0.05
6.50	−0.074	7.70	−0.075	1.18	−0.001	1.20	−0.08
6.00	−0.080	7.15	−0.074	1.19	0.006	1.15	−0.04
5.50	−0.087	6.62	−0.077	1.20	0.010	1.12	−0.03
5.00	−0.095	6.10	−0.082	1.22	0.014	1.10	−0.02
Standard Deviation (Vol)	8.07%		7.62%		0.55%		5.59%

How plausible is this outcome? As it turns out, a negative value for ρ is more plausible than it first seems. It could arise, for example, if spreads are not overly sensitive to the level of interest rates. Consider the example in Exhibit 2, in which Treasury yields rise from 5% to 8%, and then return to 5%. In the exhibit, the corporate yield spread moves in the same direction as Treasuries: The spread begins at 100 basis points when Treasuries are at 5%; it widens to 140 basis points when Treasuries rise to 8%; and then it retraces its widening as Treasuries fall. In this example, corporate spreads widen with Treasuries, but not in the same proportion. Therefore, the yield ratio declines as Treasury yields rise, and vice versa. Consequently, the correlation between changes in Treasury yields and changes in the yield ratio is negative (ρ = −0.82). Also, because vol (Ratio) is lower than vol (Treas) in this example, corporate vol is less than Treasury vol (7.62% versus 8.07%).

Real-world examples also suggest that ρ could be less than zero. In 1994, Treasury yields increased by about 200 basis points, but spreads widened only moderately. Thus, during that year, the correlation between yield ratios and Treasuries was negative. Similarly, during the hedge fund crisis in 1998, Treasury yields fell by more than 100 basis points and spreads widened sharply. During that period, the correlation between yield ratios and Treasuries was also negative. Likewise in 2000, Treasury yields moved dramatically in response to record fiscal surpluses and changing perceptions about monetary policy. During that year, spreads were unusually volatile, and ρ was less than zero. During each of these episodes, corporate vol was less than Treasury vol, in general.

The key fact to remember is that volatility is measured as the *percentage change* in yields. When corporate and Treasury yields move by the same number of basis points, the percentage change in corporate yields will be lower than percentage change in Treasuries, simply because corporate yields are greater than Treasury yields.

An element of spread volatility is necessary for corporate yield vol to be greater than Treasury yield vol. However, volatility in corporate spreads does not guarantee a large value for corporate yield vol. Spreads must be sufficiently volatile to offset the fact that yield volatility is measured as the percentage change in yields. Moreover, volatility in spreads, in itself, does not provide enough information to determine, a priori, whether corporate yield vol is greater or less than Treasury vol because corporate vol depends on both ρ and vol(Ratio)/vol(Treas). Using the same arguments, corporate vol could be higher or lower than agency vol, depending on the correlation between the two series and the volatility of their ratios. Likewise, yield volatility of AAA bonds could be higher or lower than BBB bond volatility.

HISTORICAL EVIDENCE ON CORPORATE YIELD AND SPREAD VOLATILITY

Because theory cannot give definitive answers to the volatility relationships among different bond sectors, we now turn to the evidence from historical data on yields as a guide for the future. Exhibit 3 shows volatility estimates for 10-year and 30-year Treasury, corporate, and high-yield bonds, based on data from 1988 through 2000 (the results are generally robust to alternative sample periods). Three observations are worth noting. First, all of the investment-grade corporate sectors had lower yield volatility than Treasuries. Therefore, the empirical evidence reveals that ρ is less than zero. When Treasury yields rise, yield ratios generally decline, and vice versa. This pattern in yield ratios does not imply that corporate spreads are unaffected by, or negatively correlated with, Treasury yields. Rather, it merely indicates yield spreads are not overly sensitive to the level of Treasury yields. When Treasury yields rise by 10%, for example, corporate spreads typically widen, but by less than 10%.

Second, yield volatility is slightly lower for bonds with low credit ratings. In the 10-year sector, for example, BBB bonds had a yield volatility of 11.9%, compared with 12.4% for A-rated bonds and 12.8% for AA-rated bonds. Moreover, yield volatility was lowest in the BB sector, and even the B sector had lower volatility than the investment-grade sectors. Mathematically, these relationships arise because ρ is more negative for lower-rated bonds, which effectively offsets the effect of their high spread volatility (except in the CCC sector).

Third, spread volatility increases as ratings decline. For example, in the 10-year sector, AAA bonds had a spread volatility of 19.8 basis points, compared with 34.1 basis points for BBB bonds and 154 bps for B-rated bonds. It is also interesting to observe that 30-year bonds had higher spread volatilities than 10-year bonds with the same credit rating. For example, in the single-A sector, 30-year bonds had a spread vol of 36 basis points, compared with 31 basis points for single-A 10-year bonds. These patterns in spread volatility agree with our intuition that lower-rated and longer-term bonds have greater spread risk.

In summary, investment-grade bonds with low ratings typically had higher spread volatility, but lower yield volatility, than high-rated bonds. Clearly, investors must be careful not to interpret yield volatility as a measure of credit risk or spread risk. Spread volatility is a better measure of risk, but spread volatility is not an explicit input in standard option-pricing models. Because yield volatility is measured on a percentage basis, it implicitly allows for greater spread volatility among higher-yielding, low-rated bonds.

AN ADDITIONAL COMPLICATION: RATING VOLATILITY AND CREDIT RISK

The estimates for yield volatility in Exhibit 3 were constructed from index data. That construction is somewhat flawed because investors do not usually buy options on corporate indices; rather, they buy options that are embedded into individual corporate bonds. The yield on an individual bond will not be perfectly correlated with the yield from an index because the credit quality of the bond issuer can change over time.

Exhibit 3: Estimated Yield and Spread Volatility for Selected Corporate Indexes
10-year Bonds

	Treasury	AAA	AA	A	BBB	BB	B	CCC
Yield Vol (%)	14.3	13.1	12.8	12.4	11.9	9.0	10.5	18.4
ρ		−0.45	−0.49	−0.53	−0.58	−0.78	−0.78	−0.65
Spread Vol (bps)		19.8	21.9	31.0	34.1	82.3	154.8	401.4

30-year Bonds

	Treasury	AAA	AA	A	BBB
Yield Vol (%)	11.0	10.0	9.8	9.6	9.6
ρ		−0.43	−0.47	−0.49	−0.49
Spread Vol (bps)		22.8	25.4	36.1	42.2

Estimated from monthly data, 1988–2000.
Yield volatility is the standard deviation of the percentage change in yield, annualized.
ρ is the correlation coefficient between the percentage change in Treasury yields and the percentage change in the corporate yield ratio.
Spread volatility is measured as the standard deviation of the spread.
Source: Chase Securities.

For example, consider a callable bond issued by Ford Motor Company. Ford's bonds carried a single-A rating during the 1990s, but its rating had been higher and lower in previous decades. In evaluating the call option on a Ford bond, investors should account for the fact that Ford's ratings and credit quality could change before the call date. A transition in Ford's credit quality would drive a wedge between Ford's yields and the yield on an index of single-A bonds. An investor that buys a Ford callable bond will be more interested in the volatility of Ford's yields, rather than in the volatility of a single-A yield index, because Ford may not always maintain its single-A rating.[3]

Volatility estimated from index data may be a biased measure of corporate yield volatility, but it is difficult to determine the direction of the bias. Other factors held constant, yield volatility for a specific issuer will be greater than volatility for an index. We know this to be true because an issuer may be upgraded or downgraded, but the credit quality of an index, by definition, does not change over time. Unfortunately, other factors cannot be held constant. In particular, credit ratings are cyclical: companies tend to be downgraded in recessions and upgraded in expansions. Yield levels are also cyclical: Treasury yields generally fall in recessions and rise in expansions. As a result, yield ratios tend to be negatively correlated with Treasuries, and the correlation could be more negative for individual bonds than for bond indices.

For example, suppose that Ford is downgraded in the next recession, from single-A to BBB. In this case, Ford's yield spreads would widen by more than the spread on an index of A-rated bonds. If Treasury yields are also falling in the recession, Ford's yield ratio will be rising. Thus, Ford's yield ratio and Treasury yields will be negatively correlated ($\rho < 0$), and the correlation will be stronger than the correlation between Treasuries and a single-A corporate index. Similarly, as the economy enters into a recovery phase, Ford is more likely to be upgraded and its spreads are likely to narrow. If Treasury yields are rising at that time, Ford's yield ratio will fall. Again, the correlation between Ford's yield ratio and Treasuries will be more negative than the correlation between Treasuries and a single-A index. This cyclicality in credit quality will act to offset some of the bias that arises in estimating yield volatility from index data. In general, *spreads* for specific issuers will be more volatile than spreads of a bond index. But *yield* volatility for specific issuers could be higher or lower than yield volatility of a bond index.

Furthermore, two companies that have the same rating may have different implied yield volatilities, reflecting their exposure to the business cycle. Ford and Pepsi may both be single-A rated, but Ford's earnings and yield spreads tend to be more cyclical. Finally, it is important to remember that volatility, itself, changes over time (compare, in Exhibit 1, volatilities in 1994 versus 2000). At critical periods in the business cycle, corporate yield volatility is likely to increase relative to Treasury vol and agency vol.

---

[3] The importance of credit risk in the valuation of embedded options is the subject of Chapter 17.

CONCLUSIONS

When using option valuation models, investors must be careful in interpreting the volatility input. Yield volatility is not the same as spread volatility. Spread volatility is nearly always higher for low-rated bonds than for high-rated bonds. Yield volatility, by contrast, is often lower for lower-rated, higher-yielding bonds. This does not mean that we can be complacent about the spread risk of corporate bonds, in general, and lower-rated bonds, in particular. Rather, it simply means that yield volatility implicitly allows for some spread volatility because it is measured on a percentage basis.

Chapter 8

Liquidity, Trading, and Trading Costs

A goal of active portfolio management is to achieve a better performance than a portfolio that is simply diversified broadly. To this end, portfolio managers make informed judgments about bond market risks and expected returns, and align their portfolios accordingly by trading bonds in the secondary market. By definition, portfolios that are actively managed are portfolios that are actively traded.

While trading can improve performance, any active portfolio strategy must account for the cost of trading and for the vagaries of liquidity. In this chapter, we show that trading costs and liquidity are inextricably linked though the corporate bond bid-ask spread. The cost of trading depends on that bid-ask spread, as well as duration and the frequency of turnover. While trading costs can be measured, they cannot be known with certainty because the bid-ask spread could be wide or narrow when trades are executed. In fact, the bid-ask spread changes over time, it varies across issuers, and it depends on the size of the transaction. That uncertainty about the cost of trading creates risk—liquidity risk—and that liquidity risk, in turn, gives rise to a risk premium. Consequently, illiquid bonds have higher yields than liquid bonds, not only because their wider bid-ask spreads imply a higher cost of trading but also because investors require compensation for the uncertainty about trading costs. The importance of this relation between the degree of liquidity risk and the level of yield spreads cannot be understated.

Corporate bond liquidity has a pervasive influence on portfolio management. Liquidity affects not only the cost of trading, but it also gives rise to creative trading strategies. Liquidity not only plays a role in determining the level of spreads, but also in establishing relative value between different corporate bonds, among corporate bond industry sectors, and between the corporate bond market and other fixed-income markets, such as Treasuries and mortgages. Indeed, because liquidity contributes to portfolio risks and because trading costs subtract from portfolio returns, portfolios that optimize across the spectrum of known risks and returns will have an optimal amount of liquid bonds and an optimal turnover ratio. Decisions about trading and portfolio liquidity are part of the asset allocation decision.

In this chapter, we analyze liquidity and trading costs from several perspectives. We begin with a description of the secondary market, focusing on the role of dealers in determining the bid-ask spread. We also review the spread arithmetic used to measure the excess return on a bond swap, and we build on this arithmetic to incorporate the cost of trading.

LIQUIDITY AND TRADING COSTS

Among portfolio managers, liquidity is an incessant topic of discussion. Sometimes, fluctuations in liquidity occur as a rational response to observable changes in macroeconomic trends or corporate sector risks. But more often than not, liquidity evaporates for reasons that seem hidden, trivial, or inexplicable. History teaches that liquid markets can quickly become illiquid. Corporate bond markets, in particular, have a history of alternating from periods of confidence and transparency—with multiple dealer quotes, heavy secondary market volume, and tight bid-ask spreads—to periods of gloom and uncertainty—characterized by low trading volumes and wide bid-ask spreads, or worse "offer without." At times of extreme illiquidity, corporate bond salespeople are slow to return phone calls, corporate bond traders seem to spend an inordinate amount of time in the bathroom, and corporate bond portfolio managers mutter the mantra "the Street is not my friend." Portfolio managers, most of whom are educated to believe that financial markets are efficient, learn through experience that bond market liquidity is capricious, illusive, and maddening.

Conceptual Framework

Although liquidity is difficult to understand, it does not defy analysis. Our analysis begins with a list of observations about liquidity. First and most obvious, investors need to be paid for liquidity risk. Liquidity, or to be more precise, illiquidity, can be viewed as a risk that reduces the flexibility of a portfolio. Liquidity risk should be reflected in the yield spread on a corporate bond: the greater the illiquidity, the wider the spread. In this respect, liquidity risk is no different than other corporate bond risks, such as credit risk or the market risk of embedded options. Greater risks require wider spreads.

Second and equally obvious, bonds that are difficult to analyze are less liquid than standard bonds. For example, corporate bonds are less liquid than Treasuries, and bonds with unusual redemption features are less liquid than bullet bonds. In general, bonds that are difficult to analyze trade less frequently, they have wider bid-ask spreads, and they have a narrower base of potential buyers. Investors need to be paid for the effort it takes to analyze a complex bond.

Third, market liquidity depends on the size of the transaction. An investor may find it easy to sell $2 million of bonds at the bid side of the market, but a sale of $10 million might come at a concession to the bid side, and a sale of $50 million would typically require a large concession and a good deal of patience.

Fourth, liquidity varies over time. Stable markets are usually liquid markets. In stable markets, bid-ask spreads are relatively narrow, and size does not generally imply a large concession in price. By contrast, volatile markets, especially bear markets, are notoriously illiquid. During bear markets, bid-ask spreads widen, and it often becomes all but impossible to trade in large size. Fifth, bid-side liquidity causes more angst and sleepless nights than offered-side liquidity.

The Institutional Market Structure:
Bond Dealers and the Bid-Ask Spread

Trading is costly. To understand why trading generates costs, it helps to explore the mechanics and structure of the secondary market. In the corporate bond market, most trades are directed through bond dealers, mainly investment banks, rather than through exchanges or on electronic platforms. Bond dealers serve as intermediaries between investors, standing ready to buy and sell securities in the secondary market.

The cost of trading is measured by the bid-ask spread. Most major bond dealers are willing to provide *indicative* "two-sided" (bid-ask) quotes for all but the most obscure corporate bonds. For example, a dealer might quote a Ford 5-year bond as "80-78, 5-by-10," indicating that the dealer would be willing to buy $5 million of the Ford bond at a spread of 80 basis points above the 5-year Treasury, and sell $10 million of the same bond at a 78 basis point spread. Clearly, bonds that have narrow bid-ask spreads have good liquidity. Liquidity depends not only on the magnitude of the bid-ask spread, but also on the depth of the market, as measured by the number of dealers that are willing to make markets, and also by the size that can be transacted near the quoted market. For example, an "80-78, 5-by-5" market quoted by three dealers is more liquid than an "80-78, 1-by-2" market quoted by only one dealer.

An indicative bid-ask quote is not the same as a firm market. In practice, an investor and a dealer usually haggle back and forth several times before agreeing to the terms of trade. The haggling process may take several minutes, several hours, or even several days; in many cases, the haggling concludes without an agreement to trade.

On any given day, a dealer may provide dozens of indicative quotes, but the number of actual trades may be quite small. In fact, most corporate bonds do not trade every day, or even once a month. Moreover, trading tends to be concentrated in a limited number of bonds, such as:

- bonds that have recently been placed in the new issue market
- bonds that are close substitutes for recent new issues (e.g., swapping an old GM 5-year for a new Ford 5-year)
- bonds of large and frequent corporate borrowers, such as the major banking, telecommunications, auto, and financial companies
- bonds of companies that are involved in important events, such as a merger, a rating change, an earnings surprise, or an industry shock

For these types of bonds, dealers generally provide liquid markets with tight bid-ask spreads (e.g., XYZ Corporation 10-year 97-95, $10 million-by-$10 million). Moreover, dealers prefer to hold inventories in bonds that have high turnover, deep demand, transparent pricing, and close substitutes. Dealers' preference for liquid bonds, in itself, acts to narrow the bid-ask spread. Liquidity begets liquidity.

For less liquid bonds, indicative quotes are not firm markets, bid-ask spreads are wide, and transaction amounts tend to be small. The vast majority of corporate bonds trade only infrequently. For most individual corporate bonds, the market is neither smooth nor continuous.

Coordination and Information Problems: Understanding Trading Costs

Trading costs exist because of market imperfections. Two of the most important market imperfections are coordination problems and information problems. Coordination problems arise because buy and sell orders do not arrive simultaneously; rather, dealers must hold securities in inventory until they can arrange placements with investors. Holding bond inventories is costly because inventories must be financed. In addition to the cost of carrying inventories, dealers face uncertainty about the time required to place their holdings with new investors. When a dealer buys a bond in the secondary market, he faces the risk that the bond may remain in inventory for a day, a week, a month, or even longer. At most investment banks, the cost of carrying inventories rises over time because risk managers penalize stale inventories with higher capital charges. The bid-ask spread serves to compensate dealers for the cost of holding inventory and for the uncertainty about the holding period.

Information problems are another underlying source of trading costs. The more difficult it is for dealers and investors to analyze a bond, the longer will a dealer expect to hold the bond in inventory, and the greater will be the cost of trading. The information that investors analyze can be divided into two categories: (1) information that is specific to the corporate borrower, and (2) information that is specific to the bond issue. Investors analyze a variety of types of information about a borrower, such as its leverage ratios, cash flow, management expertise, litigation risk, credit ratings, cyclical risk, and industry risk. Holding other factors constant, bid-ask spreads are wider for companies that are difficult to analyze.

Along with analyzing information that is specific to the borrower, investors also evaluate information that is specific to the bond issue, such as its face value, maturity, covenants, seniority, and option and redemption features. Other factors held constant, bonds with standard features have low information costs because they are relatively easy to evaluate. Conversely, a complicated security will have lower liquidity and higher information costs, even if other securities issued by the same borrower are very liquid.

As a consequence of these information and coordination problems, the magnitude of the bid-ask spread varies over time and across issuers due to a number of factors, such as those described as follows.

Slope of the Yield Curve

As noted, bond inventories must be financed. Inventories become more expensive to finance when the yield curve flattens, because the money market serves as dealers' main source of funding. As a result, to compensate for the higher cost of carry, dealers widen bid-ask spreads when the curve flattens. A flat yield curve may also affect liquidity and the bid-ask spread indirectly through other channels. First, a flattening of the curve often spurs investors to reallocate funds to the money markets and away from bond markets. When funds flow out of the corporate bond market, spreads must widen to equate supply and demand. Second, the yield curve generally flattens during the late stage of the business cycle, when the Fed raises short rates to quell inflationary pressures. As noted in Chapter 10, credit ratings, corporate earnings, and corporate spreads display strong cyclical patterns, and those patterns are highly correlated with the slope of the yield curve. Greater uncertainty about the economy gives rise to higher information costs and wider bid-ask spreads.

Market Volatility Orderly markets are liquid markets. When the corporate market is calm, yield spreads exhibit low volatility and bid-ask spreads are relatively narrow. At those times, dealers often carry large inventories, but inventories tend to turn over quickly. In orderly markets, dealers earn steady profits from a high volume of turnover, rather than from a wide bid-ask margin. By contrast, in times of market turmoil, such as the 1998 hedge fund crisis, dealers face greater uncertainty about the depth of investor demand for corporate bonds and about credit risk in the corporate sector. At times when markets are risky, dealers and investors become more risk averse. Consequently, in volatile markets, as dealers become reluctant to hold large inventories, bid-ask spreads widen.

Ratings During most of the 1990s, Disney's bonds were quoted with a tighter bid-ask spread than Time Warner's bonds. Both were large, well-known companies, and both were in the same industry, but Time Warner carried a lower credit rating. The risk of credit deterioration exists for all companies, but the risk becomes more crucial for lower-rated companies. For a high-rated company, a small mistake in a cash flow projection may have no discernible effect on credit risk, but for lower-rated companies the margin for error is slim. In general, low-rated bonds have wider bid-ask spreads than high-rated bonds.

Industry and Sector In some industries, each company may have unique business risks that are difficult to analyze. For example, each company in the Real Estate Investment Trust sector requires intensive credit research. In that industry, credit quality can vary markedly across companies due to differences in management, regional exposure, and tenant diversification. When the company-specific risk dominates the industry risk, information costs are high and bid-ask spreads wide. In other industries, such as oil production, the industry risk generally dominates the company-specific risks.

Name Recognition Information about large companies, such as Ford and Citigroup, is broadly disseminated in the media and financial markets. Consequently, well-known companies face lower information problems, and, other factors held equal, their bonds trade with tighter bid-ask spreads.

Structure In the secondary market, simpler is better. The bullet bond, the simplest bond, trades with a tighter bid-ask spread than a bond with a complex structure. For example, noncallable bonds typically trade with tighter bid-ask spreads than callable bonds of the same issuer. Callable bonds are less liquid because their duration can change significantly when interest rates change. Investors often disagree about which models are appropriate to analyze bonds with complex structures, and some corporate bond investors would prefer to focus solely on analyzing credit risk, rather than bond structures. As a result of these information problems, the market for complex bonds is not as deep as it is for bullet bonds, which gives rise to wider bid-ask spreads.

An Analytical Framework

The analytical tools to measure trading costs are the same tools that are used for all fixed-income investments. As usual, duration is the most important tool. Long-duration corporate bonds usually have higher trading costs than bonds with short durations.

Probability theory is the other key tool for measuring trading costs. In fixed-income strategy, investors frequently use probability distributions to characterize uncertain events (e.g., a 70% probability that the Fed cuts the funds rate by 25 basis points at the next FOMC meeting). Those same probability tools can be applied to characterize the uncertainty about trading costs. Specifically, the timing of a trade, the size of the bid-ask spread, and the depth of the market are not known with certainty, but the uncertainty can be described by probability distributions. For example, when a portfolio manager buys a bond, he knows that the bond may be sold before maturity. The bond may have a 1% probability of being sold on the next day, a 10% probability of being sold over the next month, and a 50% probability over the next year. Likewise, the portfolio manager knows that the bond's bid-ask spread may be wide or narrow at the time he wants to sell. Furthermore, the amount of bonds that can be sold at the bid side of the market also can be described by a probability distribution. For example, there may be an 80% probability of selling $1 million at the bid-side spread, but only a 30% chance of selling $10 million at that spread. These probability distributions cannot be observed directly, but they can be inferred from historical data or subjectively estimated using scenario analysis. Portfolio managers can use these probability distributions to estimate the cost of trading.

BOND SWAPS

Trading has measurable costs and potential benefits. In this section, we quantify the potential benefits, with a review of the spread arithmetic of a bond swap. Specifically, we derive the basic formulas for excess returns and breakeven spreads. In subsequent sections, we use this framework to quantify the costs of a bond swap—specifically, the trading costs—and later we expand the cost/benefit framework to a broader portfolio context.

A Review of Spread Duration Math

Investors decide to trade when they conclude that doing so will enhance portfolio returns or reduce risk. Many investors are "yield hogs." They love to swap from low-yielding to high-yielding bonds. Although yield is a key element of the decision to trade, it is not the only element, and it is often not the most important element. Indeed, one of the first lessons of fixed income is the distinction between a bond's yield and its return: because markets fluctuate, yields can differ substantially from subsequent returns.

Similarly, a key lesson in corporate bond portfolio management is that a bond's yield spread can differ substantially from its subsequent *excess return*. Frequently, corporate bonds will look "cheap" when they have a large yield spread above U.S. Treasuries or other high-quality bonds, but the realized excess return will depend on a number of factors, not just the spread.

To identify the factors that contribute to excess returns, we will begin with a simple example of a bond swap. In our example, the investor is buying Bond A and selling Bond B. Initially, we will analyze the general case where the bonds do not necessarily have equal durations, and we will not address the cost of trading. Later in this chapter, we will analyze duration-neutral swaps and trading costs, as well as the role of uncertainty.

Over a 1-year horizon, the total return on Bond A (TR_A) is approximately equal to its coupon (C_A) plus the percentage change in price ($\Delta P_A/P_A$):[1]

$$TR_A \approx C_A + \Delta P_A/P_A \tag{1}$$

Since the percentage change in price is approximately equal to the change in yield (ΔY_A) times the *end-of-period* duration $\Delta D_{A,t+1}$, or, suppressing the time subscript for now, D_A, the total return on Bond A can be rewritten as:[2]

$$TR_A \approx C_A - D_A \Delta Y_A \tag{2}$$

When Bond A is a par bond, its coupon equals the yield on its Treasury benchmark ($Y_{A,\text{Treas}}$) plus a spread (S_A):

$$C_A = Y_{A,\text{Treas}} + S_A \tag{3}$$

---

[1] In this chapter, the formulas for total returns, excess returns, and breakevens are not exact, but only approximations, in part because the returns will depend on the reinvestment rate assumption. For short investment horizons, the reinvestment rate usually has only a small effect on returns. More importantly, the return calculations do not account for convexity.

[2] Of course, the end-of-period duration cannot be known at the beginning of the investment horizon because the horizon duration will depend on the horizon Treasury yield and the horizon spread. Those horizon yields and spreads can be estimated from forward rates.

By definition, the change in the yield on Bond A (ΔY_A) is equal to the change in the Treasury yield plus the change in spread:

$$\Delta Y_A = \Delta Y_{A,\text{Treas}} + \Delta S_A \tag{4}$$

Substituting equations (3) and (4) into equation (2) results in a formula for the total return on Bond A in terms of its spread, horizon duration, and Treasury benchmark yield:

$$TR_A \approx (Y_{A,\text{Treas}} + S_A) - D_A (\Delta Y_{A,\text{Treas}} + \Delta S_A) \tag{5}$$

Similarly, the total return on Bond B can be approximated in terms of its spread, horizon duration, and Treasury benchmark yield:

$$TR_B \approx (Y_{B,\text{Treas}} + S_B) - D_B (\Delta Y_{B,\text{Treas}} + \Delta S_B) \tag{6}$$

When an investor buys Bond A and sells Bond B, the Excess Return (ER) on the swap is equal to the difference in the total returns. Subtracting equation (6) from equation (5) results in:

$$
\begin{aligned}
ER &= TR_A - TR_B \\
&\approx (Y_{A,\text{Treas}} + S_A) - D_A (\Delta Y_{A,\text{Treas}} + \Delta S_A) \\
&\quad - (Y_{B,\text{Treas}} + S_B) + D_B (\Delta Y_{B,\text{Treas}} + \Delta S_B)
\end{aligned}
\tag{7}
$$

Rearranging terms gives:

$$
\begin{aligned}
ER &\approx (Y_{A,\text{Treas}} - Y_{B,\text{Treas}}) + (S_A - S_B) - D_A (\Delta Y_{A,\text{Treas}} - \Delta Y_{B,\text{Treas}}) \\
&\quad + (D_B - D_A)\Delta Y_{B,\text{Treas}} - D_A(\Delta S_A - \Delta S_B) + (D_B - D_A)\Delta S_B
\end{aligned}
\tag{8}
$$

Equation (8) shows that the excess return on the bond swap depends on six factors:

1. the Slope of the Treasury Curve = $Y_{A,\text{Treas}} - Y_{B,\text{Treas}}$
2. the Slope of the Spread Curve = $S_A - S_B$
3. the Change in the Treasury Curve = $D_A (\Delta Y_{A,\text{Treas}} - \Delta Y_{B,\text{Treas}})$
4. the Change in the Spread Curve = $D_A (\Delta S_A - \Delta S_B)$
5. the Direction of Treasury Rates = $(D_B - D_A)\Delta Y_{B,\text{Treas}}$
6. the Direction of Spreads = $(D_B - D_A)\Delta S_B$

Four of these factors can move over the investment horizon: the change in the Treasury curve; the change in the spread curve; the direction of Treasuries; and the direction of spreads. The change in the spread curve, which is studied in more detail in Chapter 8, is only one of the moving parts that determines the return on a bond swap! Therefore, a bond swap can be an imprecise and risky strategy to capture a wide yield spread when the swapped bonds have different durations.

Duration-Neutral Swaps

Fortunately, the arithmetic of a bond swap becomes simplified when both bonds have roughly the same duration. In that case, we can make use of the following relations:

$$D_B = D_A = D \tag{9}$$

and

$$Y_{A,\text{Treas}} = Y_{B,\text{Treas}} \tag{10}$$

In words, equation (9) says that we have selected two bonds, A and B, that have the same duration, and therefore, as indicated by equation (10), both bonds are spread over the same benchmark Treasury yield. After substituting these relations into equation (8), we arrive at a simplified expression for the return pickup on a bond swap over the 1-year horizon. The excess return is equal to the spread between Bond A and Bond B minus the duration times the change in the spread:

$$ER \approx (S_A - S_B) - D(\Delta S_A - \Delta S_B) \tag{11}$$

Equation (11) shows that the excess return can be attributed to two factors: the Spread and the Market Move. The first term, $(S_A - S_B)$, is the Spread, and the second term, $D(\Delta S_A - \Delta S_B)$, is the Market Move, which captures the change in the spread curve, scaled by duration. As a result of constructing a duration-neutral swap, the excess return has only one moving part, the Market Move. In descriptive terms:

$$\text{Excess Return} = \text{Spread} + \text{Market Move} \tag{12}$$

For example, consider a swap in which the investor sells Bond B at 50 basis points and swaps into Bond A at 80 basis points. Therefore, the Spread is 30 basis points. The bonds are estimated to have a duration of about 5 after a 1-year holding period. If the spread between Bond A and Bond B tightens by 20 basis points, then the Market Move will contribute 100 basis points to the Excess Return. The excess return would sum to 130 basis points:

$$ER = (80 - 50) - 5(-20) = 130 \text{ bps} \tag{13}$$

Of course, the realized excess return may differ from the excess return that the investor expected. In our example, the investor expects to earn 130 basis points by swapping from Bond B to Bond A, but that expectation is premised on the forecast of a 20 basis point spread narrowing. The realized return could be greater or less than 130 basis points, depending on whether the spread between Bond A and Bond B tightens by more or less than the 20 basis point forecast.

Exhibit 1: Excess Return on a Bond Swap under Alternative Spread Scenarios

Spread − Duration × (Change in Spread) = Excess Return

Spread (bps)	Duration (end of Period)	Change in Spread (bps)	Excess Return (bps)	Probability
		−40	230	0.10
		−20	130	0.40
30	5	0	30	0.25
		20	−70	0.15
		40	−170	0.10
		Expected Excess Return	55 bps	

Rather than focusing on a single forecast for the excess return, some investors prefer to examine a variety of scenarios and to assign probabilities to those scenarios. For example, the horizon spread can be characterized by a probability distribution, with M different possible outcomes, each with a probability of m_i. Under this method, the excess return given by equation (11) can be rewritten as:

$$\text{Excess Return} = (S_A - S_B) - D \sum_{i=1}^{M} m_i (\Delta S_{A,\,i} - \Delta S_{B,\,i}) \qquad (14)$$

Exhibit 1 shows several scenarios for the excess return, derived from alternative views about the horizon spread between Bonds A and B. In this analysis, the investor believes a 20 basis point spread tightening has the highest probability, 40%, and under that scenario the excess return is 130 basis points. However, if the spread between Bond A and Bond B were to *widen* by 20 basis points, rather than tighten by 20 basis points, the excess return would be −70 basis points. The expected excess return, weighted by the probabilities across all scenarios, is 55 basis points. To develop a more rigorous approach to forecasting excess returns, some portfolio managers model historical data on yield spreads to estimate probability distributions.

Breakeven Analysis

In many cases, investors measure the risk of a bond swap in terms of the breakeven. The breakeven indicates how much spreads have to change in order for a bond swap to have an excess return equal to zero. Thus, by setting equation (11) equal to zero and solving for the spread change, we see that the breakeven is equal to the initial spread between Bonds A and B divided by the end-of-period duration:

$$\text{Breakeven Spread Change} \approx (S_A - S_B)/D \qquad (15)$$

To calculate a breakeven, let's continue with the example in which the investor sells Bond B at 50 basis points and swaps into Bond A at 80 basis points.

That bond swap will break even if the spread between Bond A and Bond B widens from its current level of 30 basis points to 36 basis points over the 1-year horizon:

$$\text{Breakeven Spread Change} \approx (80 - 50)/5 = 6 \text{ bps} \qquad (16)$$

In this example, the initial Spread of 30 basis points is exactly offset by a Market Move of −30 basis points.

The breakeven spread is an important concept, but it is an incomplete measure of risk. The breakeven measures how much spreads could widen before a bond swap loses money, but it does not measure the likelihood of losing money. The breakeven tells us nothing about probabilities or volatility. If spreads are very volatile, a bond swap may have a high probability of busting through the breakeven. Conversely, if volatility is low, the breakeven may have little relevance. The breakeven represents only one point on the probability distribution of possible outcomes for excess returns. The probability distribution of spreads, and the implied distribution of excess returns, provides a much more comprehensive measure of risk. Spread volatility is discussed in detail in Chapter 7.

Swaps between Corporates and Treasuries

Spread arithmetic becomes even more simplified when an investor swaps from a Treasury to a corporate bond with a similar duration. For example, if Bond B is the benchmark Treasury bond, it will have a spread of zero ($S_B = 0$), and the excess return on the bond swap simplifies to:

$$ER \approx S_A - D\Delta S_A \qquad (17)$$

Likewise, the equation for the breakeven spread to Treasuries becomes, simply, Spread divided by duration:

$$\text{Breakeven Spread to Treasury} \approx S_A/D \qquad (18)$$

For example, if Bond A has a spread of 80 basis points and an end-of-period duration of 5, its spread could widen by 16 basis points over a 1-year horizon (from 80 to 96 basis points), and the bond's return would just break even with the return on a comparable Treasury. Again, the breakeven spread to Treasuries is a limited measure of risk because it represents only one point on the distribution of possible returns versus Treasuries.

Shorter Investment Horizons

In the previous analysis, we calculated the excess return under the assumption of a 1-year investment horizon. That calculation can be modified easily to accommodate shorter investment horizons, such as one quarter or one month. Shorter investment horizons affect the calculated excess return in two ways. First, the return attributed to the Spread will be reduced because the Spread will be earned over a shorter time period. Second, the return attributed to the Market Move will be larger because the end-of-period duration will be slightly greater.

In general, to accommodate a shorter investment horizon, the excess return given by equation (11) can be re-expressed as:

$$ER \approx (S_A - S_B)(H/12) - D(\Delta S_A - \Delta S_B) \tag{19}$$

where H is the investment horizon, measured in months.

To illustrate the importance of the investment horizon, let's continue with the example where an investor sells Bond B at 50 basis points and swaps into Bond A at 80 basis points. Now, instead of using a 1-year holding period, let's assume a 3-month horizon. In this case, the expected duration at the horizon would be 5.5, larger than the duration of 5 under the 1-year investment horizon. If the spread between Bond A and Bond B tightens by 20 basis points, then the bond swap will result in a return pickup of 117.5 basis points:

$$ER \approx (80 - 50)(3/12) - 5.5 (-20) = 117.5 \text{ bps} \tag{20}$$

In this example, it is interesting to note that the 117.5 basis point return pickup over this 3-month horizon is less than the 130 basis point excess return under the previous example of the 1-year horizon, even though spreads tightened by 20 basis points in both examples. In terms of attribution, the Spread contributed 7.5 basis points over the 3-month horizon, compared with 30 basis points over the 1-year horizon, while the Market Move contributed 110 basis points, compared with 100 basis points over the longer horizon. Thus, the impact of earning 30 basis points of spread for a shorter period of time more than offset the benefit of a larger end-of-period duration. Of course, the 12.5 basis point difference in excess returns is specific to this example. By changing the assumptions about the duration, the initial spread, or the spread change, it is easy to construct alternative scenarios in which the excess return is larger over a shorter time horizon.

The formula for the breakeven spread, likewise, needs to be modified when the investment horizon is less than 1 year. Specifically, a more general expression for the breakeven spread is:

$$\text{Breakeven} \approx (S_A - S_B)(H/12)(1/D) \tag{21}$$

Likewise, a general approximation for the breakeven spread to Treasuries is:

$$\text{Breakeven Spread to Treasury} \approx S_A (H/12)(1/D) \tag{22}$$

For example, under a 3-month horizon, a bond with an 80 basis point spread to Treasuries and a 5.5 end-of-period duration could widen by 3.6 basis points (from 80 to 83.6) and just break even with Treasuries. By contrast, over a 1-year horizon, the breakeven was 16 basis points. Short investment horizons imply thin breakevens. In turn, thin breakevens barely cover the cost of trading.

Updating Spread Duration Math to Account for Trading Costs and Liquidity

Up to this point, we have calculated the excess return without accounting for liquidity risk. In effect, we have assumed that (1) trading has no cost; (2) the bid-ask spread is zero, and (3) the only factors influencing the Excess Return on a bond swap are the Spread and the Market Move. To account for trading costs, we can include them explicitly as a component of the Excess Return:

$$\text{Excess Return} \approx \text{Spread} + \text{Market Move} - \text{Trading Cost} \tag{23}$$

Trading Cost is equal to the *beginning-of-period* duration (D_t) times the bid-ask spread (BA):

$$\text{Trading Cost} = D_t \times BA \tag{24}$$

Similarly, the formula for the excess return, equation (11), can be re-expressed as:

$$ER \approx (S_A - S_B) - D_{t+1}(\Delta S_A - \Delta S_B) - D_t \times BA \tag{25}$$

Note that while both the Market Move and the Trading Cost depend on duration, these durations are not equivalent. In the analysis, Bonds A and B are traded at the beginning of the period, at time t, when their durations are D_t, but the Market Move is measured at the end of the investment horizon, at time $t+1$, when their durations are D_{t+1}. In general, D_t is greater than D_{t+1}.

To illustrate the importance of trading costs, let's continue with our example of the swap from Bond B to Bond A. Let's assume that the bid-ask for Bond A is 80-76, and that the bid-ask for Bond B is 50-47. The investor believes the bid-side spread between Bond A and Bond B will tighten by 20 basis points. Both bonds have a duration of 5.5 today, at the time they are traded, but at the end of 1 year their durations fall to 5. The investor currently owns Bond B, which can be sold at the 50 basis point bid-side spread. The investor is evaluating the expected return of swapping to Bond A, which can be purchased at the offered side spread of 76 basis points. After Bond A is purchased, it will be marked in the investor's portfolio at the bid-side spread of 80 basis points. Thus, the act of trading created an immediate, negative return of 22 basis points: the 4 basis point bid-ask spread times the 5.5 duration. Therefore, over a 1-year investment horizon, the expected excess return, inclusive of the 22 basis points in trading cost, is 108 basis points:

$$ER \approx (80 - 50) - 5(-20) - 5.5(4) = 108 \text{ bps} \tag{26}$$

Accounting for Uncertainty

The previous example assumes that the bid-ask spread is known with certainty, but for reasons outlined earlier in the chapter, bid-ask spreads change over time.

A thorough analysis of trading costs must account for the uncertainty about the bid-ask. In our example, the investor believes that Bond B, quoted at 50-47, has a 3 basis point bid-ask spread, but the exact bid-ask cannot be known for certain until a dealer makes a market. In some cases, the investor might be able to tighten the bid-ask by haggling with a dealer or by shopping around to multiple dealers. The haggling might reduce the bid-ask spread to 2 basis points or 1 basis point. However, it is also possible that the 50-47 quoted market might evaporate when it comes time for a dealer to commit capital. The real market might be 51-46, or if the size of the trade is large, 53-45. Similarly, although a dealer may quote an 80-76 market for Bond A, the true bid-ask can only be discovered by testing a dealer for a bid or offer.

One way to analyze the problem of uncertainty about the bid-ask spread is to frame the problem in terms of probabilities. Specifically, rather than assigning a single value to the bid-ask spread, we can describe it by a probability distribution in which there are N different bid-ask spreads, each with a probability of p_i. This framework allows us to rewrite equation (24) as:

$$\text{Trading Cost} = D \sum_{i=1}^{N} p_i BA_i \qquad (27)$$

In our example of the swap from Bond B to Bond A, the investor may believe the probability of executing a trade with a 4 basis point bid-ask is 60%. However, there may be a 30% probability that the tradable bid-ask spread is 5 basis points, and a 10% probability that the bid-ask is 3 basis points. Substituting these values into (27) gives an expected trading cost of about 23 basis points.

$$\text{Trading Cost} = 5.5 \times (0.6 \times 4 \text{ bps} + 0.3 \times 5 \text{ bps} + 0.1 \times 3 \text{ bps}) = 23.1 \text{ bps} \quad (28)$$

Portfolio Trading Cost

In a portfolio context, trading costs depend not only on the duration and the bid-ask spread, but also on the portfolio turnover. Specifically, the equation for trading cost (24) can be modified for the portfolio context in the following manner:

$$\text{Portfolio Trading Cost} = \text{Portfolio Duration} \times \text{Bid Ask} \times \text{Portfolio Turnover} \qquad (29)$$

where Portfolio Turnover is measured by:

$$\text{Portfolio Turnover} = (\text{Market Value of Buys} + \text{Market Value of Sells})/ (2 \times \text{Market Value of Portfolio}) \qquad (30)$$

For example, suppose an investor manages a $500 million corporate bond portfolio with a weighted average duration of 5. Over the course of a year, our investor turns the portfolio over 80% (roughly $400 million buys and $400 million sales) and pays an average bid-ask spread of 3 basis points. In this example, the cost of trading would amount to 12 basis points:

$$\text{Portfolio Trading Cost} = 5 \times 3 \text{ bps} \times 0.8 = 12 \text{ bps} \qquad (31)$$

For this $500 million portfolio, the 12 basis point cost of trading translates into $600,000 per year (which, by coincidence, just happens to equal the annual bonus of an average bond salesperson). A portfolio manager spends 12 basis points trading hopes that that cost will be recouped through prescient investment decisions. For the market as a whole, however, trading is a zero-sum game, in which the gains to portfolio managers and traders with good skills are balanced by losses to players with bad luck.[3]

Exhibit 2 shows the portfolio cost of trading for a variety of alternative assumptions about portfolio duration, turnover, and the bid-ask spread. The results are intuitive. Trading costs are high for portfolios with long durations, high turnover ratios, and wide bid-ask spreads. For example, a portfolio with an 8-year duration and a 200% turnover ratio will incur 48 basis points in trading costs per year if the average trade is executed with a 3 basis point bid-ask spread. Only skilled portfolio managers have the ability to recoup sizable trading costs.

Exhibit 2: The Portfolio Cost of Trading (basis points)
Portfolio Duration = 3

Bid-Ask Spread	Annual Portfolio Turnover				
(bps)	25%	50%	100%	200%	400%
1	0.8	1.5	3.0	6.0	12.0
3	2.3	4.5	9.0	18.0	36.0
5	3.8	7.5	15.0	30.0	60.0

Portfolio Duration = 5

Bid-Ask Spread	Annual Portfolio Turnover				
(bps)	25%	50%	100%	200%	400%
1	1.3	2.5	5.0	10.0	20.0
3	3.8	7.5	15.0	30.0	60.0
5	6.3	12.5	25.0	50.0	100.0

Portfolio Duration = 8

Bid-Ask Spread	Annual Portfolio Turnover				
(bps)	25%	50%	100%	200%	400%
1	2.0	4.0	8.0	16.0	32.0
3	6.0	12.0	24.0	48.0	96.0
5	10.0	20.0	40.0	80.0	160.0

---

[3] Actually, trading is a slightly negative-sum game due to dead weight costs, such as transfer fees and back office expenses.

Liquidity Risk in a Portfolio Context

Uncertainty pervades portfolio management. Just as investors can never be absolutely certain about the direction of the interest rates or the size of the bid-ask spread, they also face uncertainty about their portfolio turnover. An investor may plan to turn his portfolio over 80% per year, but he knows that the actual turnover ratio could be higher or lower, depending on a number of factors, such as the vagaries of monetary policy, the liquidity of bond dealers, and the incidence of negative credit events. To account for uncertainty about turnover, we can modify the previous analysis by assuming T different turnover ratios, each with a probability of q_j. This framework allows us to express the portfolio trading cost as a function of an uncertain bid-ask spread and an uncertain turnover ratio:

$$\text{Portfolio Trading Cost} = D \sum_{i=1}^{N} p_i BA_i \sum_{j=1}^{T} q_j \text{Turnover}_j \tag{32}$$

At first glance, the introduction of probabilities into the calculation of trading costs seems silly. After all, a portfolio with a 100% turnover ratio has the same expected trading cost as another portfolio with a 50% probability of 75% turnover and a 50% probability of 125% turnover. Likewise, a 4 basis point bid-ask spread with 100% certainty has the same expected cost as a 1 basis point bid-ask spread with a 25% probability and a 5 basis point spread with a 75% probability. Rather than introducing probabilities, why not just keep the analysis simple and express the bid-ask and the turnover as a weighted average?

Although it is true that the average bid-ask spread and the average turnover ratio measure the cost of trading, the averages hide the inherent uncertainty in the trading process. The most basic concept in finance is that investors do not like uncertainty. For example, corporate bond investors do not like the uncertainty that some of their bonds may be downgraded or default. To compensate for the uncertainty about credit risk, investors demand a yield premium in excess of the default and downgrade probabilities. Likewise, investors do not like uncertainty about trading in the secondary market. Investors would prefer to pay a 4 basis point bid-ask with certainty, rather than take the risk that the bid-ask could be higher or lower than 4 basis points, and only equal 4 basis points on average. To some degree, the yield spread on a corporate bond is payment to investors for the risk that the bid-ask may differ significantly from the average, or expected value.

The fact that liquidity risk, itself, commands a risk premium is of crucial importance. Yield spreads on corporate bonds compensate investors not only for the measurable costs of trading, which can be calculated with risk-neutral pricing by equation (32), but also for the uncertainty about liquidity and trading costs. Part of the spread on a corporate bond represents an uncertainty risk premium. Sometimes, the uncertainty risk premium is called a liquidity risk premium, or premium to risk-neutral pricing. Two bonds may have the same fundamental risks (e.g., they may both have BBB ratings), but if one bond is less liquid it will have a wider yield spread. This is the key reason why liquidity is important to monitor. Liquidity affects not only the size of the bid-ask spread, but also the level of the yield spread.

CONCLUSION

In the corporate bond market, we need to be paid for what we know. We know that corporate bond yields must be high enough to compensate for the cost of trading. We know that trading costs depend on duration, turnover, and the bid-ask spread. We also demand to be paid for what we don't know. We don't know the frequency of turnover or the magnitude of the bid-ask spread. And we face the risk that the bid-ask will gap wider at the moment we want to trade in size. We need to be paid for uncertainty.

Rational portfolio managers understand that trading is costly. Trading, in effect, transfers performance from investors' portfolios to the bonus pools of bond dealers. Trading eats into the yield spread on a corporate bond: it drives a wedge between a bond's spread and its expected excess return. This is not to say that portfolio managers should abandon active portfolio strategies to avoid trading costs. Rather, portfolio managers should merely recognize that the benefits of active strategies must be weighed against the costs of trading.

Chapter 9

Corporate Spread Curve Strategies

I n the corporate bond market, spread curves often differ considerably across issuers. An example of this variation is presented in Exhibit 1, which shows the spread curves for two BBB-rated corporations that we will call ABC Corporation and XYZ Inc. ABC bonds trade at wider spreads than XYZ bonds at 7-year and 20-year maturities. More importantly, the ABC spread curve is significantly steeper than the XYZ curve. The 250 basis points (bps) offered-side spread on the ABC 20-year bond is 75 bps wider than the 175 bps spread on the ABC 7-year bond. By contrast, the spread curve for XYZ is only 30 bps.

Most fixed-income investors understand the relation between the term structure of interest rates and implied forward rates. But some investors overlook the fact that a similar relation holds between the term structure of corporate spreads and forward corporate spreads. Specifically, when the spread curve is steep, the forward spreads imply that spreads will widen over time. By contrast, a flat spread curve gives rise to forwards that imply stability in corporate spreads. Essentially, the forward spread can be viewed as a breakeven spread. If spreads move to the implied forward spreads, then all bonds of the same corporate issuer will earn the same duration-adjusted returns over the investment horizon.

Exhibit 1: Spread Curves for ABC Corporation and XYZ Inc.

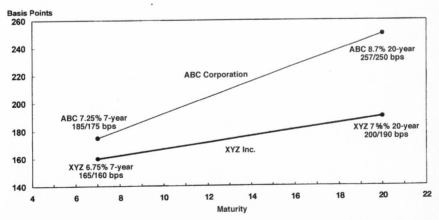

Treasury benchmark yields of 6.19% for the 7-year bonds and 6.7% for the 20-year bonds.

Sometimes, investors may disagree with the expectations implied by forward spreads, and consequently they may want to implement trading strategies to profit from reshapings of the spread curve. In many cases, these strategies are based on the belief that spread curves will converge over time. In our example, the steepness of the ABC curve implies very wide forward spreads for the ABC 20-year bond, while the flatter spread curve for XYZ implies less widening on the XYZ 20-year bond. In other words, the forward spreads suggest that the spread between ABC 20-year and XYZ 20-year will widen over time. Investors who disagree with these forward spread expectations should consider structuring their portfolios in anticipation of a convergence of the XYZ and ABC spread curves.

In this chapter, we present three spread curve strategies: (1) bond swaps; (2) a duration-neutral box trade; and (3) the spread-neutral box trade. On the surface, each of these trading strategies appears to take a position on the corporate spread curve. However, as will be shown, the first two strategies may often backfire even if spread curves move as anticipated. Only the third strategy, the spread-neutral box trade, is a pure play on the corporate spread curve.

FORWARD SPREAD ANALYSIS

At a basic level, many yield curve strategies for corporate and Treasury bonds can be analyzed in terms of forward rates. In the Treasury market, forward rates show how much yields need to change to make all bonds earn the same holding period return. The holding period return is simply a bond's coupon income and the capital gain or loss caused by yield changes over the investment horizon. When the Treasury yield curve is upward sloping, long-term bonds will earn higher returns than shorter-term bonds if yields are unchanged over the investment horizon. Therefore, to equalize holding period returns, long-term bonds would have to post capital losses to offset their initial yield advantage. The forward rate is the amount that yields have to increase to give rise to the capital loss. In this sense, the forward rate can be viewed as a breakeven yield change.[1]

Investment strategies on corporate spread curves also depend on forward rates, or, to be more specific, on forward corporate spreads. In the investment-grade corporate market, spread curves are almost always upward sloping. For example, 30-year bonds have wider spreads than 10-year bonds, which in turn have wider spreads than 5-year bonds of the same issuer, and so on. The forward spread indicates how much corporate spreads have to change over an investment horizon to equalize the duration-adjusted holding period return on all bonds of the same issuer. For a corporate bond, the holding period return is the sum of the coupon income, plus the capital gain or loss due to the change in the benchmark Treasury yield, plus the capital gain or loss due to the change in spread.

---

[1] For a review of forward rate analysis, see Antti Ilmanen, "Market Rate Expectations and Forward Rates," *Journal of Fixed Income* (September 1996).

Exhibit 2: Returns on Corporate Bonds Under Alternative Scenarios for Horizon Spreads

Today's Values			Yields at 1-Year Horizon		Returns	
Initial Maturity	Treasury (%)	Spread (bps)	Treasury (%)	Spread (bps)	Total Return (%)	Incremental Return (bps)
A. Spreads are Unchanged						
1	6.00	20	Matured		6.20	20
2	6.00	25	6.00	25	6.25	25
3	6.00	30	6.00	30	6.30	30
B. Spreads Roll Down the Spread Curve						
1	6.00	20	Matured		6.20	20
2	6.00	25	6.00	20	6.28	28
3	6.00	30	6.00	25	6.36	36
C. Spreads Move to Implied Forward Spreads						
1	6.00	20	Matured		6.20	20
2	6.00	25	6.00	31	6.20	20
3	6.00	30	6.00	37	6.20	20

* Calculations assume a 6.2% reinvestment rate.

To focus on the corporate spread curve, let's begin with the simplifying assumption that Treasury yields move to their forward rates, so that all Treasuries have the same return over the investment horizon. Under these conditions, returns on corporate bonds will not be affected by the Treasury market. The return will depend on the corporate bond's initial yield spread and on the change in the spread over the horizon. When the spread curve is upward sloping, long-term corporate bonds will earn higher returns than shorter-term bonds of the same issuer if spreads are unchanged over the investment horizon. Therefore, to equalize holding period returns, long-term corporate bonds have to post capital losses to offset their initial spread advantage. The forward spread is the amount that spreads have to widen to give rise to the capital loss. The forward spread is essentially the breakeven spread change.

An example that shows the relation between the corporate spread curve and forward spreads is presented in Exhibit 2. In this analysis, the Treasury yield curve is flat at 6% both initially and at the 1-year investment horizon.[2] Therefore, because all Treasuries have the same return, any difference in corporate returns can be attributed to corporate spreads and their movements over time. Initially, the issuer's spreads on 1-, 2-, and 3-year corporates are 20, 25, and 30 bps, respectively.

In the exhibit, we consider three scenarios over the investment horizon: (A) spreads are unchanged; (B) spreads roll down the spread curve; and (C) spreads move to forwards. If spreads are unchanged, long-term corporates will have a return advantage (panel A). The 3-year spread will remain at 30 bps over the 1-year horizon (when it becomes a 2-year corporate) and earn 30 bps over

---

[2] The assumption of a flat Treasury curve makes it easier to see the relation between the corporate spread curve and forward spreads, but it not necessary to the analysis. We could have started with initial Treasury curve of any shape and assumed that Treasuries moved to rates implied by the Treasury forward curve.

Treasuries. Similarly, the 2-year corporate will earn 25 bps of incremental return, and the 1-year corporate will earn 20 bps.

The return advantage of long-term corporates will be even greater if corporate spreads roll down the spread curve (panel B). In the rolldown scenario, the spread on the 3-year corporate tightens from 30 to 25 bps over the horizon, and it has a return of 6.36%, or 36 bps of incremental return over Treasuries. The 2-year corporate rolls down from 25 to 20 bps and earns 28 bps of incremental return.

Under the scenario that spreads move to their implied forward spreads, by definition, all bonds of the corporate issuer earn the same holding period return (panel C). In our example, all of the bonds earn 20 bps of incremental return (the return of the 1-year corporate above the 6% Treasury return). Therefore, in the forward spread scenario, spreads on the 2-year and 3-year corporates must widen. The 2-year corporate must widen from 25 bps to 31 bps, and the 3-year corporate must widen from 30 bps to 37 bps.

It is important to emphasize that the forward spread may differ from the expected future spread. An upwardly sloping spread curve *implies* wider forward spreads, but it does not necessarily imply that investors really expect spreads to widen over time. Indeed, the slope of the spread curve may also reflect a risk premium. Investors who buy long-term corporate bonds typically do not want to just break even with short corporates; rather, they want to earn a return premium for taking on the additional duration risk in the corporate market. Consequently, even when forward spreads imply spread widening, investors may be expecting that spreads will roll down the spread curve, but they may also demand a risk premium to compensate for the risk of spread volatility and of credit quality deterioration.[3] In addition, the slope of the spread curve may also reflect an illiquidity premium.

The Slope of the Spread Curve and the Forward Spread Curve

The previous example illustrates a key characteristic of corporate spread curves. When the spread curve is upward sloping, the forward spreads imply a widening of spreads. More importantly, the steeper the spread curve, the greater is the widening implied by forward spreads.

According to the arithmetic of bond math, issuers that have differently sloped spread curves will have even greater differences in their implied forward spreads. This relation between the slope of the spread curve and the implied forward spreads is shown in Exhibit 3. In this example, Company A and Company B both have 10-year bonds that trade at a 100 bps spread to Treasuries. Because both spread curves are positively sloped, the forwards for both companies imply spread widening over a 1-year horizon. But because the spread curve for Company B is more steeply sloped, the forwards imply that the spreads of Company B will widen relative to the spreads of Company A.

---

[3] For an explanation of how credit risk gives rise to an upward sloping spread curve, see Chapter 9 and Jerome S. Fons, "Using Default Rates to Model the Term Structure of Credit Spreads," *Financial Analysts Journal* (September/October 1994).

Exhibit 3: Steep Spread Curves Imply Greater Widening in Forward Spreads

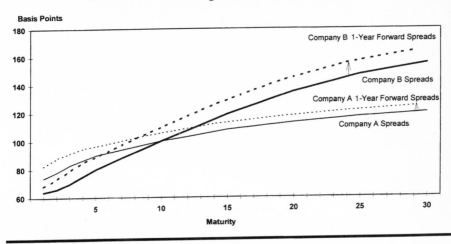

Sometimes, an investor will have a strong opinion about where spread curves are likely to move in the future. When those opinions differ significantly from the forward spread curve, the investor will find it advantageous to implement portfolio strategies that effectively bet against the forward market. If corporate spreads do not move to their forward spreads, then some bonds will earn higher duration-adjusted returns than other bonds of the same issuer. For example, an investor may expect that the spread gap between Company B and Company A will remain constant or that it may converge over time, an expectation that differs from the divergence implied by forward spreads. Two strategies that allow investors to anticipate changes in the spread curves are the bond swap and the box trade.

THE BOND SWAP

A *bond swap* is a simple, but imperfect, strategy to position a portfolio for a change in the slope of a corporate spread curve.[4] When an issuer's spread curve is expected to flatten, an investor will swap out of the issuer's shorter-term bonds and into its longer-term bonds. Continuing with our first example from Exhibit 1, an investor may believe that the steep spread curve for ABC will flatten over time. Given that view, the investor sells the ABC 7-year bond with a 185 bps spread and buys the ABC 20-year bond with 250 bps spread (Exhibit 4).[5]

---

[4] The fixed-income arithmetic of a bond swap is covered in detail in Chapter 8.

[5] In this trade, and in all of the trades that follow, we assume that bonds are sold on the bid side of the market and bought on the offered side.

Exhibit 4: ABC Bond Swap

Exhibit 5: How a Bond Swap Can Backfire Even if the Spread Curve Moves as Anticipated

Strategy: *Sell* ABC 7¼ 7-year (185 bps) and
  Buy ABC 8.7 20-year (250 bps)
    in anticipation of a flattening of the ABC spread curve

	Today's Yields		Yield at 1-Year Horizon		Yield and Spread Change		Total Return
	Treasury Benchmark Yield	Spread	Treasury Benchmark Yield	Spread	Treasury	Spread	
A. A Parallel Rise in Treasury Rates May Offset the Spread Curve Flattening							
Sell ABC 7¼ 7-year	6.19	185	6.94	185	75	0	4.93
Buy ABC 8.7 20-year	6.70	250	7.45	240	75	−10	3.78
					Give-up from Swap (bps)		−115
B. A Steepening of the Treasury Curve May Offset the Spread Curve Flattening							
Sell ABC 7¼ 7-year	6.19	185	6.04	185	−15	0	8.63
Buy ABC 8.7 20-year	6.70	250	6.95	240	25	−10	7.87
					Give-up from Swap (bps)		−76
C. The Spread Curve May Flatten at Wider Spreads							
Sell ABC 7¼ 7-year	6.19	185	6.19	255	0	70	5.13
Buy ABC 8.7 20-year	6.70	250	6.70	310	0	60	4.18
					Give-up from Swap (bps)		−95

* Calculations assume 6% reinvestment rate

Unfortunately, bond swaps have two shortcomings that could easily undermine the spread curve strategy. First, bond swaps change the duration of a portfolio. As a result, even if a corporate spread curve moves as anticipated, bond swaps may be unprofitable if Treasury rates move in an undesirable direction.

An example of this risk is shown in Exhibit 5, which gives three scenarios in which the ABC spread curve flattens 10 bps over a 1-year horizon. In panel A, the flattening of the ABC spread curve is more than offset by a 75 bps parallel widening in Treasury rates. In this scenario, the ABC 20-year bond underperforms the 7-year bond by 115 bps because of its longer duration and greater exposure to rising Treasury rates.

Panel B shows that the return on a bond swap is also sensitive to nonparallel shifts in the Treasury yield curve. In this example, the ABC spread curve flattens by 10 bps, as anticipated, but this flattening is more than counteracted by a 40 bps steepening in the Treasury yield curve. Consequently, the bond swap gives rise to a return give-up of 76 bps.

Exhibit 6: A Bond Swap Between ABC and XYZ Long-Term Bonds

A second problem with the bond swap is that it may be unprofitable even if Treasury rates are unchanged and the corporate spread curve moves in the anticipated direction. Specifically, bond swaps that anticipate a flattening (swaps from short corporates to long-term corporates) may underperform if the spread curve flattens, but at wider spread levels. Panel C of Exhibit 5 gives an example of this spread risk. In this example, the ABC 7-year bond widens by 70 bps and ABC 20-year bond widens by 60 bps, resulting in a 10 bps flattening of the ABC spread curve. Due to the general widening in ABC spreads, however, the 20-year bond underperforms the 7-year bond by 95 bps. This underperformance is attributable to the longer duration of the ABC 20-year bond.

In summary, the return on a bond swap is sensitive to four moving parts: (1) the direction of Treasury rates; (2) the slope of the Treasury curve; (3) the direction of spreads; and (4) the slope of the spread curve. Therefore, a bond swap is an imprecise and risky strategy to implement a view about the slope of a corporate spread curve because it does not neutralize the effects of duration and the direction of spreads on returns.

Duration-Neutral Bond Swaps

An alternative bond swap is shown in Exhibit 6. In this swap, the investor sells the 20-year bond of XYZ and buys the 20-year bond of ABC, based on the expectation that the XYZ and ABC spread curves will converge. The advantage of this bond swap is that it has only a minor impact on the portfolio's exposure to change in Treasury yields, as both bonds have a duration of about 9. Therefore, the swap nearly eliminates two of the four moving parts that determine the return on a bond swap (the direction of Treasury rates and the slope of the Treasury curve).

As explained in detail in Chapter 8, when two bonds have roughly equal durations, the return pickup over a 1-year horizon can be approximated by the following formula:

$$\text{Return pickup} \approx \text{Spread} - \text{Duration at horizon} \times \text{Change in spread}$$

In our example, the spread between 20-year ABC and 20-year XYZ is 50 bps, and the expected duration at a 1-year horizon is about 8.7. Therefore, if the spread between ABC and XYZ tightens by 10 bps, the return pickup from the swap will be about 137 bps:

$$\text{Return pickup} \approx 50 - 8.7 \times (-10) = 137 \text{ bps}$$

But a shortcoming of this duration-neutral bond swap is that it is sensitive to the direction of spreads, and as a result, it is not a pure play on the corporate spread curves. For example, suppose that the ABC curve flattens by 10 bps, but that the flattening occurs at wider spread levels, with the ABC 7-year bond widening from 185 to 235 bps and the ABC 20-year bond widening from 250 to 290 bps. In that scenario, the swap from XYZ 20-year to ABC 20-year will result in a 285 bps return *give-up* over a 1-year horizon. Any widening in the ABC 20-year relative to XYZ 20-year will reduce the return of the swap, irrespective of what happens to the ABC spread curve.

DURATION-NEUTRAL BOX TRADES

A *duration-neutral box trade* is an alternative strategy to structure a portfolio in anticipation of changes in corporate spread curves. A box trade is essentially a portfolio swap that is composed of two bond swaps. In one bond swap, an investor buys a long-term bond of one issuer and sells a long-term bond of another issuer. At the same time, the investor sells the shorter-term bonds of the first issuer and buys a shorter-term bond of the second issuer. By construction, the portfolio of bonds that the investor is buying has the same duration as the portfolio of bonds he or she is selling.

An example of a duration-neutral box trade is shown in Exhibit 7. Before the trade, the investor owns Portfolio 1 consisting of ABC 7-year and XYZ 20-year. After the trade, the investor owns Portfolio 2 consisting of ABC 20-year and XYZ 7-year. In this box trade, the investor buys $5 million of the ABC 20-year bond and simultaneously sells $4.6 million of the XYZ 20-year bond. At the same time, the investor sells the $5.4 million of ABC 7-year bond and buys $5 million of the XYZ 7-year bond. Notice that these amounts differ slightly from a dollar-for-dollar box trade (e.g., sell $5 million ABC 7-year for every $5 million XYZ 7-year), a difference that is necessary to make the trade duration-neutral and proceeds-neutral.[6] Both portfolios have the same expected duration of 6.5 at the 1-year investment horizon. In the base case, under which yields and spreads are unchanged, the box trade has a return pickup of 15 bps.

An attractive feature of the duration-neutral box trade is that it all but eliminates exposure to changes in the Treasury yield curve. As a result, it allows an investor to take a view on the corporate spread curve without taking on duration risk. For example, suppose that Treasury rates rise by 50 bps over a 1-year horizon, and that the ABC credit curve flattens by 10 bps (see Exhibit 8). Thus, all yields rise by 50 bps, except for the ABC 20-year bond yield, which rises by 40 bps. In this scenario, Portfolio 2 (ABC 20-year and XYZ 7-year) has a return of 5.75%, compared with a return of 5.19% for Portfolio 1 (ABC 7-year and XYZ

---

[6] The end-of-period duration is not unique, of course, because the bonds' durations depend on Treasury yields and spreads at the horizon. In our examples, the duration-neutral weightings reflect a base case assumption that yields and spreads are unchanged over the horizon.

20-year). Therefore, if the ABC curve flattens by 10 bps at the long end, the duration-neutral box trade has a return pickup of 57 bps.

Not all box trades are pure plays on the corporate spread curve. In fact, in our example, the profitability of the box trades is sensitive to the direction of the spreads, as well as the slope of the spread curves. To illustrate this sensitivity, suppose that the ABC curve flattens, but that the flattening takes place at wider spread levels. (In Exhibit 8, by contrast, the ABC spread curve flattened at tighter levels, as Treasury rates rose by 50 bps.) Exhibit 9 shows the return profile of the box trade when ABC spread curve flattens by 10 bps, with the ABC 7-year bond widening by 40 bps and the ABC 20-year bond widening by 30 bps. For simplicity, we've assumed that Treasury yields and XYZ spreads are unchanged over a 1-year horizon. Even though the ABC curve has flattened in this scenario, the return on Portfolio 2 is 21 bps less than the return on Portfolio 1.

Exhibit 7: A Duration-Neutral Box Trade

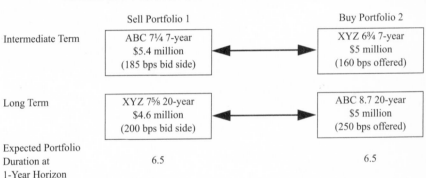

	Sell Portfolio 1		Buy Portfolio 2
Intermediate Term	ABC 7¼ 7-year $5.4 million (185 bps bid side)	◄──►	XYZ 6¾ 7-year $5 million (160 bps offered)
Long Term	XYZ 7⅝ 20-year $4.6 million (200 bps bid side)	◄──►	ABC 8.7 20-year $5 million (250 bps offered)
Expected Portfolio Duration at 1-Year Horizon	6.5		6.5

Exhibit 8: Return on Duration-Neutral Box Trade When Treasury Rates Rise by 50 Basis Points and the ABC Spread Curve Flattens by 10 Basis Points

Issuer	Coupon (%)	Maturity in Years	Duration at 1-Year Horizon*	Market Value ($ millions)	Spread (bps)	Yield Change over Horizon (bps)	Total Return (%)
Buy Portfolio 2							
ABC	8.700	20	8.71	5.0	250	40	5.80
XYZ	6.750	7	4.20	5.0	160	50	5.70
Portfolio 2			6.45	10.0			5.75
Sell Portfolio 1							
XYZ	7.625	20	9.08	4.6	200	50	4.28
ABC	7.250	7	4.23	5.4	185	50	5.94
Portfolio 1			6.45	10.0			5.18
						Return Pickup (bps)	56.60

* Horizon durations for base case that yields and spreads are unchanged.

Exhibit 9: Return on Duration-Neutral Box Trade When the ABC Spread Curve Flattens 10 Basis Points at Wider Levels

Issuer	Coupon (%)	Maturity in Years	Duration at 1-Year Horizon*	Market Value ($ millions)	Spread (bps)	Yield Change over Horizon (bps)	Total Return (%)
Buy Portfolio 2							
ABC	8.700	20	8.71	5.0	250	30	6.62
XYZ	6.750	7	4.20	5.0	160	0	7.76
Portfolio 2			6.45	10.0			7.19
Sell Portfolio 1							
XYZ	7.625	20	9.08	4.6	200	0	8.65
ABC	7.250	7	4.23	5.4	185	40	6.35
Portfolio 1			6.45	10.0			7.40
						Return Pickup (bps)	−21.40

* Horizon durations for base case that yields and spreads are unchanged.

Furthermore, Portfolio 2 will perform poorly if the long-term and intermediate-term ABC bonds widen in parallel. For example, if ABC 7-year and 20-year bonds widen by 50 bps in parallel, then Portfolio 2 will underperform Portfolio 1 by 81 basis points. Similarly, if XYZ spreads tighten in 50 bps in parallel, with ABC spreads unchanged, Portfolio 2 will underperform Portfolio 1 by 90 bps. These scenarios illustrate that box trades do not always allow investors to profit from a convergence of spread curves and that the profitability can be sensitive to parallel shifts of spread curves. In our particular example, the trade is biased to enhance returns when the ABC curve flattens at tighter spread levels, or alternatively when the XYZ curve steepens at wider levels.

THE SPREAD-NEUTRAL, DURATION-NEUTRAL BOX TRADE

A *spread-neutral box trade* is a pure strategy to position a portfolio for a realignment of corporate spread curves. When properly designed, the trade will be profitable if spread curves move in the anticipated direction, regardless of whether Treasury benchmark yields rise or fall and regardless of whether the spread curve convergence occurs at wider or tighter spread levels. In this respect, a spread-neutral box trade is superior to a bond swap and other duration-neutral box trades because the profitability of the strategy depends only on the slope of the spread curves.

The key in constructing the trade lies in choosing the relative amounts of intermediate and long-term bonds that are swapped. In the previous example, we arbitrarily decided to buy roughly $5 million of intermediate and long-term bonds of ABC and XYZ. By changing these dollar weightings, we can construct a portfolio that is neutral with respect to parallel shifts in the spread curve. With a little bit of algebra, it's straightforward to show that the portfolio weightings are a function of the bonds' durations.[7] Specifically, the trade is designed to be duration-neutral across each issuer's spread curve.

Exhibit 10 illustrates the spread-neutral box trade for our example of ABC and XYZ. In this trade, the portfolio-weighted duration of the ABC bonds that the investor buys is equal to the portfolio-weighted duration of the ABC bonds that the investor sells. The investor sells $6.9 million of the ABC 7-year bond (bond market value × duration/portfolio market value = 6.9 × 4.23/10 = 2.93) and buys $3.4 million of the ABC 20-year bond (3.4 × 8.71/10 = 2.93). Likewise, the XYZ bonds also have the same portfolio-weighted duration at the investment horizon. The investor sells $3.1 million of the XYZ 20-year bond and swaps into $6.6 million of the XYZ 7-year bond.

In short, the investor swaps Portfolio 3 (ABC 7-year and XYZ 20-year) for Portfolio 4 (ABC 20-year and XYZ 7-year). Because both the ABC/ABC and XYZ/XYZ bond swaps have the same portfolio-weighted duration, Portfolio 3 and Portfolio 4 have the same horizon duration, 5.7. Exhibit 11 shows that the trade has a return pickup of about 2 bps under the base case that spreads and Treasury rates are unchanged over the 1-year horizon.[8]

To see that the trade is spread neutral, consider the example in Exhibit 12, in which ABC spreads widen in parallel by 25 basis points, but XYZ spreads are unchanged. Under that scenario, the return pickup of Portfolio 4 over Portfolio 3 is about 3 basis points, almost the same as the 2 bps pickup in Exhibit 11. The total returns are not exactly the same because, although Portfolios 3 and 4 are spread neutral and duration neutral, they are not neutral with respect to convexity.

Exhibit 10: A Spread-Neutral, Duration-Neutral Box Trade

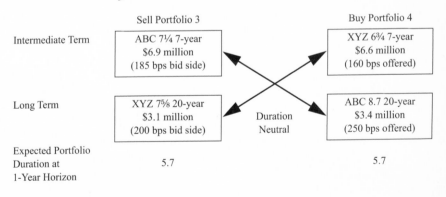

	Sell Portfolio 3		Buy Portfolio 4
Intermediate Term	ABC 7¼ 7-year $6.9 million (185 bps bid side)		XYZ 6¾ 7-year $6.6 million (160 bps offered)
Long Term	XYZ 7⅝ 20-year $3.1 million (200 bps bid side)	Duration Neutral	ABC 8.7 20-year $3.4 million (250 bps offered)
Expected Portfolio Duration at 1-Year Horizon	5.7		5.7

---

[7] Some people may find it interesting that the weightings do not depend on the spreads, except for the relatively minor effect of spreads on duration. See the Appendix for the algebraic derivation of the portfolio weights in the spread-neutral box trade.

[8] It is only by coincidence that the spread-neutral trade about breaks even under the base case that yields are unchanged. The coincidence arises from our particular example of ABC and XYZ. Other spread-neutral box trades can result in return pickups or return give-ups in the base case.

Exhibit 11: Return on Spread-Neutral Box Trade in Base Case: Yields and Spreads Unchanged Over 1-Year Horizon

Issuer	Coupon (%)	Maturity in Years	Duration at 1-Year Horizon*	Market Value ($ millions)	Spread (bps)	Yield Change over Horizon (bps)	Total Return (%)
Buy Portfolio 4							
ABC	8.700	20	8.71	3.4	250	0	9.13
XYZ	6.750	7	4.20	6.6	160	0	7.76
Buy Portfolio			5.72	10.0			8.22
Sell Portfolio 3							
XYZ	7.625	20	9.08	3.1	200	0	8.65
ABC	7.250	7	4.23	6.9	185	0	8.00
Sell Portfolio			5.72	10.0			8.20
						Return Pickup (bps)	2.10

* Horizon durations for base case that yields and spreads are unchanged.

Exhibit 12: Return on Spread-Neutral Box Trade When ABC Spreads Widen 25 Basis Points in Parallel

Issuer	Coupon (%)	Maturity in Years	Duration at 1-Year Horizon*	Market Value ($ millions)	Spread (bps)	Yield Change over Horizon (bps)	Total Return (%)
Buy Portfolio 4							
ABC	8.700	20	8.71	3.4	250	25	7.03
XYZ	6.750	7	4.20	6.6	160	0	7.76
Buy Portfolio			5.72	10.0			7.52
Sell Portfolio 3							
XYZ	7.625	20	9.08	3.1	200	0	8.65
ABC	7.250	7	4.23	6.9	185	25	6.97
Sell Portfolio			5.72	10.0			7.48
						Return Pickup (bps)	3.10

* Horizon durations for base case that yields and spreads are unchanged.

Spread-neutral box trades are structured to position a portfolio for a convergence of spread curves. In our example, Portfolio 4 will outperform Portfolio 3 if either the ABC spread curve flattens or the XYZ spread curve steepens. Exhibit 13 shows that the return on Portfolio 4 exceeds that of Portfolio 3 by 33 bps in a scenario where the ABC curve flattens by 10 bps. As derived as follows, the return on this spread-neutral box trade will increase about 3 bps for every 1 bp of flattening in the ABC spread curve, and by a similar amount for every 1 bp steepening in the XYZ spread curve.

THE OPTIMAL BOX TRADE

By definition, duration-neutral box trades do not alter the interest rate risk of a corporate portfolio; rather, they merely alter the sensitivity of a portfolio to changes in corporate bond spreads and spread curves. The duration of a box trade is not unique. It can vary over a wide range, but the duration range is bounded. Indeed, in our ABC/XYZ example, there is a continuum of duration-neutral box trades that involve swaps from intermediate and long-term bonds of ABC and XYZ.

In general, the duration of a box trade is bounded at one extreme by the duration of the bond with the second shortest duration and, at the other extreme, by the bond with the second longest duration. In our example, the XYZ 7⅝% 20-year bond has the longest duration at the 1-year horizon, 9.08 (Exhibit 14). Due to that long duration, it is impossible to buy a portfolio of the XYZ 6¾% 7-year and the ABC 8.7% 20-year that has the same duration as the XYZ 7⅝% 20-year bond. At the other extreme, the XYZ 6¾% 7-year bond has the shortest duration, 4.2. However, no portfolio of the ABC 7¼% 7-year and the XYZ 7⅝% 20-year can be structured with a duration below 4.23.

The bond with the second longest horizon duration is the ABC 8.7% 20-year bond, 8.71 duration. With some arithmetic, it is easy to show that a portfolio of the ABC 7¼% 7-year and the XYZ 7⅝% 20-year can be designed to have a 8.71 horizon duration. In terms of market values, that portfolio will include $92 of the XYZ 7⅝% 20-year bonds for every $8 of the ABC 7¼% 7-year bonds. This trade could be described as a "triangle-trade" rather than a box trade, because the trade has a zero weighting on the XYZ 6¾% 7-year. The strategy behind this trade is straightforward: the investor believes that the ABC spread curve will flatten *and* that ABC spreads will tighten relative to XYZ spreads. Given those expectations, the investor wants to buy long-term ABC and sell long-term XYZ, with the constraint that the trade must remain duration neutral. As a result of this constraint, the investor also sells a small amount of the intermediate-term ABC.

Exhibit 13: Return on Spread-Neutral Box Trade When the ABC Spread Curve Flattens 10 Basis Points at Wider Levels

Issuer	Coupon (%)	Maturity in Years	Duration at 1-Year Horizon*	Market Value ($ millions)	Spread (bps)	Yield Change over Horizon (bps)	Total Return (%)
Buy Portfolio 4							
ABC	8.700	20	8.71	3.4	250	40	5.80
XYZ	6.750	7	4.20	6.6	160	0	7.76
Buy Portfolio			5.72	10.0			7.10
Sell Portfolio 3							
XYZ	7.625	20	9.08	3.1	200	0	8.65
ABC	7.250	7	4.23	6.9	185	50	5.94
Sell Portfolio			5.72	10.0			6.77
						Return Pickup (bps)	32.6

* Horizon durations for base case that yields and spreads are unchanged.

Exhibit 14: Duration Continuum of Box Trades

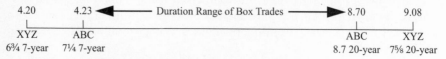

	Sell Portfolio		Buy Portfolio		
	ABC 7.25 7-year	XYZ 7.625 20-year	ABC 8.7 20-year	XYZ 6.75 7-year	
Expected Duration at Horizon	4.23	9.08	8.70	4.20	
Portfolio Duration	Portfolio Weighting (%)				Strategy
8.70	8	92	100	0	ABC curve will flatten relative to XYZ curve. ABC spreads will tighten relative to XYZ spreads.
5.72	31	69	34	66	ABC curve will flatten relative to XYZ curve.
4.23	100	0	1	99	ABC curve will flatten relative to XYZ curve. ABC spreads will widen relative to XYZ spreads.

At the other extreme, the bond with the second shortest horizon duration is the ABC 7¼% 7-year bond, 4.23 duration. A portfolio that has the same horizon duration as that bond would include $99 of the XYZ 6¾% 7-year for every $1 of the ABC 8.7% 20-year. In this triangle trade, the XYZ 7⅝% 20-year has a zero weighting. In this trading strategy, the investor believes that the ABC spread curve will flatten, *but* that ABC spreads will widen relative to XYZ spreads. Under that scenario, the investor reduces his exposure to ABC risk by effectively replacing ABC 7-year bonds with XYZ 7-year bonds. The small exposure to the ABC 8.7% 20-year bond is necessary to make the trade duration neutral. If a portfolio manager believes strongly that ABC spreads will widen, he or she could also make the trade duration neutral by buying other long corporates or long Treasuries, rather than ABC.

In between these two extremes lies the spread-neutral box trade, with a duration of 5.7. The spread-neutral box trade is a unique duration-neutral swap that is also neutral with respect to parallel shifts in the spread curves. The implicit expectation in the spread-neutral box trade is that the ABC and XYZ curves will converge, but the investor has no opinion on whether the convergence will take place at wider or tighter levels. As a result, the spread-neutral box trade may not be the optimal trade because, in many cases, an investor may have an opinion about both the relative slope of an issuer's spread curves and about the direction of spreads.

Exhibit 15: A Box Trade for a Corporate/Treasury Portfolio

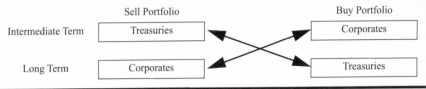

In summary, a variety of box trades can be constructed by varying the relative amounts of intermediate and long-term bonds that are swapped. While all of these box trades are duration neutral, only one is neutral with respect to the direction spreads. The optimal box trade will reflect an investor's view about spread curves and spread direction. As a practical matter, we recognize that it can be difficult for investors to buy and sell odd lots. Nevertheless, in our example, an investor could come close to approximating a spread-neutral box trade by swapping roughly $3 million and $7 million of intermediate and long-term bonds of XYZ and ABC. The key feature of a spread-neutral trade is that the amount of bonds swapped will usually differ from a dollar-for-dollar box trade, and as a result of that difference, the trades will have different exposures to the slope and direction of spread curves.

CONCLUSION

We have presented several strategies that allow investors to take a view on the slope of corporate spread curves. The bond swap, the most basic strategy, is simple to implement, but it is not a pure play on the spread curve. Some bond swaps may be unprofitable because they change the duration of a portfolio, and all bond swaps are sensitive to the direction of spreads. The box trade, by contrast, can be used to tailor a portfolio to match an investor's opinion about both the slope of the spread curve and the direction of spreads.

Although we have concentrated on a specific example of two corporate spread curves that have different slopes, spread curve strategies can also be applied more generally on a portfolio basis. For example, consider an investor who manages a portfolio of corporates and Treasuries. The portfolio manager may believe that corporate spread curves are poised to steepen, which would argue for an underweighting of long-term corporates. However, the investor may want to keep some of the portfolio invested in the corporate market to pick up incremental return, and the investor also may want to maintain the portfolio's duration. Given these parameters, the investor should consider a corporate/Treasury box trade (see Exhibit 15). In that portfolio trade, the investor would swap long corporates for short corporates, and swap short Treasuries for long Treasuries. That portfolio box trade would leave the portfolio's duration unchanged, maintain an exposure to spread product, but reduce the exposure to a steepening of the spread curve.

APPENDIX

The Algebra of a Spread-Neutral, Duration-Neutral Box Trade

In this box trade, the investor notices that Issuer A has a steeper spread curve than Issuer B. The investor believes that the curves will converge over time: the spread curve of Issuer A will flatten or the spread curve of Issuer B will steepen. The investor buys Portfolio 1 and sells Portfolio 2 in a spread-neutral box trade. The trade involves four securities, indexed by the subscripts 1 through 4 in the following table:

Buy: Portfolio 1

Issuer	Issue	Market Value	Spread	Horizon Duration
A	1	V_1	S_1	D_1
B	2	V_2	S_2	D_2
		V		

Sell: Portfolio 2

Issuer	Issue	Market Value	Spread	Horizon Duration
B	3	V_3	S_3	D_3
A	4	V_4	S_4	D_4
		V		

Because Issuer A's spread curve is expected to flatten relative to that of Issuer B, the investor swaps from a short-duration bond into a long-duration bond of Issuer A, and makes the opposite swap with the bonds of Issuer B: $D_1 > D_4$ and $D_3 > D_2$.

Relationships:

Proceeds Neutral

Dollar amount bought = Dollar amount sold

$$V_1 + V_2 = V_3 + V_4 = V$$

Spread Neutral

$$V_1 \times D_1 \times \Delta S_A = V_4 \times D_4 \times \Delta S_A$$
$$V_2 \times D_2 \times \Delta S_B = V_3 \times D_3 \times \Delta S_B$$

Duration Neutral (implied by above)

$$V_1 \times D_1 / V + V_2 \times D_2 / V = V_3 \times D_3 / V + V_4 \times D_4 / V = \text{Portfolio duration}$$

Solution:

$$V_1 = V \times D_4 \times (D_2 - D_3)/(D_2 \times D_4 - D_1 \times D_3)$$
$$V_2 = V - V_1$$
$$V_3 = V_2 \times D_2 / D_3$$
$$V_4 = V - V_3$$

Notice that the solution depends only on the bonds' durations. It is independent of the spreads, except for the relatively minor effect that spreads have on duration.

If spreads are unchanged, the return pickup over a 1-year horizon is approximately:

Return pickup = Weighted spread of portfolio bought
          − Weighted spread of portfolio sold
$$\approx (V_1 S_1 + V_2 S_2)/V - (V_3 S_3 + V_4 S_4)/V$$

For every 1 bp of flattening in the spread curve for Issuer A, the incremental return pickup over a 1-year horizon is:

$$\text{Pickup for 1 bp flattening of Issuer A's spread curve} \approx (V_1 D_1 + V_4 D_4)/(2V)$$

Likewise, for every 1 bp of steepening in the spread curve for Issuer B, the incremental return pickup over a 1-year horizon is:

$$\text{Pickup for 1 bp steepening of Issuer B's spread curve} \approx (V_2 D_2 + V_3 D_3)/(2V)$$

Chapter 10

Business Cycles, Profit Cycles, and Corporate Bond Strategies

I n the previous two chapters, we showed that portfolio managers can improve performance by anticipating changes in yield spreads and spread curves. Clearly, understanding the fundamental factors that drive corporate spreads is the first step in the process of anticipating spread movements. Fundamentals can be categorized as either macro or micro. In this chapter, we focus on the macro fundamentals, specifically on the patterns of spreads and industry profits over the business cycle. In Chapters 11 and 12, we explore the micro fundamentals of credit risk and credit analysis.

CORPORATE BOND SPREADS OVER THE BUSINESS CYCLE

The economic business cycle has a profound and reasonably reliable effect on corporate bond spreads. Evidence that spreads move with the business cycle is shown in Exhibit 1, which depicts the spread between Baa-rated and Aaa-rated bonds over business cycles dating back to 1919. The shaded areas in the exhibit represent periods of economic recession, as defined by the National Bureau of Economic Research (NBER). In general, spreads tightened during the early stages of economic expansions, and spreads widened sharply during economic recessions. In fact, spreads typically began to widen before the official end of an economic expansion. In 1990, for example, the Baa-Aaa spread began the year at 85 basis points, but it widened to 96 basis points when the expansion ended in July, and subsequently widened to 140 basis points in January 1991.

Exhibit 2 gives further evidence that spreads respond to the business cycle. The vertical line indicates the month of the business cycle peak. The exhibit shows the change in the Baa-Aaa spread in the months surrounding the cycle peak, based on the average of the 10 cycles since World War II. In the months leading up to a recession, the Baa-Aaa spread typically widened by 5 to 10 basis points. Spreads usually continued to widen after a recession began, with the widening peaking roughly 10 to 14 months into the cycle.

While recessions almost always cause spreads to widen, the timing and magnitude of the spread peak varies from cycle to cycle. In the 1990–1991 recession, for example, spreads peaked just 7 months after the recession started, as investors began to anticipate that that recession would be relatively short-lived. By contrast, in other recessions that had longer durations, the peak in spreads occurred much later, and the magnitude of spread widening was also greater.

Exhibit 1: Yield Spread Between Baa and Aaa Bonds

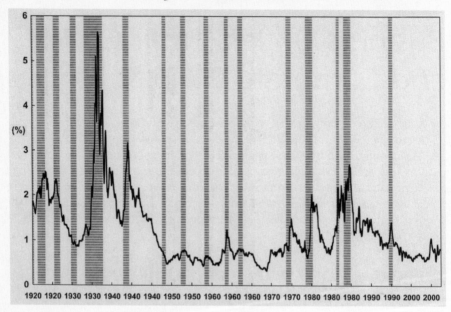

Exhibit 2: Average Change in Baa-Aaa Spread Around Business Cycle Peak

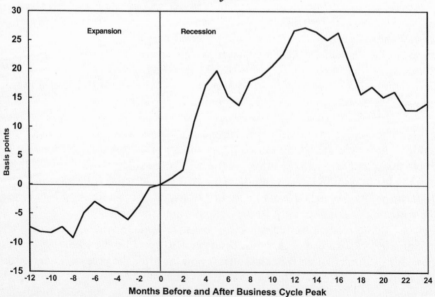

The cyclical behavior of yield spreads demonstrates that the corporate bond market anticipates future economic events. Investors don't wait for the NBER to declare that a recession has begun. When evidence begins to gather that the economy is weakening, that corporate profits are slowing, that rating downgrades are more probable, and that lending standards are tightening, then investors rationally become more risk averse and, consequently, spreads widen.

The corporate bond market is forward looking. Its forecasting power is not perfect, of course, because spreads sometimes give false signals of recessions that never materialize. For example, spreads widened after the 1987 stock market crash and after the 1998 hedge fund crisis, but in both episodes spreads quickly retraced the widening when it became clear that those crises would not precipitate a recession. Nevertheless, the ability of spreads to anticipate economic cycles is more reliable than most cyclical indicators. Indeed, in October 1990, three months after that recession began, many prominent economists were still debating whether the economy might be vulnerable to a recession. In the corporate bond market, there was no debate.

Implications for Corporate Bond Portfolio Managers

The cyclical behavior of spreads has clear implications for corporate bond portfolio managers. Specifically, portfolio managers should reduce exposures to lower-rated companies as expansions age, and increase exposures when they anticipate the beginning of a new expansion. In practice, it is difficult for portfolio managers to implement that contrarian strategy because it requires a discipline of reducing risk during times of euphoria and increasing risk in times of panic.

Economic Indicators

For several decades, economists have researched the causes of business cycles and identified economic indicators that often lead the cycle. That research, while not always conclusive, can be used by portfolio managers as a guide to anticipate the next phase of the cycle and to position their portfolios accordingly. More importantly, the economic research has highlighted a number of key patterns in economic and financial data that repeat over cycles. Some of the more reliable leading indicators are:

Rising short-term interest rates
Flattening (or inversion) of the U.S. Treasury yield curve
Rising bond defaults, loan delinquencies, bankruptcies, and credit rating
    downgrades
Weak readings for the purchasing managers index
Low savings rates
Deteriorating quantity and quality of corporate earnings
Rising inventories
Slower growth of monetary and credit aggregates
Deteriorating consumer and business confidence
Rising claims for unemployment insurance

Exhibit 3: Corporate Profits as a Share of GDP
Averaged and Normalized over 10 Business Cycles between WWII and 2000

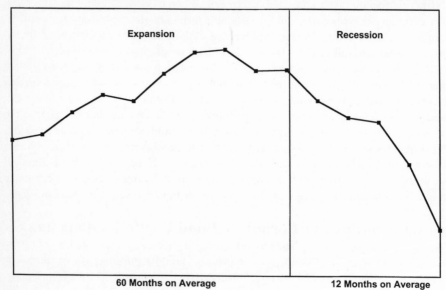

Source: National Income and Product Accounts

Economists do not always agree about the theoretical causes of cycles, but as a practical matter, when a cycle dies, two suspicious characters are often spotted near the seen of the crime: the Fed and energy prices.

CORPORATE PROFITS OVER THE BUSINESS CYCLE

Spreads are cyclical because profits are cyclical. Exhibit 3 displays corporate profits as a share of GDP. By taking the average of that profit share over post-World War II business cycles, and then normalizing for the length of the cycle, the exhibit reveals that profits are pro-cyclical. That is, profits not only move in tandem with the strength of the economy, but they also move with greater amplitude.

When the economy is growing, each sector of the economy benefits from that growth. The labor sector, of course, benefits from a growing economy, as jobs become more plentiful and wages rise. Nevertheless, the gains to the labor sector are more than matched by the gains to the corporate sector. During economic expansions, an increasing share of national income goes to the bottom line in the corporate sector. In recessions, conversely, all sectors of the economy usually suffer, as unemployment rises and profits fall. While recessions undoubtedly hurt the labor sector, a decline in economic activity has a more dramatic impact on the corporate sector, as is evident by the decline in the share of profits relative to GDP.

The U.S. economy experienced 10 business cycles between World War II and the end of the century, with the expansion phase lasting an average of 60 months. Expansions have displayed considerable variation around that average, however, as expansions in the 1960s, 1980s, and 1990s lasted more than 90 months, while expansions in the 1950s and 1970s had much shorter lives. Recessions had an average length of 12 months, with some lasting only 7 months while a couple of recessions stretched out for 17 months. Notwithstanding the fact that cycles vary in length, corporate spreads and profits have displayed a reasonably consistent correlation during past cycles.

INDUSTRY SECTOR STRATEGIES OVER THE BUSINESS CYCLE

A key element of corporate bond strategy is the decision about which industry sectors to emphasize in a portfolio and which industries to avoid.[1] Clearly, decisions about industry overweights and underweights must be driven by fundamental credit research.[2] In addition, industry decisions should be shaped by business cycle analysis. Because some sectors of the economy display strong cyclical patterns, portfolio managers can usually improve performance by actively rotating their industry weightings as the business cycle evolves.

To illustrate the industry decision, consider the automobile sector. Autos are a durable good, which typically require sizable downpayments and a significant commitment to monthly financing. A consumer's decision to purchase a new vehicle is discretionary. Consequently, during periods of economic expansion, auto companies usually record strong sales and profits, as rising wages and high levels of employment give consumers the financial resources and confidence to purchase a new car. In a recession, conversely, consumers naturally become less confident and more risk averse. In recessions, savings rates rise, as consumers decide to delay or forego purchases of durable goods, such as autos. When the economy emerges from a recession, the pent-up demand for autos leads to a rebound in consumer spending and a surge in auto company profits. Therefore auto company profits generally exhibit greater amplitude than profits in other corporate sectors.

The cycle in auto company profits is shown in Exhibit 4. Specifically, this exhibit measures auto company profits as a share of total corporate profits over the cycles since World War II. Auto profits exhibit relative strength early in the expansion phase, when an economic rebound gives consumers confidence to satisfy their pent-up demand for cars. As an economic expansion ages, auto profits usually remain strong, but the share of auto profits to total corporate profits declines, as other industries benefit increasingly from the rebound. In a recession, auto profits decline precipitously, both as a share of total corporate profits and absolutely.

---

[1] A framework for allocating to sectors is explained in Chapter 13.
[2] Credit analysis is the subject of Chapter 12.

Exhibit 4: Auto Sector Profits as a Percentage of Total Corporate Profits

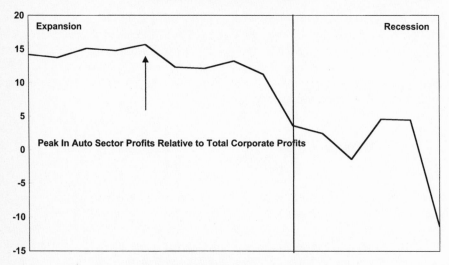

Source: National Income and Product Accounts

Exhibit 5 displays peak profits for the major sectors of the corporate bond market. The exhibit identifies the phase in the cycle when the profits for a particular industry are highest relative to total corporate profits. Like auto companies, banking companies usually enjoy a profit rebound in the early phase of the recovery. That rebound in bank profitability is a direct consequence of counter-cyclical Federal Reserve policy, which results in low interest rates, a steep yield curve, regulatory forbearance, and a purging of bad loans. Later, as the cycle ages, the bank profit share slips, as interest rates rise, the yield curve normalizes, and bank loan officers become more lax.

Consumer staple companies register a peak in relative profits during economic recessions. The demand for consumer staples, such as food and beverages, is not highly sensitive to the strength of the economy. During recessions, consumers cut back on large discretionary purchases, such as new cars and vacations, but expenditures on staple goods do not decline markedly. Consequently, although profits for consumer staple companies are not robust in recessions, profits for other sectors fall more sharply, resulting in an increase in consumer staples' profit share during recessions. Similarly, utility company profits typically peak in relative terms during recessions. That relative stability of utility company profits reflects regulated pricing and moderate sensitivity of their sales to economic growth.

Oil company profits also peak in recessions. In the business cycles since the 1970s, high oil prices played a role in killing economic expansions. Essentially, the strength in oil company profits during recessions has represented a transfer of wealth and income from other sectors of the economy to the oil sector.

Exhibit 5: Peaks in Sector Profits Over the Business Cycle

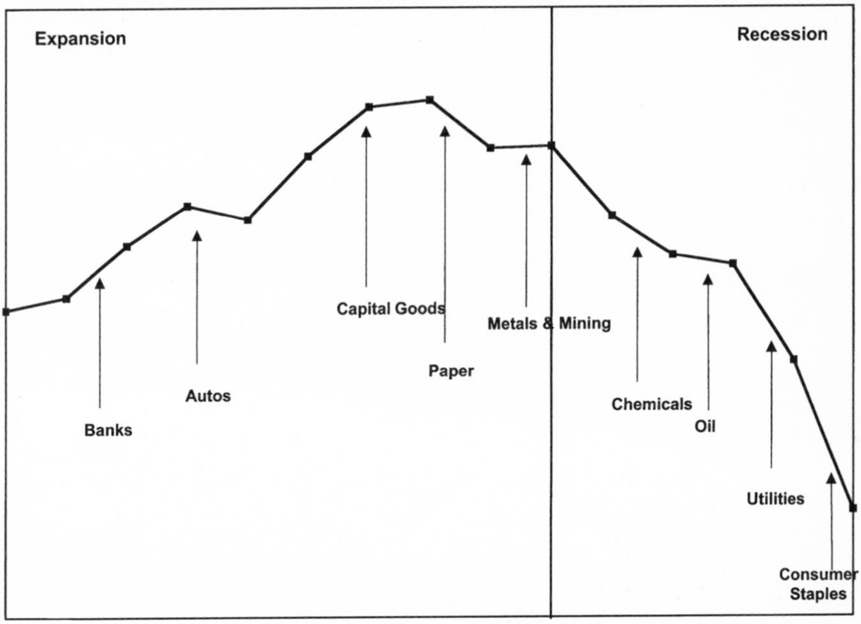

Source: National Income and Product Accounts

Capital goods companies, paper companies, and metals and mining companies each produce goods that are closely geared to the level of economic activity. For example, the demand for paper products is highest when the economy is operating near full capacity, with high volumes of shipping and packaging. For these industries, the peak in relative profits usually occurs in the late stage of an economic expansion.

These patterns in industry profits suggest some obvious strategies for corporate bond portfolio managers. Strategic investors should actively adjust industry exposures in advance of the profit cycle. Industry spreads should reflect identifiable risks, such as recession risk and profit cycle risk. When economic indicators warn of recession risk, investors should either underweight cyclical industries or demand very high-yield spreads on cyclical bonds. Likewise, investors should increase exposures to defensive sectors, such as utilities and consumer staples, when recession risk is high, and rotate away from defensive sectors when economic conditions are poised to improve.

While portfolio managers can improve performance by anticipating industry profit cycles, a word of warning is in order. A formulaic implementation of portfolio strategies will not guarantee success. Every business cycle has unique features that may run counter to historical patterns. Oil prices have played a role in ending many business cycles, but that role could be reversed in the next cycle. Utility profits have been relatively stable over most business cycles, but that pattern could change with deregulation and re-regulation. Likewise, sector profits might exhibit greater amplitude and longer duration in future cycles due to globalization of industries, such as finance, autos, and telecom. Moreover, while spreads are undoubtedly influenced by the outlook for corporate profits, spreads are also impacted by many other market forces, such as new issue supply and monetary policy. Still, despite the standard warning that "past performance is no guarantee of future results," the past has served well as the first and best guide to the future.

Section III

Corporate Credit Risk

Chapter 11

Credit Risk

An investor who lends funds by purchasing a corporate bond issue is exposed to three types of credit risk: (1) default risk, (2) credit spread risk, and (3) downgrade risk. In this chapter we discuss these risks. At the end of the chapter we introduce instruments to protect against credit risk.

DEFAULT RISK

Traditionally, credit risk is defined as the risk that the issuer will fail to satisfy the terms of the obligation with respect to the timely payment of interest and repayment of the amount borrowed. This form of credit risk is called *default risk*. If a default does occur, this does not mean the investor loses the entire amount invested. There is a certain percentage of the investment that can be expected to be recovered. This is called the *recovery rate*.

Credit Ratings

Professional money managers use various techniques to analyze information on companies and bond issues in order to estimate the probability that the issuer will live up to its future contractual obligations (i.e., to assess their risk of default) and the severity of a loss if one occurs. (This activity is known as *credit analysis* and we'll cover this topic in Chapter 12.)

Some institutional investors and most investment banking firms have their own credit analysis departments to assess default risk. Institutional investors also rely on nationally recognized statistical rating organizations that perform credit analysis and issue their conclusions in the form of ratings. These organizations, commonly referred to as "rating agencies," are (1) Moody's Investors Service, (2) Standard & Poor's Corporation, and (3) Fitch. The rating systems use similar symbols, as shown in Exhibit 1.

In all rating systems the term "high grade" means low credit risk, or conversely, high probability of future payments. The highest-grade bonds are designated by Moody's by the letters Aaa, and by the others as AAA. The next highest grade is Aa (Moody's) or AA; for the third grade all rating agencies use A. The next three grades are Baa (Moody's) or BBB, Ba (Moody's) or BB, and B, respectively. There are also C grades. Bonds rated triple A (AAA or Aaa) are said to be "prime"; double A (AA or Aa) are of "high quality"; single A issues are called "upper medium grade"; and triple B are "medium grade." Lower-rated bonds are said to have "speculative elements" or be "distinctly speculative."

Exhibit 1: Summary of Corporate Bond Rating Systems and Symbols

Moody's	S&P	Fitch	Summary Description
Investment Grade — High Creditworthiness			
Aaa	AAA	AAA	Gilt edge, prime, maximum safety
Aa1	AA+	AA+	
Aa2	AA	AA	High-grade, high-credit quality
Aa3	AA–	AA–	
A1	A+	A+	
A2	A	A	Upper-medium grade
A3	A–	A–	
Baa1	BBB+	BBB+	
Baa2	BBB	BBB	Lower-medium grade
Baa3	BBB–	BBB–	
Speculative — Lower Creditworthiness			
Ba1	BB+	BB+	
Ba2	BB	BB	Low-grade, speculative
Ba3	BB–	BB–	
B1		B+	
B2	B	B	Highly speculative
B3		B–	
Predominantly Speculative, Substantial Risk or in Default			
	CCC+	CCC+	
Caa	CCC	CCC	Substantial risk, in poor standing
Ca	CC	CC	May be in default, very speculative
C	C	C	Extremely speculative
	CI		Income bonds — no interest being paid
		DDD	
		DD	Default
	D	D	

Bond issues that are assigned a rating in the top four categories are referred to as *investment-grade bonds*. Issues that carry a rating below the top four categories are referred to as *noninvestment-grade bonds* or more popularly as *high-yield bonds* or *junk bonds*. Thus, the corporate bond market can be divided into two sectors: the investment grade and noninvestment-grade markets.

All rating agencies use rating modifiers to provide a narrower credit quality breakdown within each rating category. S&P and Fitch use a rating modifier of plus and minus. Moody's uses 1, 2, and 3 as its rating modifiers.

Bankruptcy and Creditor Rights

The holder of a corporate debt instrument has priority over the equity owners in the case of bankruptcy of a corporation. There are creditors who have priority over other creditors. Here we provide an overview of the bankruptcy process and then look at what actually happens to creditors in bankruptcies.

The Bankruptcy Process

The law governing bankruptcy in the United States is the Bankruptcy Reform Act of 1978 as amended.[1] One purpose of the act is to set forth the rules for a corporation to be either liquidated or reorganized. The *liquidation* of a corporation means that all the assets will be distributed to the holders of claims of the corporation and no corporate entity will survive. In a *reorganization*, a new corporate entity will result. Some holders of the claim of the bankrupt corporation will receive cash in exchange for their claims, others may receive new securities in the corporation that results from the reorganization, and others may receive a combination of both cash and new securities in the resulting corporation.

Another purpose of the bankruptcy act is to give a corporation time to decide whether to reorganize or liquidate and then the necessary time to formulate a plan to accomplish either a reorganization or liquidation. This is achieved because when a corporation files for bankruptcy, the act grants the corporation protection from creditors who seek to collect their claims. The petition for bankruptcy can be filed either by the company itself, in which case it is called a *voluntary bankruptcy*, or be filed by its creditors, in which case it is called an *involuntary bankruptcy*. A company that files for protection under the bankruptcy act generally becomes a "debtor-in-possession" (DIP), and continues to operate its business under the supervision of the court.

The bankruptcy act consists of 15 chapters, each chapter covering a particular type of bankruptcy. Of particular interest to us are two of the chapters, Chapter 7 and Chapter 11. Chapter 7 deals with the liquidation of a company; Chapter 11 deals with the reorganization of a company.

Absolute Priority: Theory and Practice

When a company is liquidated, creditors receive distributions based on the "absolute priority rule" to the extent assets are available. The absolute priority rule is the principle that senior creditors are paid in full before junior creditors are paid anything. For secured creditors and unsecured creditors, the absolute priority rule guarantees their seniority to equity holders.

In liquidations, the absolute priority rule generally holds. In contrast, a good body of literature argues that strict absolute priority has not been upheld by the courts or the SEC.[2] Studies of actual reorganizations under Chapter 11

---

[1] For a discussion of the Bankruptcy Reform Act of 1978 and a nontechnical description of its principal features, see Jane Tripp Howe, "Investing in Chapter 11 and Other Distressed Companies," Chapter 18 in Frank J. Fabozzi (ed.), *The Handbook of Corporate Debt Instruments* (New Hope, PA: Frank J. Fabozzi Associates, 1998).

[2] See, for example, William H. Meckling, "Financial Markets, Default, and Bankruptcy," *Law and Contemporary Problems*, 41, 1977, pp. 124–177; Merton H. Miller, "The Wealth Transfers of Bankruptcy: Some Illustrative Examples," *Law and Contemporary Problems*, 41, 1977, pp. 39–46; Jerold B. Warner, "Bankruptcy, Absolute Priority, and the Pricing of Risky Debt Claims," *Journal of Financial Economics*, 4, 1977, pp. 239–276; and, Thomas H. Jackson, "Of Liquidation, Continuation, and Delay: An Analysis of Bankruptcy Policy and Nonbankruptcy Rules," *American Bankruptcy Law Journal*, 60, 1986, pp. 399–428.

have found that the violation of absolute priority is the rule rather than the exception.[3]

Several hypotheses have been suggested as to why in a reorganization the distribution made to claimholders will diverge from that required by the absolute priority principle.

The *incentive hypothesis* argues that the longer the negotiation process among the parties, the greater the bankruptcy costs and the smaller the amount to be distributed to all parties. This is because in a reorganization, a committee representing the various claimholders is appointed with the purpose of formulating a plan of reorganization. To be accepted, a plan of reorganization must be approved by at least two-thirds of the amount and a majority of the number of claims voting and at least two-thirds of the outstanding shares of each class of interests. Consequently, a long-lasting bargaining process is expected. The longer the negotiation process among the parties, the more likely that the company will be operated in a manner that is not in the best interest of the creditors and, as a result, the smaller the amount to be distributed to all parties. Since all impaired classes including equityholders generally must approve the plan of reorganization, creditors often convince equityholders to accept the plan by offering to distribute some value to them.

The *recontracting process hypothesis* argues that the violation of absolute priority reflects a recontracting process between stockholders and senior creditors that gives recognition to the ability of management to preserve value on behalf of stockholders.[4] According to the *stockholders' influence on reorganization plan hypothesis* creditors are less informed about the true economic operating conditions of the firm than management. Because the distribution to creditors in the plan of reorganization is based on the valuation by the firm, creditors without perfect information easily suffer the loss.[5] According to Wruck, managers generally have a better understanding than creditors or stockholders about a firm's internal operations, while creditors and stockholders can have better information about industry trends. Management may therefore use its superior knowledge to present the data in a manner that reinforces its position.[6]

The essence of the *strategic bargaining process hypothesis* is that the increasing complexity of firms that declare bankruptcy will accentuate the negoti-

---

[3] See Julian R. Franks and Walter N. Torous, "An Empirical Investigation of U.S. Firms in Reorganization," *Journal of Finance* (July 1989), pp. 747–769; Lawrence A. Weiss, "Bankruptcy Resolution: Direct Costs and Violation of Priority of Claims," *Journal of Financial Economics* (1990), pp. 285–314; and Frank J. Fabozzi, Jane Tripp Howe, Takashi Makabe, and Toshihide Sudo, "Recent Evidence on the Distribution Patterns in Chapter 11 Reorganizations," *Journal of Fixed Income* (Spring 1993), pp. 6–23.

[4] Douglas G. Baird and Thomas H. Jackson, "Bargaining After the Fall and the Contours of the Absolute Priority Rule," *University of Chicago Law Review*, 55, 1988, pp. 738–789.

[5] L.A. Bebchuk, "A New Approach to Corporate Reorganizations," *Harvard Law Review*, 101, 1988, pp. 775–804.

[6] Karen Hooper Wruck, "Financial Distress, Reorganization, and Organizational Efficiency," *Journal of Financial Economics*, 27, 1990, pp. 419–444.

ating process and result in an even higher incidence of violation of the absolute priority rule. The likely outcome is further supported by the increased number of official committees in the reorganization process as well as the increased number of financial and legal advisors.

There are some who argue that creditors will receive a higher value in reorganization than they would in liquidation in part because of the costs associated with liquidation.[7] Finally, the lack of symmetry in the tax system (negative taxes are not permitted, although loss deductions may be carried forward) results in situations in which the only way to use all current loss deductions is to merge.[8] The tax system may encourage continuance or merger and discourage bankruptcy.

Consequently, while investors in the debt of a corporation may feel that they have priority over the equity owners and priority over other classes of debtors, the actual outcome of a bankruptcy may be far different from what the terms of the debt agreement state.

One study examined the extent of violation of the absolute priority rule among three broad groups: secured creditors, unsecured creditors, and equityholders, and also among various types of debt and equity securities.[9] The study also provided evidence on which asset class bears the cost of violations of absolute priority and an initial estimate of total distributed value relative to liquidation value. The findings of this study suggest that unsecured creditors bear a disproportionate cost of reorganization, and that more senior unsecured creditors may bear a disproportionate cost relative to the junior unsecured creditors while equityholders often benefit from violations of absolute priority.

Default and Recovery Statistics

There is a good deal of research published on default rates by the rating agencies and academicians.[10] From an investment perspective, default rates by themselves are not of paramount significance: it is perfectly possible for a portfolio of corporate bonds to suffer defaults and to outperform Treasuries at the same time, provided the yield spread of the portfolio is sufficiently high to offset the losses from default. Furthermore, because holders of defaulted bonds typically recover a percentage of the face amount of their investment, the *default loss rate* can be substantially lower than the default rate.

The default loss rate is defined as follows:

default loss rate = default rate × (100% − recovery rate)

---

[7] Michael C. Jensen, "Eclipse of the Public Corporation," *Harvard Business Review*, 89, 1989, pp. 61–62 and Wruck, "Financial Distress, Reorganization, and Organizational Efficiency."

[8] J.I. Bulow and J.B. Shoven. "The Bankruptcy Decision," *Bell Journal of Economics*, 1978. For a further discussion of the importance of NOLs and the current tax law, see Fabozzi et al., "Recent Evidence on the Distribution Patterns in Chapter 11 Reorganizations."

[9] Fabozzi, Howe, Makabe, and Sudo, "Recent Evidence on the Distribution Patterns in Chapter 11 Reorganizations."

For instance, a default rate of 5% and a recovery rate of 30% means a default loss rate of only 3.5% (5% of 70%).

Therefore, focusing exclusively on default rates merely highlights the worst possible outcome that a diversified portfolio of corporate bonds would suffer, assuming all defaulted bonds would be totally worthless.

Default Rates

First, let's look at what research has found for the default rate experience of corporate bonds. We begin with a discussion of the experience for high-yield corporate bonds. We do this because what will be apparent is that there are various ways to define default rates that are clearly illustrated by these studies of high-yield corporate bonds.

In their 1987 study, Altman and Nammacher found that the annual default rate for low-rated corporate debt was 2.15%, a figure that Altman has updated since to 2.40%. Drexel Burnham Lambert's (DBL) estimates have also shown default rates of about 2.40% per year. Asquith, Mullins, and Wolff, however, found that nearly one out of every three high-yield corporate bonds defaults. The large discrepancy arises because the researchers use three different definitions of "default rate"; even if applied to the same universe of bonds (which they are not), all three results could be valid simultaneously.[11]

Altman and Nammacher define the default rate as the par value of all high-yield bonds that defaulted in a given calendar year, divided by the total par value outstanding during the year. Their estimates (2.15% and 2.40%) are simple averages of the annual default rates over a number of years. DBL took the cumu-

---

[10] See, for example, Edward I. Altman, "Measuring Corporate Bond Mortality and Performance," *Journal of Finance* (September 1989), pp. 909–922; Edward I. Altman, "Research Update: Mortality Rates and Losses, Bond Rating Drift," unpublished study prepared for a workshop sponsored by Merrill Lynch Merchant Banking Group, High Yield Sales and Trading, 1989; Edward I. Altman and Scott A. Nammacher, *Investing in Junk Bonds* (New York: John Wiley, 1987); Paul Asquith, David W. Mullins, Jr., and Eric D. Wolff, "Original Issue High Yield Bonds: Aging Analysis of Defaults, Exchanges, and Calls," *Journal of Finance* (September 1989), pp. 923–952; Marshall Blume and Donald Keim, "Risk and Return Characteristics of Lower-Grade Bonds 1977-1987," Working Paper (8-89), Rodney L. White Center for Financial Research, Wharton School, University of Pennsylvania, 1989; Marshall Blume and Donald Keim, "Realized Returns and Defaults on Lower-Grade Bonds," Rodney L. White Center for Financial Research, Wharton School, University of Pennsylvania, 1989; Bond Investors Association, "Bond Investors Association Issues Definitive Corporate Default Statistics," press release dated August 15, 1989; Gregory T. Hradsky and Robert D. Long, "High Yield Default Losses and the Return Performance of Bankrupt Debt," *Financial Analysts Journal* (July-August 1989), pp. 38–49; "Historical Default Rates of Corporate Bond Issuers 1970-1988," *Moody's Special Report*, July 1989 (New York: Moody's Investors Service); "High-Yield Bond Default Rates," Standard & Poor's *Creditweek*, August 7, 1989, pp. 21–23; David Wyss, Christopher Probyn, and Robert de Angelis, "The Impact of Recession on High-Yield Bonds," DRI-McGraw-Hill (Washington, D.C.: Alliance for Capital Access, 1989); and the 1984-1989 issues of *High Yield Market Report: Financing America's Futures* (New York and Beverly Hills: Drexel Burnham Lambert, Incorporated).

[11] As a parallel, we know that the mortality rate in the United States is currently less than 1% per year, but we also know that 100% of all humans (eventually) die.

lative dollar value of all defaulted high-yield bonds, divided by the cumulative dollar value of all high-yield issuance, and further divided by the weighted average number of years outstanding to obtain an average annual default rate. Asquith, Mullins, and Wolff use a cumulative default statistic. For all bonds issued in a given year, the default rate is the total par value of defaulted issues as of the date of their study, divided by the total par amount originally issued to obtain a cumulative default rate. Their result (that about one in three high-yield bonds default) is not normalized by the number of years outstanding.

Although all three measures are useful indicators of bond default propensity, they are not directly comparable. Even when restated on an annualized basis, they do not all measure the same quantity. The default statistics from all studies, however, are surprisingly similar once cumulative rates have been annualized. Exhibit 2 shows the default rates by year for the period 1971 to 1997 as reported in a study by Altman and Kishore.[12] The bottom of the exhibit reports that the arithmetic average default rate for the entire period was 2.6% and the weighted average default rate (i.e., weighted by the par value of the amount outstanding for each year) was 3.3%. For a more recent time period, 1985 to 1997, the arithmetic average default rate was higher, 3.7%.

Historical Recovery Rates

Next let's look at the historical loss rate realized by investors in high-yield corporate bonds. This rate, referred to earlier as the *default loss rate*, is reported in the last column of Exhibit 2. The methodology for computing the default loss rate by Altman and Kishore is as follows. First, the *default loss of principal* is computed by multiplying the default rate for the year by the average loss of principal. The average loss of principal is computed by first determining the recovery per $100 of par value. They quantify the recovery per $100 of par value using the weighted average price of all issues after default. The difference between par value of 100 and the recovery of principal is the default loss of principal.

For example, in 1997, the weighted average price after default per $100 par value was $54.2, as reported in the fifth column of Exhibit 2. The recovery of principal was therefore $54.2 and the default loss of principal for 1997 was therefore $45.8. The default loss from principal for 1997 is then the product of the default rate for 1997 of 1.25% (fourth column of Exhibit 2) and the default loss of principal of $45.8. The product is 0.573%. Next the default loss of coupon interest is computed. This is found by multiplying the default rate by the weighted average coupon rate divided by 2 (because the coupon payments are semiannual). Again, looking at 1997, the weighted average coupon is shown in the next-to-the- last column in the exhibit to be 11.87%. The default loss of coupon is then the product of the default rate of 1.25% and one-half of 11.87%, or 0.074%. The default loss rate is then the sum of the default rate and the default loss rate of principal. For 1997, it is 0.65%.

---

[12] Edward I. Altman and Vellore M. Kishore, "Defaults and Returns on High Yield Bonds," Chapter 14 in *The Handbook of Corporate Debt Instruments* (New Hope, PA: Frank J. Fabozzi Associates, 1998).

Exhibit 2: Default Rates and Default Losses for High-Yield Corporate Bonds: 1978–1997

Year	Par Value Outstanding* ($ Millions)	Par Value Defaults ($ Millions)	Default Rates (%)	Weighted Price After Default ($)	Weighted Coupon (%)	Default Loss (%)
1997	$335,400	4,200	1.25	54.2	11.87	0.65
1996	271,000	3,336	1.23	51.9	8.92	0.65
1995	240,000	4,551	1.90	40.6	11.83	1.24
1994	235,000	3,418	1.45	39.4	10.25	0.96
1993	206,907	2,287	1.11	56.6	12.98	0.56
1992	163,000	5,545	3.40	50.1	12.32	1.91
1991	183,600	18,862	10.27	36.0	11.59	7.16
1990	181,000	18,354	10.14	23.4	12.94	8.42
1989	189,258	8,110	4.29	38.3	13.40	2.93
1988	148,187	3,944	2.66	43.6	11.91	1.66
1987	129,557	7,486	5.78	75.9	12.07	1.74
1986	90,243	3,156	3.50	34.5	10.61	2.48
1985	58,088	992	1.71	45.9	13.69	1.04
1984	40,939	344	0.84	48.6	12.23	0.48
1983	27,492	301	1.09	55.7	10.11	0.54
1982	18,109	577	3.19	38.6	9.61	2.11
1981	17,115	27	0.16	12.0	15.75	0.15
1980	14,935	224	1.50	21.1	8.43	1.25
1979	10,356	20	0.19	31.0	10.63	0.14
1978	8,946	119	1.33	60.0	8.38	0.59

Default Rate Summary

		Default Rates (%)	Standard Deviation
Arithmetic Average Default Rate	1971 to 1997	2.613	2.554
	1978 to 1997	2.849	2.808
	1985 to 1997	3.745	3.059
Weighted Average Default Rate**	1971 to 1997	3.311	3.452
	1978 to 1997	3.342	3.066
Median Annual Default Rate	1971 to 1997	1.500	

* As of mid-year.
** Weighted by par value of amount outstanding for each year.

Default Loss Rate Summary

	Default Rate (%)	Weighted Price After Default ($)	Weighted Coupon (%)	Default Loss (%)
Arithmetic Average 1978-1997:	2.85	42.9	11.48	1.83
Weighted Average 1978-1997:	3.34			2.18

Sources: Adapted from Exhibits 1 and 7 in Edward I. Altman and Vellore M. Kishore, "Defaults and Returns on High Yield Bonds," Chapter 14 in Frank J. Fabozzi (ed.), *The Handbook of Corporate Debt Instruments* (New Hope, PA: Frank J. Fabozzi Associates, 1998).

Historical Recovery Rates and Seniority Several studies have found that the recovery rate is closely related to the bond's seniority. Exhibit 3 shows the weighted average recovery rate for the 777 bond issues studied by Altman and

Kishore that defaulted between 1978 and 1997 for the following bond classes: (1) senior secured, (2) senior unsecured, (3) senior subordinated, (4) subordinated, and (5) discount and zero coupon.[13] The recovery rate for senior-secured bonds averaged 59% of face value, compared with 49% for senior-unsecured, 35% for senior-subordinated, and 32% for subordinated bonds.

In an analysis of bond and preferred stock defaults between 1970 and 1995, Carty and Lieberman also found a close association between seniority and recovery rates.[14] The recovery rates from that study range from 53% for senior-secured bonds to 29% for subordinated bonds, and only 6% for preferred stock. In general, the recovery rates in the Carty and Lieberman study are about 2% to 4% lower than those in the Altman and Kishore study, a relatively small difference that may be attributed to differences in the sample period and sample methodology.

The recovery rates reported in the studies by Altman and Kishore and Carty and Lieberman are only indirect estimates of the value of seniority. Not all firms that default have multiple levels of senior and subordinated debt. A more direct estimate of seniority is obtained by comparing prices of senior and subordinated bonds of the same company at the time of default. The Carty and Lieberman study found that subordinated bonds typically recover about $20 less than senior bonds of the same company. Clearly, because subordinated bonds have lower recovery rates, they should trade at wider yield spreads than senior bonds of the same issuer. In Chapter 14, we develop a model that estimates the yield spread difference between bonds with different recovery values.

Exhibit 3: Weighted Average Recovery Rates on Defaulted Debt by Seniority Per $100 Face Value (1978–1997)

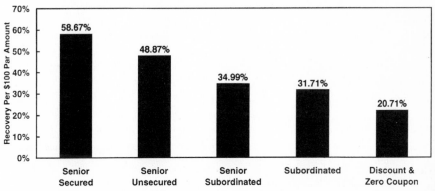

Source: From Exhibit 8 in Edward I. Altman and Vellore M. Kishore, "Defaults and Returns on High Yield Bonds," Chapter 14 in Frank J. Fabozzi (ed.), *The Handbook of Corporate Debt Instruments* (New Hope, PA: Frank J. Fabozzi Associates, 1998).

[13] Altman and Kishore, "Defaults and Returns on High Yield Bonds."
[14] Lea V. Carty and Dana Lieberman, "Corporate Bond Defaults and Recovery Rates: 1938-1995," Moody's Investors Service (January 1996).

Recovery Rates for Different Industries Seniority is not the only factor that affects recovery values. In general, recovery values will vary with the types of assets and competitive conditions of the firm, as well as the economic environment at the time of bankruptcy. In addition, recovery rates will also vary across industries. For example, some manufacturing companies, such as petroleum and chemical companies, have assets with a high tangible value, such as plant, equipment, and land. These assets usually have a significant market value, even in the event of bankruptcy. In other industries, however, a company's assets have less tangible value, and bondholders should expect low recovery rates.

To understand why recovery rates might vary across industries, consider two extreme examples: a software company and an electric utility. In the event of bankruptcy, the assets of a software company will probably have little tangible value. The company's products will have a low liquidation value because of the highly competitive and dynamic nature of the industry. The company's major intangible asset, its software developers, may literally disappear as employees move to jobs at other companies. In general, in industries that spend heavily on research and development and in which technological changes are rapid, a company's liquidation value will decline sharply when its products lose their competitive edge. In these industries, bondholders can expect to recover little in the event of default.

At the other extreme, electric utility bonds will likely have relatively high recovery values. The assets of an electric company (e.g., generation, transmission, and distribution) usually continue to generate a stream of revenues even after a bankruptcy. In most cases, a bankruptcy of a utility can be solved by changing the company's capital structure, rather than by liquidating its assets. In addition, regulators have a vested interest in maintaining the company as a going concern.

In a study covering defaulted bonds from 1971–1995, Altman and Kishore present detailed data on recovery rates stratified by industry sector and seniority.[15] The results of that study, summarized in Exhibit 4, agree with our economic intuition about recovery rates and tangible asset values. Public utilities had a high recovery rate, 71.5% of par for senior-unsecured bonds. Also, the 81.7% recovery rate for petroleum, chemicals, and related products was significantly higher than the rates for other industries. In most other industries, recovery rates for senior-unsecured bonds averaged around 45% of par, while subordinated bond recoveries averaged about 30% of par.[16]

---

[15] Edward I. Altman and Vellore M. Kishore, "Almost Everything You Wanted to Know about Recoveries on Defaulted Bonds," *Financial Analysts Journal* (November/December 1996), pp. 57–64.

[16] Nearly all bonds are rated speculative-grade at the time of default, but 23% of the bonds in the Altman and Kishore study were originally rated investment-grade and were subsequently downgraded to speculative-grade before the default. Interestingly, the original rating of the bond had no effect on the bond's recovery rate, after accounting for seniority.

Exhibit 4: Weighted Average Recovery Rates Per $100 Face Value by Industry and Seniority (1971-1995)

Industry	Weighted Average Recovery Rate		Number of Observations	
	Senior Unsecured	Subordinated	Senior Unsecured	Subordinated
Mining and petroleum drilling	$37.37	$27.48	9	21
Construction and real estate	39.16	22.79	12	12
Food and kindred products	48.27	36.68	6	6
Textile and apparel products	36.24	24.80	8	6
Wood, paper, leather products, and publishing	58.54	47.14	3	5
Chemicals, petroleum, rubber and plastic products	81.71	31.46	16	6
Building materials, metals, and fabricated products	36.55	31.83	20	28
Machinery, instruments, and related products	51.36	41.60	11	15
Diversified manufacturing	82.37	21.58	3	10
Transportation and transportation equipment	36.28	15.00	22	8
Services–business and personal	n/a	43.06	0	2
Communications, broadcasting, and movie production	53.73	35.56	12	21
Public utilities	71.53	43.06	0	2
Wholesale and retail trade	33.50	47.17	2	7
General merchandise stores	45.59	28.83	26	26
Financial institutions	42.70	21.28	37	11
Lodging, hospitals, and nursing facilities	19.39	18.63	4	9
Casino, hotel, and recreation	100.00	26.22	1	4

We caution that the historical recovery rates should be viewed as rough estimates, rather than guaranteed prices, because recovery rates can vary significantly from company to company even within a particular industry. In addition, the recovery rates are based on a small sample of defaults for some industries, such as paper companies and commercial banks. More importantly, recovery rates in the future may differ significantly from the past experience.

This note of caution is particularly important for bonds issued by banks and bank holding companies. The Altman and Kishore study found that the weighted average recovery price for bank bonds was 22% of face value. In the future, recovery values may be substantially lower, particularly for securities issued at the bank holding company level. In the event of a bank insolvency, the claim of investors in holding company securities is generally subordinate to the claims of the bank's creditors, including its depositors, its general creditors, and its subordinated creditors. Essentially, investors in holding company securities have no claim until the claims of bank level creditors are satisfied. Also, under Federal Reserve Board policy, a bank holding company is expected to act as a "source of strength" to each subsidiary bank and to commit resources to support a subsidiary bank when it might not do so absent such policy. As a result, in the event of a bank holding company bankruptcy, we would expect low recovery values for all bank holding company bonds, regardless of whether the bonds are senior, subordinated, or deeply subordinated deferrable bonds.[17]

CREDIT SPREAD RISK

Even in the absence of default, an investor is concerned that the market value of a bond will decline and/or the price performance of that bond will be worse than that of other bonds against which the investor is compared. This is because the price of a bond changes in the opposite direction to the change in the yield required by the market. Thus, if yields increase, the price of a bond declines, and vice versa.

The yield on a corporate bond is made up of two components: (1) the yield on a similar default-free bond issue and (2) a premium above the yield on a default-free bond issue necessary to compensate for the risks associated with the corporate bond. The risk premium is referred to as a spread. In the United States, Treasury issues are the benchmark yields because they are believed to be default free, they are highly liquid, and Treasury issues are not callable (with the exception of some old issues). The part of the risk premium or spread attributable to default risk is called the *credit spread*.

The price performance of a corporate bond issue and its return that the investor will realize by holding that issue over some time period will depend on how the credit spread changes. If the credit spread increases (i.e., the spread has "widened"), the market price of the corporate bond issue will decline (assuming Treasury rates have not changed). The risk that an issuer's debt obligation will decline due to an increase in the credit spread is called *credit spread risk*. Spread volatility is not the same as yield volatility, and consequently, spread risk is not the same as interest rate risk. In Chapter 7, we explore the theoretical and empirical relations between spread volatility and yield volatility.

This risk exists for an individual issue, for issues in a particular industry or economic sector, and for all corporate bond issues in the economy. For example, in general during economic recessions investors are concerned that corpora-

---

[17] As a result of the Financial Institutions Reform, Recovery, and Enforcement Act of 1989, any subsidiary bank of a bank holding company can generally be held liable for any expected loss incurred by the FDIC in connection with the appointment of a conservator or receiver of any other subsidiary bank of the bank holding company. Therefore, any losses to the FDIC may result in losses to the bank holding company's other subsidiary banks or a reduction in the ability of subsidiary banks to transfer funds to the holding company to service holding company bonds.

Under the Federal Deposit Insurance Corporation Improvement Act of 1991, a bank holding company is required to guarantee a capital restoration plan of an undercapitalized subsidiary bank up to certain limits. In addition, under the Crime Control Act of 1990, in the event of a bank holding company's bankruptcy, any commitment by the bank holding company to a federal bank regulatory agency to maintain the capital of a subsidiary bank will be assumed by the bankruptcy trustee and entitled to a priority of payment.

tions will face a decline in cash flows that would be used to service their debt obligations. As a result, the credit spread tends to widen for corporate issuers and the prices of all such issues throughout the economy will decline. In Chapter 10 we review the evidence on credit spreads and the business cycle.

DOWNGRADE RISK

While there are portfolio managers who seek to allocate funds among different sectors of the bond market to capitalize on anticipated changes in credit spreads, an analyst investigating the credit quality of an individual issue is concerned with the prospects of the credit spread increasing for that particular issue. But how does the analyst assess whether he or she believes the market will change the credit spread attributed to the issue?

As explained previously, market participants gauge the default risk of an issue by looking at the credit ratings assigned to issues by the rating agencies. Once a credit rating is assigned to a debt obligation, a rating agency monitors the credit quality of the issuer and can reassign a different credit rating. An improvement in the credit quality of an issue or issuer is rewarded with a better credit rating, referred to as an *upgrade*; a deterioration in the credit rating of an issue or issuer is penalized by the assignment of an inferior credit rating, referred to as a *downgrade*. An unanticipated downgrading of an issue or issuer increases the credit spread and results in a decline in the price of the issue or the issuer's bonds. This risk is referred to as *downgrade risk* and is closely related to credit spread risk.

A useful tool for gauging downgrade risk is a *rating transition matrix* published by rating agencies. Exhibit 5 provides information on historical experience of issues being upgraded and downgraded. The experience is based on the ratings by Standard & Poor's. A rating transition matrix is available for different holding periods. Exhibit 5 shows a 1-year, 2-year, 5-year, and 10-year rating transition matrix. Let's use the 1-year rating transition matrix (the first matrix in the exhibit) to explain how to interpret the values.

The rows indicate the rating at the beginning of a year. The columns show the rating at the end of the year. For example, look at the third row. This row shows the transition for A-rated bonds at the beginning of a year. The number 87.94 in the third row means that on average 87.94% of A-rated bonds at the beginning of the year remained A-rated at year end. The value of 2.16 means that on average 2.16% of A-rated bonds at the beginning of the year were upgraded to AA. The value of 4.97 means that on average 4.97% of A-rated bonds at the beginning of the year were downgraded to a BBB rating by the end of the year.

From Exhibit 5 two points are noteworthy. First, the probability of a downgrade is higher than for an upgrade for investment-grade bonds. Second, the longer the transition period, the lower the probability that an issuer will retain its original rating.

Exhibit 5: Selected Transition Matrices Based on S&P Rated Issues

Average 1-Year Transition Rates	Rating at end of first year (%)								
Initial rating	AAA	AA	A	BBB	BB	B	CCC	D	N.R.
AAA	90.34	5.62	0.39	0.08	0.03	0.00	0.00	0.00	3.54
AA	0.64	88.78	6.72	0.47	0.06	0.09	0.02	0.01	3.21
A	0.07	2.16	87.94	4.97	0.47	0.19	0.01	0.04	4.16
BBB	0.03	0.24	4.56	84.26	4.19	0.76	0.15	0.22	5.59
BB	0.03	0.06	0.40	6.09	76.09	6.82	0.96	0.98	8.58
B	0.00	0.09	0.29	0.41	5.11	74.62	3.43	5.30	10.76
CCC	0.13	0.00	0.26	0.77	1.66	8.93	53.19	21.94	13.14

Average 2-Year Transition Rates	Rating at end of second year (%)								
Initial rating	AAA	AA	A	BBB	BB	B	CCC	D	N.R.
AAA	81.51	10.14	1.05	0.18	0.06	0.03	0.00	0.00	7.04
AA	1.18	79.41	11.87	1.07	0.16	0.18	0.01	0.04	6.09
A	0.10	3.86	77.57	8.60	1.07	0.41	0.03	0.11	8.26
BBB	0.10	0.47	8.44	70.48	6.80	1.46	0.33	0.48	11.44
BB	0.03	0.11	0.87	10.79	56.21	10.11	1.61	2.95	17.32
B	0.00	0.14	0.54	0.92	8.88	53.85	3.83	11.01	20.84
CCC	0.14	0.00	0.57	1.72	2.15	11.61	32.09	28.37	23.35

Average 5-Year Transition Rates	Rating at end of fifth year (%)								
Initial rating	AAA	AA	A	BBB	BB	B	CCC	D	N.R.
AAA	60.60	17.32	3.41	0.93	0.14	0.11	0.00	0.11	17.39
AA	2.32	57.01	22.06	3.26	0.53	0.44	0.08	0.24	14.08
A	0.16	6.45	56.74	13.79	2.30	1.12	0.17	0.50	18.78
BBB	0.23	1.25	14.52	44.64	8.47	2.38	0.58	1.76	26.18
BB	0.05	0.30	2.35	15.16	24.23	9.37	1.45	9.14	37.94
B	0.00	0.15	0.87	2.53	10.41	19.42	2.05	19.98	44.59
CCC	0.18	0.00	0.35	2.65	3.36	6.54	7.77	39.22	39.93

Average 10-Year Transition Rates	Rating at end of 10th year (%)								
Initial rating	AAA	AA	A	BBB	BB	B	CCC	D	N.R.
AAA	37.30	20.22	7.84	3.02	0.12	0.00	0.00	0.64	30.85
AA	2.88	33.41	28.09	6.49	0.84	0.24	0.11	0.95	27.00
A	0.37	6.29	37.47	15.23	3.34	1.16	0.11	1.75	34.29
BBB	0.35	1.77	15.71	26.17	6.48	1.57	0.20	4.30	43.45
BB	0.16	0.08	3.44	11.77	7.55	3.32	0.44	18.14	55.12
B	0.00	0.10	0.85	3.07	4.77	3.92	0.38	29.48	57.43
CCC	0.26	0.00	0.26	1.05	3.67	1.83	0.00	46.86	46.07

Source: Table 16 in Leo Brand and Reza Bahar, "Corporate Defaults: Will Things Get Worse Before They Get Better?" *Special Report*, Standard & Poor's Corporation.

A more detailed transition matrix by rating modifier is used in practice. Exhibit 6 is an example for a 1-year rating transition matrix as reported by S&P. In Chapter 13, we show how investors can use rating transition matrices to formulate portfolio strategies.

Event Risk

Occasionally the ability of an issuer to make interest and principal payments changes seriously and unexpectedly because of (1) a natural or industrial accident or some regulatory change, or (2) a takeover or corporate restructuring. These risks are referred to generically as *event risk* and will result in a downgrading of the issuer by the rating agencies. Two examples of the first type of event risk are (1) a change in the accounting treatment of loan losses for commercial banks and (2) the cancellation of nuclear plants by public utilities. An example of the second type of event risk is the takeover in 1988 of RJR Nabisco for $25 billion through a financing technique known as a leveraged buyout (LBO). The new company took on a substantial amount of debt to finance the acquisition of the firm. In the case of RJR Nabisco, the debt and equity after the leveraged buyout were $29.9 and $1.2 billion, respectively. Because of the need to service a larger amount of debt, the company's credit rating was reduced. RJR Nabisco's rating as assigned by Moody's dropped from A1 to B3. As a result, investors demanded a higher credit spread because of this new capital structure with a greater proportion of debt. The yield spread to a benchmark Treasury rate increased from about 100 basis points to 350 basis points.[18]

CREDIT DERIVATIVES

Treasury futures contracts can be used to control interest rate risk with respect to changes in the level of interest rates (as measured by Treasury yields). However, there are also changes in the spread that must be controlled for corporate bonds. Agency note futures contracts can be used to partially control the spread risk for corporate bonds. However, the correlation between the spread on agency debentures and corporate bonds (both investment grade and noninvestment grade) is not perfect. Moreover, agency note futures contract is relatively new as of this writing. What has developed in the over-the-counter or dealer market are derivative products that provide protection against credit risk. These products are referred to as *credit derivatives*. There are three main types of credit derivatives that we describe: credit options, credit forwards, and credit swaps.

---

[18] Leland Crabbe, "Event Risk: An Analysis of Losses to Bondholders and 'Super Poison Put' Bond Covenants," *Journal of Finance* (June 1991), pp. 689–706.

Exhibit 6: Average 1-Year Rating Transition Matrix by Rating Modifier

Initial rating	Rating at year end (%)																		
	AAA	AA+	AA	AA−	A+	A	A−	BBB+	BBB	BBB−	BB+	BB	BB−	B+	B	B−	CCC	D	N.R.
AAA	90.34	3.13	2.13	0.36	0.14	0.19	0.06	0.06	0.03	0.00	0.00	0.03	0.00	0.08	0.00	0.00	0.00	0.00	3.54
AA+	2.19	81.89	8.83	2.94	0.38	0.68	0.08	0.00	0.15	0.08	0.00	0.00	0.00	0.08	0.00	0.00	0.00	0.00	2.72
AA	0.68	1.22	83.78	6.76	2.34	1.44	0.24	0.39	0.20	0.10	0.02	0.02	0.02	0.02	0.00	0.02	0.05	0.00	2.68
AA−	0.00	0.32	3.22	79.86	8.63	2.88	0.52	0.14	0.14	0.03	0.03	0.03	0.00	0.00	0.14	0.00	0.00	0.03	4.03
A+	0.02	0.07	0.64	4.08	80.63	7.32	2.31	0.51	0.36	0.16	0.04	0.13	0.02	0.11	0.07	0.00	0.02	0.02	3.48
A	0.08	0.09	0.48	0.72	4.83	79.14	5.13	2.99	1.00	0.35	0.17	0.20	0.15	0.14	0.02	0.00	0.00	0.05	4.48
A−	0.10	0.03	0.10	0.42	0.99	7.16	75.07	7.06	2.85	0.78	0.21	0.37	0.13	0.18	0.05	0.03	0.00	0.05	4.42
BBB+	0.00	0.03	0.06	0.18	0.51	1.80	6.99	73.95	7.68	2.61	0.48	0.33	0.12	0.27	0.21	0.00	0.15	0.12	4.50
BBB	0.05	0.02	0.07	0.10	0.42	0.77	1.90	6.52	74.60	5.21	2.02	1.01	0.44	0.32	0.25	0.00	0.05	0.22	6.02
BBB−	0.03	0.00	0.07	0.21	0.17	0.49	0.49	2.05	7.41	71.90	5.15	2.85	0.97	0.73	0.31	0.31	0.28	0.35	6.23
BB+	0.11	0.00	0.00	0.06	0.11	0.33	0.28	0.55	3.22	11.43	64.00	5.05	3.38	1.55	0.89	0.11	0.83	0.44	7.65
BB	0.00	0.00	0.09	0.04	0.00	0.21	0.17	0.26	1.24	3.72	6.11	66.10	6.93	2.69	1.15	0.56	0.68	0.94	9.11
BB−	0.00	0.00	0.00	0.00	0.06	0.03	0.13	0.26	0.42	0.75	2.95	7.52	65.43	7.49	2.50	1.17	1.23	1.33	8.72
B+	0.00	0.02	0.00	0.09	0.00	0.07	0.17	0.11	0.11	0.22	0.46	1.54	4.90	69.69	5.36	2.10	1.69	2.91	10.57
B	0.00	0.00	0.10	0.00	0.00	0.24	0.24	0.00	0.24	0.10	0.48	0.71	1.76	6.86	61.31	4.24	4.76	8.38	10.58
B−	0.00	0.00	0.00	0.00	0.11	0.00	0.00	0.22	0.11	0.11	0.22	0.33	0.44	3.73	6.26	56.86	9.11	10.32	12.18
CCC	0.13	0.00	0.00	0.00	0.13	0.00	0.13	0.51	0.26	0.00	0.26	0.38	1.02	1.91	3.19	3.83	53.19	21.94	13.14

N.R.–Rating withdrawn

Source: Table 12 in Leo Brand and Reza Bahar, "Corporate Defaults: Will Things Get Worse Before They Get Better?" *Special Report*, Standard & Poor's Corporation.

Credit Options

There are two types of credit options. The first type is a credit option written on an underlying issue. For this type of credit option the payout is determined based on whether a default occurs for the underlying issue. The amount of the payout is a fixed amount determined at the time the option is purchased. If a default does not occur by the option's expiration date, there is no payout.

The same type of credit option—which is basically a "binary option" because it has only two possible payoffs, zero if there is no default and the predetermined fixed sum if there is a default—can also be written where the payoff is based on whether or not the issue is downgraded. Then the payoff is specified by the amount of the loss expected if there is a downgrade. Credit options can also be written in which a default is defined in broader terms than simply failure to meet an interest or principal payment. For example, the event that could trigger a payoff can be defined in terms of whether some financial measure is above or below a certain value. For example, a minimum net worth can be specified. This form of a credit option can specify that if the issuer's book value falls below $150 million or less, for example, then there is a payoff.

For the second type of credit option, the payoff is determined by the level of the credit spread over a referenced security, typically a Treasury security. The strike is specified in terms of the level of the credit spread. The payoff can specify that if the credit spread for the issue is greater than the strike spread, there is a payoff. For example, suppose that the referenced issue is a bond of company XYZ. Suppose the current spread is 200 basis points. The strike spread can be specified as 250 basis points and that if the credit spread by the expiration date exceeds that strike spread there is a payoff. Alternatively, the payoff can specify that if the credit spread is less than the strike there is a payoff.

The tricky part of the payoff for an option written on a credit spread is the determination of the payoff. Remember that if interest rates in general increase, the price of the issue underlying the option will decline, and vice versa. What the payoff must do is separate the change in the price of the underlying issue due to a change in the general level of rates and the change in the credit spread. This is done by having the payoff based on the difference in the actual credit spread and the strike spread multiplied by a specified notional amount and by a risk factor. The risk factor is a quantitative measure that is derived from two important analytical concepts, duration and convexity that we discussed in Chapter 6. For purposes of our discussion, it is not necessary to understand how the risk factor is computed. Instead, let's see how the payoff is determined. The payoff function is determined as follows if the credit option is based on the credit spread being greater than the strike spread:

$$(\text{credit spread} - \text{strike spread}) \times \text{notional amount} \times \text{risk factor}$$

where the credit spread and the strike spread are expressed in decimal form.

For example, suppose that for the issue of company XYZ the strike spread is 250 basis points and that the notional amount of the credit option is $10 million. Suppose also that the risk factor for this issue is 5. If at the expiration date of this option the credit spread for this issue is 300 basis points, then the payoff is:

$$(0.030 - 0.025) \times \$10,000,000 \times 5 = \$250,000$$

If the credit spread at the expiration date is 250 basis points or less, then there is no payoff.

If the credit spread option had a payoff based on the credit spread narrowing, then the payoff function would be:

(strike spread − credit spread) × notional amount × risk factor

Credit Forward Contracts

The underlying for a credit forward contract is the credit spread. The payoff depends on the credit spread at the settlement date of the contract. The payoff is positive (i.e., the party receives cash) if the credit spread moves in favor of the party at the settlement date. The party makes a payment if the credit spread moves against the party at the settlement date.

For example, suppose that a manager has a view that the credit spread will increase (i.e., widen) to more than the current 250 basis points in one year for an issue of company XYZ. Then the payoff function for this credit forward contract would be:

(credit spread at settlement date − 250) × notional amount × risk factor

Assuming that the notional amount is $10 million and the risk factor is 5, then if the credit spread at the settlement date is 325 basis points, the amount that will be received by the manager is:

$$(0.0325 - 0.025) \times \$10,000,000 \times 5 = \$375,000$$

Instead, suppose that the credit spread at the settlement date decreased to 190 basis points, then the manager would have to pay out $300,000 as shown below:

$$(0.019 - 0.025) \times \$10,000,000 \times 5 = -\$300,000$$

In general, if a manager takes a position in a credit forward contract to benefit from an increase in the credit spread, then the payoff would be as follows:

(credit spread at settlement date − credit spread in contract)
    × notional amount × risk factor

For a manager taking a position that the credit spread will decrease, the payoff is:

(credit spread in contract − credit spread at settlement date)
× notional amount × risk factor

Credit Swaps

There are two different types of credit swaps: credit default swaps and total return swaps. *Credit default swaps* are used by a manager to shift credit exposure to a credit protection seller. A *total return swap* is used by a manager to increase credit exposure.

Credit default swaps come in two forms: credit insurance and swapping risky credit payments for certain fixed payments. With credit insurance, the buyer pays a fee to enter into a credit default swap. The buyer receives a payment every period for the life of the contract if a referenced credit defaults on a payment. While this contract is called a "swap," it is basically a package of credit options. Rather than a payment being contingent on an individual referenced credit, the referenced credit can be a portfolio of bonds. The second form of credit default swap is one in which a manager agrees to exchange the total return on a credit risky asset for known periodic payments from the counterparty. The payments are exchanged based on what happens to the value of the credit risky asset. If it declines in value, the manager receives a payment to compensate for the decline in value plus a periodic payment from the counterparty.

With a total return credit swap the manager agrees to pay all cash flows from the referenced asset or assets, including the change in the value of the referenced asset or assets. The manager receives in exchange a floating rate plus any depreciation of the referenced asset from the credit swap seller.

Chapter 12

Introduction to Corporate Bond Credit Analysis

C redit analysis is the indispensable element of corporate bond portfolio management. The ultimate goal of credit analysis is to reduce risks in the portfolio and to identify mispriced opportunities. By delving deeply into the operations and financial condition of a corporate borrower, the credit analyst strives to identify which companies should be avoided due to their risks of fundamental deterioration, credit rating downgrades, or default. The skills of a credit analyst are both quantitative and qualitative. The job of the credit analyst involves both art and science because the credit quality of a corporate borrower depends not only on the measurable strength of the company's financial statements but also on intangibles, such as the strategic vision of management and the "animal spirits" of competitive markets. In this chapter, we introduce some of the elements of credit analysis.

Good credit analysts do their own, independent research. They monitor corporate developments, they use financial statements to model financial risk, and they meet with company management. In addition, credit analysts also need to understand the methodology of the rating companies—Standard & Poor's Corporation, Moody's Investors Service, Inc., and Fitch. Ratings can differ from issue to issue for the same issuer because each issue may give the bondholder a different priority of claim in a bankruptcy. Once a credit rating is assigned to a corporate debt obligation, a rating agency monitors the credit quality of the issuer and can reassign a different credit rating. An improvement in the credit quality of an issue or issuer is rewarded with a better credit rating, referred to as an *upgrade*; a deterioration in the credit quality of an issue or issuer is penalized by the assignment of an inferior credit rating, referred to as a *downgrade*. An unanticipated downgrading of an issue or issuer increases the credit spread sought by the market, resulting in a decline in the price of the issue or the issuer's debt obligation. This risk is referred to as *downgrade risk*.

A credit rating is not a measure of the other aspects of credit risk (i.e., credit ratings do not measure credit spread risk and downgrade risk). Yet, an analyst must be aware of how rating agencies gauge default risk for purposes of assigning ratings in order to understand downgrade risk. When an analyst assesses the credit quality of an issuer, he or she often evaluates quantitative measures such as financial ratios as well as the priority of claim in a bankruptcy in terms of what the rating agencies require to achieve a certain rating. When an analyst expresses a view that the credit quality has deteriorated, typically the analyst

183

means that the analysis suggests that the issue may be downgraded because the quantitative measures identified are inferior to the benchmarks for the issue to maintain its current credit rating.

ELEMENTS OF CORPORATE CREDIT ANALYSIS

In conducting this credit examination, the analyst considers the four C's of credit:

- character
- capacity
- collateral
- covenants

Character of management is the foundation of sound credit. This includes the ethical reputation as well as the business qualifications and operating record of the board of directors, management, and executives responsible for the use of the borrowed funds and repayment of those funds. *Capacity* is the ability of an issuer to repay its obligations. *Collateral* is looked at not only in the traditional sense of assets pledged to secure the debt, but also to the quality and value of those unpledged assets controlled by the issuer. In both senses the collateral is capable of supplying additional aid, comfort, and support to the debt and the debtholder. Assets form the basis for the generation of cash flow, which services the debt in good times as well as bad. *Covenants* are the terms and conditions of the lending agreement. They lay down restrictions on how management operates the company and conducts its financial affairs. Covenants can restrict management's discretion. A default or violation of any covenant may provide a meaningful early warning alarm, enabling investors to take positive and corrective action before the situation deteriorates further. Covenants have value because they play an important part in minimizing risk to creditors. They help prevent the transfer of wealth from debtholders to equityholders.

ANALYSIS OF AN ISSUER'S CHARACTER

Character analysis involves the analysis of the quality of management. In discussing the factors it considers in assigning a credit rating, Moody's Investors Service notes the following regarding the quality of management:[1]

> Although difficult to quantify, management quality is one of the most important factors supporting an issuer's credit strength. When the unexpected occurs, it is a management's ability to react appropriately that will sustain the company's performance.

---

[1] "Industrial Company Rating Methodology," *Moody's Investors Services: Global Credit Research* (July 1998), p. 6.

In assessing management quality, the analysts at Moody's, for example, try to understand the business strategies and policies formulated by management. Following are factors that are considered:[2]

1. strategic direction
2. financial philosophy
3. conservatism
4. track record
5. succession planning
6. control systems

ANALYSIS OF THE CAPACITY TO PAY

A corporation will generate the funds to service its debt from its cash flow. The cash flow is generated from revenues and reduced by the costs of operations. Therefore, in assessing the ability of an issuer to pay, an analysis of the financial statements as discussed later in this chapter is undertaken. In addition to management quality, the factors examined by analysts at Moody's are:[3]

1. industry trends
2. the regulatory environment
3. basic operating and competitive position
4. financial position and sources of liquidity
5. company structure (including structural subordination and priority of claim)
6. parent company support agreements
7. special event risk

In considering industry trends, analysts look at the vulnerability of the company to economic cycles, the barriers to entry, and the exposure of the company to technological changes. For firms in regulated industries, proposed changes in regulations must be analyzed to assess their impact on future cash flows. At the company level, diversification of the product line and the cost structure are examined in assessing the basic operating position of the firm.

In addition to the measures described later in this chapter for assessing a company's financial position over the past 3 to 5 years, an analyst must look at the capacity of a firm to obtain additional financing and backup credit facilities. There are various forms of backup credit facilities. The strongest forms of backup credit facilities are those that are contractually binding and do not include provisions that permit the lender to refuse to provide funds. An example of such a pro-

---

[2] "Industrial Company Rating Methodology," p. 7.
[3] "Industrial Company Rating Methodology," p. 3.

vision is one that allows the bank to refuse funding if the bank feels that the borrower's financial condition or operating position has deteriorated significantly. (Such a provision is called a *material adverse change clause*.) Non-contractual facilities such as lines of credit that make it easy for a bank to refuse funding should be of concern to the analyst. The analyst must also examine the quality of the bank providing the backup facility.

Analysts should also assess whether the company can use securitization as a funding source for generating liquidity. Asset securitization involves using a pool of loans or receivables as collateral for a security. The decision of whether to securitize assets to borrow or use traditional borrowing sources is done on the basis of cost. However, if traditional sources dry up when a company faces a liquidity crisis, securitization may provide the needed liquidity. An analyst should investigate the extent to which management has considered securitization as a funding source.

Other sources of liquidity for a company may be third-party guarantees, the most common being a contractual agreement with its parent company. When such a financial guarantee exists, the analyst must undertake a credit analysis of the parent company.

In the analysis of an issuer's ability to pay, the analyst will analyze the issuer's financial statements (income statement, balance sheet, and statement of cash flows), project future financial statements based on certain assumptions, and compute various measures. These measures include traditional ratio measures and cash flow measures. In the following section we review these measures and explain how an analysis of cash flows provides a better early warning alarm of potential financial difficulties than traditional ratios.

Traditional Ratios

Traditional ratios to evaluate the ability of an issuer to meet its obligations include:

- profitability ratios
- debt and coverage ratios

Profitability Ratios

Equity analysts focus on the earnings of a firm, particularly the earnings per share. While a holder of the debt obligation of a firm does not have the opportunity to share in the economic growth of the firm, this does not mean that a credit analyst should ignore a firm's profitability. It is from revenues that a firm will continue to grow in order to generate cash flow to meet obligations.

Profitability ratios are utilized to explore the underlying causes of a change in the company's earnings. They show the combined effects of liquidity and asset and debt management on the profitability of the firm. These ratios break earnings per share into its basic determinants for purposes of assessing the factors underlying the profitability of the firm. They help assess the adequacy of historical profits and project future profitability through better understanding of its underlying causes.

Standards for a given ratio will vary according to operating characteristics of the company being analyzed and general business conditions; such standards cannot be stated as fixed and immutable. It is assumed that the analyst has made all adjustments deemed necessary to reflect comparable and true earning power of the corporation before calculating the ratios discussed as follows. It is important to stress that ratios are utilized to raise significant questions requiring further analysis, not to provide answers. Ratios must be viewed in the context of other ratios and other facts, derived from sources other than the financial statements, such as the statement of cash flows.

Equity analysts use the DuPont formula (explained in textbooks on equity analysis) to assess the determinants of a company's earnings per share. The profitability ratios analyzed to assess earnings per share are:

- return on stockholders' equity
- return on total assets
- profit margin
- asset turnover

Each of these measures and their limitations are explained in textbooks on financial statement analysis and equity analysis, so they will not be repeated here.

Debt and Coverage Analysis
Three sets of ratios are used by credit analysts as indicators to assess the ability of a firm to satisfy its debt obligations:

- short-term solvency ratios
- capitalization (or financial leverage) ratios
- coverage ratios

In addition to these ratios, an analyst should look at the maturity structure of the issuer's debt.

Short-Term Solvency Ratios Short-term solvency ratios are used to judge the adequacy of liquid assets for meeting short-term obligations as they come due. Firms go bankrupt, or get into financial difficulty, because they cannot pay obligations as they come due, not necessarily because they are not profitable.

A complete analysis of the adequacy of working capital for meeting current liabilities as they come due and assessing management's efficiency in using working capital would require a thorough analysis of cash flows and forecasts of fund flows in future periods that are discussed in the next section. However, ratios provide a crude but useful assessment of working capital. The following two ratios are calculated to assess the adequacy of working capital for a firm:

• the current ratio
• the acid-test ratio

The current ratio is calculated by dividing current assets by current liabilities:

$$\text{current ratio} = \frac{\text{current assets}}{\text{current liabilities}}$$

The current ratio indicates the company's coverage of current liabilities by current assets. For example, if the ratio were 2:1, the firm could realize only half of the values stated in the balance sheet in liquidating current assets and still have adequate funds to pay all current liabilities.

A general standard for this ratio (such as 2:1) is *not* useful. Such a standard fails to recognize that an appropriate current ratio is a function of the nature of a company's business and would vary with differing operating cycles of different businesses.

A *current asset* is one that is expected to be converted into cash in the ordinary operating cycle of a business. Inventory, therefore, is a current asset. In a tobacco or liquor manufacturing company, inventory may be as much as 80% to 90% of current assets. However, for a liquor company, that inventory may have to age 4 years or more before it can be converted into a salable asset. Such a company typically would require a much higher current ratio than average to have adequate liquidity to meet current liabilities maturing in 1 year. For a public utility company where there is no inventory or receivables collection problem, a current ratio of 1.1 or 1.2 to 1 has proved satisfactory. Industry averages, such as those produced by organizations like Dun & Bradstreet or Robert Morris Associates, should be looked at rather than considering an overall standard. Industry averages have their faults, but they are preferable to general standards that do not recognize operating differences among classes of companies.

The current ratio has a major weakness as an analytical tool. It ignores the composition of current assets, which may be as important as their relationship with current liabilities. Therefore, current ratio analysis must be supplemented by other working capital ratios.

Since the problem in meeting current liabilities may rest on slowness or even inability to convert inventories into cash to meet current obligations, the acid-test ratio (also called the quick ratio) is recommended. This is the ratio of current assets minus inventories, accruals, and prepaid items to current liabilities; that is:

$$\text{acid-test ratio} = \frac{\text{current assets} - \text{inventories} - \text{accruals} - \text{prepaid items}}{\text{current liabilities}}$$

This ratio does assume that receivables are of good quality and will be converted into cash over the next year.

Capitalization Ratios Credit analysts also calculate *capitalization ratios* to determine the extent to which the corporation is trading on its equity, and the resulting financial leverage. These ratios, also called *financial leverage ratios*, can be interpreted only in the context of the stability of industry and company earnings and cash flow. The assumption is that the greater the stability of industry and company earnings and cash flow, the more the company is able to accept the risk associated with financial leverage, and the higher the allowable ratio of debt to total capitalization (the total dollar amount of all long-term sources of funds in the balance sheet).

There are many variations to be found within the industry to calculate capitalization ratios. Two such ratios are shown below:

long-term debt to capitalization

$$= \frac{\text{long-term debt}}{\text{long-term debt + shareholders' equity including minority interest}}$$

total debt to capitalization

$$= \frac{\text{current liabilities + long-term debt}}{\text{long-term debt + shareholders' equity including minority interest}}$$

where shareholders' equity includes preferred stock.

For both ratios, the higher the ratio, the greater the financial leverage. The value used to measure debt in both ratios is book value. It is useful to calculate stockholders' equity at market as well as at book value for the purpose of determining these ratios. A market calculation for common equity may indicate considerably more or less financial leverage than a book calculation.

Commercial rating companies and most Wall Street analysts rely heavily on the long-term debt to capitalization ratio, and this is often provided in research reports sent out to clients. While this ratio can be useful, it should be noted that in recent years, given the uncertain interest rate environment, many corporations have taken to financing a good deal of their business with short-term debt. Indeed, an imaginative treasurer with a keen insight into money market activities can earn as much for a company as a plant manager, simply by switching debt from long term to short term and vice versa, at the right time.

Other considerations in using the long-term debt to capitalization ratio involves leased assets. Many corporations rent buildings and equipment under long-term lease contracts. Required rental payments are contractual obligations similar to bond coupon and repayment obligations. However, assets acquired through leasing (i.e., those leases classified as operating leases) may not be capitalized and shown in the balance sheet. Two companies, therefore, might work with the same amount of fixed assets and produce the same profits before interest or rental payments, but the one leasing a high proportion of its productive equipment could show significantly lower financial leverage.

Coverage Tests *Coverage ratios* are used to test the adequacy of cash flows generated through earnings for purposes of meeting debt and lease obligations. The four most commonly used coverage ratios are:

- EBIT interest coverage ratio
- EBITDA interest coverage ratio
- funds from operations/total debt ratio
- free operating cash flow/total debt ratio

EBIT stands for "earnings before interest and taxes." The *EBIT interest coverage ratio* is simply EBIT divided by the annual interest expense. (Interest expense includes "capitalized interest." This is effectively interest expense imputed for capitalized assets, the most important of which is leased assets.) Interest expense is tax deductible and, therefore, all earnings before taxes are available for paying such charges. Also, the interest should be added back to determine the amount available to meet annual interest expenses.

EBITDA stands for "earnings before interest, taxes, depreciation, and amortization." The *EBITDA interest coverage ratio* is simply the ratio of EBITDA divided by the annual interest expense.

The last two ratios listed above indicate the amount of funds from operations relative to the amount of total debt. The funds from operations includes net income plus the following: depreciation, amortization, deferred income taxes, and other noncash items. The definition of free operating cash flows varies by rating agency. In the next section we describe one variant of free operating cash flow.

Suggested standards for coverage ratios are based on experience and empirical studies relating the incidence of defaults over a number of years to such ratios. Different standards are needed for a highly cyclical company than for a stable company.

Cash Flow Analysis

Will the ratios just described be sufficient to help an analyst identify companies that may encounter financial difficulties? Consider the study by Largay and Stickney who analyzed the financial statements of W.T. Grant during the 1966–1974 period preceding its bankruptcy in 1975 and ultimate liquidation.[4] They noted that financial indicators such as profitability ratios, turnover ratios, and liquidity ratios showed some down trends, but provided no definite clues to the company's impending bankruptcy. A study of cash flows from operations, however, revealed that company operations were causing an increasing drain on cash, rather than providing cash.[5] This necessitated an increased use of external financing, the

---

[4] J.A. Largay III and C.P. Stickney, "Cash Flows, Ratio Analysis and the W.T. Grant Company Bankruptcy," *Financial Analysts Journal* (July-August 1980), pp. 51–54.

[5] For the period investigated, a statement of changes of financial position (on a working capital basis) was required prior to 1988.

required interest payments on which exacerbated the cash flow drain. Cash flow analysis clearly was a valuable tool in this case since W.T. Grant had been running a negative cash flow from operations for years. Yet none of the traditional ratios discussed previously take into account the cash flow from operations.

Dugan and Samson examined the use of operating cash flow as an early warning signal of a company's potential financial problems.[6] The subject of the study was Allied Products Corporation because for a decade this company exhibited a significant divergence between cash flow from operations and net income. For parts of the period, net income was positive while cash flow from operations was a large negative value. In contrast to W.T. Grant that went into bankruptcy, the auditor's report in the 1991 annual report of Allied Products Corporation did issue a going concern warning. Moreover, the stock traded in the range of $2 to $3 per share. There was then a turnaround of the company by 1995. In its 1995 annual report, net income increased dramatically from prior periods (to $34 million) and there was a positive cash flow from operations ($29 million). The stock traded in the $25 range by the Spring of 1996.[7] As with the W.T. Grant study, Dugan and Samson found that the realities of a firm are better reflected in its cash flow from operations.

Martin Fridson has documented how the typical cash flow generation and uses of companies in different stages of their business life cycle (startup, emerging growth, established growth, mature industry, and declining industry) relate to their statement of cash flows.[8] In addition, he explains how the statement of cash flows allows the analyst to assess a firm's "financial flexibility." An analysis of this statement provides an analyst with the information needed to answer such questions as:

- How "safe" is the company's dividend?
- Could the company fund its needs internally if external sources of capital suddenly become scarce or prohibitively expensive?
- Would the company be able to continue meeting its obligations if its business turned down sharply?

These questions can be answered by computing a measure called *discretionary cash flow*. Fridson defines this measure as follows:[9]

> Cash flow that remains available to a company after it has funded its basic operating requirements. There is no universally

---

[6] Michael T. Dugan and William D. Samson, "Operating Cash Flow: Early Indicators of Financial Difficulty and Recovery," *The Journal of Financial Statement Analysis* (Summer 1996), pp. 41–50.

[7] As noted for the W.T. Grant study by Largay and Stickney, cash flow from operations had to be constructed from the statement of changes in financial positions that companies were required to report prior to 1988.

[8] Chapter 4 in Martin S. Fridson, *Financial Statement Analysis: a Practitioner's Guide* (New York: John Wiley & Sons, 1995).

[9] Fridson, *Financial Statement Analysis*, p. 273.

accepted, precise definition of discretionary cash flow, but conceptually it includes funds from operations less required new investment in working capital and nondiscretionary capital expenditures. The latter figure is difficult to quantify with precision, but it exceeds the required 'maintenance' level required to keep existing plant and equipment in good working order. Ordinarily, some additional expenditures, which may be designated 'semi-discretionary' are necessary to keep a company competitive with respect to capacity, costs, and technology.

The computation of discretionary cash flow begins with the basic cash flow, which includes net earnings, depreciation, and deferred income taxes, less items in net income that do not provide cash. From the basic cash flow, nondiscretionary items are deducted. Subtracting from the basic cash flow increases in working capital (excluding cash and payables) gives *operating cash flow*. Deducting from operating cash flow the capital expenditures gives the company's discretionary cash flow. As noted in the above quote, capital expenditures that are nondiscretionary must be estimated. It is common for an analyst to use the capital expenditures reported in the financial statement. This is summarized in Exhibit 1.

For example, consider a company with a basic cash flow of $800 million and operating cash flow of $500 million. Suppose that this company pays dividends of $130 million and that its capital expenditure is $300 million. Then the discretionary cash flow for this company is $200 million, found by subtracting the capital expenditure ($300 million) from the operating cash flow ($500 million). This means that even after maintaining a dividend payment of $130 million, its cash flow would be positive. Notice that asset sales and other investing activity are not needed to generate cash to meet the dividend payments because in Exhibit 1 these items are subtracted after accounting for the dividend payments. In fact, if this company planned to increase its capital expenditures, an analyst can use the format in Exhibit 1 to assess how much that expansion can be before impacting dividends and/or increasing financing needs.

Exhibit 1: Computing a Company's Discretionary Cash Flow *

	Basic cash flow[1]
Less:	Increase in adjusted working capital[2,3]
	Operating cash flow
Less:	Capital expenditures[3]
	Discretionary cash flow

[1] The basic cash flow includes net earnings, depreciation, and deferred income taxes, less items in net income not providing cash.

[2] The increase in adjusted working capital excludes cash and payables.

[3] Nondiscretionary needs.

* This format was suggested by Martin S. Fridson, *Financial Statement Analysis: A Practitioner's Guide* (New York: John Wiley & Sons, 1995).

A useful ratio to help further assess a company's cash flow is the *cash flow from operations to capital expenditures ratio*. This ratio gives the analyst information about the financial flexibility of the company and is particularly useful for capital-intensive firms and utilities.[10] The larger the ratio, the greater the financial flexibility. The analyst, however, must carefully examine the reasons why this ratio may be changing over time and why it might be out of line with comparable firms in the industry. For example, a declining ratio can be interpreted in two ways. First, the firm may eventually have difficulty adding to capacity via capital expenditures without the need to borrow funds. The second interpretation is that the firm may have gone through a period of major capital expansion and therefore it will take time for revenues to be generated that will increase the cash flow from operations to bring the ratio to some normal long-run level.

ANALYSIS OF COLLATERAL AND COVENANTS

A corporate debt obligation can be secured or unsecured. In our discussion of creditor rights in a bankruptcy, we explained that in the case of a liquidation, proceeds from a bankruptcy are distributed to creditors based on the absolute priority rule. However, in the case of a reorganization, the absolute priority rule rarely holds. That is, an unsecured creditor may receive distributions for the entire amount of his or her claim and common stockholders may receive something, while a secured creditor may receive only a portion of its claim. The reason is that a reorganization requires approval of all the parties. Consequently, secured creditors are willing to negotiate with both unsecured creditors and stockholders in order to obtain approval of the plan of reorganization.

The question is then, what does a secured position mean in the case of a reorganization if the absolute priority rule is not followed? The claim position of a secured creditor is important in terms of the negotiation process. However, because absolute priority is not followed and the final distribution in a reorganization depends on the bargaining ability of the parties, some analysts place less emphasis on collateral compared to the other factors discussed earlier and covenants discussed later.

In Chapter 2 we discussed the various types of collateral used for a corporate debt issue and features that analysts should be cognizant of in looking at an investor's secured position. Bond covenants also contain important details that limit or restrict the borrower's activities. Covenants, which can be either negative or affirmative, are also discussed in detail in Chapter 2.

---

[10] Fridson, *Financial Statement Analysis*, p. 273.

SPECIAL CONSIDERATIONS FOR
HIGH-YIELD CORPORATE BONDS

The discussion thus far has focused on credit analysis for any issuer regardless of credit rating. Some unique factors should be considered in the analysis of high-yield bonds. We discuss the following:

- analysis of debt structure
- analysis of corporate structure
- analysis of covenants

In addition, we discuss the reasons why an equity analysis approach to high-yield bond issuers is being used.

Analysis of Debt Structure

In January 1990, the Association for Investment Management and Research held a conference on high-yield bonds. One of the presenters at the conference was William Cornish, then President of Duff & Phelps Credit Rating Company. In his presentation he identified a unique factor in the credit analysis of high-yield issuers—the characteristics of the types of debt obligations comprising a high-yield issuer's debt structure.[11]

Cornish explained why it was necessary for an analyst to examine a high-yield issuer's debt structure. At the time of his presentation, new types of bonds were being introduced into the high-yield market such as deferred coupon bonds. He noted that the typical debt structure of a high-yield issuer includes:

- bank debt
- broker's loans or "bridge loans"
- reset notes
- senior debt
- senior subordinated debt
- subordinated debt (payment in kind bonds)

Cornish then went on to explain the importance of understanding the characteristics of the diverse debt obligations that are included in a typical high-yield debt structure.

Consider first bank loans. While investment-grade issuers also have bank debt in their capital structure, high-yield issuers rely to a greater extent on this form of debt because of a lack of alternative financing sources. Banks' loans have three key characteristics. First, holders of bank debt have a priority over other debtholders on the firm's assets. Second, bank debt is typically short-term (usu-

---

[11] William A. Cornish, "Unique Factors in the Credit Analysis of High-Yield Bonds," in Frank K. Reilly (ed.), *High-Yield Bonds: Analysis and Risk Assessment* (Charlottesville, VA: Association for Invesment Management and Research, 1990).

ally it is not greater than 2 years). Finally, the rate on bank debt floats with the level of interest rates.

There are three implications of these characteristics of bank debt for the analysis of the credit worthiness of high-yield issuers. First, because the cost of this source of debt financing is affected by changes in short-term interest rates, the analyst must incorporate changing interest rate scenarios into cash flow projections. A rise in short-term interest rates can impose severe cash flow problems for an issuer heavily financed by bank debt.

Second, because the debt is short term, bank debt must be repaid in the near future. The challenge that the analyst faces is determining where the funds will be obtained to pay off maturing bank debt. There are three sources available:

1. repayment from operating cash flow
2. refinancing
3. sale of assets

Typically, a high-yield issuer will use a combination of the above three sources. The implication is that the analyst must carefully examine the timing and amount of maturing bank debt and consider the sources for repayment.

If the repayment is to come from operations, the projections of cash flow from operations become even more critical than for a high-grade issuer, which can rely on a wider range of funding sources such as commercial paper. When refinancing is the source of funds for loan repayment, there is the issue discussed earlier that future conditions in the financial market must be incorporated into the analyst's projections in order to assess future funding costs.

If the source of the loan repayment is the sale of assets, the analyst must consider which assets will be sold and how the sale of such assets will impact future cash flow from operations. If key assets must be sold to pay off maturing bank debt, management is adversely impacting the ability to repay other debt in the future from operating cash flow. In leveraged buyouts, the new management will have a specific plan for the disposal of certain assets in order to pay off bank debt and other debt or related payments. One credit analyst, Jane Tripp Howe, suggests that the analyst ask the following questions regarding asset sales:[12]

"Can the company meet its cash obligations if the sale of assets is delayed?
How liquid are the assets that are scheduled for sale?
Are the appraised value for these assets accurate?"

Banks will not provide short-term funds where there are insufficient assets to cover a loan in the case of liquidation. If short-term to intermediate-term

---

[12] Jane Tripp Howe, "Credit Considerations in Evaluating High-Yield Bonds," Chapter 21 in Frank J. Fabozzi (ed.), *Handbook of Fixed Income Securities* (Burr Ridge, IL: Irwin Professional Publishing, 1997), p. 408.

funds are needed, a high-yield issuer will turn to broker loans (or bridge loans) and/or reset notes. A reset note is a security where the coupon rate is reset periodically such that the security price will trade at some specified premium above par value. The presence of reset notes in the debt structure is of particular concern to the analyst for two reasons. First, there is the need to analyze the impact of future interest rates and spreads to assess the impact of higher borrowing costs. Second, to avoid a higher reset rate when interest rates rise due to rising interest rates in general and/or because of a higher spread demanded by the market for the particular issuer, the issuer may seek to dispose of assets. Again the assets sold may have an adverse impact on future operating cash flow.

While there are typically longer-term bonds referred to as "senior bonds" in a high-yield issuer's debt structure, the term "senior bonds" is misleading in the presence of bank loans. Moreover, there are deferred coupon bonds. One such bond structure is a zero-coupon bond. Deferred coupon bonds permit the issuer to postpone interest payment to some future year. As a result, the interest burden is placed on future cash flow to meet the interest obligations. Because of this burden, the presence of deferred coupon bonds may impair the ability of the issuer to improve its credit quality in future periods. Moreover, if senior bonds have deferred coupon payments, the subordinated bonds will be adversely affected over time as the amount of senior bonds grows over time relative to the amount of subordinated bonds. For example, one type of deferred coupon bond that was commonly issued at one time was the payment-in-kind (PIK) bond. With this bond structure, a high-yield issuer has the option to either pay interest in cash or pay the equivalent of interest with another bond with the same coupon rate. If the issuer does not have the ability to pay the interest in cash, payment with another bond will increase future interest expense and thereby adversely impact the issuer's future cash flow. If the PIK bonds are senior bonds, subordinated bonds are adversely affected over time as more senior bonds are added to the capital structure and future interest expense is increased further.

Analysis of Corporate Structure

High-yield issuers usually have a holding company structure. The assets to pay creditors of the holding company will come from the operating subsidiaries. Cornish explains why it is critical to analyze the corporate structure for a high-yield issuer. Specifically, the analyst must understand the corporate structure in order to assess how cash will be passed between subsidiaries and the parent company and among the subsidiaries. The corporate structure may be so complex that the payment structure can be confusing.

Cornish provides an illustration of this. At the time of his presentation (January 1990), Farley Inc. had the following debt structure: senior subordinated debt, subordinated notes, and junior subordinated debt. The question raised by Cornish was where Farley Inc. was going to obtain cash flow to make payments to its creditors. One possibility was to obtain funds from its operating subsidiaries. At the time, Farley Inc. had three operating subsidiaries: Fruit of the Loom, Acme Boot, and West Point Pepperell. An examination of the debt structure of Fruit of the Loom (20% owned by Farley Inc.) indicated that there was bank debt and no intercompany loans were permitted. While there were restrictions on dividend payments, none were being paid at the time. An examination of the Acme Boot (100% owned by Farley Inc.) showed that there was bank debt and while there were restrictions but no prohibitions on intercompany loans, Farley Inc. had in fact put cash into this operating subsidiary. Finally, West Point Pepperell (95% owned by Farley Inc.) had bridge loans that restricted asset sales and dividend payments. Moreover, any payments that could be made to Farley Inc. from West Point Pepperell had to be such that they would not violate West Point Pepperell's financial ratio requirements imposed by its bridge loan. The key point of the illustration is that an analyst evaluating the ability of Farley Inc. to meet its obligations to creditors would have to look very closely at the three operating subsidiaries. Just looking at financial ratios for the entire holding company structure would not be adequate. At the time, it was not likely that the three operating subsidiaries would be able to make any contribution to assist the parent company in paying off its creditors.

Analysis of Covenants

While an analyst should of course consider covenants when evaluating any bond issue (investment grade or high yield), it is particularly important for the analysis of high-yield issuers. The importance of understanding covenants was summarized by one high-yield portfolio manager, Robert Levine, as follows:[13]

> Covenants provide insight into a company's strategy. As part of the credit process, one must read covenants within the context of the corporate strategy. It is not sufficient to hire a lawyer to review the covenants because a lawyer might miss the critical factors necessary to make the appropriate decision. Also, loopholes in covenants often provide clues about the intentions of management teams.

Equity Analysis Approach

Historically, the return on high-yield bonds has been greater than that of high-grade corporate bonds but less than that of common stocks. The risk (as measured in terms of the standard deviation of returns) has been greater than the risk of high-grade bonds but less than that of common stock. Moreover, high-yield bond returns have been found to be more highly correlated to equity returns than to investment grade bond returns. This is why, for example, managers hedging high-yield bond portfolios have found that a combination of stock index futures con-

[13] Robert Levine, "Unique Factors in Managing High-Yield Bond Portfolios," in Frank K. Reilly (ed.), *High-Yield Bonds: Risk Analysis and Risk Assessment* (Charlottesville, VA: Association for Investment Management and Research), p. 35.

tracts and Treasury futures contracts has offered a better hedging alternative than just hedging with Treasury bond futures.[14]

Consequently, some portfolio managers strongly believe that high-yield bond analysis should be viewed from an equity analyst's perspective. As Stephen Esser notes:[15]

> Using an equity approach, or at least considering the hybrid nature of high-yield debt, can either validate or contradict the results of traditional credit analysis, causing the analyst to dig further.

He further states:[16]

> For those who work with investing in high-yield bonds, whether issued by public or private companies, dynamic, equity-oriented analysis is invaluable. If analysts think about whether they would want to buy a particular high-yield company's stock and what will happen to the future equity value of that company, they have a useful approach because, as equity values go up, so does the equity cushion beneath the company's debt. All else being equal, the bonds then become better credits and should go up in value relative to competing bond investments.

We will not review the equity analysis framework here. But, there has been strong sentiment growing in the investment community that an equity analysis approach will provide a better framework for high-yield bond analysis than a traditional credit approach.

---

[14] Kenneth S. Choie, "How to Hedge a High-Yield Bond Portfolio," Chapter 13 in Frank J. Fabozzi (ed.), *The New High-Yield Debt Market* (New York: HarperBusiness, 1990).

[15] Stephen F. Esser, "High-Yield Bond Analysis: The Equity Perspective," in Ashwinpaul C. Sondhi (ed.), *Credit Analysis of Nontraditinal Debt Securities* (Charlottesville, VA: Association for Investment Management and Research, 1995), p. 47.

[16] Esser, "High-Yield Bond Analysis: The Equity Perspective," p. 54.

Chapter 13

A Rating Transition Framework for Corporate Bond Strategy

The goal of corporate bond portfolio strategy is to identify sectors of the market that are likely to earn high excess returns. This chapter shows that excess returns can be attributed to three component variables: initial yield spreads; the change in yield spreads over the investment horizon; and changes in credit quality.

Portfolio returns can be significantly impacted by changes in credit quality, even if yield spreads for generic bond sectors remain constant over time. The framework in this chapter posits that upgraded bonds will appreciate in value and that downgraded bonds will record price declines. The net effect on excess returns will depend on the proportions of upgrades and downgrades, as well as on the slope of credit quality curves.

Using historical statistics on rating transition probabilities, expected excess returns are estimated for the major sectors of the investment-grade corporate bond market. Given these estimates for excess returns, sectors are ranked according to their relative value. In many cases, sectors with the highest initial yield spreads do not have the greatest potential for earning high excess returns.

WHY YIELD SPREADS DIFFER FROM EXCESS RETURNS

The primary reason for owning investment-grade corporate bonds is to achieve returns that exceed those of Treasury securities with comparable durations. In seeking high excess returns, some investors load up on bonds with wide yield spreads. Unfortunately, this strategy may not achieve the desired result because realized excess returns may differ from initial yield spreads, just as realized returns do not always equal quoted yields.

Over an investment horizon, two factors can drive a wedge between yield spreads and realized excess returns:

- The general level of yield spreads may change.
- The credit quality of the portfolio may change.

To see the importance of these two factors, consider a portfolio of A-rated bonds, priced at an average spread of 60 basis points over Treasuries. Over a 1-year horizon, the portfolio's excess return may differ substantially from the average spread. For example, the excess return will be greater than 60 basis points if single-A spreads narrow, and less if spreads widen.

Even if spreads on single-A bonds do not change, however, the excess return may differ from the initial 60 basis point spread because the credit quality of the portfolio may change through time. Suppose that 20% of the bonds are downgraded to triple-B, while the remaining 80% maintain single-A ratings. Because prices of the downgraded bonds will fall to triple-B levels, the excess return on the portfolio will likely be much less than 60 basis points.

Although changes in credit quality cannot be predicted with perfect certainty, it is not reasonable to assume that the credit profile of a corporate bond portfolio will remain static. Each year, some bonds will migrate to higher rating categories, while others will be downgraded. In this process, portfolio returns will be influenced by the frequency and severity of transitions in credit quality.

A RATING TRANSITION MATRIX: THE HISTORICAL DATA

Exhibit 1 presents the historical experience of credit quality changes in the form of a rating transition matrix. The data are based on a Moody's study of rating changes over the period 1970–1993.[1] The rows in the table give the rating at the beginning of the year, and the columns indicate the rating at the end of the year.

For example, the first row gives rating transitions for triple-A rated bonds. On average, 91.9% maintained their triple-A rating from the beginning of the year to the end (Column 1). However, 7.38% of the triple-As were downgraded to double-A, and 0.72% were downgraded to single-A (Columns 2 and 3).

---

[1] See Lea V. Carty and Jerome S. Fons, "Measuring Changes in Corporate Credit Quality," *Journal of Fixed Income*, June 1994, pp. 27–41. The data in Exhibit 1 are a transformation of Exhibit 11 in Carty and Fons. In their transition matrix, 2% to 3% of investment-grade issuers had their rating withdrawn at the end of the year, due to retirement of all rated debt, completion of an exchange offer, or other reasons. The credit quality of the issuer with a withdrawn rating could have improved, deteriorated, or stayed the same, but it is difficult to know which outcome is more likely without conducting a separate study of issuers with withdrawn ratings. In Exhibit 1, we have distributed the percentage in the withdrawn categories on a market-weighted basis to the other rating categories. Implicitly, this treatment assumes that the transition distribution of the credit quality of withdrawn issuers is the same as the distribution for issuers that maintained their ratings.

Another difference between the Carty and Fons study and this paper is that their rating transition probabilities are calculated at the *issuer* level, whereas the analysis in this paper is based on *issue* probabilities. This distinction will not have a significant effect on the inferences about corporate bond strategy unless large, active borrowers have dramatically different risk characteristics than small borrowers.

Transitions of Standard & Poor's ratings display a pattern similar to that of the Moody's data. See Leo Brand, Thomas C. Kitto, and Reza Bahar, "1993 Corporate Default, Rating Transition Study Results," *Standard & Poor's CreditReview*, May 2, 1994, pp. 1–12. For an analysis of autocorrelation in rating changes on portfolio returns, see Edward I. Altman and Duen-Li Kao, "The Implications of Corporate Bond Rating Drift," *Financial Analysts Journal*, May-June 1992, pp. 64–75.

Exhibit 1: One-Year Rating Transition Probabilities (%)

Rating at Start of Year	Rating at end of year							
	Aaa	Aa	A	Baa	Ba	B	C or D	Total
Aaa	91.90	7.38	0.72	0.00	0.00	0.00	0.00	100%
Aa	1.13	91.26	7.09	0.31	0.21	0.00	0.00	100%
A	0.10	2.56	91.20	5.33	0.61	0.20	0.00	100%
Baa	0.00	0.21	5.36	87.94	5.46	0.82	0.21	100%

The largest numbers in Exhibit 1 are along the diagonal, indicating that a large percentage of bonds maintain their ratings from year to year. Yet the numbers in the off-diagonal cells are not trivial, and several are greater than 5%. These statistics have several implications for portfolio managers. First, it will be difficult to avoid holding downgraded bonds. Second, portfolio returns will be affected by changes in credit quality, and not just by changes in the general level of spreads. Third, although the historical transition matrix can be used as a base case for identifying relative value, future changes in credit quality may differ from the historical data. To achieve superior returns, portfolio managers must make an effort to anticipate emerging trends in credit quality and to position their portfolios to take advantage of those trends.

In Exhibit 1, and throughout this chapter, the analysis is restricted to the investment-grade corporate bond market, but this restriction is made for convenience rather than necessity. Indeed, the analytical framework of this chapter can also be used to make relative value assessments for other asset classes, such as speculative-grade bonds, bank loans, and derivative securities. Moreover, we selected U.S. Treasury securities as the benchmark for measuring excess returns on corporate bonds, but the framework can be easily generalized to other benchmarks, such as U.S. agencies or swaps.

USING RATING TRANSITION MATRICES TO CALCULATE EXPECTED EXCESS RETURNS

For a specific sector in the corporate bond market, expected excess returns can be estimated in a three-step procedure: (1) determine rating change probabilities for the sector, given by a rating transition matrix; (2) estimate the increase in prices of upgraded bonds and the decrease for downgraded bonds; and (3) calculate the expected return as the sum of the coupon interest plus the weighted price change for the sector, where the weights are given by the rating transition probabilities.

The calculation of expected excess returns is best illustrated by way of an example (Exhibit 2). Consider a portfolio of double-A rated, 3-year bonds, which in this example trade at 30 basis points over 3-year Treasuries. Historically, 91.26% of double-A bonds maintain their rating each year. Hence, 91.26% of the portfolio can be expected to earn an excess return of 30 basis points over a 1-year horizon (Row

2). On average, 1.13% of double-A bonds are upgraded to triple-A each year. In the analysis, the upgraded bonds appreciate in value, as their spreads narrow from the double-A spread of 30 basis points to the triple-A spread of 25 basis points. These upgraded bonds will earn an excess return of 38 basis points: 30 basis points of incremental coupon income, plus 8 basis points due to the price appreciation (Row 1). Similarly, 7.09% of double-A bonds are typically downgraded to single-A. The analysis projects that spreads on the downgraded bonds will widen to the single-A spread of 35 basis points, producing an excess return of 21 basis points (Row 3). By calculating excess returns for each rating transition and weighing the returns by the transition probabilities, the last line in Exhibit 2 shows that the portfolio is expected to earn 28.9 basis points over Treasuries.

Notice that the excess return on the double-A portfolio, 28.9 basis points, is less than the initial spread of 30 basis points. The difference reflects two influences. First, the probability of an upgrade to triple-A is lower than the probability of a downgrade to single-A and below. Second, the credit curve punishes downgraded bonds more than it benefits upgraded bonds. Double-A bonds that fall to single-A and below suffer price declines that range from 0.1% to 1.8%, while those upgraded to triple-A record price increases of less than 0.1%.

To summarize, expected excess returns depend on three variables: the initial yield spread, the probability of a rating change, and the increase or decrease in price at the end of the investment horizon. Relative-value analysis must consider each of these variables. Interestingly, even if a sector has a low probability of default and a wide yield spread, it could have a low expected return.

For example, among investment-grade bonds, the Baa sector has the lowest probability of a downgrade (6.49%), the highest probability of an upgrade (5.57%), and the widest yield spreads. In the triple-A sector, by contrast, 8.1% are downgraded and none are upgraded. When a Baa bond is downgraded, it will experience a substantial decline in price as its spread gaps to speculative-grade levels. When a triple-A bond is downgraded, however, it usually suffers a relatively small price decline because only a small percentage of triple-A bonds fall below double-A. Hence, to compensate investors for the total effect that credit downgrades have on portfolio returns, Baa bonds need to have wider spreads than higher-rated bonds.

Exhibit 2: Expected Excess Return Estimates for 3-Year, AA-Rated Bonds Over a 1-Year Horizon

Initial Spread	Horizon Rating	Horizon Spread	Return over Treasuries	×	Transition Probability	=	Contribution to Excess Return
30	Aaa	25	38 bp		1.13%		0.43 bp
30	Aa	30	30		91.26		27.38
30	A	35	21		7.09		1.49
30	Baa	60	−24		0.31		−0.07
30	Ba	130	−147		0.21		−0.31
Portfolio Excess Return over Treasuries						=	28.9 bp

Exhibit 3: Expected Excess Returns Over Treasuries When Rating Transitions Match Historical Experience (1-Year Horizon)

Rating at Start of Year	3-Year		5-Year		10-Year		30-Year	
	Initial Spread	Excess Return	Initial Spread	Excess Return	Initial Spread	Excess Return	Initial Spread	Excess Return
Aaa	25 bp	24.2 bp	30 bp	28.4 bp	35 bp	31.7 bp	45 bp	34.6 bp
Aa	30	28.9	35	31.4	40	30.3	55	34.8
A	35	31.1	45	37.3	55	37.9	75	42.7
Baa	60	46.3	70	39.9	85	21.9	115	27.4

RELATIVE-VALUE ANALYSIS

Exhibit 3 extends the calculation of 1-year excess returns to the major rating and maturity categories in the investment-grade corporate market. In calculating excess returns, we use the transition matrix in Exhibit 1, and we assume that generic sector spreads do not change over the 1-year investment horizon (the same assumptions used in Exhibit 2). These assumptions are relaxed in subsequent sections in this chapter.

Notice that for each rating and maturity category the excess returns are less than the initial spreads. This difference mainly reflects the slope of the corporate credit curve. For example, when Baa bonds migrate to Ba, their spreads generally widen by 70 basis points or more, but when they are upgraded to single-A their spreads narrow by just 25 to 40 basis points. On net, the rating transitions reduce excess returns because the price appreciation of upgraded bonds is more than offset by the price drop of downgraded bonds.

The calculations in Exhibit 3 make it easy to identify which sectors of the corporate market offer the greatest relative value. In the 3-year sector, for example, Baa-rated bonds have the largest 1-year excess return, 46.3 basis points, while triple-A bonds have the smallest, 24.2 basis points. For corporates with short maturities, the Baa sector has the greatest relative value because investors are being compensated for the risk of credit deterioration. Three-year, Baa-rated bonds also have wider spreads than higher-rated bonds, but as we will see, bonds with the wide spreads do not always offer the greatest potential for producing high excess returns.

Compared to the 3-year sector, the 10-year sector gives substantially different inferences about relative value. Although 10-year, Baa-rated bonds have an average yield spread of 85 basis points, their 1-year excess return over Treasuries is expected to be just 21.9 basis points. Interestingly, Baa-rated bonds are expected to underperform all other rating classes in the 10-year sector, although Baa-rated bonds trade at much wider spreads than higher-rated bonds. In the 30-

year sector, Baa bonds also underperform higher-rated bonds. The excess return for 30-year Baa bonds is 27 basis points, compared with 35 basis points for double-A and triple-A bonds, and 43 basis points for single-As.

At first glance, it seems paradoxical that Baa bonds offer the greatest value in the 3-year sector, but the least value in the 10- and 30-year sectors. The Baa spread curve increases with maturity, rising from 60 basis points at 3 years to 115 basis points at 30 years. Moreover, the spread between Baa and single-A bonds is 40 basis points at the 30-year maturity, and just 25 basis points for 3-year bonds.

Although spreads on Baa bonds increase with maturity, this is more than offset by their long durations. A 10 basis point spread change has a much larger effect on a portfolio of 10- and 30-year bonds than on a portfolio of 3- and 5-year bonds. Consequently, rating transitions and the associated spread changes have a larger impact on bonds with long durations. Duration has its largest impact on the Baa sector because of the steepness in the credit curve between the Baa and Ba sectors. To have the same expected returns as 30-year single-A bonds, 30-year Baa bonds would need to sell at even wider spreads.

The impact of duration is evident in the ratio of the excess return to the initial yield spread. In the 30-year sector, the excess return on Baa bonds is only 24% as large as the initial spread (27 basis points vs. 115 basis points). In the 3-year sector, however, the excess return for Baa bonds is 77% as large as the initial spread (46 basis points vs. 60 basis points).

In the preceding analysis, we have examined which rating class offers the greatest relative value in a particular maturity sector. An investor may also be interested in examining which maturity sector offers the greatest value for a particular rating category. Consider bonds with Baa ratings. Three-year Baa bonds have the highest excess return, 46.3 basis points, while the 10-year Baa's have the lowest, 21.9 basis points. In the triple-A category, in contrast, the 30-year sector offers the greatest relative value and the 3-year sector the lowest.

It is important to emphasize that these inferences about relative value depend critically on initial yield spreads. The example in Exhibit 3 uses data from the mid-1990s, when yield spreads were very tight by historical standards. At that time, moreover, the credit quality curves were compressed, with Baa-rated bonds trading tight to single-A bonds, and single-A's tight to double-A's. Under the market conditions of the mid-1990s, Baa-bond spreads had very little cushion to absorb rating transition risk. Similarly, 30-year bond spreads for all rating categories were too tight to compensate for unfavorable rating migrations.

By contrast, in 1990–1991 and in 1999–2000, yield spreads for most sectors were significantly wider and credit quality curves were much steeper. For example, Baa-bond spreads were more than 100 basis points wider than the 85 basis point level used in Exhibit 3. The wider spreads at the end of the decade gave the market a larger cushion to absorb losses due to downgrades.

USING MODIFIED RATING TRANSITION MATRICES TO FINE-TUNE PORTFOLIO STRATEGY

We have so far used a rating transition matrix based on more than 20 years of historical data, and we assumed no change in the general level of spreads. Now, we show how the rating transition matrix can be modified to reflect an investor's view about credit quality, and in later sections we'll introduce the effect of spread changes.[2]

There are several reasons why an investor may want to use a rating transition matrix that differs from the one based on the average from historical data. First, the historical average matrix includes several recession years, in which downgrades outnumbered upgrades by a wide margin. If the economy is unlikely to sink into a recession over the investment horizon, an investor may want to use a transition matrix that includes fewer downgrades and more upgrades than the historical norm. In addition, the historical data contain several episodes when entire industries suffered from deteriorating credit quality. Some of the major episodes include industrial downgrades in the merger/LBO wave in the late 1980s; utility downgrades during the nuclear crisis in the early 1980s; financial company downgrades during the credit crunch of the early 1990s; and telecommunications downgrades in 2000 and 2001. These episodes may introduce a bias to the calculation of excess returns, leading to incorrect inferences about relative value.

A second shortcoming of the historical transition matrix is that it only reports the average of the distribution, but investors may also want to assess relative value under best-case and worst-case rating scenarios. For example, by how much do rating transitions differ in recession years versus expansion years? By examining different scenarios for rating transitions, investors can gauge the potential risks and rewards of alternative portfolio weightings. It is easy to examine alternative transition scenarios because the rating agencies publish year-by-year transition matrixes.

Also, the historical rating transition matrix summarizes rating activity for all sectors of the corporate market, but an investor's view about credit quality may differ from sector to sector. For example, an investor may believe that industrial bonds are poised to improve in credit quality, that utilities will suffer a large number of downgrades, and that financials will be stable. Given this outlook for credit quality, the investor should use a customized rating transition matrix for each industry sector.

Portfolio Returns in a "Good Year" for Credit Quality

Exhibit 4 gives the rating transition matrix for a "good year" in credit quality. Compared with the historical average transition matrix given in Exhibit 1, the "good-year" matrix includes twice the percentage of upgrades and half the percentage of

---

[2] The calculations in Exhibit 3 assume that the single, semiannual coupon payment is reinvested at the original coupon rate in the final 6 months of the horizon. Excess returns would be 0.2 to 1.8 basis points lower with a reinvestment rate of 5%. However, inferences about *relative value* are not sensitive to the assumed reinvestment rate.

downgrades (e.g., whereas 7.38% of double-A bonds are downgraded to single-A in the historical matrix, the percentage is 3.69 in the "good-year" matrix).

Excess returns calculated from the "good-year" transition matrix, presented in Exhibit 5, differ in several ways from the returns based on the historical data. First, not surprisingly, returns for the "good year" are greater for each maturity and for each rating category. Second, Baa bonds outperform all other rating categories in all maturity sectors.

Third, long-term and low-quality bonds benefit most from the favorable transitions in credit quality. For example, using the "good-year" transitions, the excess return of Baa-rated, 30-year bonds is 108 basis points, or 94% of the initial spread. Using historical transitions, the excess return is only 27 basis points, or 24% of the initial spread. In contrast, the excess return on 3-year, triple-A bonds is about 24 basis points under both scenarios.

Despite the improved performance under the "good-year" transitions, excess returns for the "good-year" and "base-case" scenarios have one aspect in common: In both cases, excess returns are less than initial spreads. Essentially, despite the low number of downgrades under the "good-year" scenario, rating changes still have a negative net effect on portfolio returns. To produce excess returns that exceed initial yield spreads, the rating transition matrix would need to have a combination of even more upgrades or fewer downgrades.

Portfolio Returns in a "Bad Year" for Credit Quality

Exhibit 6 gives a "bad-year" matrix of rating transitions. Compared with the historical average matrix, the "bad-year" matrix has twice the number of downgrades and half the number of upgrades.

Exhibit 4: Rating Transitions During a "Good Year" for Corporate Credit Quality (%)

Rating at Start of Year	Rating at end of year							
	Aaa	Aa	A	Baa	Ba	B	C or D	Total
Aaa	95.95	3.69	0.36	0.00	0.00	0.00	0.00	100%
Aa	2.26	93.94	3.55	0.16	0.11	0.00	0.00	100%
A	0.20	5.12	91.61	2.67	0.31	0.10	0.00	100%
Baa	0.00	0.42	10.72	85.62	2.73	0.41	0.11	100%

Exhibit 5: Expected Excess Returns Over Treasuries During a "Good Year" for Corporate Credit Quality (1-Year Horizon)

Rating at Start of Year	3-Year		5-Year		10-Year		30-Year	
	Initial Spread	Excess Return	Initial Spread	Excess Return	Initial Spread	Excess Return	Initial Spread	Excess Return
Aaa	25 bp	24.6 bp	30 bp	29.2 bp	35 bp	33.4 bp	45 bp	39.8 bp
Aa	30	29.6	35	33.5	40	35.7	55	46.8
A	35	33.4	45	42.5	55	50.3	75	67.8
Baa	60	57.0	70	62.1	85	69.6	115	107.9

Exhibit 6: Rating Transitions During a "Bad Year" for Corporate Credit Quality (%)

Rating at Start of Year	Rating at end of year							
	Aaa	Aa	A	Baa	Ba	B	C or D	Total
Aaa	83.8	14.8	1.4	0.0	0.0	0.0	0.0	100%
Aa	0.6	84.2	14.2	0.6	0.4	0.0	0.0	100%
A	0.1	1.3	86.4	10.7	1.2	0.4	0.0	100%
Baa	0.0	0.1	2.7	84.2	10.9	1.6	0.4	100%

Exhibit 7: Expected Excess Returns Over Treasuries During a "Bad Year" for Corporate Credit Quality (1-Year Horizon)

Rating at Start of Year	3-Year		5-Year		10-Year		30-Year	
	Initial Spread	Excess Return	Initial Spread	Excess Return	Initial Spread	Excess Return	Initial Spread	Excess Return
Aaa	25 bp	23.4 bp	30 bp	26.7 bp	35 bp	28.5 bp	45 bp	24.1 bp
Aa	30	27.6	35	27.6	40	20.1	55	12.8
A	35	26.7	45	28.2	55	16.9	75	1.4
Baa	60	28.7	70	2.5	85	−57.5	115	−96.9

Excess returns derived from the "bad-year" matrix are given in Exhibit 7. Baa bonds display the most interesting pattern in relative value. In the 3-year sector, Baa bonds still outperform the other rating categories, albeit by only a slight margin, as rating downgrades are not severe enough to offset the ample initial spreads. In the 5-year sector, however, Baa bonds significantly underperform higher-rated bonds, producing an excess return of just 2.5 basis points. Baa bonds post exceptionally poor results in the 10- and 30-year sectors, where they underperform Treasuries by −57 and −97 basis points, respectively.

Strategic Implications

From these examples, it is clear that optimal portfolio strategies depend critically on an investor's view about credit quality. Indeed, the portfolio strategies of two investors may differ radically if they have different credit outlooks. Under the "good-year" scenario for credit quality, the optimal strategy overweights the long end of the corporate market and overweights the Baa sector at all maturities. Under the historical or "base-case" scenario, the optimal portfolio has a balanced mix of short, intermediate, and long corporates, but Baa bonds are overweighted at the short end and underweighted at the long end. Under the "bad-year" scenario, triple-A's and double-A's are overweighted at the long end, and Baa bonds are avoided at all but the shortest maturities.

Again, it is worth reiterating that these strategic recommendations depend on initial spreads. If 30-year, Baa spreads were substantially wider, the sector may be expected to produce superior returns even in the "bad-year" scenario.

ADJUSTING ESTIMATES OF EXCESS RETURNS: ACCOUNTING FOR THE ROLL

A key assumption in the previous analysis is that the generic sector spreads do not change over the investment horizon. Consider a 3-year triple-A bond that trades at a spread of 25 basis points today. The analysis has assumed that the spread will remain at 25 basis points at the end of the 1-year investment horizon, provided that the bond remains triple-A rated.

A shortcoming of this approach is that it does not account for the shape of the corporate credit curve. Assuming that the corporate credit curve has a positive slope, spreads can be expected to tighten as they roll down the curve over the investment horizon. Thus, today's 3-year, triple-A bond that becomes a 2-year, triple-A in 1 year will roll down to the 2-year spread of, say, 23 basis points. Likewise, a 3-year, triple-A bond that migrates to double-A will roll to the 2-year, double-A spread of 28 basis points.

Exhibit 8 displays the expected excess returns calculated under the assumption that the portfolio of bonds rolls down the corporate credit curve over the 1-year investment horizon. Compared with the base case in Exhibit 3, excess returns are higher for all rating and maturity sectors under the rolldown scenario. This improved outlook is to be expected, given that corporate spreads generally increase with maturity.

The adjustment for the rolldown also gives rise to different inferences about relative value. Under the base case that assumes no rolldown (Exhibit 3), Baa bonds have the lowest expected returns in both the 10- and 30-year sectors. Under the rolldown scenario (Exhibit 8), however, Baa bonds have the second highest expected returns in the 10-year sector and the third highest in the 30-year sector.

A COMPREHENSIVE FRAMEWORK FOR STRATEGIC PORTFOLIO ALLOCATIONS

The analysis described to this point has shown that rating transitions can play a major role in portfolio strategy, even if sector spreads do not change. This analysis differs from the traditional approach to corporate bond strategy, which focuses mainly on the impact of spread movements, while ignoring the effect of rating transitions. Clearly, both approaches are flawed because portfolio returns will be affected by both spread movements and rating transitions. In this section, after a quick review of the traditional approach, we present a comprehensive framework that integrates both the traditional and the new approach to strategy.

Exhibit 8: Expected Excess Returns Over Treasuries When Corporate Spreads Roll Down the Credit Curve Over the Investment Horizon (1-Year Horizon)

Rating at Start of Year	3-Year			5-Year			10-Year			30-Year		
	Initial Spread	Horizon Spread	Excess Return	Initial Spread	Horizon Spread	Excess Return	Initial Spread	Horizon Spread	Excess Return	Initial Spread	Horizon Spread	Excess Return
Aaa	25 bp	23 bp	27.9 bp	30 bp	28 bp	36.9 bp	35 bp	34 bp	39.7 bp	45 bp	45 bp	40.1 bp
Aa	30	28	32.8	35	33	40.0	40	39	38.3	55	54	43.0
A	35	32	36.8	45	40	54.3	55	53	53.7	75	74	53.4
Baa	60	55	55.9	70	65	56.7	85	81	45.2	115	114	42.8

Exhibit 9: A Static Rating Transition Matrix

Rating at Start of Year	Rating at end of year							
	Aaa	Aa	A	Baa	Ba	B	C or D	Total
Aaa	100	0	0	0	0	0	0	100%
Aa	0	100	0	0	0	0	0	100%
A	0	0	100	0	0	0	0	100%
Baa	0	0	0	100	0	0	0	100%

The Effect of Spread Changes on Excess Returns: The Traditional Approach

The traditional approach to portfolio strategy analyzes how spread changes affect portfolio returns. In general, the analysis implicitly assumes a rating transition matrix with 100% in the diagonal elements and zeros in the off-diagonal elements (Exhibit 9). With a diagonal transition matrix, the calculation of expected excess returns is almost trivial. Suppose that a portfolio has an average spread of 70 basis points today and that spreads are not expected to change over the 1-year horizon. In this case, the excess return on the portfolio will equal the initial spread, 70 basis points.

Suppose that spreads for all sectors are expected to narrow by 5 basis points over the next year. How will this narrowing affect portfolio returns? As a rule of thumb, the excess return will equal the initial spread minus the change in the spread multiplied by the duration of the portfolio at the end of the period. Hence, if spreads narrow 5 basis points and the end-of-period duration is 5 years, the portfolio with a 70 basis point initial spread will record an excess return of 95 basis points.[3]

Exhibit 10 presents the effect of a 5 basis point spread narrowing for various sectors of the corporate market. The spread change has a disproportionately large impact on the long maturity corporates. For example, 30-year, Baa bonds earn an excess return of 167 basis points, compared with 69 basis points for 3-year, Baa bonds. This finding is not surprising: it merely reflects the long duration of longer-term corporates.

For each maturity sector, the analysis indicates that Baa bonds have the highest excess returns and triple-A bonds have the lowest. For parallel shifts in spreads, the traditional approach always gives the same relative value recommendation: buy low-rated bonds and sell high-rated bonds.

The Effect of Spread Changes on Excess Returns: A Comprehensive Approach

A comprehensive approach to corporate strategy accounts for both spread changes and rating transitions. Exhibit 11 shows the effect of a 5 basis point spread narrowing under the comprehensive approach. In the table, the excess returns are calculated under the assumption that ratings migrate according to historical experience (i.e., Exhibit 3 transitions).

---

[3] Excess return = Initial spread − Change in spread × Duration
= 70 bps − (−5 bps) × 5 = 95 bps

Exhibit 10: Expected Excess Returns Over Treasuries When Corporate Spreads Narrow 5 Basis Points and Ratings Do Not Change Over the Investment Horizon (1-Year Horizon)

Rating at Start of Year	3-Year			5-Year			10-Year			30-Year		
	Initial Spread	Horizon Spread	Excess Return	Initial Spread	Horizon Spread	Excess Return	Initial Spread	Horizon Spread	Excess Return	Initial Spread	Horizon Spread	Excess Return
Aaa	25 bp	20 bp	34.2 bp	30 bp	25 bp	47.1 bp	35 bp	30 bp	67 bp	45 bp	40 bp	100.7 bp
Aa	30	25	39.2	35	30	52.1	40	35	72.0	55	50	110.1
A	35	30	44.2	45	40	62.0	55	50	86.8	75	70	129.1
Baa	60	55	69.2	70	65	86.9	85	80	116.4	115	110	167.2

Exhibit 11: Expected Excess Returns Over Treasuries When Corporate Spreads Narrow 5 Basis Points and Rating Transitions Match Historical Experience (1-Year Horizon)

Rating at Start of Year	3-Year			5-Year			10-Year			30-Year		
	Initial Spread	Horizon Spread	Excess Return	Initial Spread	Horizon Spread	Excess Return	Initial Spread	Horizon Spread	Excess Return	Initial Spread	Horizon Spread	Excess Return
Aaa	25 bp	20 bp	33.4 bp	30 bp	25 bp	45.5 bp	35 bp	30 bp	63.7 bp	45 bp	40 bp	90.1 bp
Aa	30	25	38.1	35	30	48.5	40	35	62.2	55	50	89.8
A	35	30	40.3	45	40	54.3	55	50	69.6	75	70	96.5
Baa	60	55	55.4	70	65	56.8	85	80	53.0	115	110	78.9

The results in Exhibit 11 differ meaningfully from those in the traditional approach (Exhibit 10), where spreads narrow but the portfolio does not experience rating changes. For all maturities and all sectors, the comprehensive approach gives lower estimates for excess returns, a result that occurs because the traditional approach does not account for the probability rating transitions. In addition to giving different estimates of absolute value, the two approaches also give different inferences about relative value. Under the traditional approach, Baa bonds have the greatest relative value in the 30-year sector, 167 basis points. In contrast, under the comprehensive approach, Baa bonds offer the lowest relative value in the 30-year sector, 79 basis points, while single-A bonds give the greatest value, 96 basis points. Clearly, portfolio allocations that focus solely on the outlook for spreads, while ignoring the impact of evolving credit quality, may not perform as expected.

Spread Shifts and Relative Value

In making sector allocation decisions in the corporate bond market, we recommend that investors approach the market with opinions about future credit trends and spread movements. When these opinions are made explicit, it is straightforward to determine which sectors offer the greatest relative value. For example, as discussed in the previous section, if an investor believes that spreads will be 5 basis points tighter and that credit trends will match the historical experience, then the portfolio allocation should overweight long-term and high-rated corporate bonds.

Exhibit 12 gives excess return estimates for a scenario in which spreads widen by 5 basis points and rating transitions follow the historical experience. If an investor believes that this scenario is likely to happen, he or she should overweight short-term corporates and avoid the long end of the corporate sector altogether. Notably, all investment-grade sectors with 30-year maturities underperform Treasuries if spreads widen by 5 basis points over the 1-year investment horizon. Essentially, based on this analysis that used spread data from the mid-1990s, corporate spreads at the long end of the market were not wide enough to cushion against the risk of even a slight widening.

Exhibit 13 presents excess returns when the corporate credit curve steepens. Under this scenario, triple-A spreads are unchanged over the 1-year horizon, double-A spreads are 2 basis points wider, single-A are 4 wider, Baa are 6 wider, and so on. As expected, a steepening of the credit curve, combined with the rating transitions, indicates that Baa bonds should be underweighted in all but the 3-year sector. In addition, single-A bonds also would be underweighted in long maturities relative to the base case, which assumes no spread changes.

In Exhibit 14, excess returns are computed under the assumptions that the spread curve flattens in 2 basis point increments and that rating transitions mirror the historical statistics. In the flattening scenario, Baa bonds have the highest relative value in the 3-, 5-, and 30-year sectors.

Exhibit 12: Expected Excess Returns Over Treasuries When Corporate Spreads Widen 5 Basis Points and Rating Transitions Match Historical Experience (1-Year Horizon)

Rating at Start of Year	3-Year			5-Year			10-Year			30-Year		
	Initial Spread	Horizon Spread	Excess Return	Initial Spread	Horizon Spread	Excess Return	Initial Spread	Horizon Spread	Excess Return	Initial Spread	Horizon Spread	Excess Return
Aaa	25 bp	30 bp	15.0 bp	30 bp	35 bp	11.3 bp	35 bp	40 bp	−0.1 bp	45 bp	50 bp	−20.5 bp
Aa	30	35	19.7	35	40	14.4	40	45	−1.5	55	60	−19.6
A	35	40	21.9	45	50	20.3	55	60	6.3	75	80	−10.7
Baa	60	65	37.1	70	75	23.0	85	90	−9.2	115	120	−23.7

Exhibit 13: Expected Excess Returns Over Treasuries When the Spread Curve Steepens and Rating Transitions Match Historical Experience (1-Year Horizon)

Rating at Start of Year	3-Year			5-Year			10-Year			30-Year		
	Initial Spread	Horizon Spread	Excess Return	Initial Spread	Horizon Spread	Excess Return	Initial Spread	Horizon Spread	Excess Return	Initial Spread	Horizon Spread	Excess Return
Aaa	25 bp	25 bp	23.9 bp	30 bp	30 bp	27.8 bp	35 bp	35 bp	30.6 bp	45 bp	45 bp	32.7 bp
Aa	30	32	25.0	35	37	24.1	40	42	16.7	55	57	11.5
A	35	39	23.6	45	49	23.4	55	59	12.1	75	79	−0.8
Baa	60	66	35.3	70	76	19.6	85	91	−15.4	115	121	−33.6

Exhibit 14: Expected Excess Returns Over Treasuries When the Spread Curve Flattens and Rating Transitions Match Historical Experience (1-Year Horizon)

Rating at Start of Year	3-Year			5-Year			10-Year			30-Year		
	Initial Spread	Horizon Spread	Excess Return	Initial Spread	Horizon Spread	Excess Return	Initial Spread	Horizon Spread	Excess Return	Initial Spread	Horizon Spread	Excess Return
Aaa	25 bp	25 bp	24.5 bp	30 bp	30 bp	29.0 bp	35 bp	35 bp	32.9 bp	45 bp	45 bp	36.5 bp
Aa	30	28	32.8	35	33	38.7	40	38	44.0	55	53	58.2
A	35	31	38.6	45	41	51.2	55	51	63.8	75	71	86.4
Baa	60	54	57.3	70	64	60.2	85	79	59.3	115	109	89.1

These examples illustrate how an investor can translate a well-articulated view of market trends into a strategy for sector allocation. To fine-tune sector allocation decisions, investors should also make projections about spreads and credit trends for the various industry sectors, such as industrials, utilities, financials, and Yankees.

CONCLUDING REMARKS

Yield spreads are a useful starting point for relative-value analysis, but it is essential to recognize that spreads may differ substantially from subsequent excess returns. Over a given investment horizon, excess returns will be partly determined by yield spreads, but they will also be affected by transitions in credit quality and changes in spread relationships. This chapter has developed a methodology that accounts for all of these factors in a framework that ranks sectors according to their expected excess returns. In this framework, a corporate bond sector is not necessarily cheap just because its spreads are wide relative to other sectors. The sector's spreads may be wide for a good reason: if the credit quality of the sector is expected to deteriorate, then spreads need to be wide to compensate for the price risk associated with rating downgrades.

This framework for corporate strategy is analogous to the analysis used in other fixed-income markets. In formulating investment strategy in the Treasury market, for example, investors have become accustomed to viewing forward interest rates as embodying the market's expectation of future interest rates. If forward rates imply that short-term interest rates are expected to rise, an investor may buy or sell longer-term bonds, depending on whether they believe the market is over or underestimating the likelihood of higher future rates. An analogous strategic approach can be implemented in the corporate bond market.

Specifically, today's sector spreads can be interpreted as the market's assessment of future credit trends and spread movements. Thus, when spreads on Baa-rated bonds are tight on a historical basis, the tight spreads can be interpreted as reflecting the market's belief that the Baa sector will experience a combination of few downgrades, an unusually large number of upgrades, or spread narrowing. Basically, tight spreads imply a favorable outlook for credit quality, and wide spreads imply a negative outlook. An investor with a different outlook would bet against the market by shifting their portfolio allocations to other sectors.

Chapter 14
Valuation of Subordinated Structures

Corporate bond portfolio management is a dynamic process in which investors continually reevaluate which sectors of the market have the most attractive tradeoff between risk and expected return. The analysis of corporate bond risk is complicated because risk has many dimensions (see Exhibit 1). The first and most important dimension of risk is the company's financial leverage. Low-leveraged companies with AAA or AA balance sheets have very low risk of default, and as a result their bonds trade at only modest yield premiums to Treasuries. A second dimension of risk is that default rates generally rise over time. Consequently, the term structure of credit spreads is almost always upward sloping for investment-grade companies. Third, earnings volatility varies across industries. That earnings risk usually implies that spreads for cyclical companies are wider than spreads for noncyclical companies, even after accounting for differences in leverage.

A fourth dimension of risk is the seniority of a bond in the company's capital structure. In the event of bankruptcy, holders of senior-secured bonds have first claim on the company's assets, followed by senior-unsecured bonds, subordinated bonds, preferred stock, and, finally, common equity. Subordinated bonds should trade at wider spreads than senior bonds, all other things being equal, because of the risk of a low recovery in the event of default.

Exhibit 1: Dimensions of Corporate Bond Risk

	Low Risk ⟶ High Risk					
Leverage	Low Leverage ⟶ High Leverage					
	AAA	AA	A	BBB	BB	B
Maturity	Short term ⟶ Long Term					
	1-year	3-year	5-year	10-year	30-year	100-year
Industry	Noncyclical ⟶ Cyclical					
	Electrics, Phones	Consumer Products	Services	Banks	Chemicals, Paper	Autos
Seniority	High Seniority ⟶ Low Seniority					
	Senior Secured	Senior Unsecured	Senior Subordinated	Subordinated	Deferrable	Preferred Stock
	Narrow Spreads ⟶ Wide Spreads					

Until recently, buyers of investment-grade bonds rarely analyzed the seniority dimension of risk because the vast majority of corporate bonds were senior-unsecured or, in the case of electric utilities, senior-secured first mortgage bonds. However, the recent explosive growth of the market for deeply subordinated securities has added a new dimension of risk to the corporate market. These securities have similar structures but many names: *trust preferreds*, *debt/equity hybrids*, *deferrable bonds*, *TOPrS*, *MIPS*, and *capital securities*. In this chapter, we refer to these securities as *deferrable bonds*.

In general, deferrable bonds are deeply subordinated in the corporate capital structure. They also give the issuing company the option to defer coupons for up to 5 years in the event of financial distress. The growth of this sector has created the need for a framework to analyze the relative value of deferrable bonds.

This chapter presents a model of valuing subordinated securities. The valuation of most subordinated notes is fairly straightforward because they differ from senior notes only in their recovery value in the event of default. In the case of deferrable bonds, the valuation is slightly more complicated, because it must capture both the low seniority and the risk of deferral before a default. The model in this chapter allows us to estimate a breakeven spread between deferrable bonds and more senior bonds. For example, for Aa-rated companies, the breakeven spread is only 5 basis points (bps) between 30-year deferrable bonds and senior bonds, using a 45% recovery rate for senior bonds, 20% for deferrable bonds, and a 2-year period of deferral before a default. With the same maturity, recovery, and deferral assumptions, the breakeven spread is 9 bps for A-rated companies, 22 bps for Baa-rated companies, and 92 bps for Ba-rated companies. We emphasize that breakeven spreads should vary across industries because default risk, recovery risk, and deferral risk vary across industries. We also emphasize that the model gives only a rough estimate of the risks of deferral and subordination, and that fair value spreads will generally be wider than breakeven spreads.

HISTORICAL RECOVERY RATES AND SENIORITY

The major risk of buying bonds with subordinated priority is that investors have a junior claim in the event of bankruptcy. In general, the more junior the claim, the lower is the post-default price, or recovery value. As discussed in detail in Chapter 11, that risk of a low recovery value can be substantial. In general, bonds with a senior-secured claim have recovered more than 50% in the event of bankruptcy, on average, and some recovery rates have been much higher. By contrast, bonds with a senior-unsecured claim typically recover between 40% and 50% of par, while subordinated bonds have recovery rates that are much lower, often less than 30% of par. Those differences in recoveries imply that bonds with different priorities should be priced with different spreads. Even though a single-A company may have a low probability of default, the yield spread on the company's subordinated securities should be greater than the spread on its senior securities. More-over, the pricing between senior and subordinated securities should mainly reflect the expected difference between senior and subordinated recovery rates, rather than the absolute level of recoveries.

A historical perspective on recovery rates is also important in the analy-sis of deferrable bonds. Deferrable bonds have a very low priority in the corporate capital structure, ranking just above preferred stock. As a result, in the event of bankruptcy, holders of deferrable bonds should expect to recover much less than holders of senior bonds, and even less than subordinated bondholders.

Like preferred stock, deferrable bonds give the issuing company the option to defer coupon payments without triggering a default. In general, coupons can be deferred up to 5 years. However, unlike preferred stock, if coupons are deferred for longer than 5 years, the bond would be in default, which would likely force a bank-ruptcy. In this sense, deferrable bonds have economic characteristics of debt instru-ments, rather than equity, because a company could conceivably defer paying dividends on preferred stock indefinitely without triggering a bankruptcy.

A BREAKEVEN SPREAD MODEL OF CREDIT RISK

Our goal is to build an analytical framework to help understand credit risk, subor-dination, and deferral risk. For senior corporate bonds, the major source of credit risk is the risk of default. For subordinated bonds, investors must also be com-pensated for the risk of a low recovery value in the event of default. Therefore, subordinated bonds should trade at wider spreads than senior bonds, all other things being equal. For deeply subordinated deferrable bonds, investors must be compensated not only for default and recovery risk, but also for the risk that interest may be deferred up to 5 years before a default. Hence, spreads on defer-rable bonds should be wider than spreads on senior bonds and subordinated bonds of the same issuer.

One way to model the credit risk of corporate bonds is to calculate the breakeven spread. The breakeven spread, by definition, tells us the spread that is required on a portfolio of corporate bonds such that the present value of the corpo-rate portfolio will equal the present value of Treasuries. To calculate the breakeven spread, we use a model of the term structure of credit spreads, described in greater detail by Fons.[1] A key parameter in the Fons model is the recovery rate assump-tion. By changing the recovery rate, we can estimate the breakeven spread between senior bonds and subordinated bonds. To analyze deferrable bonds, how-ever, we must modify the Fons model to capture the risk that coupons could be deferred before a default. We use the results from this new model to calculate the breakeven spread between deferrable bonds and standard corporate bonds.

---

[1] Jerome S. Fons, "Using Default Rates to Model the Term Structure of Credit Spreads," *Financial Analysts Journal* (September/October 1994), pp. 25–32.

A Model of Breakeven Spreads for Senior and Subordinated Bonds

In the Fons model of corporate spreads, the breakeven spread depends on the probability of default and the recovery rate in the event of default. A key assumption of the model is that, after a corporate bond is purchased, it is held to maturity or until default. In the event of default, the bond is sold immediately, and the investor receives a fraction (μ_{corp}) of the bond's face value (F) and accrued coupon (C). Given these assumptions, the formula to price the credit risk of a corporate bond with N years to maturity that promises to pay an annual coupon of C is:

$$P_{corp} = \sum_{t=1}^{N} \frac{S_t C + S_{t-1} d_t \mu_{corp}(C+F)}{(1+i)^t} + \frac{S_N F}{(1+i)^N} \tag{1}$$

where

$$S_t = \prod_{j=1}^{t}(1-d_j) = (1-D_t)$$

S_t = the probability of surviving to year t without defaulting (one minus the cumulative default rate for year t; $1 - D_t$)

d_t = the probability that a corporate bond defaults in year t given that the bond has survived to year t without defaulting

i = the yield on a Treasury bond with N years to maturity

C = the coupon on a corporate bond with N years to maturity

F = the face value of the corporate bond

μ_{corp} = the recovery value of the corporate bond in the event of default

$Spread_{corp}$ = $C - i$ = the breakeven spread for a corporate par bond

By using historical data on corporate bond defaults and recovery rates, this model gives the breakeven spread between a portfolio of corporate bonds and a default-free Treasury bond of the same maturity. For par bonds, the breakeven spread is $C - i$. That breakeven spread can be calculated by rearranging the terms in equation (1) and solving for C. Although the model in equation (1) is applicable for bonds with annual coupons, it can be easily modified for bonds with semiannual or quarterly coupons. All the results in this chapter assume that bonds pay interest semiannually.

Cumulative corporate bond default rates are presented in Exhibit 2. This historical data on defaults, which corresponds to D_t in equation (1), was obtained from the Moody's annual default study, covering the period 1970–1995. The default rates are based on the issuer's senior rating. For example, according to the Moody's study, 5.3% of single-A issuers defaulted over a 20-year period ($D_{A\text{-rated},20}$ = 5.3%). Conversely, 94.7% of the single-A issuers survived for the 20-year period without defaulting ($S_{A\text{-rated},20} = 1 - D_{A\text{-rated},20}$ = 94.7%).

Exhibit 2: Cumulative Default Rates on Corporate Bonds

Years	Senior Bond Rating					
	Aaa	Aa	A	Baa	Ba	B
1	0.0%	0.0%	0.0%	0.1%	1.4%	7.6%
2	0.0%	0.0%	0.1%	0.4%	3.8%	14.0%
3	0.0%	0.1%	0.2%	0.7%	6.3%	19.8%
4	0.0%	0.3%	0.4%	1.2%	8.8%	24.7%
5	0.1%	0.4%	0.6%	1.7%	11.5%	28.9%
6	0.2%	0.6%	0.7%	2.2%	13.7%	32.3%
7	0.3%	0.8%	0.9%	2.8%	15.5%	35.1%
8	0.5%	1.0%	1.2%	3.4%	17.4%	37.5%
9	0.6%	1.1%	1.4%	4.0%	19.0%	39.5%
10	0.8%	1.2%	1.8%	4.6%	20.7%	41.6%
11	1.0%	1.3%	2.1%	5.3%	22.5%	42.7%
12	1.2%	1.5%	2.4%	6.1%	24.6%	43.3%
13	1.4%	1.6%	2.7%	6.8%	26 7%	43.7%
14	1.5%	2.0%	3.0%	7.5%	28.4%	44.1%
15	1.7%	2.1%	3.3%	8.3%	30.0%	44.5%
16	1.8%	2.2%	3.7%	9.1%	31.8%	45.0%
17	2.0%	2.5%	4.1%	10.0%	33.2%	45.6%
18	2.2%	2.6%	4.6%	10.8%	34.5%	45.6%
19	2.2%	2.8%	5.1%	11.5%	35.9%	45.6%
20	2.2%	3.0%	5.3%	12.0%	37.3%	45.6%

Source: Moody's Investors Service. Based on data from 1970–1995.

Unfortunately, the Moody's default data is available for only 20 years, but most deferrable bonds have maturities of 30 years or longer. In terms of equation (1), we need values for d_1 through d_{30} but we only have historical data up to d_{20}. To address this problem, we make the simplifying assumption that the *marginal* default rate is constant from year 21 to year 30. Specifically, we set the marginal rate after year 20 equal to the average marginal rate between years 11 and 20:

$$d_t = d = 1 - (S_{20}/S_{11})^{1/10} \quad \text{for all } t > 20$$

Our assumption is consistent with academic studies, which have found that marginal default rates usually flatten out over time, particularly after 10 years.

Breakeven Spreads between Senior and Subordinated Bonds

The breakeven spread model indicates the minimum spread that investors need to be compensated for the risks of default and recovery. For example, consider a portfolio of Baa-rated senior-unsecured bonds. The Moody's default data indicates that about 4.6% of Baa-rated bonds default over a 10-year period. The historical recovery rate for senior-unsecured bonds is about 45% of par. Therefore, using these values in equation (1), the breakeven spread to Treasuries for a portfolio of Baa-rated, senior bonds is 25 basis points (see Exhibit 3). In contrast to 10-year bonds, the breakeven spread for 30-year Baa-rated bonds is 33 bps, a difference that reflects the fact that marginal default rates rise over time. Similarly, the breakeven spread for 10-year and 30-year single-A bonds are 9 bps and 14 bps, respectively.

Exhibit 4 gives breakeven spreads to Treasuries for subordinated bonds. The only difference between these spreads and the spreads for senior bonds in Exhibit 3 is that we use a lower recovery rate, 30% of par in this example. Because they have a lower recovery rate, subordinated bonds have wider breakeven spreads than senior bonds. For example, the breakeven spread for 30-year, Baa-rated subordinated bonds is 42.2 bps, compared with 33.1 bps for 30-year Baa-rated senior bonds.

It is important to note that the breakeven spreads for subordinated bonds are calculated using the recovery rates for subordinated bonds but the default probabilities for senior bonds. Moody's historical default statistics are derived from the issuer's senior rating. Our analysis assumes that default rates are the same for all the bonds of a company, regardless of the bonds' seniority. For our purposes, it does not matter if the subordinated bonds are rated one or two notches lower. All that matters is that they have a lower recovery rate than senior bonds in the event of default.[2]

Exhibit 3: Breakeven Spreads to Treasuries for Corporate Bonds with a 45% Recovery Rate

| | Senior Bond Rating | | | | | |
Years to Maturity	Aaa	Aa	A	Baa	Ba	B
2	0.0	1.4	1.9	11.2	109.4	427.9
3	0.0	2.0	4.5	13.6	121.2	418.8
5	1.3	4.6	6.3	18.4	134.8	394.7
10	3.9	6.5	9.2	25.1	131.4	335.7
30	5.7	8.0	13.9	33.1	131.5	228.2

Exhibit 4: Breakeven Spreads to Treasuries for Bonds with a 30% Recovery Rate

| | Senior Bond Rating | | | | | |
Years to Maturity	Aaa	Aa	A	Baa	Ba	B
2	0.0	1.8	2.5	14.3	139.4	547.6
3	0.0	2.6	5.8	17.3	154.6	536.0
5	1.7	5.9	8.0	23.4	171.9	505.0
10	5.0	8.3	11.7	31.9	167.5	429.2
30	7.3	10.2	17.7	42.2	167.6	291.3

[2] Credit risk depends on both the probability of default and the recovery value in the event of default. In most rating categories, the probability of default is the dominant risk. Fridson points out that while a subordinated bond may have a B-rating, the company's senior bonds will generally be rated one or two notches higher. (See Martin Fridson and M. Christopher Garman, "Valuing Like-Rated Senior and Subordinated Debt," *Journal of Fixed Income* (December 1997), pp. 83–93.) Historical default statistics are based on the senior rating. As a result, the default risk of a B-rated senior bond of one company is higher than the default risk of a B-rated subordinated bonds of another company. Fridson finds that B-rated senior bonds generally trade at wider spreads than B-rated subordinated bonds.

*Exhibit 5: Breakeven Spreads Between Bonds with a 30%
Recovery Rate and Bonds with a 45% Recovery Rate*

Years to Maturity	Senior Bond Rating					
	Aaa	Aa	A	Baa	Ba	B
2	0.0	0.4	0.5	3.1	30.0	119.8
3	0.0	0.6	1.2	3.7	33.3	117.2
5	0.4	1.3	1.7	5.0	37.1	110.3
10	1.1	1.8	2.5	6.9	36.1	93.5
30	1.6	2.2	3.8	9.1	36.1	63.1

Exhibit 5 gives the breakeven spread between portfolios of senior bonds and portfolios of subordinated bonds for selected ratings and maturities. These breakeven spreads are simply the difference between the spreads in Exhibits 3 and 4. Notice that the breakeven spreads are wider for bonds with lower ratings. For example, in the 30-year sector, the breakeven spread between subordinated and senior debt is 2.2 bps for Aa-rated companies, compared with 3.8 bps for single-A companies, 9.1 bps for Baa companies, and 36.1 bps for Ba companies. This widening across ratings reflects the fact that lower-rated companies have a greater risk of default, which implies a greater risk that holders of sub debt will actually realize a low recovery value.

A MODEL OF BREAKEVEN SPREADS FOR SUBORDINATED, DEFERRABLE BONDS

The analysis of deferrable bonds differs slightly from that of standard bonds. The deferral feature should be viewed as an option that the company would exercise only if it falls into financial distress. In the event of financial distress, a company would institute measures to conserve cash. First, it will stop paying dividends on common stock, and, if its financial position deteriorates further, it may defer dividends on preferred stock. If the financial distress becomes acute, the company may also stop paying coupons on its deferrable bonds. During a deferral period, the coupons on a deferrable bond accrue interest at the coupon rate.

Once a company defers coupons, the situation could be resolved in one of two ways. First, the company could recover from financial distress. In that event, holders of deferred bonds will be made whole because they will receive the coupons that were deferred, plus interest-on-interest.

Second, if the measures to conserve cash fail to alleviate the financial distress, the company may eventually default on its debt and be forced into bankruptcy. In that event, holders of deferrable bonds will have a junior claim relative to senior bondholders and other senior lenders. The claim will be equal to the face value of the deferrable bonds, plus the deferred coupons, plus the interest-on-interest on the deferred coupons.

Therefore, to estimate the breakeven spread on deferrable bonds, we must modify the Fons model to account for the possibility that coupons may be deferred for as long as 5 years before a default. In this modified model, the price of a deferrable bond is given by the following formula:

$$P_{defer} = \sum_{t=1}^{N} \frac{S_t C_{defer,\,t} + S_{t-1} d_t \mu_{defer}(C_{defer,\,t} + F)}{(1+i)^t} + \frac{S_N F}{(1+i)^N}$$

$$- \sum_{h=1}^{H} \sum_{t=1}^{N} \frac{S_{t-1} d_t C_{defer,\,t-h}}{(1+i)^{t-h}}$$

$$+ \sum_{h=1}^{H} \sum_{t=1}^{N} \frac{S_{t-1} d_t \mu_{defer} C_{defer,\,t-h}(1 + C_{defer,\,t-h})^h}{(1+i)^t} \qquad (2)$$

where

H = the number of years that interest is deferred before a default in year t

$C_{defer,t}$ = the coupon in year t on a deferrable bond with N years to maturity ($C_{defer,t} = 0$ for all $t \leq 0$)

μ_{defer} = the recovery value of the deferrable bond in the event of default

$Spread_{defer}$ = $C_{defer} - i$ = the breakeven spread on a deferrable bond sold at par

This modified model includes two terms that did not appear in the previous model of breakeven spreads. First, suppose a company defaults in year t. In that event, the model captures the risk that the company may have deferred coupons in years $t-1$, $t-2$, and up to year $t-H$. That risk is captured by the following term:

$$\sum_{h=1}^{H} \sum_{t=1}^{N} \frac{S_{t-1} d_t C_{defer,\,t-h}}{(1+i)^{t-h}}$$

where $C_{defer,t} = 0$ for all $t \leq 0$.

Second, in a bankruptcy, the investor's claim will include the deferred coupons and the accrued interest on deferred coupons. That claim is given by the following term:

$$\sum_{h=1}^{H} \sum_{t=1}^{N} \frac{S_{t-1} d_t \mu_{defer} C_{defer,\,t-h}(1 + C_{defer,\,t-h})^h}{(1+i)^t}$$

where $C_{defer,t} = 0$ for all $t \leq 0$.

Note that the model accounts for the risk that the recovery value for a deferrable bond (μ_{defer} in equation (2)) may be much lower than the recovery rate for a senior bond (μ_{corp} in equation (1)).

Exhibit 6: Breakeven Spreads to Treasuries on 30-Year Deferrable Bonds with a 10% Recovery Rate in the Event of Default

Years between Deferral and Default	Senior Bond Rating					
	Aaa	Aa	A	Baa	Ba	B
0	9.4	13.2	22.8	54.3	216.0	376.1
1	10.0	14.1	24.5	58.3	234.6	407.5
2	10.8	15.1	26.2	62.4	253.3	435.3
3	11.5	16.0	27.9	66.7	271.8	459.3
4	12.3	17.0	29.7	71.0	290.0	479.7
5	13.1	18.0	31.5	75.4	307.7	496.8

Breakeven Spreads on Deferrable Bonds

Exhibit 6 gives breakeven spreads to Treasuries on 30-year deferrable bonds for various ratings under the assumption of a 10% recovery in the event of default. Again, we emphasize that the calculations are based on the senior rating of the issuer because the senior rating is the measure of default risk that is relevant in equation (2). In the exhibit, the breakeven spreads are based on alternative assumptions for the number of years of deferral before a default. For example, for a portfolio of A-rated issuers, the breakeven spread is 31.5 bps if coupons are deferred for 5 years before the default, but the breakeven spread is only 24.5 bps if the deferral period is only 1 year. If there is no deferral period ($H = 0$), then the model is exactly the same equation (1), and the breakeven spread is 22.8 bps for A-rated issuers.

As expected, the model indicates that deferral risk has a greater impact on lower-rated bonds. For example, consider bonds that defer coupons 1 year before a default. For Aaa-rated companies, the breakeven spread is 10.0 bps, while for Baa-rated companies the spread is 58.3 bps, a difference of 48.3 bps. Now consider bonds that defer 5 years before a default. In this case, Aaa companies have a 13.1 bps breakeven spread, while Baa companies have a 75.4 bps breakeven spread, a difference of 62.3 bps. The impact of deferral risk on breakeven spreads is even greater for bonds rated below investment-grade.

Determining the Expected Length of a Deferral Period

These alternative estimates of the breakeven spread raise a fundamental question: How long would a company defer coupons before a default? Our answer cannot be guided by historical data because the market for deferrable bonds was only created in recent years with the advent of MIPS and TOPrS. However, it is important to remember that deferral is a precarious state of existence. We expect that most companies will either fail or recover within 1 or 2 years after deferring coupons. It is possible, but not likely, that a company could survive on the knife edge of bankruptcy for up to 5 years.

Although there is no history of deferrals on corporate bonds, it is helpful to look at the deferral history in the preferred stock market. According to a

Moody's study, 53% of preferred issues that deferred dividends subsequently defaulted.[3] Among those issuers that defaulted, 43% of the defaults occurred simultaneously with the deferral ($H = 0$), 29% of the defaults occurred within 1 year after the deferral ($H = 1$), 14% between 1 and 2 years ($H = 2$), 3% between 2 and 3 years ($H = 3$), 2% between 3 and 4 years ($H = 4$), and 2% between 4 and 5 years ($H = 5$). The remaining 7% of the defaults occurred more than 5 years after the preferred dividend deferral. This history from the preferred stock market suggests that defaults on deferred bonds are likely to occur within 1 or 2 years after a coupon deferral.

BREAKEVEN SPREADS BETWEEN DEFERRABLE BONDS AND STANDARD CORPORATE BONDS

What is the breakeven spread between deferrable bonds and standard bonds? The previous analysis indicates that there is no single answer. The breakeven spread should be wider for low-rated issuers because of their greater risk of default. In addition, the breakeven spread should vary across industries to reflect differences in expected recovery rates and in the expected length of a deferral period. We believe prudent investors will examine a variety of assumptions for recovery values and deferral periods.

In Exhibit 7, we present a menu of breakeven spreads between deferrable securities and more senior standard bonds. All of the breakeven spreads are calculated for semiannual bonds with 30-year maturities, the most common maturity for deferrable bonds. In the exhibit, the recovery rates for senior bonds range from 75%, 60%, 45%, 30%, and 10%, deferrable bond recoveries range from 30%, 20%, 10%, and 0, and the deferral periods before a default range from 0 to 5 years.

The key finding of this analysis is that the spread premium is more sensitive to the difference between expected recovery rates on deferrable bonds and senior bonds than it is to the absolute level of recovery rates. This can be seen by comparing two panels in Exhibit 7: (1) senior recovery rates of 60% and deferrable recoveries of 30%, and (2) senior recovery rates of 30% and deferrable recoveries of 0%. In both scenarios, the difference between senior and deferrable recoveries is 30%. For investment-grade companies, the breakeven spreads in this first scenario are generally only 1 to 4 bps tighter than the spreads in the second scenario. By contrast, breakeven spreads change by larger amounts in other scenarios that vary the *difference* between senior and deferrable recoveries (e.g., 60% senior recovery and 30% deferrable versus 60% senior and 10% deferrable). This finding has important implications for the relative value of deferrable bonds in different industries.

---

[3] Lea V. Carty, "Moody's Preferred Stock Ratings and Dividend Impairment," *Journal of Fixed Income* (December 1995), pp. 95–103.

Exhibit 7: Breakeven Spreads between 30-Year Deferrable Bonds and Senior Bonds

Recovery Rate on Senior Bond   75%
Recovery Rate on Deferrable Bond   30%

Years between Deferral and Default	Aaa	Aa	A	Baa	Ba	B
0	4.7	6.6	11.4	27.1	108.1	188.2
1	5.2	7.3	12.7	30.2	121.6	210.1
2	5.8	8.0	14.0	33.3	134.9	229.1
3	6.3	8.8	15.3	36.5	147.8	245.1
4	6.9	9.6	16.7	39.8	160.3	258.3
5	7.5	10.3	18.1	43.1	172.3	269.1

Recovery Rate on Senior Bond   75%
Recovery Rate on Deferrable Bond   20%

Years between Deferral and Default	Aaa	Aa	A	Baa	Ba	B
0	5.7	8.1	14.0	33.2	132.2	230.5
1	6.3	8.9	15.4	36.7	148.2	257.0
2	7.0	9.7	16.9	40.3	164.1	280.1
3	7.6	10.6	18.4	44.1	179.7	299.8
4	8.3	11.5	20.0	47.9	194.9	316.4
5	9.0	12.3	21.6	51.7	209.6	330.1

Recovery Rate on Senior Bond   75%
Recovery Rate on Deferrable Bond   10%

Years between Deferral and Default	Aaa	Aa	A	Baa	Ba	B
0	6.8	9.5	16.5	39.2	156.5	273.0
1	7.4	10.4	18.1	43.2	175.1	304.3
2	8.1	11.4	19.8	47.4	193.7	332.2
3	8.9	12.4	21.6	51.6	212.2	356.2
4	9.7	13.4	23.3	56.0	230.4	376.6
5	10.5	14.3	25.2	60.4	248.2	393.7

Recovery Rate on Senior Bond   75%
Recovery Rate on Deferrable Bond   0%

Years between Deferral and Default	Aaa	Aa	A	Baa	Ba	B
0	7.8	11.0	19.0	45.3	180.7	315.6
1	8.6	12.0	20.8	49.8	202.1	352.3
2	9.3	13.1	22.7	54.4	223.8	385.3
3	10.2	14.2	24.7	59.2	245.4	414.1
4	11.0	15.3	26.7	64.1	267.0	438.9
5	11.9	16.4	28.7	69.1	288.2	460.1

Recovery Rate on Senior Bond   60%
Recovery Rate on Deferrable Bond   30%

Years between Deferral and Default	Aaa	Aa	A	Baa	Ba	B
0	3.1	4.4	7.6	18.1	72.2	125.9
1	3.6	5.1	8.9	21.1	85.7	147.8
2	4.2	5.8	10.2	24.3	99.0	166.7
3	4.8	6.6	11.5	27.5	111.9	182.7
4	5.4	7.4	12.9	30.8	124.5	195.9
5	6.0	8.1	14.3	34.1	136.4	206.7

Exhibit 7 (Continued)

Recovery Rate on Senior Bond   60%
Recovery Rate on Deferrable Bond   20%

Years between Deferral and Default	Aaa	Aa	A	Baa	Ba	B
0	4.2	5.9	10.1	24.1	96.3	168 1
1	4.8	6.7	11.6	27.7	112.3	194.6
2	5.4	7.5	13.1	31.3	128.2	217.8
3	6.0	8.4	14.6	35.0	143.8	237.5
4	6.7	9.3	16.2	38.8	159.0	254.0
5	7.4	10.1	17.8	42.7	173.7	267.7

Recovery Rate on Senior Bond   60%
Recovery Rate on Deferrable Bond   10%

Years between Deferral and Default	Aaa	Aa	A	Baa	Ba	B
0	5.2	7.3	12.7	30.2	120.6	210.6
1	5.9	8.2	14.3	34.2	139.2	242.0
2	6.6	9.2	16.0	38.3	157.8	269.8
3	7.3	10.2	17.7	42.6	176.3	293.8
4	8.1	11.2	19.5	46.9	194.5	314.2
5	8.9	12.1	21.3	51.3	212.3	331.3

Recovery Rate on Senior Bond   60%
Recovery Rate on Deferrable Bond   0%

Years between Deferral and Default	Aaa	Aa	A	Baa	Ba	B
0	6.3	8.8	15.2	36.2	144.8	253.2
1	7.0	9.8	17.0	40.7	166.2	289.9
2	7.8	10.9	18.9	45.4	187.9	322.9
3	8.6	12.0	20.9	50.2	209.5	351.7
4	9.5	13.1	22.9	55.1	231.1	376.6
5	10.4	14.2	24.9	60.1	252.3	397.7

Recovery Rate on Senior Bond   45%
Recovery Rate on Deferrable Bond   30%

Years between Deferral and Default	Aaa	Aa	A	Baa	Ba	B
0	1.6	2.2	3.8	9.1	36.1	63.1
1	2.1	2.9	5.1	12.1	49.6	85.0
2	2.6	3.6	6.4	15.2	62.9	104.0
3	3.2	4.4	7.7	18.5	75.9	120.0
4	3.8	5.2	9.1	21.7	88.4	133.2
5	4.4	5.9	10.5	25.0	100.4	144.0

Recovery Rate on Senior Bond   45%
Recovery Rate on Deferrable Bond   20%

Years between Deferral and Default	Aaa	Aa	A	Baa	Ba	B
0	2.6	3.7	6.3	15.1	60.3	105.4
1	3.2	4.5	7.8	18.6	76.3	131.9
2	3.8	5.3	9.3	22.2	92.2	155.0
3	4.5	6.2	10.8	26.0	107.8	174.8
4	5.2	7.1	12.4	29.8	123.0	191.3
5	5.9	7.9	14.0	33.6	137.7	205.0

Exhibit 7 (Continued)

Recovery Rate on Senior Bond   45%
Recovery Rate on Deferrable Bond   10%

Years between Deferral and Default	Aaa	Aa	A	Baa	Ba	B
0	3.7	5.1	8.9	21.1	84.5	147.9
1	4.3	6.0	10.5	25.1	103.2	179.2
2	5.0	7.0	12.2	29.3	121.8	207.1
3	5.8	8.0	13.9	33.5	140.3	231.1
4	6.5	9.0	15.7	37.9	158.5	251.5
5	7.3	9.9	17.5	42.3	176.3	268.6

Recovery Rate on Senior Bond   45%
Recovery Rate on Deferrable Bond   0%

Years between Deferral and Default	Aaa	Aa	A	Baa	Ba	B
0	4.7	6.6	11.4	27.2	108.8	190.5
1	5.4	7.6	13.2	31.7	130.2	227.2
2	6.2	8.7	15.1	36.3	151.8	260.2
3	7.1	9.8	17.1	41.1	173.5	289.0
4	7.9	10.9	19.1	46.0	195.0	313.8
5	8.8	12.0	21.1	51.0	216.3	335.0

Recovery Rate on Senior Bond   30%
Recovery Rate on Deferrable Bond   30%

Years between Deferral and Default	Aaa	Aa	A	Baa	Ba	B
0	0.0	0.0	0.0	0.0	0.0	0.0
1	0.5	0.7	1.3	3.0	13.5	21.9
2	1.1	1.5	2.6	6.2	26.8	40.9
3	1.6	2.2	3.9	9.4	39.8	56.8
4	2.2	3.0	5.3	12.7	52.3	70.0
5	2 8	3.7	6.7	16.0	64.2	80.9

Recovery Rate on Senior Bond   30%
Recovery Rate on Deferrable Bond   20%

Years between Deferral and Default	Aaa	Aa	A	Baa	Ba	B
0	1.0	1.5	2.5	6.0	24.2	42.3
1	1.6	2.3	4.0	9.5	40.1	68.7
2	2.3	3.1	5.5	13.2	56.0	91.9
3	2.9	4.0	7.0	16.9	71.6	111.6
4	3.6	4.9	8.6	20.7	86.9	128.2
5	4.3	5.7	10.2	24.6	101.5	141.9

Recovery Rate on Senior Bond   30%
Recovery Rate on Deferrable Bond   10%

Years between Deferral and Default	Aaa	Aa	A	Baa	Ba	B
0	2.1	2.9	5.1	12.1	48.4	84.8
1	2.7	3.8	6.7	16.1	67.0	116.1
2	3.5	4.8	8.4	20.2	85.6	144.0
3	4.2	5.8	10.1	24.5	104.2	168.0
4	5.0	6.8	11.9	28.8	122.4	188.3
5	5.8	7.8	13.7	33.2	140.1	205.4

Exhibit 7 (Continued)

Recovery Rate on Senior Bond　　　30%
Recovery Rate on Deferrable Bond　0%

Years between Deferral and Default	Aaa	Aa	A	Baa	Ba	B
0	3.1	4.4	7.6	18.1	72.7	127.4
1	3.9	5.4	9.4	22 6	94.1	164.1
2	4.7	6.5	11.3	27.3	115.7	197.1
3	5.5	7.6	13.3	32.1	137.4	225.9
4	6.4	8.7	15.3	37.0	158.9	250.7
5	7.2	9.8	17.3	42.0	180.1	271.9

Recovery Rate on Senior Bond　　　10%
Recovery Rate on Deferrabie Bond　10%

Years between Deferral and Default	Aaa	Aa	A	Baa	Ba	B
0	0.0	0.0	0.0	0.0	0.0	0.0
1	0.7	0.9	1.6	4.0	18.6	31.4
2	1.4	1.9	3.3	8.1	37.3	59.2
3	2.1	2.9	5.1	12.4	55.8	83.2
4	2.9	3.9	6.8	16.7	74.0	103.6
5	3.7	4.8	8.7	21.2	91.7	120.7

Recovery Rate on Senior Bond　　　10%
Recovery Rate on Deferrable Bond　0%

Years between Deferral and Default	Aaa	Aa	A	Baa	Ba	B
0	1.0	1.5	2.5	6.0	24.3	42.6
1	1.8	2.5	4.4	10.5	45.7	79.3
2	2.6	3.6	6.3	15.2	67.3	112.3
3	3.4	4.7	8.2	20.0	89.0	141.1
4	4.3	5.8	10.2	24.9	110.5	166.0
5	5.1	6.8	12.2	29.9	131.7	187.1

The breakeven spreads in Exhibit 7 can be tailored to a specific industry, such as banks, electric utilities, and industrials. Let's start with banks. Nearly all long-term bank holding company bonds are subordinated. Thus, in the case of bank holding companies, our analysis should focus on the spread between subordinated bonds and deferrable bonds. Given the junior status of holding company debt relative to bank-level debt, we expect that subordinated bonds of bank holding companies would have a small recovery value of, say, 10% or less. Deferrable bonds would probably have an even lower recovery rate. Furthermore, banks and other financial institutions usually cannot survive for long without access to the capital markets. As a result, a deferral of coupons would probably be resolved quickly, with either a full payment of coupons or a default.

Therefore, in the case of bank holding companies, we believe investors should expect low recovery rates and a short deferral period. For example, let's assume a 10% recovery rate on subordinated debt, a 0% recovery rate on deferrable bonds, and a 1-year period of deferral before a default. Under those assumptions, the breakeven spreads between deferrable bonds and subordinated notes for Aa-rated 30-

year bank holding company bonds is only 2.5 bps (see the last panel in Exhibit 7). The spread is small because (1) Aa-rated companies have a low probability of default, even over 30 years; (2) subordinated bonds and deferrable bonds are assumed to have similar (low) recovery rates; and (3) the assumed period of deferral before a default is only 1 year. Using these same recovery and deferral assumptions, the breakeven spreads would be 4.4 bps for single-A banks, 10.5 bps for Baa banks, and 45.7 bps for Ba-rated banks. In summary, when analyzing bank holding company bonds, investors should require a relatively small breakeven spread between deferrable bonds and subordinated notes because of the combination of a small difference in recovery values and the relatively short period of deferral.

In the electric utility sector, the relative value of deferrable bonds will reflect different assumptions for recovery and deferral. In contrast to banks, most electric utility bonds are senior and secured by first mortgages. When an electric company falls into bankruptcy, first mortgage bonds usually have a high recovery value at the time of default. In addition, unlike financial institutions, an electric utility may be able to survive for several years after invoking a deferral option during a period of financial distress. For example, in the mid-1980s, several electrics with nuclear problems deferred dividends and subsequently recovered.

For the electric utility bonds, we would advise using relatively high recovery rates. As a base case, let's assume a 60% recovery rate on senior bonds, 30% on deferrable bonds, and a 3-year period of interest deferral before a default. These recovery and deferral assumptions give rise to breakeven spreads of 6.6 bps for Aa-rated electric portfolios, 11.5 bps for single-A electrics, 27.5 bps for Baa electrics, and 111.9 bps for Ba-rated electrics. These spreads are wider than the breakeven spreads that we calculated for banks. Even though we have assumed higher recovery rates for electric bonds, we have also assumed a larger *difference* in recovery rates between senior bonds and deferrable bonds. As noted, breakeven spreads between deferrable and senior bonds depend mainly on the difference in recovery rates, rather than the absolute level of recoveries. In addition, the wider breakevens for electric bonds reflect the assumption of a longer period of coupon deferral.

Finally, for most industrial companies, we believe that historical studies provide a reasonable benchmark for expected recovery rates and deferral periods. Let's consider a 45% recovery rate for senior bonds, 20% for deferrable bonds, and a 2-year period of deferral before a default. These assumptions give rise to breakeven spreads of 5.3 bps for double-A issuers, 9.3 bps for single-A, 22.2 bps for Baa, and 92.2 bps for Ba-rated issuers.

LIMITATIONS OF BREAKEVEN SPREAD ANALYSIS

Breakeven spreads should be interpreted with caution. Our estimates of breakeven spreads depend critically on the assumptions of the model (hold to maturity or until default) and on the historical data for default rates and recovery rates. Specifically, the model uses default rates based on the experience over the last 25 years, but investors are concerned about default risk over the next 30 years.

A number of factors could cause default rates and recovery values in the future to differ significantly from the past. For example, Congress could tinker with the tax law that favors debt financing over equity; legislative changes in the bankruptcy code could either improve or harm the rights of bondholders; further deregulation, or even re-regulation, of banks, utilities, and other industries could have a dramatic impact on sector risk characteristics; and the growth rate of the economy will no doubt have some impact on the rate of corporate bond defaults. In addition, mergers between high-rated and low-rated companies often result in significant changes in bond ratings, as well as discontinuous jumps in default risk. While it is important to have an analytical framework for analyzing bonds with different risk characteristics, it is also important to remember that a lot of things can change during the life of a 30-year bond. Predicting defaults and recoveries is an imprecise science.

We also emphasize that breakeven spreads are not fair value spreads. Specifically, the breakeven spread model assumes risk neutrality, but most investors are not risk neutral. Buyers of investment-grade bonds do not want to break even with Treasuries. Buyers of deferrable bonds should not want to just break even with other investors who buy senior bonds. Investors should require that deferrable bonds include an additional spread premium as compensation for the uncertainty of default, recovery, deferral, and liquidity. As demonstrated in Chapter 7, the spread premium to compensate for trading costs and liquidity can be substantial.

Furthermore, breakeven spread analysis assumes that investors care only about default risk. The analysis does not account for other events that may affect the timing of cash flows or the market value of a deferrable bond. For example, in some circumstances, a company that defers coupons may recover from its financial distress, rather than falling into bankruptcy. That event does not affect the breakeven spread because, if a company recovers, investors will receive deferred coupons plus interest-on-interest, an outcome that has the same present value as an uninterrupted payment of coupons. Also, because the analysis focuses solely on default, it ignores the risk of a downgrade. Some investors face internal or regulatory guidelines that compel them to sell bonds that are downgraded to below investment-grade.

In light of these limitations, the breakeven spread is only a rough measure of the credit risk on a deferrable bond, and it should not be interpreted as a fair value spread. The fair value spreads will be wider than the breakeven spread because investors will want to receive some reward for risk taking. In the mid-1990s, when deferrable bonds were introduced to a broad cross-section of investors, the credit environment was benign, spreads were relatively tight, and the spread premium on deferrable bonds was low because investors had a high tolerance for risk. In the late 1990s, when the credit environment became less friendly, the spread premium on deferrable bonds increased because investors demanded a higher premium for taking risk.

SUMMARY AND CONCLUSIONS

Deferrable bonds have two risks that are not present in plain vanilla corporate bonds. First, most are deeply subordinated in the corporate capital structure, indicating that bondholders would have a very junior claim on the company's assets in the event of default and bankruptcy. Second, most structures allow companies to defer coupons for up to 5 years. In this chapter, we have presented a model that accounts for these risks and calculates breakeven spreads between deferrable bonds and senior corporate bonds.

We do not recommend that investors use the model to make pinpoint estimates of the fair value spread on a deferrable bond. The model has too many limitations and the future is too uncertain. Rather, the point of the model is to develop an intuitive framework for analyzing the relative value of deferrable bonds. Accordingly, our model gives rise to several intuitive findings.

First, deferrable bonds with low ratings should trade at wider spreads than higher-rated bonds, regardless of whether spreads are measured relative to Treasuries or to senior bonds of the same company. The lower the rating, the greater is the risk of default.

Second, deferrable bonds with low expected recovery values should trade at wider spreads to Treasuries than deferrable bonds with high recovery values, all other things being equal. The lower the recovery value, the greater is the severity of loss.

Third, the spread between a deferrable bond and a senior bond is more sensitive to the difference between their expected recovery values than it is to the *absolute level* of recoveries. The greater the difference, the greater is the severity of loss, and the wider the spread.

Fourth, the spread between deferrable bonds and senior bonds should vary across industries because recoveries vary across industries. For the banking industry, the largest sector in the deferrable bond market, a default would probably result in low recoveries for all bonds (senior, subordinate, or deeply subordinated deferrable bonds). Consequently, in the case of bank holding company bonds, low recovery values to all bondholders imply a relatively small spread between deferrable bonds and subordinated bonds.

Fifth, the spread on a deferrable bond should be relatively wide when it seems possible that the company could defer coupons for a long period before a default. The longer expected period of deferral, the greater is the investor's risk of lost cash flows.

Sixth, although most structures give the issuer the option to defer coupons for up to 5 years, we believe that a deferral would usually be resolved within 1 or 2 years, with either a full recovery of deferred coupons or a default. Deferral is a precarious state that would only happen to companies in financial distress.

Finally, the expected period of deferral may vary across industries. Financial companies, in particular, are unlikely to defer coupons for a long period because they rely heavily on access to the capital markets.

Section IV

Redemption Analysis

Chapter 15

Early Redemption Features

Included in the indenture of a bond issue may be provisions allowing the redemption of the issue prior to the stated maturity date. There can be a provision granted to the issuer to redeem the bond issue early and/or a provision that grants the bondholder the right to force the issuer to redeem the bond prior to the stated maturity date. These provisions are commonly referred to as "embedded options." In this chapter we describe these embedded options. In later chapters we see how these options affect the value and the interest rate risk of a corporate bond. In Chapter 4 we covered one embedded option, the right of the bondholder to convert to common stock.

CALL AND REFUNDING PROVISIONS

A call provision in a corporate bond gives the issuing company the option of retiring outstanding principal before the stated maturity date. In most cases, the provision allows for the redemption in whole or in part. The method of redemption is usually stated as "by such method as it shall deem fair and appropriate" or "fair and equitable," and is left to the discretion of the trustee. Most directly or privately placed issues provide for pro rata redemption in case of partial calls. This means that all holders will have the same percentage of their holdings redeemed (subject to the restrictions imposed by the minimum denominations). Very few publicly issued bonds have pro rata redemption features; rather, the redemption is done "by lot." This is, essentially, the random selection of bonds through the use of computer programs. In practice, most bonds are called in full, rather than in part.

Redemption dates are usually stated as "on or after" a certain date. In some cases, however, the bonds may only be redeemed on certain dates, often the interest payment dates. Prior notice must be given—usually 30 to 45 days preceding the redemption date.

Critical Features of a Call Provision

The critical features of a call provision are (1) the exercise price, (2) the date the issuer is allowed to exercise the option, and (3) any restrictions on exercising the option.

The Exercise Price

A company wanting to retire a debt issue prior to maturity usually must pay a premium over the par value for the privilege.

Exhibit 1: Redemption Schedule for
Anheuser-Busch Companies, Inc.
10% Sinking Fund Debentures due July 1, 2018

Redemption

The Debentures will be redeemable at the option of the Company at any time in whole or in part, upon not fewer than 30 nor more than 60 days' notice, at the following redemption prices (which are expressed in percentages of principal amount) in each case together with accrued interest to the date fixed for redemption:

If redeemed during the 12 months beginning July 1,

1988	110.0%	1999	104.5%
1989	109.5%	2000	104.0%
1990	109.0%	2001	103.5%
1991	108.5%	2002	103.0%
1992	108.0%	2003	102.5%
1993	107.5%	2004	102.0%
1994	107.0%	2005	101.5%
1995	106.5%	2006	101.0%
1996	106.0%	2007	100.5%
1997	105.5%	2008 and thereafter	100.0%
1998	105.0%		

provided, however, that prior to July 1, 1998, the Company may not redeem any of the Debentures pursuant to such option, directly or indirectly, from or in anticipation of the proceeds of the issuance of any indebtedness for money borrowed having an interest cost of less than 10% per annum.

Source: Prospectus dated June 23, 1988.

Regular versus Special Redemption Prices The initial call premium on long-term debt traditionally has been the interest coupon plus par or the initial reoffering price. Exhibit 1 shows a call schedule for Anheuser-Busch Companies 10% Sinking Fund Debentures due July 1, 2018. The prices shown in an issue's call schedule are called *regular* or *general redemption prices*.

There are also *special redemption prices* for debt redeemed through the sinking fund and through other provisions such as the maintenance and replacement fund, with the proceeds from the confiscation of property through the right of eminent domain, and through the release and substitution of property clauses. The special redemption price is usually par.

Date the Issuer Is Allowed to Exercise the Option

The Anheuser-Busch debentures are *currently callable* (i.e., the company may redeem the bonds at any time at the above general redemption prices subject only to the 10-year prohibition against lower cost refunding). Other issues may not be called for any reason for a certain number of years. For example, there may be a 5-year noncallable period for long-term debt.

If a debt does not have any protection against early call, then it is said to be a currently callable issue, as is the Anheuser issue. But most new bond issues, even if currently callable, usually have some restrictions against certain types of early redemption. The most common restriction is prohibiting the refunding of the bonds with lower-cost debt for a certain number of years. Both call prohibitions and refunding prohibitions may be for a certain number of years or for the issue's life. Bonds that are noncallable for the issue's life are more common than bonds that are nonrefundable for life but otherwise callable.

Restrictions on Exercising: Callable versus Noncallable

Many investors are confused by the terms "noncallable" and "nonrefundable." Call protection is much more absolute than refunding protection. While there may be certain exceptions to absolute or complete call protection in some cases (such as sinking funds and the redemption of debt under certain mandatory provisions), it still provides greater assurance against premature and unwanted redemption than does refunding protection. Refunding prohibition merely prevents redemption only from certain sources, namely the proceeds of other debt issues sold at a lower cost of money. The holder is only protected if interest rates decline, and the borrower can obtain lower-cost money to pay off the debt. The Anheuser bonds could not be redeemed prior to July 2, 1998, if the company raises the funds from a new issue with an interest cost lower than 10%. There is nothing to prevent the company from calling the bonds within the 10-year refunding protected period from debt sold at a higher rate (although it normally wouldn't do so) or from funds obtained through other means. And that is exactly what Anheuser did. Between December 1993 and June 1994, it called $68.8 million of these relatively high-coupon bonds at 107.5% of par with funds from its general operations.

Some prospectuses specifically clarify refunding and redemption. For example, Cincinnati Gas & Electric Company's prospectus for the 10⅛% First Mortgage Bonds due in 2020 states:

> The Offered Bonds are redeemable (though CG&E does not con-
> template doing so) prior to May 1, 1995 through the use of earn-
> ings, proceeds from the sale of equity securities and cash
> accumulations other than those resulting from a refunding oper-
> ation such as hereinafter described. The Offered Bonds are not
> redeemable prior to May 1, 1995 as a part of, or in anticipation
> of, any refunding operation involving the incurring of indebted-
> ness by CG&E having an effective interest cost (calculated to
> the second place in accordance with generally accepted financial
> practice) of less than the effective interest cost of the Offered
> Bonds (similarly calculated) or through the operation of the
> Maintenance and Replacement Fund.

Refunding means to replace an old bond issue with a new one, often at a lower interest cost. In the Florida Power & Light case a judge said:

> The terms "redemption" and "refunding" are not synonymous. A
> "redemption" is simply a call of bonds. A "refunding" occurs

when the issuer sells bonds in order to use the proceeds to redeem an earlier series of bonds. The refunding bond issue being sold is closely linked to the one being redeemed by contractual language and proximity in time so that the proceeds will be available to pay for the redemption. Otherwise, the issuer would be taking an inordinate risk that market conditions would change between the redemption of the earlier issue and the sale of the later issue.

Beginning in early 1986 a number of industrial companies issued long-term debt with extended call protection and refunding protection. A number are noncallable for the issue's life, such as Dow Chemical Company's 8⅝% debentures due in 2006 and Atlantic Richfield's 9⅞% debentures due in 2016. The prospectuses for both issues expressly prohibit redemption prior to maturity. These noncallable-for-life issues are referred to as "bullet bonds."

Redemption dates are usually stated as "on or after" a certain date. In some cases, however, the bonds may only be redeemed on certain dates, often the interest payment dates. Prior notice must be given—usually 30 to 45 days preceding the redemption date.

Some high-yield bond issues started to appear in 1992 granting the issuer a limited right to redeem a portion of the bonds during the noncall period if the proceeds are from an initial public stock offering. In a few cases, proceeds from a secondary stock offering are also a permissible source of funds. Called "claw-back" provisions, they merit careful attention by inquiring bond investors since they can lose bonds at the point in time just when the issuer's finances have been strengthened through access to the equity market. Also, the redemption may reduce the amount of the outstanding bonds to a level at which their liquidity in the aftermarket may suffer.

Make Whole Provisions Since the mid-1990s, a sizable percentage of new corporate bond offerings have included *make-whole call provisions*. These provisions differ considerably from standard call provisions. Under a make-whole call provision, the call price is set as a yield spread over a reference Treasury security. Therefore, the call price varies with the price of the reference Treasury security. Under a standard call provision, by contrast, the call price is set in stone along a rigid schedule that does not depend on the level of Treasuries or any other security.

The economics of a make-whole call provision are best illustrated by way of example. On December 12, 1998, Service Corporation issued a 6% bond due December 15, 2005, at a spread of 150 basis points to the U.S. Treasury 5⅞% of November 2005. That Service Corp. bond included a make-whole call provision that allowed the company to redeem the issue at 15 basis points above a comparable Treasury (i.e., the 5⅞s of November 2005).

The effective price at which this bond could be called has changed significantly since the bond was first issued. For example, on February 21, 2000, the yield of the U.S. Treasury 5⅞s of 2005 had risen to 6.75%, indicating that the Service Corp. bond could be called at a yield of 6.90%, or a price of $95.74. Less than 1 year later, the yield on the comparable U.S. Treasury had fallen to 4.80%, implying a call price for the Service Corp. bond of $104.53.

Almost always, the make-whole call spread is only a fraction of the new issue spread. In the Service Corp example, the make-whole spread of 15 basis points was only one-tenth the 150 basis point spread at new issue. Thus, investors will almost always benefit from the exercise of a make-whole call, just as they would benefit if a bond dealer made a bid for their bonds at an unusually tight spread. By contrast, a corporation's decision to exercise a standard call provision does not depend on the spread to Treasuries, but on the level of interest rates. When interest rates fall and corporate borrowers exercise standard call options, investors lose.

Although make-whole call provisions have become a standard feature in the market, they are rarely exercised. Because the spreads on make-whole call provisions are generally set at very tight levels, corporations find it uneconomical to exercise these options and refinance at wider spreads. Nevertheless, make-whole call provisions do serve an important function: they make a corporation's capital structure more flexible. Modern corporations are constantly reshaping their businesses through mergers, spin-offs, and divestitures. These M&A transactions are often coupled with financial restructurings, such as the retirement of outstanding debt. Rather than retire debt through tender-offers (discussed later in this chapter), which are costly and have a low success ratio, companies find it preferable to retire debt by exercising make-whole call options. When this happens, investors win.

Outright Redemptions

For want of a better term we will use *outright redemptions* to mean the retirement of debt at the general redemption price. The proceeds for the outright redemption need not come from lower-cost borrowings, nor is the redemption triggered by the maintenance and replacement fund, the sinking fund, or the release and substitution of property provisions found in bonded debt. Outright redemptions are also known by some as "cash calls," but this term could also be applied to other types of debt calls. The point to remember is that they can occur at any time unless there are call prohibitions; investors should not be lulled by a nonrefunding provision.

Archer-Daniels-Midland Company (ADM) presents an interesting case. On May 12, 1981, the company sold $250 million of 7% debentures due May 15, 2011, and $125 million of 16% sinking fund debentures, also maturing on May 15, 2011. Both issues were currently callable, the 7% to original issue discounts at par and the full coupon 16s at a premium. The 16% debentures also had the standard 10-year prohibition against lower-cost refunding. Subsequent to these offerings ADM raised money in 1982 and 1983 through lower-cost borrowings. It also sold common equity on January 28, 1983, raising more than $131 million, and again on June 1, 1983, raising another $15.45 million. At 6:19 p.m. on June 1, 1983, the Dow Jones Capital Markets News Wire Service announced that the company would redeem on August 1, at 113.95 plus accrued interest of $33.78, all of the outstanding 16% sinking fund debentures due May 15, 2011.

The corporate bond market was in an uproar. This call was well within the 10-year refunding protected period. One investment banking firm sued to bar the redemption, claiming that "investors expected the debentures to continue on the market until 1991 (which) kept the trading value of the debt at about $1,250 per $1,000 face value and misled investors into believing the debentures would continue to be traded . . . it wouldn't have purchased the debentures if it believed Archer-Daniels would redeem the bonds so soon." People don't often sue in debt redemptions unless they stand to lose money. Here, the plaintiff lost money. Several weeks before the call, it purchased $15,518,000 face amount of the debentures at 125.25 each, and the day before, another $500,000 principal amount at 120. If these bonds were held to the call date, the principal loss would have been nearly $1,784,000.

The company said that the proceeds for this redemption came from the sale of the common stock. The shelf registration prospectus dated March 22, 1983, may have indicated that the high-coupon debt might be in jeopardy when it said in the Use of Proceeds section, "The proceeds will be used, as required, for general corporate purposes, including working capital, capital expenditures and possible acquisitions of, or investments in, businesses and assets, and the repayment of indebtedness originally incurred for general corporate purposes." The debenture prospectus said that "The proceeds will be used, as required, for general corporate purposes." This is part of the standard boilerplate found in many financing documents. The plaintiff claimed that ADM was not allowed, by the issue's terms, to call the bonds from lower-cost funds, and it pointed to the 1982 and 1983 debt financings. It contended that the money raised from the common stock sales was little more than a subterfuge for circumventing the refunding protection provided in the indenture. It also alleged securities fraud by ADM, as the company did not reveal its own interpretation of the redemption language and would contemplate redemption if it felt that doing so was in its own best interests.

The court upheld ADM's right to call the sinking fund debentures with the proceeds from the sales of common shares, saying the redemption was within the company's legal rights and in accordance with the indenture. It pointed to the strict "source" of funds argument, which came up several years earlier in the case of the redemption of preferred stock with the proceeds of common stock. The ADM decision was an important event in the modern corporate bond world because it substantially eroded the effectiveness of standard refunding provisions. The ADM episode, and others like it, also contributed to a structural change in the market toward bullet bonds, discussed as follows.

Why Companies Issue Callable Bonds

Why do companies include call provisions in bond deals? The most simple, obvious, and straightforward answer is that companies would like to have the ability to refinance high-coupon debt if interest rates fall. However, academic research has rejected the idea that interest rate volatility plays a role in a firm's decision to issue callable bonds. In an efficient market, according to the academics, the refinancing of high-cost bonds with low-cost bonds is a zero-sum game, where the gains to a company that refinances bonds are equal to, and exactly offset by, the losses to bond investors. Presumably, bond investors are rational enough to understand the rules of the game. Bondholders should demand higher yields on callable bonds than on noncallable bonds, with the yield difference equal to the value of the embedded call option. In this framework, companies gain nothing by issuing callable bonds because investors will force them to pay full value for the option.

To explain why callable bonds exist, financial academics have developed several interesting theories. The theories argue that companies include call provisions to reduce the so-called agency costs of debt. For example, one theory is based on the idea that companies possess unique and favorable information about their future earnings prospects. According to this theory of asymmetric information, because bond investors do not have access to the favorable information, the company is forced to pay too high an interest rate on its bonds. A company can solve this problem by selling bonds with embedded call options. Specifically, after the favorable information is later revealed, investors will re-evaluate the company's credit quality, allowing the company to call old bonds and refinance with lower-cost bonds.

Agency theories provide elegant answers to the callable bond puzzle. Unfortunately, the theories fall down in the face of rigorous empirical analysis. For example, the asymmetric information theory predicts that companies issuing callable bonds will release favorable information at a future date, but there is no evidence that good news is revealed more frequently for callable bonds than for noncallable bonds. Similarly, if companies really wanted to minimize their cost of debt, they would select a call date that corresponds to the date when favorable information is later revealed. However, the data show no meaningful variation in call dates. For academics, the existence of callable bonds remains a mystery.[1]

Investment-Grade Callable Bonds: A Vanishing Breed

Before the 1980s, nearly all investment-grade bonds included call options. In the late 1970s and early 1980s, less than 5% of new corporate bond offerings were noncallable before maturity (see Exhibit 2). However, noncallable bonds became more common in the early 1980s, particularly after 1982, the year the Securities and Exchange Commission passed Rule 415, when 21% of new offerings provided call protection for life. From 1982 forward, the frequency of corporate bonds that included call provisions declined further, and by the early 1990s, callable bonds had almost vanished from the new issue market for investment-grade bonds.

---

[1] Leland E. Crabbe and Jean Helwege, "Alternative Tests of Agency Theories of Callable Corporate Bonds," *Financial Management* (Winter 1994), pp. 3–20.

Exhibit 2: Noncallable Have Supplanted Callable Bonds
Noncallable Bonds as a Percentage of All New Issues with Investment-Grade Ratings

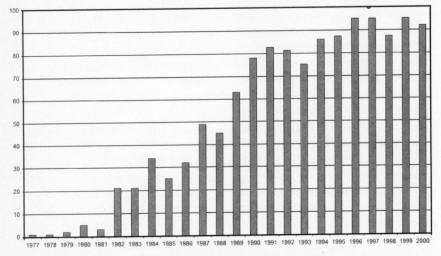

Source: Chase Securities

During the 1980s and 1990s, the maturity structure of the corporate bond market also changed dramatically. In the late 1970s, new corporate bond issues had an average maturity of 25 years, but the average fell to less than 13 years by the 1990s. The near disappearance of callable bonds, therefore, is partly a consequence of the shortening of maturities because bonds with shorter maturities are less likely to include call provisions. The shortening of bond maturities does not adequately explain the trend toward noncallable bonds, however, because the proportion of noncallable offerings increased at all maturities, including longer maturities. Indeed, bonds with 30-year maturities almost always included call options until the late 1980s, but since that time the vast majority of 30-year bonds are noncallable for life (see Exhibit 3). New issues of bonds with 5-year and 10-year maturities displayed an equally dramatic disappearance of the callable structure.

The Reasons Why Callable Bonds Nearly Vanished

The shift toward noncallable bonds coincided with several important developments in the fixed-income markets. One such development was the emergence in the late 1980s of the market for swap options. The swap market has made it easier for investors and borrowers to determine the market value of call options embedded in corporate bonds. The value of embedded call options cannot be observed directly because the provisions cannot be resold. However, options on interest rate swaps, which can be bought and sold in the open market, can be tailored to replicate the terms of embedded call options. The price of a swap option, therefore, serves as a close proxy for the price of an embedded call option. Consequently, investors and bond dealers can now engage in arbitrage, which narrows price discrepancies between the bond market and the swap market.

The rapid growth of the market for mortgage-backed securities is another development that may have indirectly caused the shift toward noncallable corporate bonds. The mortgage market has several features in common with the corporate bond market. As with callable corporate bonds, redemptions of mortgage-backed securities become more likely when interest rates fall. The major investors in corporate bonds, such as insurance companies, pension funds, and investment companies, also are the major investors in mortgage-backed securities. To reduce the risk of a mismatch between the duration and convexity of their assets and the duration and convexity of their liabilities, these investors typically would prefer to hold noncallable securities. However, as a result of the growth of the market for mortgage-backed securities—outstandings of mortgage pools and trusts increased from $95 billion in 1979 to $870 billion in 1989 and $2292 billion in 1999—the proportion of fixed-income securities that is subject to refinancing risk has increased dramatically. Investors in fixed-income securities may have responded to the increase in aggregate call risk by demanding higher yields on their holdings of callable debt, including callable corporate bonds. Faced with an increased cost of issuing callable bonds, many corporations have decided to shift their financing toward noncallable debt.

Exhibit 3: Long Maturity Bonds are Now Mostly Noncallable
Noncallable Bonds as a Percentage of All New Issues with Investment-Grade Ratings and Maturities of 30 Years or Longer

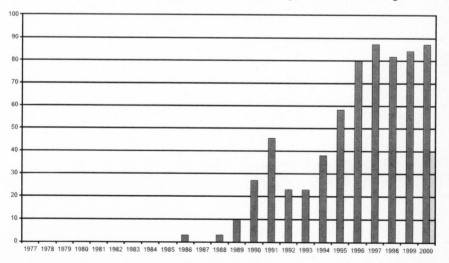

Source: Chase Securities

Another important development was the decline in market interest rates since the early 1980s, which allowed corporations to refinance billions of dollars of high-coupon debt. In particular, in 1986 and 1993, when rates fell to cyclical lows, calls of corporate bonds soared to record levels. In response to this unpleasant learning experience with bond calls, investors may have subsequently demanded higher compensation for holding callable bonds.

Finally, the establishment of the swap and mortgage-backed securities markets has spawned a large volume of theoretical and empirical research devoted to the analysis of duration, convexity, and options on fixed-income securities. That research, and the accompanying development of applied computer software, has provided investors with more effective tools for valuing embedded call options. It is likely that increased knowledge about option pricing prompted investors to demand more compensation for holding callable securities.

The emergence of the swap market, the growth of the market for mortgage-backed securities, the large volume of bond calls in the 1980s and 1990s, and the development of option-pricing models all made investors more aware of call risk in the corporate bond market. Whether one or more of these factors was more important than the others in causing the shift toward noncallable offerings and the increase in call prices is difficult to determine because they all developed concurrently and gradually. Moreover, because all of the developments are interrelated, it seems likely that each played a role in reshaping the structure of the corporate bond market.

Sinking and Purchase Funds

A *sinking fund* is a provision allowing for a debt's periodic retirement or amortization over its life span. It can also require the periodic deposit of funds or property into a reserve for the loan's eventual retirement or the maintenance of the value of the collateral securing it; this is called an *improvement fund* or a *sinking and improvement fund*. It is more common to have the sinking fund applied to the current extinguishment of debt and not to have the funds build up for use at maturity.

A variety of sinking fund types are found in publicly issued debt. They include mandatory specific sinking fund, nonmandatory specific sinking fund, and nonspecific sinking funds. We discuss each as follows.

Mandatory Specific Sinking Fund

The most common is the *mandatory specific sinking fund*, requiring the periodic redemption of a certain amount of a specific debt issue. The 10¼% May Department Stores Company Debentures due 2018 has a typical mandatory specific sinking fund as follows:

> The Company will provide for the retirement by redemption of $12,500,000 of the principal amount of the Debentures Due 2018 on June 15 of each of the years 1999 to and including 2017 at the principal amount thereof, together with accrued interest to the date

of redemption. The Company may also provide for the redemption of up to an additional $25,000,000 principal amount . . . annually, . . . such optional right being non-cumulative. The Company may (1) deliver outstanding Debentures Due 2018 (other than Debentures Due 2018 previously called for redemption) and (2) apply as a credit Debentures Due 2018 which have been redeemed either at the election of the Company or through the application of a permitted optional sinking fund payment, in each case in satisfaction of all or any part of any required sinking fund payment, provided that such Debentures Due 2018 have not been previously so credited.

The above tells us that the company must retire 5% of the $250 million issue each year starting June 15, 1999 (1 year after the refunding protection expires). The May Company payments retire 95% of the issue prior to maturity, leaving $12,500,000 as the final amount due on June 15, 2018. The company has the right to increase sinking fund payments by another $25,000,000, for a total of $37,500,000. This is a "triple-up" option. More often, issues have a "double-up" option allowing the retirement of bonds in an additional amount equal to the mandatory requirement. This provision is often referred to as an *accelerated sinking fund provision*, and the value of this benefit to the issuer must be priced into a bond, as with a call provision.

Usually the issuer may deliver debentures acquired by it instead of paying cash and calling the required bonds at par. In high interest rate periods, when the bonds are trading below par, companies would normally prefer to buy the bonds through open market purchases instead of calling them at the higher price; this can lend price support to the bonds. In times of lower interest rates, open market purchases are costly and unnecessary. The company can merely deposit cash with the trustee for a par call; this could depress the bond's price. Thus, depending on the coupon rate relative to the current market rate, a sinking fund may have varying effects on the bond's price and liquidity.

Nonmandatory Specific Sinking Fund

There is also the *nonmandatory specific sinking fund*, the most prevalent type in electric utility company issues. The $100 million 7½% bonds of Public Service Electric and Gas Company due on March 1, 2023, require the retirement of $2.5 million principal amount of bonds each March 1, 1994, through 2022. The company may satisfy the sinking fund, in whole or in part, by delivering bonds acquired through open market purchases or other means, by paying cash to the trustee who will call bonds for redemption at 100, or by the utilization of unfunded property additions or improvements at 60% of their cost. Property credits so utilized cannot be further employed under the mortgage.

Utilities are usually considered consumers of capital, for they engage in large, ongoing construction projects. As they need to borrow fairly regularly, the application of property credits helps reduce the demands on the capital markets. (It makes no sense to pay off debt on the one hand only to have to go back to the market to raise the money that was just paid out.) Utilization of property credits conserves cash and still helps maintain the integrity of the collateral behind the bonds. In some cases, a company may be able to authenticate and simultaneously cancel new bonds specifically authorized for this purpose. This usually is done against unfunded property additions and thus reduces the amount of new debt the company can issue.

Nonspecific Sinking Funds

Specific sinking funds apply to just the named issue. There are also *nonspecific sinking funds* of both the mandatory and nonmandatory variety. The nonspecific sinking fund, also known as a *funnel*, *tunnel*, *blanket*, or *aggregate sinking fund*, is based on the outstanding amount of a company's total bonded indebtedness. If mandatory, the sinking fund must be satisfied by bonds of any issue or issues selected by the company. If nonmandatory, the company may utilize certain property credits in fulfilling the sinking fund requirement. In most cases the redemption price for bonds called under the funnel sinking fund is par, but for some it could be the general or regular redemption prices.

The funnel sinking fund may be deceptive. Usually 1% of all bonds outstanding, this can amount to a large requirement, especially if the total amount is applied against a single issue. For example, if bonded debt of $3 billion consists of issues ranging in size from $50 million to $200 million, the annual funnel requirement is $30 million; this equals 15% to 60% of any one issue. When interest rates and cash needs are high, companies normally utilize unfunded property additions if they are able to do so. But actual bond retirement provides a way to redeem high-coupon debt (usually at par) when interest rates are down. In some cases, however, a maximum of 1% of a specific issue may be retired in any one year if the call is within 5 years of issuance (the refunded protected period).

Most sinking funds operate annually, but some are effective semiannually. Again, most sinking funds are based on a specific percentage of the original amount issued, or a fixed amount of bonds, which remains the same until the entire issue is retired. But other issues' sinking fund payments may increase periodically. Each payment may be higher than the preceding one, or payments might be level for several years, then step up for another few years, and so forth. There are even some sinking funds that increase for several years and then decrease for a few more years.

Because of the risk of exhausting gas supplies, some gas pipeline company indentures provide for the acceleration of the sinking fund in the event that estimates of the reserve lives of the company's proven gas reserves decline.

Maintenance and Replacement Funds

A *maintenance and replacement fund* requires a company to annually determine the amounts needed to satisfy the fund and any shortfall. (Not all utility indentures provide for them, and some companies have eliminated or sharply modified them in recent years.) The requirement is based on a formula, usually 15% or so of adjusted gross operating revenues, but some are based on a much smaller percentage (such as 2% to 2.5%) of depreciable mortgaged property or a percentage of bonded debt. The difference between what is required and the actual amount expended on maintenance is the shortfall. The shortfall is usually satisfied with unfunded property additions, but it can be satisfied with cash or, in some cases, maintenance and replacement fund credits from prior years. The cash can be used for the retirement of debt or withdrawn upon the certification of unfunded property credits.

Redemption Through the Sale of Assets and Eminent Domain

Bondholders want the borrower to maintain and preserve the value of the collateral securing the debt. The fact that the debt may be overcollateralized does not necessarily mean that management has free rein over the use and disposition of the excess collateral and any proceeds therefrom. But the lender has no right to impose undue restrictions on the borrower's ability to sell plant and property if doing so is deemed desirable from the standpoint of sound business practices. The secured lender has the right to adequate protection. If a company has $100 million of bonded debt outstanding secured by $200 million of plant, property, and equipment, the $100 million surplus collateral provides additional protection for the bond owner. If the company feels that it is prudent to sell some of the property securing that debt, it should be allowed to do so (release the property from the mortgage lien) and substitute either cash or other property so that the total value of the collateral will not be reduced. The cash can be used to retire bonds or buy additional collateral. This type of situation is covered by *release and substitution of property clauses.*

The release and substitution of property clause of Arizona Public Service as described in its prospectuses is fairly clear.

> When not in default under the Mortgage, the Company may obtain the release from the lien thereof of (a) property that has become unserviceable, obsolete or unnecessary for use in the Company's operations, provided that it replaces such property with, or substitutes for the same, an equal value of other property and (b) other property that has been sold or otherwise disposed of, provided that the Company deposits with the Trustee cash in an amount, or utilizes as a credit net Property Additions acquired by the Company within the preceding five years and having a fair value (not more than Cost), equal to the fair value of the property to be released.

Arizona has utilized this method of debt redemption a couple of times. In late 1984, it retired $100 million of its 16% First Mortgage Bonds due 1994 at 100, with the proceeds from the sale of its gas distribution assets. In early 1987, it redeemed $150 million of its 11½% First Mortgage Bonds due June 1, 2015, also at par. The proceeds for this redemption came from the sale and leaseback of its portion in the Unit #2 of the Palo Verde nuclear power plant. These bonds had been issued only in June 1985.

Of course, investors are hurt most when their high-yield, premium-priced bonds are called at par or the special redemption price, and most electric utility mortgage issues use the special redemption price for these special calls. A few provide for the regular redemption prices. Because the redemption prices used in any special redemption may vary between issues of the same company, prudent investors should carefully review the bonds' documentation to ascertain the call prices and the issues' vulnerability to special call.

Unsecured debt usually has no special redemption prices or requirements for prepayment in the event of asset sales. However, there may be exceptions, especially in the case of some sub investment-grade debt. Remember, do not confuse call protection with refunding protection. Redemptions of unsecured debt do occur within the refunding-protected period where the funds came from the sale of assets.

Many utility bond issues contain provisions regarding the taking or confiscation of assets by a governmental body through its right of eminent domain or the disposition of assets by order of or to any governmental authority. In a number of cases, bonds must be redeemed if the company receives more than a certain amount in cash.

Net Worth, Merger, and Other Redemptions

The great increase in merger and acquisition activity, including leveraged buyouts and other corporate restructurings, has caused some companies to include other special debt retirement features in their indentures. For example, the maintenance of net worth clause is included in the indentures of many lower-rated bond issues of the 1980s. In this case, an issuer covenants to maintain its net worth above a stipulated level. If its net worth falls below that specified amount for a certain period (usually two consecutive quarters), the company must begin redeeming its debt at par. The redemptions, often 10% of the original issue, are mostly on a semi-annual basis and must continue until the net worth recovers to an amount above the stated figure. In many cases, the company is only required to "offer to redeem" the stated amount. An offer to redeem is not mandatory on the bondholders' part; only those holders who want their bonds redeemed need do so. In a number of instances in which the issuer is required to call bonds, the bondholders may elect not to have bonds redeemed. This is not much different from an offer to redeem. It may "protect" bondholders from the redemption of the high-coupon debt at lower interest rates. However, if a company's net worth declines to a level low enough to activate such a call, it would probably be prudent to have one's bonds redeemed.

The minimum net worth requirement varies from approximately 45% to 65% of the issuer's net worth at the time the debt was issued, depending on the company. The definition of net worth, or net tangible assets, will also vary among issuers. The prospectuses talk about generally accepted accounting principles and frequently include only common shareholders' net worth, but some also include preferred stock. Intangible assets, such as goodwill, patents, trademarks, and unamortized deferred charges, normally are excluded from the calculation of tangible net worth. But again, definitions vary among issues. Obviously the definition is very important, and one cannot always rely on the prospectus since it may include no definition or only an incomplete one.

There are a few other ways companies can (or must) extinguish debt prior to maturity. The issues of some finance companies and others with a considerable amount of accounts receivable have provisions allowing the issues to be redeemed if the receivables decline below a certain amount. While not mandatory, this provision can protect debtholders from a weakening of credit due to a substantial decline in the issuer's asset base. It allows the issuer to reduce its debt burden, assuming that it still has the wherewithal to do so. Of course, if the company elects to redeem debt, it will most likely choose from the higher-coupon issues. This provision has been infrequently invoked—if ever—by major debt issuers. A call could occur if there were a serious recession and receivables declined by a substantial amount. It could also be activated if a company sold or transferred receivables to another corporation as part of a reorganization, restructuring, or liquidation.

Tenders

Another debt retirement method is the *tender*. While it may be more costly for the borrower than a straight cash call, it allows debt to be retired even if it is noncallable. Also, tenders don't force the holder to give up the bonds. To encourage holders to tender their bonds, the issuer must offer a price above what others are willing to offer, namely a buyback price above the market.

Most tenders allow a company to retire debt at a fixed or predetermined price, and rather quickly since tenders are usually open for only a limited time. A simple open-market purchase of bonds usually occurs over a longer period, leaving the purchaser subject to changes in market conditions. Open-market purchases may prove to be less costly than a tender offer if interest rates rise and prices decline, but it is less likely to permit a company to achieve its debt retirement goals. Of course, the market can go against the company using a fixed-price tender offer, with the result that few bonds are repurchased. Therefore, in recent years, an increasing number of issuers are using a "fixed-spread tender offer," which allays its interest rate risk during the tender period. In this type of tender the purchase price of the bond is based on the yield to maturity of some other issue (most often a U.S. Treasury issue) maturing on or close to the first refunding or call date of the subject corporate bond plus a fixed spread expressed in basis points.

With the Dutch auction tender, the sellers rather than the buying company set the prices they wish to receive. At the end of the tender period, the buyer reviews all of the tenders received and determines the highest price it is willing to pay. It then buys all of the bonds tendered at and below the maximum acceptable tender price. The Dutch auction allows the market to set the tender price.

Proceeds for a tender can come from any source. Holders need not tender their bonds, and the company is within its rights to offer to repurchase them even within the refunding-protected period.

In general, it makes good sense for investors to consider tender offers because if enough bonds are repurchased, the few remaining could very well become virtually unmarketable, or at least, very illiquid. If listed, they could be delisted. Traders will not ordinarily take into their positions bonds that can't be readily resold. Also, with fewer bonds outstanding the holder is more likely to lose a greater percentage of its holdings through the sinking fund.

PUT PROVISIONS

A put provision gives the investor the option to either ask for repayment on a certain date(s) prior to the stated maturity or to hold the bond to either the next put date (if any) or maturity. This provision benefits the investor in a rising interest rate environment should the market rate rise above the issue's coupon rate.

Most put bonds are putable at par during a 30-day window 1 month before the put date. For example, holders of the J.C. Penney Company 6.9% of 8/15/2026, putable in 8/15/2003, must notify the company of their intention to put between 6/15/2003 and 7/15/2003. Most putable bonds have only one put option and a fixed coupon rate; there are some issues with multiple put options and issues with step-up putables in which the coupon rate increases after the put date.

Some put provisions have certain restrictions on the holder's right of redemption. For example, a few issues provide that not more than a certain amount of bonds will be repurchased from any holder at any one put date. In addition, there may be an aggregate limitation on the total amount of bonds that may be redeemed at any one time.

Structure of the Putable Bond Market

Investment-grade companies issued a wide variety of putable bond structures. By structure we mean the maturity and the amount of time since issues when the issue can be put. This is commonly denoted by X PUT Y where X is the number of years to maturity at issuance and Y is the number of years before the issue can be put by the bondholder. The structure of the putable bond market has changed over time. For example, in the 1980s, 42% of the new issues were putable within 5 years after the time of issuance. During that period, bonds with 10PUT5 structures accounted for 22% of the put bond volume, while bonds with 30PUT10 structures were less common, representing less than 8% of the volume. Between 1994 and 1996, by contrast, only 20% of the new issues were putable within 5 years. In the recent period, 10PUT5 bonds have accounted for 10% of the volume, while 30PUT10 bonds have garnered a 36% share of the market. Moreover, the 20PUT10 bond, a common structure in the 1980s, has all but disappeared in recent years.

The final maturity of putable bonds has also lengthened over time. In the 1980s, 72% of the put bonds had final maturities of 20 years or less, but between 1994 and 1996 these bonds represented just 21% of the putable bond volume. In addition, about 8% of the putable bonds in the 1980s also included call options, but only one corporate bond in recent years has been both callable and putable.

These changes in the structure of the putable market mainly reflect a shift in investor demand, rather than a change in issuer preferences. In the late 1980s, many corporations were willing to issue putable bonds with long maturities and long periods before the first put, but the investor bid was concentrated in the short end of the market. In recent years, investor demand for long-dated, high-duration, and highly convex bonds (concepts that we describe in Chapter 6) is evident not only in the structure of the putable market, but also in the overall corporate market, as is manifested by the strong demand for 30-, 40-, and 100-year bullet bonds.

Understanding Quoted Spreads on Putable Bonds

Yields on putable bonds are quoted as a spread above a benchmark Treasury yield. In practice, the pricing of putable bonds can seem confusing because some bonds are quoted as a spread-to-put-date, while other bonds are quoted as a spread-to-maturity. For example, consider the case of a 30PUT10 bond, such as the 7.35% put bond issued by KN Energy Inc. in July 1996. That bond was sold at par to yield 7.35%. The spread-to-put-date was 51 bps above the 10-year Treasury yield, while the spread-to-maturity was 29 basis points above the 30-year Treasury yield.

There is no "correct" way to quote the spread on a putable bond. The price of a putable bond is the same regardless of whether its yield is quoted as a spread-to-put-date or a spread-to-maturity. However, the choice of quoting as a spread-to-put-date or a spread-to-maturity reveals how investors perceive the benefits of the embedded option. When a bond is quoted as a spread-to-put-date, the investor is viewing the bond as a short-term bond with an option to extend into a longer maturity bond. When a bond is quoted as a spread-to-maturity, then the investor is viewing the bond as a long-term bond with an option to shorten the maturity to the put date.

For example, a 30PUT10 bond can be analyzed as either:

1. a 10-year bond with an option to extend the bond's maturity by 20 years, or
2. a 30-year bond with an option to shorten the bond's maturity by 20 years.

Under the first view, the putable bond is a substitute for a 10-year bond with greater upside if rates fall. Under the second view, the putable bond is viewed as a substitute for a 30-year bullet, with downside protection in the event that rates rise.

Putable bonds trade at tighter spreads than bullet bonds of the same issuing company. For example, the spread-to-put-date on a 30PUT10 bond will be tighter than the spread of a 10-year bullet bond. Investors are willing to accept a lower spread because they own an option to extend the maturity in the event that rates fall. The spread-to-maturity on a 30PUT10 will also be tighter than the spread on a 30-year bullet. Investors are willing to give up some spread as compensation for the option to shorten the bond's maturity if rates rise.

From either perspective, the investor has a long position in an option. In the case of a 30PUT10 bond, the investor's long position is reflected in the price of a putable bond or, equivalently, in its yield spread:

> Price of 30PUT10 = Price of 30-year bullet + Value of put option
> Price of 30PUT10 = Price of 10-year bullet + Value of extension option

or

> Spread-to-Maturity = 30-year bullet spread − Value of put option (bps)
> Spread-to-Put-Date = 10-year bullet spread − Value of extension option (bps)

Poison Puts

About 1986, in reaction to the increased merger and acquisition activity, some companies incorporated "poison puts" in their indentures. These were designed to thwart unfriendly takeovers by making the company proposed to be acquired unpalatable to the acquirer. All too often companies have been taken over or drastically restructured and debt substantially increased with the result that the bond ratings get lowered and bond prices decline. The common shareholder might come out all right, but the bondholders do not. Bondholders consider this an unfair transfer of wealth from one class of investors to another.

Basically, poison put provisions may not deter a proposed acquisition but could make it more expensive. In addition, uncertainty is increased because the put payment is not made, in most cases, until 100 days after the change in control occurs. Thus, the management has no way of knowing exactly how many bonds will be tendered for redemption. Of course, if the board of directors approves the change in control (i.e., it is a "friendly" transaction, and most takeovers are friendly if the price is right), the poison put provisions do not become effective. The designated event of change in control generally means either that continuing directors no longer constitute a majority of the board of directors or that a person, including affiliates, becomes the beneficial owner, directly or indirectly, of stock with at least 20% of the voting rights. In a couple of cases (such as in ITT Corporation's 7⅞% Notes due 1993 and Kerr-McGee Corporation's 9¾% Debentures due 2016) a rating change is also part of the requirement to set the put in motion.

The prospectus for ICN Pharmaceuticals, Inc. Debenture offering commented on the Change-in-Control Put as follows:

> The Change-in-Control Put may deter certain mergers, tender offers or other present or future takeover attempts and may thereby adversely affect the market price of the Common Stock.

Since a Change-in-Control Put may deter takeovers where the person attempting the takeover views itself as unable to finance the repurchase of the principal amount of Debentures which may be delivered to the Company for repurchase upon occurrence of such Change-in-Control. To the extent that the Debentures are repurchased pursuant to the Change-in-Control Put, the Company will be unable to utilize the financing provided by the sale of the Debentures. In addition, the ability of the Company to obtain additional Senior Debt based on the existence of the Debentures may be similarly adversely affected.

These poison puts lacked teeth, and in 1988 investors got particularly upset at the continuing activity in corporate restructurings. It was the leveraged buyout of RJR Nabisco Inc. that was "the straw that broke the camel's back." The whole industrial bond market was affected as bond buyers withdrew from the market and new issues were postponed. Trading of industrials in the secondary market nearly came to a standstill as prospectuses and indentures were checked and rechecked for protective covenants. Bond analysts sharpened their pencils and performed event risk studies to try to identify companies that appeared vulnerable for some type of restructuring. Investors demanded better covenants in public issues and, in some cases, got them. New poison put language was developed and incorporated into the new indentures. Essentially, if both a designated event and a rating downgrade to below investment-grade occur within a certain period, the company is obligated to repurchase the bonds at par. It does not matter if the takeover is friendly or hostile. One issue provided that if the market value of the debentures was less than par due to the event and rating downgrade, it could elect to redeem all of the issue at par. If it failed to redeem the bonds, it would have to reset the interest rate to such a level that would have resulted in the bonds being worth par on the day after the downgrading date.[2]

MOPPRS AND OTHER PUT/CALL BONDS

Since the late 1990s, "put/call" features have been included in a significant share of new corporate issues. Sometimes these put/call structures are known by their clever Wall Street acronyms, such as Mopprs™ (Mandatory Par Put or Remarketed Securities). Regardless of their names, all put/call bonds have the same essential features. Most important, on the date of the put/call, the investor expects to receive par. For investors, put/call bonds have no optionality. In fact, put/call bonds were designed with the specific intent of creating a structure that would have the same liquidity, credit risk, and yield spread as a short-term bullet bond.

---

[2] Leland Crabbe, "Event Risk: An Analysis of Losses to Bondholders and 'Super Poison Put' Bond Covenants," *Journal of Finance* (June 1991), pp. 689–706.

The final maturity on the bond's indenture will be greater than the put/call date, but that final maturity is immaterial from the point of view of the investor. Legally and economically, the investor owns a short-term bullet bond with short-term credit risk.

For example, a Mopprs may have a final maturity of 10 years but a put/call date in 3 years. At the date of the put/call, the investor is entitled to receive par. Thus, that Mopprs would be priced off the 3-year Treasury benchmark. Because that Mopprs has the same legal and economic risks as a 3-year bullet bond, investment bankers would argue that the Mopprs should trade with a spread comparable to that of a 3-year bullet of the same corporate issuer. However, as a practical matter, Mopprs are less liquid than traditional bullet bonds, and therefore they typically trade 5 to 20 basis points wide to traditional bullet bonds.

Although investors do not have to be concerned about optionality, put/call bonds do contain interest rate options that matter to the corporate issuer. In fact, from the issuer's point of view, put/call bonds are very similar to putable bonds. In a putable bond, the interest rate option is owned by the corporate bond investor. At the put date, the corporate bond investor has the option to either put the bond to the issuer at par or to extend the bond to the final maturity. By contrast, in a put/call bond, the option is owned by an investment bank. At the put/call date, the investment bank will have the option to extend the bond's life, but in that event the bond would have to be remarketed to new investors at prevailing market rates.

To understand the structure, let's continue with an example where Investor A buys an XYZ Corporation Mopprs, with a put/call date in 3 years and a final maturity of 10 years. In 3 years, Investor A will mandatorily receive par in all interest rate scenarios. If rates are high, XYZ Corporation will pay Investor A par and the bond will be retired. If rates are low, Investor A will receive par from an investment bank. In that event, the investment bank has the option to remarket the bond to new investors (Investor B) as a high-coupon bullet bond, with a maturity of 7 years. Of course, in a low rate environment, a high-coupon bond will have a price above par. The difference between the price Investor B pays for the remarketed bond and the price (par) paid to Investor A is the value of the put/call option on the put/call date. If the investment bank does not or cannot remarket the bond, it will be mandatorily put back to the issuer. If the investment bank has gone out of business, then the bonds will be mandatorily put back to the issuer. Therefore, from the point of view of Investor A, in all scenarios, put/call bonds have the credit risk of the corporate issuer, XYZ Corporation, not of the investment bank.

At the time a put/call bond is issued, the investment bank pays the corporate issuer the value of the extension option. The value paid by the investment bank is determined competitively in the market for swaptions, and, as a result, that value is often greater than what the company would receive from corporate bond investors in a traditional putable bond. In other words, interest rate extension options are typically valued more highly in the swaptions market than in the corporate bond market. In fact, put/call structures came into existence precisely to exploit the valuation differences between the putable bond market and the swaptions market. (Putable bonds are analyzed in detail in Chapters 16 and 17.) Mopprs and other put/call structures are also carefully designed with appropriate legal language that gives corporate issuers favorable tax and accounting treatment.

Chapter 16

Valuing Corporate Bonds with Embedded Options and Structured Notes

I n Chapter 5, our focus was on the valuation of corporate bonds where neither the issuer nor the bondholder has the option to alter a bond's cash flow. In this chapter, we look at how to value a corporate bond with one or more embedded options and structured notes. The model used to value the structures is the lattice model. We explain how to apply one particular form of this model, the binomial model, in this chapter. In addition, we explain a yield spread measure that takes into account the embedded option in a corporate bond, the option-adjusted spread.

COMPONENTS OF A CORPORATE BOND WITH EMBEDDED OPTIONS

To develop an analytical framework for valuing a corporate bond with one or more embedded options, it is necessary to decompose it into its component parts. Consider, for example, the most common bond with an embedded option, a callable bond. A callable bond is a bond in which the bondholder has sold the issuer an option (more specifically, a call option) that allows the issuer to repurchase the contractual cash flows of the bond from the time of the bond's first call date until the maturity date.

Consider the following two bonds: (1) a callable bond with an 8% coupon, 20 years to maturity, and callable in 5 years at 104 and (2) a 10-year 9% coupon bond callable immediately at par. For the first bond, the bondholder owns a 5-year option-free bond and has sold a call option granting the issuer the right to call away from the bondholder 15 years of cash flows 5 years from now for a price of 104. The investor who owns the second bond has a 10-year option-free bond and has sold a call option granting the issuer the right to immediately call the entire 10-year contractual cash flows, or any cash flows remaining at the time the issue is called, for 100.

Effectively, the owner of a callable bond is entering into two separate transactions. First, the investor buys an option-free bond from the issuer for which he pays some price. Then, he sells the issuer a call option for which he receives the option price. Therefore, we can summarize the position of a callable bond-holder as follows:

long a callable bond = long an option-free bond + sold a call option

In terms of value, the value of a callable bond is therefore equal to the value of the two component parts. That is,

value of a callable bond
  = value of an option-free bond − value of a call option

The reason the call option's value is subtracted from the value of the option-free bond is that when the bondholder sells a call option, he receives the option price. Actually, the position is more complicated than we just described. The issuer may be entitled to call the bond at the first call date and anytime thereafter, or at the first call date and any subsequent coupon anniversary date. Thus the investor has effectively sold an American-type call option to the issuer, but the call price may vary with the date the call option is exercised. This is because the call schedule for a bond may have a different call price depending on the call date. Moreover, the underlying bond for the call option is the remaining coupon payments that would have been made by the issuer had the bond not been called. For exposition purposes, it is easier to understand the principles associated with the investment characteristics of a callable bond by describing the investor's position as long an option-free bond and short a call option.

The same logic applies to putable bonds. In the case of a putable bond, the bondholder has the right to sell the bond to the issuer at a designated price and time. A putable bond can be broken into two separate transactions. First, the investor buys an option-free bond. Second, the investor buys a put option from the issuer that allows the investor to sell the bond to the issuer. Therefore, the position of a putable bondholder can be described as:

long a putable bond = long an option-free bond + long a put option

In terms of value,

value of a putable bond = value of an option-free bond + value of a put option

LATTICE MODEL

Several models have been proposed to value bonds with embedded options. Of interest to us are those models that provide an "arbitrage-free value" for a security. In the previous chapter we explained that an arbitrage-free value for an option-free bond was obtained by first generating the spot rates (or forward rates). The spot rates are the rates that would produce a value for each on-the-run Treasury issue that is equal to its observed market price. In developing the interest rates that should be used to value a bond with an embedded option, the same principle must be maintained. That is, no matter how complex the valuation model, when each on-the-run Treasury issue is valued using the model, the value produced should be equal to the on-the-run issue's market price. This is because it is assumed that the on-the-run issues are fairly priced.

The first complication in building a model to value bonds with embedded options is that the future cash flows will depend on what happens to interest rates in the future. This means that future interest rates must be considered. This is incorporated into a valuation model by considering how interest rates can change based on some assumed interest rate volatility. In Chapter 7 we explained what interest rate volatility is and how it is estimated. Given the assumed interest rate volatility, an interest rate "tree" representing possible future interest rates consistent with the volatility assumption can be constructed. Since the interest rate tree looks like a lattice, these valuation models are commonly referred to as *lattice models*. It is from the interest rate tree (or lattice) that two important elements in the valuation process are obtained. First, the interest rates on the tree are used to generate the cash flows, taking into account the embedded option. Second, the interest rates on the tree are used to compute the present value of the cash flows.

For a given interest rate volatility, several interest rate models have been used in practice to construct an interest rate tree. An *interest rate model* is a probabilistic description of how interest rates can change over the life of the bond. An interest rate model does this by making an assumption about the relationship between the level of short-term interest rates and the interest rate volatility as measured by the standard deviation. A discussion of the various interest rate models that have been suggested in the finance literature and that are used by practitioners in developing valuation models is beyond the scope of this chapter.[1] What is important to understand is that the interest rate models commonly used are based on how short-term interest rates can evolve (i.e., change) over time. Consequently, these interest rate models are referred to as *one-factor models*, where "factor" means only one interest rate is being modeled over time. More complex models would consider how more than one interest rate changes over time. For example, an interest rate model can specify how the short-term interest rate and the long-term interest rate can change over time. Such a model is called a *two-factor model*.

Given an interest rate model and an interest rate volatility assumption, it can be assumed that interest rates can realize one of two possible rates in the next period. A valuation model that makes this assumption in creating an interest rate tree is called a *binomial lattice model*, or simply *binomial model*. There are valuation models that assume that interest rates can take on three possible rates in the

---

[1] For a discussion of interest rate models used in bond valuation models, see Philip O. Obazee, "Understanding the Building Blocks for OAS Models," in Frank J. Fabozzi (ed.), *Professional Perspectives on Fixed Income Portfolio Management: Volume 3* (New Hope, PA: Frank J. Fabozzi Associates, 2001).

next period. These models are called *trinomial lattice models*, or simply *trinomial models*. There are even more complex models that assume in creating an interest rate tree that more than three possible rates in the next period can be realized. Regardless of the assumption about how many possible rates can be realized in the next period, the interest rate tree generated must produce a value for the on-the-run Treasury issue that is equal to its observed market price (i.e., it must produce an arbitrage-free value). Moreover, the intuition and the methodology for using the interest rate tree (i.e., the backward induction methodology described later) are the same.

Once an interest rate tree is generated that (1) is consistent with both the interest rate volatility assumption and the interest rate model and (2) generates the observed market price for each on-the-run issue, the next step is to use the interest rate tree to value a bond with an embedded option. The complexity here is that a set of rules must be introduced to determine, for any period, when the embedded option will be exercised. For a callable bond, these rules are called the "call rules." The rules vary from model builder to model builder.

At this stage, all of this sounds terribly complicated. While the building of a model to value bonds with embedded options is more complex than building a model to value option-free bonds, the basic principles are the same. In the case of valuing an option-free bond, the model that is built is simply a set of spot rates that are used to value cash flows. The spot rates will produce an arbitrage-free value. For a model to value a bond with embedded options, the interest rate tree is used to value future cash flows, and the interest rate tree is combined with the call rules to generate the future cash flows. Again, the interest rate tree will produce an arbitrage-free value.

Let's move from theory to practice. Only a few practitioners will develop their own model to value bonds with embedded options. Instead, it is typical for a portfolio manager or analyst to use a model developed by either a dealer firm or a vendor of analytical systems. A fair question is then: Why bother covering a valuation model that is readily available from a third party? The answer is that a valuation model should not be a black box to portfolio managers and analysts. The models in practice share all of the principles described in this chapter, but differ with respect to certain assumptions that can produce quite different results. The reasons for these differences in valuation must be understood. Moreover, third-party models give the user a choice of changing the assumptions. A user who has not "walked through" a valuation model has no appreciation of the significance of these assumptions and therefore how to assess the impact of these assumptions on the value produced by the model. There is "modeling risk" when we use the output of a valuation model. This is the risk that the underlying assumptions of a model may be incorrect. Understanding a valuation model permits the user to effectively determine the significance of an assumption.

An example of understanding the assumptions of a model is the volatility used. Suppose that the market price of a bond is $89. Suppose further that a valuation model produces a value for a bond with an embedded option of $90 based on a 12% interest rate volatility assumption. Then, according to the valuation model, this bond is cheap by one point. However, suppose that the same model produces a value of $87 if a 15% volatility is assumed. This tells the portfolio manager or analyst that the bond is two points rich. Which is correct?

Below we use the binomial model to demonstrate all of the issues and assumptions associated with valuing a bond with embedded options. Specifically, it is used to value agency debentures, corporates, and municipal bond structures with embedded options.

BINOMIAL MODEL

To illustrate the binomial valuation model, we start with the on-the-run yield curve for the particular issuer whose bonds we want to value. The starting point is the Treasury's on-the-run yield curve. To obtain a particular issuer's on-the-run yield curve, an appropriate credit spread is added to each on-the-run Treasury issue. The credit spread need not be constant for all maturities. For example, as explained in the previous chapter, the credit spread may increase with maturity.

In our illustration, we use the hypothetical on-the-run issues for an issuer shown in Exhibit 1. Each bond is trading at par value (100), so the coupon rate is equal to the yield to maturity. We simplify the illustration by assuming annual-pay bonds. Using the bootstrapping methodology, the spot rates are those shown in the last column of Exhibit 1.

Binomial Interest Rate Tree[2]

Once we allow for embedded options, consideration must be given to interest rate volatility. This can be done by introducing a *binomial interest rate tree*. This tree is nothing more than a graphical depiction of the one-period or short rates over time based on some assumption about interest rate volatility. How this tree is constructed is illustrated as follows.

Exhibit 1: On-the-Run Yield Curve and Spot Rates for an Issuer

Maturity (Years)	Yield to Maturity (%)	Market Price ($)	Spot Rate (%)
1	3.5	100	3.5000
2	4.2	100	4.2147
3	4.7	100	4.7345
4	5.2	100	5.2707

---

[2] The model described in this section was presented in Andrew J. Kalotay, George O. Williams, and Frank J. Fabozzi, "A Model for the Valuation of Bonds and Embedded Options," *Financial Analysts Journal* (May–June 1993), pp. 35–46.

Exhibit 2: Four-Year Binomial Interest Rate Tree

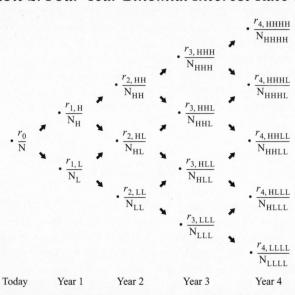

| Today | Year 1 | Year 2 | Year 3 | Year 4 |

Exhibit 2 provides an example of a binomial interest rate tree. In this tree, each node (bold circle) represents a time period that is equal to 1 year from the node to its left. Each node is labeled with an N, representing node, and a subscript that indicates the path that the 1-year rate took to get to that node. L represents the lower of the two 1-year rates and H represents the higher of the two 1-year rates. For example, node N_{HH} means to get to that node the following path for 1-year rates occurred: the 1-year rate realized is the higher of the two rates in the first year and then the higher of the 1-year rates in the second year.[3]

Look first at the point denoted by just N in Exhibit 2. This is the root of the tree and is nothing more than the current 1-year spot rate, or equivalently the current 1-year rate, which we denote by r_0. What we have assumed in creating this tree is that the 1-year rate can take on two possible rates the next period and the two rates have the same probability of occurring. One rate will be higher than the other. It is assumed that the 1-year rate can evolve over time based on a random process called a lognormal random walk with a certain volatility.

We use the following notation to describe the tree in Year 1. Let

σ = assumed volatility of the 1-year rate

$r_{1,L}$ = the lower 1-year rate 1 year from now

$r_{1,H}$ = the higher 1-year rate 1 year from now

---

[3] Note that N_{HL} is equivalent to N_{LH} in the second year and that in the third year N_{HHL} is equivalent to N_{HLH} and N_{LHH} and that N_{HLL} is equivalent to N_{LLH}. We have simply selected one label for a node rather than clutter up the exhibit.

The relationship between $r_{1,L}$ and $r_{1,H}$ is as follows:

$$r_{1,H} = r_{1,L}(e^{2\sigma})$$

where e is the base of the natural logarithm 2.71828.

For example, suppose that $r_{1,L}$ is 4.4448% and σ is 10% per year, then:

$$r_{1,H} = 4.4448\%(e^{2 \times 0.10}) = 5.4289\%$$

In Year 2, there are three possible values for the 1-year rate, which we will denote as follows:

$r_{2,LL}$ = 1-year rate in Year 2 assuming the lower rate in Year 1 and the lower rate in Year 2

$r_{2,HH}$ = 1-year rate in Year 2 assuming the higher rate in Year 1 and the higher rate in Year 2

$r_{2,HL}$ = 1-year rate in Year 2 assuming the higher rate in Year 1 and the lower rate in Year 2 or equivalently the lower rate in Year 1 and the higher rate in Year 2

The relationship between $r_{2,LL}$ and the other two 1-year rates is as follows:

$$r_{2,HH} = r_{2,LL}(e^{4\sigma}) \text{ and } r_{2,HL} = r_{2,LL}(e^{2\sigma})$$

So, for example, if $r_{2,LL}$ is 4.6958%, then assuming once again that σ is 10%, then

$$r_{2,HH} = 4.6958\%(e^{4 \times 0.10}) = 7.0053\%$$

and

$$r_{2,HL} = 4.6958\%(e^{4 \times 0.10}) = 5.7354\%$$

In Year 3 there are four possible values for the 1-year rate, which are denoted as follows: $r_{3,HHH}$, $r_{3,HHL}$, $r_{3,HLL}$, and $r_{3,LLL}$, and whose first three rates are related to the last as follows:

$$r_{3,HHH} = (e^{6\sigma}) \, r_{3,LLL}$$
$$r_{3,HHL} = (e^{4\sigma}) \, r_{3,LLL}$$
$$r_{3,HLL} = (e^{2\sigma}) \, r_{3,LLL}$$

Exhibit 2 shows the notation for a 4-year binomial interest rate tree. We can simplify the notation by letting r_t be the 1-year rate t years from now for the lower rate since all the other short rates t years from now depend on that rate. Exhibit 3 shows the interest rate tree using this simplified notation.

Exhibit 3: Four-Year Binomial Interest Rate Tree with 1-Year Rates*

$$\cdot \frac{r_4 e^{8\sigma}}{N_{HHHH}}$$

$$\cdot \frac{r_3 e^{6\sigma}}{N_{HHH}}$$

$$\cdot \frac{r_2 e^{4\sigma}}{N_{HH}}$$

$$\cdot \frac{r_4 e^{6\sigma}}{N_{HHHL}}$$

$$\cdot \frac{r_1 e^{2\sigma}}{N_H}$$

$$\cdot \frac{r_3 e^{4\sigma}}{N_{HHL}}$$

$$\cdot \frac{r_0}{N}$$

$$\cdot \frac{r_2 e^{2\sigma}}{N_{HL}}$$

$$\cdot \frac{r_4 e^{4\sigma}}{N_{HHLL}}$$

$$\cdot \frac{r_1}{N_L}$$

$$\cdot \frac{r_3 e^{2\sigma}}{N_{HLL}}$$

$$\cdot \frac{r_2}{N_{LL}}$$

$$\cdot \frac{r_4 e^{2\sigma}}{N_{HLLL}}$$

$$\cdot \frac{r_3}{N_{LLL}}$$

$$\cdot \frac{r_4}{N_{LLLL}}$$

| Today | Year 1 | Year 2 | Year 3 | Year 4 |

* r_t equals forward 1-year lower rate

It can be shown that the standard deviation of the 1-year rate is equal to $r_0\sigma$.[4] The standard deviation is a statistical measure of volatility. It is important to see that the process that we assumed generates the binomial interest rate tree (or equivalently the short rates), implies that volatility is measured relative to the current level of rates. For example, if σ is 10% and the 1-year rate (r_0) is 4%, then the standard deviation of the 1-year rate is 4% × 10% = 0.4% or 40 basis points. However, if the current 1-year rate is 12%, the standard deviation of the 1-year rate would be 12% × 10% or 120 basis points.

Determining the Value at a Node

To find the value of the bond at a node, we first calculate the bond's value at the two nodes to the right of the node we are interested in. For example, in Exhibit 3, suppose we want to determine the bond's value at node N_H. The bond's value at node N_{HH} and N_{HL} must be determined. Hold aside for now how we get these two values because as we will see, the process involves starting from the last year in the tree and working backwards to get the final solution we want, so these two values will be known.

Effectively what we are saying is that if we are at some node, then the value at that node will depend on the future cash flows. In turn, the future cash

---

[4] This can be seen by noting that $e^{2\sigma} \approx 1 + 2\sigma$. Then the standard deviation of the 1-year rate is

$$\frac{re^{2\sigma} - r}{2} \approx \frac{r + 2\sigma r - r}{2} = \sigma r$$

flows depend on (1) the bond's value 1 year from now and (2) the coupon payment 1 year from now. The latter is known. The former depends on whether the 1-year rate is the higher or lower rate. The bond's value depending on whether the rate is the higher or lower rate is reported at the two nodes to the right of the node that is the focus of our attention. So, the cash flow at a node will be either (1) the bond's value if the short rate is the higher rate plus the coupon payment, or (2) the bond's value if the short rate is the lower rate plus the coupon payment. For example, suppose that we are interested in the bond's value at N_H. The cash flow will be either the bond's value at N_{HH} plus the coupon payment or the bond's value at N_{HL} plus the coupon payment.

To get the bond's value at a node we follow the fundamental rule for valuation: the value is the present value of the expected cash flows. The appropriate discount rate to use is the 1-year rate at the node. Now there are two present values in this case: the present value if the 1-year rate is the higher rate and one if it is the lower rate. Since it is assumed that the probability of both outcomes is equal, an average of the two present values is computed. This is illustrated in Exhibit 4 for any node assuming that the 1-year rate is r_* at the node where the valuation is sought and letting:

V_H = the bond's value for the higher 1-year rate
V_L = the bond's value for the lower 1-year rate
C = coupon payment

Using our notation, the cash flow at a node is either:

$V_H + C$ for the higher 1-year rate

$V_L + C$ for the lower 1-year rate

Exhibit 4: Calculating the Value at a Node

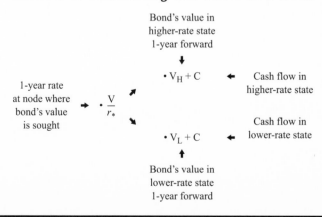

Exhibit 5: The 1-Year Rates for Year 1 Using the 2-Year 4.2% On-the-Run Issue: First Trial

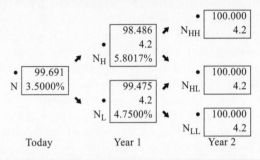

Today	Year 1	Year 2

The present value of these two cash flows using the 1-year rate at the node, r_*, is:

$$\frac{V_H + C}{(1 + r_*)} = \text{present value for the higher 1-year rate}$$

$$\frac{V_L + C}{(1 + r_*)} = \text{present value for the lower 1-year rate}$$

Then, the value of the bond at the node is found as follows:

$$\text{value at a node} = \frac{1}{2}\left[\frac{V_H + C}{(1 + r_*)} + \frac{V_L + C}{(1 + r_*)}\right]$$

Constructing the Binomial Interest Rate Tree

To see how to construct the binomial interest rate tree, let's use the assumed on-the-run yields in Exhibit 1. We will assume that volatility, σ, is 10% and construct a 2-year tree using the 2-year bond with a coupon rate of 4.2%.

Exhibit 5 shows a more detailed binomial interest rate with the cash flow shown at each node. We'll see how all the values reported in the exhibit are obtained. The root rate for the tree, r_0, is simply the current 1-year rate, 3.5%.

In the first year there are two possible 1-year rates, the higher rate and the lower rate. What we want to find is the two 1-year rates that will be consistent with the volatility assumption, the process that is assumed to generate the short rates, and the observed market value of the bond. There is no simple formula for this. It must be found by an iterative process (i.e., trial-and-error). The steps are described and illustrated as follows.

Step 1: Select a value for r_1. Recall that r_1 is the lower 1-year rate. In this first trial, we *arbitrarily* selected a value of 4.75%.

Step 2: Determine the corresponding value for the higher 1-year rate. As explained earlier, this rate is related to the lower 1-year rate as follows: $r_1 e^{2\sigma}$.

Since r_1 is 4.75%, the higher 1-year rate is 5.8017% (= 4.75% $e^{2\times0.10}$). This value is reported in Exhibit 5 at node N_H.

Step 3: Compute the bond's value in Year 1. This value is determined as follows:

     3a. Determine the bond's value in Year 2. In our example, this is simple. Since we are using a 2-year bond, the bond's value is its maturity value ($100) plus its final coupon payment ($4.2). Thus, it is $104.2.

     3b. Calculate the present value of the bond's value found in Step 3a for the higher rate in Year 2. The appropriate discount rate is the higher 1-year rate, 5.8017% in our example. The present value is $98.486 (= $104.2/ 1.058017). This is the value of V_H that we referred to earlier.

     3c. Calculate the present value of the bond's value found in Step 3a for the lower rate. The discount rate assumed for the lower 1-year rate is 4.75%. The present value is $99.475 (= $104.2/1.0475) and is the value of V_L.

     3d. Add the coupon to both V_H and V_L to get the cash flow at N_H and N_L, respectively. In our example we have $102.686 for the higher rate and $103.675 for the lower rate.

     3e. Calculate the present value of the two values using the 1-year rate r_*. At this point in the valuation, r_* is the root rate, 3.50%. Therefore,

$$\frac{V_H + C}{1 + r_*} = \frac{\$102.686}{1.035} = \$99.213$$

and

$$\frac{V_L + C}{1 + r_*} = \frac{\$103.675}{1.035} = \$100.169$$

Step 4: Calculate the average present value of the two cash flows in Step 3. This is the value we referred to earlier as

$$\text{value at a node} = \frac{1}{2}\left[\frac{V_H + C}{(1 + r_*)} + \frac{V_L + C}{(1 + r_*)}\right]$$

In our example, we have

$$\text{value at a node} = \frac{1}{2}(\$99.213 + \$100.169) = \$99.691$$

Step 5: Compare the value in Step 4 to the bond's market value. If the two values are the same, then the r_1 used in this trial is the one we seek. This is the 1-year rate that would then be used in the binomial interest rate tree for the lower rate and to obtain the corresponding higher rate. If, instead, the value found in Step 4 is not equal to the market value of the bond, this means that the value r_1 in this trial is not the 1-year rate that is consistent with (1) the volatility assumption, (2) the process assumed to generate the 1-year rate, and (3) the observed market value of the bond. In this case, the five steps are repeated with a different value for r_1.

When r_1 is 4.75%, a value of $99.691 results in Step 4, which is less than the observed market price of $100. Therefore, 4.75% is too high and the five steps must be repeated trying a lower rate for r_1.

Let's jump right to the correct rate for r_1 in this example and rework Steps 1 through 5. This occurs when r_1 is 4.4448%. The corresponding binomial interest rate tree is shown in Exhibit 6.

Step 1: In this trial we select a value of 4.4448% for r_1, the lower 1-year rate.

Step 2: The corresponding value for the higher 1-year rate is 5.4289% (= 4.4448% $e^{2 \times 0.10}$).

Step 3: The bond's value in Year 1 is determined as follows:

> *3a.* The bond's value in Year 2 is $104.2, just as in the first trial.

> *3b.* The present value of the bond's value found in Step 3a for the higher 1-year rate, V_H, is $98.834 (= $104.2/1.054289).

> *3c.* The present value of the bond's value found in Step 3a for the lower 1-year rate, V_L, is $99.766 (= $104.2/1.044448).

> *3d.* Adding the coupon to V_H and V_L, we get $103.034 as the cash flow for the higher rate and $103.966 as the cash flow for the lower rate.

Exhibit 6: The 1-Year Rates for Year 1 Using the 2-Year 4.2% On-the-Run Issue

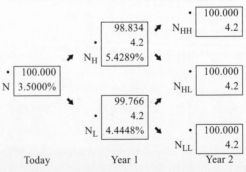

Exhibit 7: Information for Deriving the 1-Year Rates for Year 2 Using the 3-Year 4.7% On-the-Run Issue

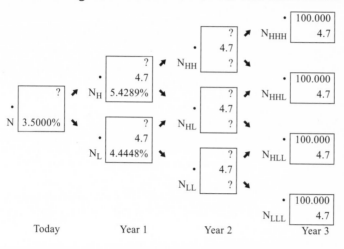

Today	Year 1	Year 2	Year 3

3e. The present value of the two cash flows using the 1-year rate at the node to the left, 3.5%, gives

$$\frac{V_H + C}{1 + r_*} = \frac{\$103.034}{1.035} = \$99.550$$

and,

$$\frac{V_L + C}{1 + r_*} = \frac{\$103.966}{1.035} = \$100.450$$

Step 4: The average present value is $100, which is the value at the node.

Step 5: Since the average present value is equal to the observed market price of $100, r_1 or $r_{1,L}$ is 4.4448% and $r_{1,H}$ is 5.4289%.

We can "grow" this tree for one more year by determining r_2. Now we will use the 3-year on-the-run issue, the 4.7% coupon bond, to get r_2. The same five steps are used in an iterative process to find the 1-year rates in the tree in Year 2. Our objective is now to find the value of r_2 that will produce a bond value of $100 (since the 3-year on-the-run issue has a market price of $100) and is consistent with (1) a volatility assumption of 10%, (2) a current 1-year rate of 3.5%, and (3) the two rates 1 year from now of 4.4448% (the lower rate) and 5.4289% (the higher rate).

We explain how this is done using Exhibit 7. Let's look at how we get the information in the exhibit. The maturity value and coupon payment are shown in the boxes at the four nodes at Year 3. Since the 3-year on-the-run issue has a maturity value of $100 and a coupon payment of $4.7, these values are the same in the box shown at each node. For the three nodes at Year 2 the coupon payment of $4.7 is shown. Unknown at these three nodes are (1) the three rates in Year 2 and (2) the value of the bond at Year 2. For the two nodes in Year 1, the coupon payment is known, as are the 1-year rates. These are the rates found earlier. The value of the bond, which depends on the bond values at the nodes to the right, are unknown at these two nodes. All of the unknown values are indicated by a question mark.

Exhibit 8 is the same as Exhibit 7 but complete with the values previously unknown. As can be seen from Exhibit 8, the value of r_2, or equivalently $r_{2,LL}$, which will produce the desired result, is 4.6958%. We showed earlier that the corresponding rates $r_{2,HL}$ and $r_{2,HH}$ would be 5.7354% and 7.0053%, respectively. To verify that these are the 1-year rates in Year 2, work backwards from the four nodes at Year 3 of the tree in Exhibit 8. For example, the value in the box at N_{HH} is found by taking the value of $104.7 at the two nodes to its right and discounting at 7.0053%. The value is $97.846. (Since it is the same value for both nodes to the right, it is also the average value.) Similarly, the value in the box at N_{HL} is found by discounting $104.70 by 5.7354% and at N_{LL} by discounting at 4.6958%. The same procedure used in Exhibits 5 and 6 is used to get the values at the other nodes.

In the balance of this chapter we see how to value various bond structures using the binomial model.

Exhibit 8: The 1-Year Rates for Year 2 Using the 3-Year 4.7% On-the-Run Issue

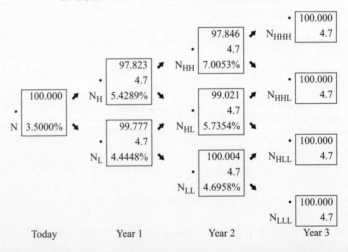

Exhibit 9: Binomial Interest Rate Tree for Valuing Up to a 4-Year Corporate Bond for Issuer (10% Volatility Assumed)

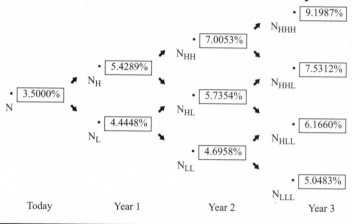

VALUING AN OPTION-FREE CORPORATE BOND

Consider an option-free corporate bond with 4 years remaining to maturity and a coupon rate of 6.5%. The value of this bond can be calculated by discounting the cash flow at the spot rates in Exhibit 1 as shown below:

$$\frac{\$6.5}{(1.035)^1} + \frac{\$6.5}{(1.042147)^2} + \frac{\$6.5}{(1.047345)^3} + \frac{\$100 + \$6.5}{(1.052707)^4} = \$104.643$$

An option-free bond that is valued using the binomial interest rate tree should have the same value as discounting by the spot rates.

Exhibit 9 shows the 1-year rates or binomial interest rate tree that can then be used to value any bond for this issuer with a maturity up to 4 years. To illustrate how to use the binomial interest rate tree, consider once again the 6.5% option-free bond with 3 years remaining to maturity. Also assume that the issuer's on-the-run yield curve is the one in Exhibit 1, hence the appropriate binomial interest rate tree is the one in Exhibit 9. Exhibit 10 shows the various values in the discounting process, and produces a bond value of $104.643.

This value is identical to the bond value found when we discounted at the spot rates. This clearly demonstrates that the valuation model is consistent with the standard valuation model for an option-free corporate bond.

VALUING A CALLABLE CORPORATE BOND

Now we will demonstrate how the binomial model can be applied to value a callable corporate bond. The valuation process proceeds in the same fashion as in the case of an option-free bond, but with one exception: when the call option may be exercised by the issuer, the bond value at a node must be changed to reflect the lesser of its values if it is not called (i.e., the value obtained by applying the recursive valuation formula described previously) and the call price.

For example, consider a 6.5% corporate bond with 4 years remaining to maturity that is callable in 1 year at $100. Exhibit 11 shows two values at each node of the binomial tree. The discounting process explained earlier is used to calculate the first of the two values at each node. The second value is the value based on whether the issue will be called. *For simplicity*, let's assume that this issuer calls the issue if it exceeds the call price. Then, in Exhibit 11 at nodes N_L, N_H, N_{LL}, N_{HL}, N_{LLL}, and N_{HLL} the values from the recursive valuation formula are $101.968, $100.032, $101.723, $100.270, $101.382, and $100.315, respectively. These values exceed the assumed call price ($100) and therefore the second value is $100 rather than the calculated value. The second value is used in subsequent calculations. The root of the tree indicates that the value for this callable bond is $102.899.

The question that we have not addressed in our illustration, which is nonetheless important, is the circumstances under which the issuer will call the bond. A detailed explanation of the call rule is beyond the scope of this chapter. Basically, it involves determining when it would be economic for the issuer to call the issue on an after-tax basis.

Exhibit 10: Valuing an Option-Free Corporate Bond with 4 Years to Maturity and a Coupon Rate of 6.5% (10% Volatility Assumed)

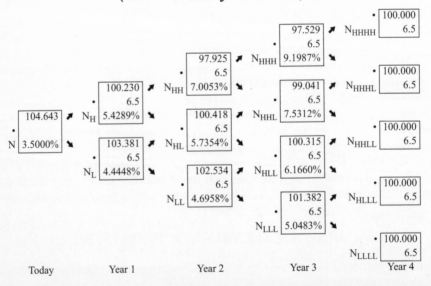

Exhibit 11: Valuing a Callable Bond with 4 Years to Maturity, a Coupon Rate of 6.5%, and Callable in 1 Year at 100 (10% Volatility Assumed)

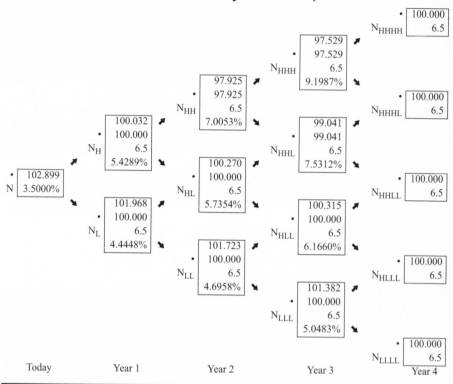

Suppose instead that the call price schedule is $102 in Year 1, $101 in Year 2, and $100 in Year 3. Also assume that the corporate bond will not be called unless it exceeds the call price for that year. Exhibit 12 shows the value at each node and the value of the callable bond. The call price schedule results in a greater value for this callable corporate bond, $103.942 versus $102.899 when the call price is $100 in each year.

Determining the Call Option Value

As explained earlier in the chapter, the value of a callable bond is equal to the value of an option-free bond minus the value of the call option. This means that:

value of a call option = value of an option-free bond − value of a callable bond

We have just seen how the value of an option-free corporate bond and the value of a callable corporate bond can be determined. The difference between the two values is therefore the value of the call option.

Exhibit 12: Valuing a Callable Corporate Bond with 4 Years to Maturity, a Coupon Rate of 6.5%, and with a Call Price Schedule (10% Volatility Assumed)

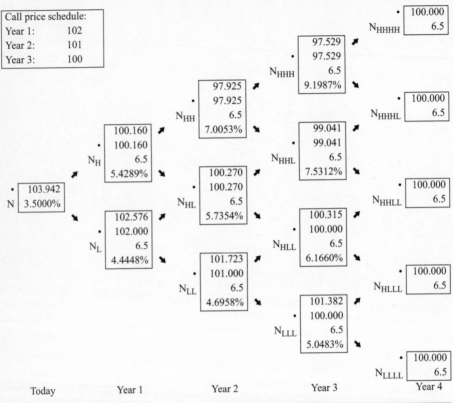

In our illustration, the value of the option-free corporate bond is $104.643. If the call price is $100 in each year, the value of the callable corporate bond is $102.899. Therefore, the value of the call option is $1.744 (= $104.634 − $102.899).

VALUING A PUTABLE CORPORATE BOND

A putable bond is one in which the bondholder has the right to force the issuer to pay off the bond prior to the maturity date. To illustrate how the binomial model can be used to value a putable bond, suppose that a 6.5% bond with 4 years remaining to maturity is putable in 1 year at par ($100). Also assume that the appropriate binomial interest rate tree for this issuer is the one in Exhibit 9 and the bondholder exercises the put if the bond's price is less than par.

Exhibit 13: Valuing a Putable Corporate Bond with 4 Years to Maturity, a Coupon Rate of 6.5%, and Putable in 1 Year at 100 (10% Volatility Assumed)

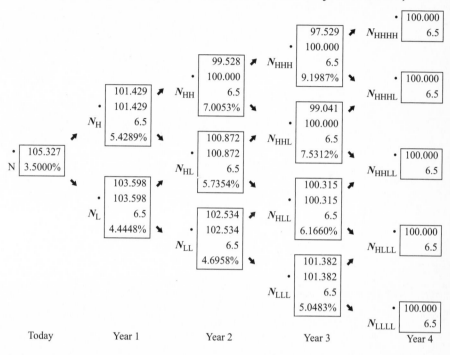

Exhibit 13 shows the binomial interest rate tree with the bond value altered at three nodes (N_{HH}, N_{HHH}, and N_{HHL}) because the bond value at these nodes is less than $100, the assumed value at which the bond can be put. The value of this putable bond is $105.327.

Since the value of an option-free bond can be expressed as the value of a putable bond minus the value of a put option on that bond, this means that:

value of a put option = value of an option-free bond − value of a putable bond

In our example, since the value of the putable bond is $105.327 and the value of the corresponding option-free bond is $104.643, the value of the put option is −$0.684. The negative sign indicates the issuer has sold the option, or equivalently, the investor has purchased the option.

The binomial model can also be used to value a bond that is both callable and putable.

Exhibit 14: Valuing a Floating-Rate Corporate Note with No Cap

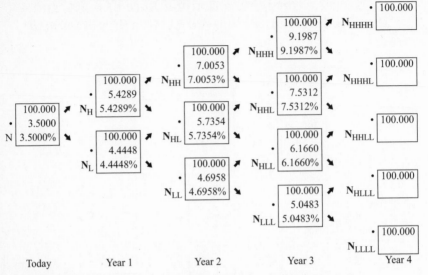

Note: The coupon rate shown at a node is the coupon rate to be received in the next year.

VALUING A CAPPED FLOATING-RATE CORPORATE NOTE

The valuation of a capped floating-rate corporate note using the binomial model requires that the coupon rate be adjusted based on the 1-year rate (which is assumed to be the reference rate). Exhibit 14 shows the binomial tree and the relevant values at each node for a floater whose coupon rate is the 1-year rate flat and in which there are no restrictions on the coupon rate.

The valuation procedure is identical to that for the other callable and putable bonds described previously with one exception. While the coupon rate is set at the beginning of the period, it is paid in arrears. In the valuation procedure, the coupon rate set for the next period is shown in the box at which the rate is determined. For example, in Exhibit 14, the coupon rate shown in the top box in Year 2 is 7.0053 as determined by the 1-year rate at that node. Since the payment will not be made until the next year, the value of 100 shown in the same box is determined by using the standard procedure but discounting the coupon rate in the same box. For example, let's see how we get the value of 100 in the top box in Year 2. The procedure is to calculate the average of the two present values of the bond value and coupon. Since the bond values and coupons are the same, the present value is simply:

$$\frac{100 + 7.0053}{7.0053} = 100$$

Suppose that the floater has a cap of 7.25%. Exhibit 15 shows how this floater would be valued. At each node where the short rate exceeds 7.25%, a coupon of $7.25 is substituted. The value of this capped floater is 99.724. Thus, the cost of the cap is the difference between par and 99.724. If the cap for this floater was 7.75% rather than 7.25%, it can be shown that the value of this floater would be 99.858. That is, the higher the cap, the closer the capped floater will trade to par.

VALUING STRUCTURED NOTES

As explained in Chapter 3, structured notes have an unusual coupon rate formula. The coupon rate can be based on either an interest rate, a noninterest rate financial index, or a nonfinancial index. Structured notes for which the coupon rate is based on an interest rate can generally be valued using the binomial model We will illustrate how using a common structured note: a *step-up callable note*.

Step-up callable notes are callable instruments whose coupon rate is increased (i.e., "stepped up") at designated times. When the coupon rate is increased only once over the security's life, it is said to be a *single step-up callable note*. A *multiple step-up callable note* is a step-up callable note whose coupon is increased more than one time over the life of the security.

To illustrate how the binomial model can be used to value a single step-up callable note, suppose that a 4-year step-up callable note pays 4.25% for 2 years and then 7.5% for 2 more years. Assume that this note is callable at par at the end of Year 2 and Year 3. We will use the binomial interest rate tree given in Exhibit 9 to value this note.

Exhibit 15: Valuing a Floating-Rate Corporate Note with a 7.25% Cap

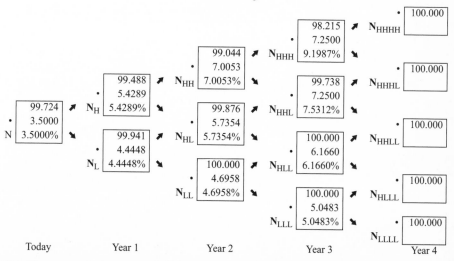

Note: The coupon rate shown at a node is the coupon rate to be received in the next year.

Exhibit 16: Valuing a Single Step-Up Noncallable Note with 4 Years to Maturity (10% Volatility Assumed)

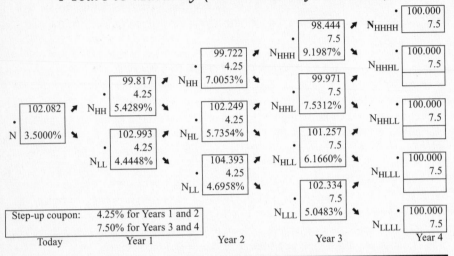

Exhibit 16 shows the value of a corresponding single step-up noncallable note. The valuation procedure is identical to that performed in Exhibit 11 except that the coupon in the box at each node reflects the step-up terms. The value is $102.082. Exhibit 17 shows that the value of the single step-up callable note is $100.031. The value of the embedded call option is equal to the difference in the step-up noncallable note value and the step-up callable note value, $2.051.

VOLATILITY AND THE THEORETICAL VALUE

In our illustrations, interest rate volatility was assumed to be 10%. The volatility assumption has an important impact on the theoretical value. More specifically, the higher the expected volatility, the higher the value of an option. The same is true for an option embedded in a bond. Correspondingly, this affects the value of the bond with an embedded option.

For example, for a callable bond, a higher interest rate volatility assumption means that the value of the call option increases and, since the value of the option-free bond is not affected, the value of the callable bond must be lower. For a putable bond, higher interest rate volatility means that its value will be higher.

To illustrate this point, suppose that a 20% volatility is assumed rather than 10%. The value of the hypothetical callable bond is $102.108 if volatility is assumed to be 20%, compared to $102.899 if volatility is assumed to be 10%. The hypothetical putable bond at 20% volatility has a value of $106.010, compared to $105.327 at 10% volatility.

Exhibit 17: Valuing a Single Step-Up Callable Note with 4 Years to Maturity, Callable in 2 Years at 100 (10% Volatility Assumed)

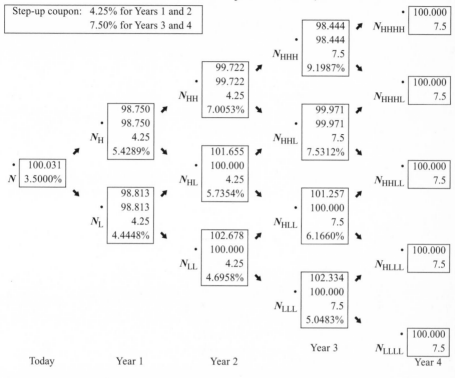

In the construction of the binomial interest rate, it was assumed that volatility is the same for each year. The model can be extended to incorporate a short-long volatility or a more elaborate term structure of volatility.

OPTION-ADJUSTED SPREAD

Suppose the market price of the 4-year 6.5% callable bond is $102.218 and the theoretical value assuming 10% volatility is $102.899. This means that this bond is cheap by $0.681 according to the valuation model. The option-adjusted spread (OAS) is the constant spread that when added to all the 1-year rates on the binomial interest rate tree will make the arbitrage-free value (i.e., the value produced by the binomial model) equal to the market price.

In our illustration, if the market price is $102.218, the OAS would be the constant spread added to every rate in Exhibit 9 that will make the arbitrage-free value equal to $102.218. The solution in this case would be 35 basis points. This can be verified in Exhibit 18, which shows the value of this issue by adding 35 basis points to each rate.

As with the value of a bond with an embedded option, the OAS will depend on the volatility assumption. For a given bond price, the higher the interest rate volatility assumed, the lower the OAS for a callable corporate bond. For example, if volatility is 20% rather than 10%, the OAS would be −6 basis points. This illustration clearly demonstrates the importance of the volatility assumption. Assuming volatility of 10%, the OAS is 35 basis points. At 20% volatility, the OAS declines and, in this case, is negative and therefore the bond is overvalued relative to the model.

How do we interpret the OAS? In general, a nominal spread between two yields reflects differences in the:

1. credit risk of the two issues
2. liquidity risk of the two issues
3. option risk of the two issues

Exhibit 18: Demonstration that the Option-Adjusted Spread is 35 Basis Points for a 6.5% Callable Corporate Bond Selling at 102.218 (Assuming 10% Volatility)

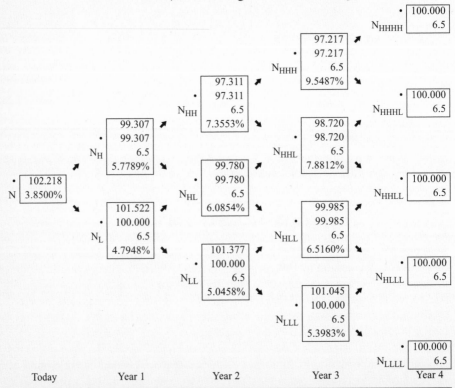

For example, if one of the issues is a BBB industrial issue with an embedded option and the benchmark interest rates are the rates for the U.S. Treasury on-the-run securities, then the nominal spread is a measure of the difference due to the:

1. credit risk of the BBB industrial issue
2. liquidity risk associated with the BBB industrial issue
3. option risk associated with the BBB industrial issue that is not present in Treasury issues

What the OAS seeks to do is remove from the nominal spread the amount that is due to the option risk. The measure is called an OAS because (1) it is a spread and (2) it adjusts the cash flows for the option when computing the spread to the benchmark interest rates. The second point can be seen from Exhibits 11 and 12. Notice that at each node the value obtained from the backward induction method is adjusted based on the call option and the call rule. Thus, the resulting spread is "option adjusted."

Consequently, if the Treasury on-the-run issues are used as the benchmark, because the embedded option has been taken into account, the OAS is measuring the compensation for the:

1. credit risk of the BBB industrial issue
2. liquidity risk associated with the BBB industrial issue

So, for example, an OAS of 160 basis points for a callable BBB industrial issue would mean that based on the valuation model (including the volatility assumption), the OAS is compensation for the credit risk and the lower liquidity of the industrial issue relative to the Treasury benchmark issues. The OAS has removed the compensation for the call feature present in the industrial issue that is not present in the Treasury benchmark interest rates.

However, suppose that the benchmark interest rates are the on-the-run interest rates for the issuer, as in our illustration of how to use the binomial model to value a bond with an embedded option. Then there is no difference in the credit risk between the benchmark interest rates and the corporate issue. That is, the OAS reflects only the difference in the liquidity of an issue relative to the on-the-run issues. The valuation has removed the spread due to the option risk and using the issuer's own benchmark interest rates removes the credit risk.

Suppose instead that the benchmark interest rates used are not of that particular issuer but the on-the-run issues for issuers in the same sector of the bond market and the same credit rating of the issue being analyzed. For example, suppose that the callable bond issue being analyzed is that issued by the XYZ Manufacturing Company, a BBB industrial company. An on-the-run yield curve can be estimated for the XYZ Manufacturing Company. Using that on-the-run yield curve, the OAS reflects the difference in the liquidity risk between the particular callable bond of the XYZ Manufacturing Company analyzed and the on-the-run issues of the XYZ

Manufacturing Company. However, if instead the benchmark interest rates used to value the callable bond of the XYZ Manufacturing Company are those of a generic BBB industrial company, the OAS reflects (1) the difference between the liquidity risk of the XYZ Manufacturing Company's callable bond and that of a generic BBB industrial company and (2) differences between event risk/credit risk specific to XYZ Manufacturing Company's issue beyond generic BBB credit risk. Note that the difference between XYZ and the BBB sector could be positive or negative.

Consequently, we know that an OAS is a spread after adjusting for the embedded option. But we know nothing else until the benchmark interest rates are identified. Without knowing the benchmark used—Treasury on-the-run yield curve, an issuer's on-the-run yield curve, or a generic on-the-run yield curve for issuers in the same sector of the bond market and of the same credit rating—we cannot interpret what the OAS is providing compensation for. Some market participants might view this as unrealistic since most of the time the on-the-run Treasury yield curve is used and therefore the OAS reflects credit risk and liquidity risk. However, vendors of analytical systems and most dealer models allow an investor to specify the benchmark interest rates to be used. The default feature in these systems (i.e., what the model uses as the benchmark interest rates if the investor does not specify the benchmark) is the Treasury on-the-run yield curve.

So, once an investor is told what the OAS is of a particular bond, the first question should be: Relative to what benchmark interest rates? This is particularly important in non-U.S. markets where the OAS concept is beginning to be used with greater frequency. It also means that comparing OAS values across global markets is difficult because different benchmark interest rates are being used and therefore the OAS is capturing different risks.

Funded investors (i.e., investors who borrow funds and seek to earn a spread over their funding costs) use LIBOR as their benchmark interest rates. Most funded investors borrow funds at a spread over LIBOR. Consequently, if a yield curve for LIBOR is used as the benchmark interest rates, the OAS reflects a spread relative to their funding cost. The OAS reflects credit risk relative to the credit risk associated with LIBOR and liquidity risk of the issue. So, if a callable bond has an OAS of 80 basis points and the LIBOR yield curve is the benchmark, then the OAS is compensation relative to LIBOR after adjusting for the embedded call option. A funded investor will then compare the OAS to the spread it must pay over its funding costs. So, if an investor's funding cost is 25 basis points over LIBOR, then a callable bond with an OAS of 80 basis points would be acceptable. Whether or not a funded investor would purchase the callable bond depends on whether the credit risk and the liquidity risk are acceptable and whether the compensation for these risks (as measured by the OAS) in the opinion of the investor is adequate.

Finally, let's take a closer look at the interpretation of the OAS as a spread relative to benchmark interest rates. This does *not* mean that it is a spread over one maturity for the benchmark interest rates. For example, consider the 35 basis point OAS for the 4-year 6.5% callable issue. The yield for the 4-year on-the-run issue is

5.2%. An OAS of 35 basis points does *not* mean that this callable issue is offering an option-adjusted *yield* of 5.55% (5.2% plus 35 basis points). Rather, to understand how it is spread off the benchmark interest rates, look at Exhibit 18.

First, the benchmark interest rates are used to construct the interest rate at each node of the interest rate tree. Next, recall that the rate at each node in the interest rate tree is the 1-year forward rate. (In general, they are the one-period forward rates). Now, to get the OAS we must determine the spread that must be added to each of the 1-year forward rates in the interest rate tree so that the backward induction method will produce a value equal to the market value. So, while it is often stated that the OAS is a spread relative to the benchmark interest rates, strictly speaking, it is a spread over the one-period forward rates in the interest rate tree that are constructed from the benchmark interest rates.

COMPUTING EFFECTIVE DURATION AND CONVEXITY WITH THE BINOMIAL MODEL

Let's look at how to calculate the effective duration using the binomial model. The procedure for calculating the value of V_+ to use in the duration formula—equation (1) of Chapter 6—is as follows:

Step 1: Calculate the option-adjusted spread (OAS) for the issue.

Step 2: Shift the on-the-run yield curve up by a small number of basis points (Δy).

Step 3: Construct a binomial interest rate tree based on the new yield curve in Step 2.

Step 4: To each of the one-period rates in the binomial interest rate tree, add the OAS to obtain an "adjusted tree."

Step 5: Use the adjusted tree found in Step 4 to determine the value of the bond, which is V_+.

To determine the value of V_-, the same five steps are followed except that in Step 2, the on-the-run yield curve is shifted down by a small number of basis points (Δy).

To illustrate how V_+ and V_- are determined in order to calculate effective duration and effective convexity, we use the same on-the-run yield curve shown in Exhibit 1 assuming a volatility of 10%. The hypothetical 4-year callable corporate bond with a coupon rate of 6.5%, callable at par, and selling at 102.218 used to illustrate the binomial model is used in this illustration to demonstrate how to calculate the effective duration. As shown earlier in this chapter, the OAS for this issue is 35 basis points.

Exhibit 19: Determination of V_+ for Calculating Effective Duration and Convexity*

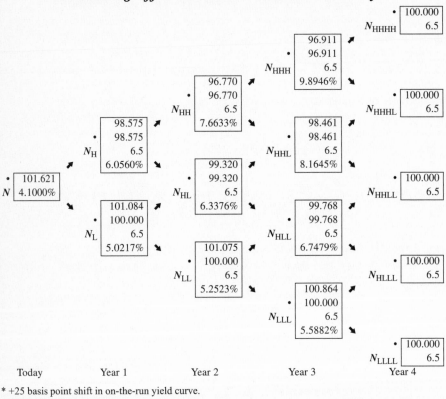

| | Today | Year 1 | Year 2 | Year 3 | Year 4 |

* +25 basis point shift in on-the-run yield curve.

Exhibit 19 shows the adjusted tree by shifting the yield curve up by an arbitrarily small number of basis points, 25 basis points, and then adding 35 basis points (the OAS) to each 1-year rate. The adjusted tree is then used to value the bond. The resulting value, V_+, is 101.621. Exhibit 20 shows the adjusted tree by shifting the yield curve down by 25 basis points and then adding 35 basis points to each 1-year rate. The resulting value, V_-, is 102.765.

Therefore, Δy is 0.0025, V_+ is 101.621, V_- is 102.765, and V_0 is 102.218. The effective duration is then

$$\text{Effective duration} = \frac{102.765 - 101.621}{2(102.218)(0.0025)} = 2.24$$

When the binomial model is used to value a security, the values used in the duration formula to calculate effective duration can be used to calculate effective convexity. That is, the same five steps discussed earlier to get the relevant values must be followed. For our hypothetical 4-year callable corporate bond, the effective convexity is:

*Exhibit 20: Determination of V_ for Calculating Effective Duration and Convexity**

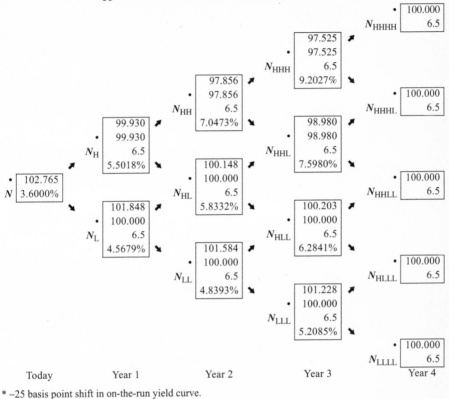

| Today | Year 1 | Year 2 | Year 3 | Year 4 |

* −25 basis point shift in on-the-run yield curve.

$$\text{Effective convexity} = \frac{101.621 + 102.765 - 2(102.218)}{2(102.218)(0.0025)^2} = -39.1321$$

Notice that this callable bond exhibits negative convexity.

Chapter 17

Credit Risk and Embedded Options

V olatility in Treasury yields is the key factor that influences the value of interest rate options. For corporate bonds, the value of an embedded option also depends on the credit risk of the bond issuer, because the issuer's credit quality may change between the time an investor buys a bond and the date of next call or put. The risk of a change in credit quality will affect the probability that an option will be exercised. For example, when a company's credit quality improves, its spreads will narrow and its callable bonds have a greater chance of being redeemed, which increases the value of the call option. Conversely, a decline in a company's credit quality will reduce the value of the option by decreasing the chance of a call. Thus, the value of an embedded option, and its implied volatility, will depend on the risk that spreads will widen or narrow in response to an improvement or deterioration in the issuer's credit quality.

In Chapter 16, we showed that embedded options can be valued using a binomial interest rate model. A key feature of the binomial model is that the value of embedded options depends on yield volatility. To value an option embedded in a corporate bond, we need to model the two components of the corporate bond yield: the Treasury yield plus the corporate yield spread. In Chapter 7, we demonstrated that corporate yield volatility can be attributed to volatility in Treasury yields, volatility in the corporate spread, and to the correlation between Treasury yields and corporate spreads. In this chapter, we maintain the binomial framework for modeling Treasury rates, and we examine how option values are affected by spread volatility that arises from credit risk.

An assumption about credit risk is implicit in most option-pricing models. In this chapter, we show that a model's assumption about credit risk can be translated into an explicit prediction about an issuer's future credit spread. For example, some models implicitly assume that the bond issuer's credit quality will not change over time, and that its future spreads will equal current spreads. Other models assume that credit quality and forward spreads may differ from current levels. In this chapter, we show that these assumptions can give rise to significantly different estimates of option values and implied volatility. In addition, we present an approach to option valuation that depends on the probability of a rating transition.

To illustrate the relationships among credit risk, implied volatility, and option values, this chapter looks at several practical, relatively simple examples of bonds with credit risk. The calculations for the option values are particular to the specific examples of bonds with 10-noncall-5 and 10-put-5 structures. Option values would be different for bonds with different option and maturity structures, and they also depend critically on the forward rates implied by the Treasury yield curve. However, our inferences about the effect of credit risk on option values are generally robust to other common structures in the investment-grade market, such as 30NC10 bonds.

THE EFFECT OF CREDIT RISK ON EMBEDDED OPTIONS

The effect of credit risk is easy to illustrate by way of an example. Let's assume that we have a choice of buying two bonds: a 7% Treasury bond and a 7½% single-A corporate bond. Both bonds are selling at par and both have the same structure: a 10-year maturity with a call option after 5 years, or 10NC5 (see Exhibit 1).

Suppose in 5 years that the yield on 5-year Treasuries falls to 6.5%. In this case, the Treasury would call the 7% bond and refinance at the lower interest rate. Will the single-A company also call its 7.5% bond? To a large measure, the answer depends on the company's credit quality 5 years from now. If the company maintains its single-A rating, then the decline in Treasury yields would likely spur the company to call the bond. However, if the company's credit quality declines, it may not be economical to call the bond because its new issue spread may have widened. For example, if the single-A company's rating falls to BBB or below, the cost of refinancing may be higher than 7.5%. Even if the company maintains its single-A rating, it may not call its bond if corporate spreads widen, in general, over the next 5 years. For example, the company would not call the bond if spreads widen by 100 basis points or more.

The value of an embedded option depends not only on the future path of Treasury rates, but also on the path of the company's yield spreads, which in turn depend on the path of the company's credit quality. In other words, to evaluate a corporate bond option, we need to model not only forward Treasury yields but also the forward credit quality and forward yield spreads of the issuer. In the investment-grade market, the risk of a change in credit quality is not trivial. Based on data from S&P from 1980–1993, there is a 28.57% historical probability that a single-A company will have its rating downgraded over a 5-year period (see Exhibit 2).[1] Moreover, there is a 0.93% probability that a single-A will default.

---

[1] See Leo Brand, Thomas C. Kitto, and Reza Bahar, "1993 Corporate Default Rating Transition Study Results," *Standard & Poor's CreditReview*, May 2, 1994. The data in Exhibit 2 are a transformation of Table 13 in the S&P study. In the S&P transition matrix, 12% to 25% of investment-grade issuers had their rating withdrawn over a 5-year period, due to retirement of all rated debt, completion of an exchange offer, or other reasons. The credit quality of the issuer with a withdrawn rating could have improved, deteriorated, or stayed the same, but it is difficult to know which outcome is more likely without conducting a separate study of issuers with withdrawn ratings. In Exhibit 2, we have distributed the percentage in the withdrawn categories on a market-weighted basis to the other rating categories, but we maintained the S&P default probabilities. Implicitly, this treatment assumes that the transition distribution of the credit quality of withdrawn issuers is the same as the distribution for issuers that maintained their ratings.

Exhibit 1: Bonds with Similar Structures but Different Credit Risks

Issuer	Coupon	Price	Structure	Call Price
Treasury	7.0%	100	10NC5	Par
A Rated Corporate	7.5%	100	10NC5	Par

Exhibit 2: Adjusted 5-Year Rating Transition Probabilities

Rating at Beginning of Period	Rating at End of Five Years							
	AAA	AA	A	BBB	BB	B	CCC	D
AAA	58.47	31.48	6.80	1.75	0.97	0.53	0.00	0.00
AA	3.71	60.19	26.15	5.82	1.65	1.61	0.18	0.70
A	0.22	10.00	61.21	19.79	4.54	2.87	0.44	0.93
BBB	0.59	1.74	22.66	51.03	13.90	5.82	1.59	2.66

ALTERNATIVE METHODS OF VALUING OPTIONS WITH CREDIT RISK

In this section, we present three methods of valuing a call option in a corporate bond. Each method makes different assumptions about the corporate issuer's future credit quality and its future credit spread. In the first method, the option value is estimated under the assumptions that the corporate issuer's credit quality will not change over time and that the issuer's future spread will be the same as the current yield spread. Under the second method, the corporate issuer's credit quality could be upgraded, downgraded, or remain unchanged at the time of the option exercise date, and consequently its spreads could be tighter, wider, or unchanged. Using historical data on rating transition probabilities, the second method prices the option based on the issuer's expected future rating and spread. Under the third method, the option value depends on the issuer's forward spread, which is implied by the current term structure of bullet spreads.

Under each valuation method, we will assume that Treasury yield volatility is 10%. Later, we explore the relationship between implied corporate yield volatility and credit risk.

Method 1: Static Credit Quality and Static Spreads

To illustrate these three methods, let's consider an example of an 8.3%, 10-year, BBB-rated bond with a European call option in 5 years. As shown in Exhibit 3, the BBB company could sell a 5-year bullet bond today at a spread of 85 basis points over the 5-year Treasury. Under the first method of valuing the option, the future spread is assumed to be the same as the current spread on a 5-year bullet, 85 basis points. Given that future spread, and assuming Treasury yield volatility of 10%, the option value is 2.13% of par.[2] The key assumption in this valuation method is that the future spread on a 5-year bond equals the current spread. Implicitly, Method 1 assumes that the BBB company will remain BBB rated in 5 years, and that BBB spreads will not change over time.

Method 2: Credit Quality and Future Spreads Reflect Rating Transition Probabilities

The second method of valuing the option recognizes that a company's credit quality may change over time. In this method, the future spread depends on the company's credit rating. Although the future credit rating of the company is unknown today, we can use the historical data on rating transitions to assign a probability to a rating category. The first row in Exhibit 4 gives the 5-year rating transition probabilities for BBB companies. For example, over a 5-year period, a BBB company has a 0.59% probability of an upgrade to AAA, a 51.03% probability of remaining BBB, and a 2.66% probability of default. The second row of Exhibit 4 gives spreads on 5-year bullets for the rating categories, ranging from 40 basis points for a 5-year AAA to 350 basis points for a 5-year single-B. These bullet spreads are used as proxies for the future spread in valuing the option.

For each rating scenario, the value of the option depends on the future spread on a 5-year new issue, which in turn depends on the company's future credit rating. For example, if the company is upgraded to AAA, the future spread is 40 basis points. Under this scenario, and maintaining the 10% Treasury yield volatility assumption, the option value is 3.02% of par (column 1, row 3). Similarly, if the company remains BBB rated, the future spread is 85 basis points and the option value is 2.13% of par, the same as the value under Method 1 given in Exhibit 3.

Exhibit 3: Call Option Value Estimation Using the Current Spread as the Forward Spread
Bond Description

Coupon	8.30%	Call Date	5 years
Maturity	10 years	Call Type	European
Price	100	Call Price	100

Option Valuation

Treasury Yield Volatility	10%
Current Spread on 5-year Bullet	85 bps
Static Estimate of Spread on a 5-year Bullet, 5 years Forward	85 bps
Estimated Option Value (% of par)	2.13

---

[2] To value the embedded options, we used a one-factor, arbitrage-free term structure model that utilizes the whole yield curve and assumes that the spot interest rate is lognormally distributed. Thus, the value of an embedded option depends partly on the slope of the Treasury yield curve and its implied forward rates. In the examples in this chapter, we used the following assumptions for the Treasury yield curve: 3 months = 5.83%, 6 months = 6.05%, 1 year = 6.33%, 2 years = 6.71%, 3 years = 6.81%, 5 years = 7.01%, and 10 years = 7.10%. This one-factor model is discussed in greater detail in Chapter 7.

Exhibit 4: Call Option Value Estimation Based on Rating Transitions

Bond: 8.3% 10-year BBB rated, European call in 5 years.
Priced at par.
Treasury yield volatility: 10%

	Rating at 5-Year Horizon								
	AAA	AA	A	BBB	BB	B	C	D	
5-Year Rating Transition Probability (%)	0.59	1.74	22.66	51.03	13.90	5.82	1.59	2.66	Estimated
5-Year Bullet Spreads (bps)	40	45	50	85	250	350	NA*	NA*	Option
Option Value (% of par)	3.02	2.90	2.79	2.13	0.31	0.04	0	0	Value
Option Value × Probability	0.02	0.05	0.63	1.09	0.04	0.00	0.00	0.00	1.83

* If the company's rating falls to C or D, the option is assumed to have zero value.

Exhibit 5: Call Option Value Estimation Based on the Implied Forward Spread

Bond: 8.3% 10-year, BBB rated, European call in 5 years.
Priced at par.
Treasury yield volatility: 10%

Spread Curve

3 year	75 bps
5 year	85 bps
10 year	95 bps

Implied 5-year spread, 5 years forward   109 bps

Estimated option value (% of par)   1.71

These estimates agree with our intuition about the relationship between credit risk and option values. The call option has a high value under scenarios where the issuer's rating is upgraded, because the narrowing of spreads in these scenarios increases the value of the option by increasing the probability of exercise. If the company's rating falls to a C or D rating, the analysis assumes the option has zero value. In summary, under Method 2, the value of the option is equal to the expected value under the rating scenarios, weighted by the transition probabilities (row 4). In our example, the option value is 1.83% of par.

Method 3: Credit Quality and Forward Spreads Reflect the Slope of the Bullet Spread Curve

Exhibit 5 presents a third method of valuing the call option, which is based on the forward yield spread.[3] In Method 3, the forward spread is derived from the term structure of bullet spreads. There are a variety of algorithms to estimate forward spreads, ranging from the simple bootstrap procedure to a variety of spline

[3] Forward spreads are covered in Chapter 9.

models.[4] The forward spread shown in the exhibit is estimated from the Merrill Lynch exponential spline model.[5] Specifically, we input the Treasury coupon yield curve into the exponential spline model to estimate zero-coupon spot rates. Similarly, we used the bullet yield curve for the BBB company to estimate its zero-coupon spot rates. Next, we used these spot curves to construct 5-year forward par coupon curves for both the Treasury and the BBB corporate. The forward spread is equal to the difference between the BBB company's forward yield and the Treasury forward yield.

In this framework, the main factor that determines the forward spread is the slope of the spread curve. In general, when the spread curve is upward sloping, forward spreads will be higher than current bullet spreads. In our example, the spread on a 5-year bullet is 85 basis points and the spread on a 10-year bullet is 95 basis points. In the spline model, these bullet spreads imply that the spread on a 5-year bullet, 5 years forward is 109 basis points. Using that 109 basis point forward spread and maintaining the 10% Treasury yield volatility assumption, Exhibit 5 shows that the option value is 1.71% of par.

These three examples illustrate that the value of an embedded call option depends critically on the assumptions about the issuer's future credit quality and yield spreads. The option value is highest under Method 1, which assumes that credit quality will not change and that future spreads equal current spreads. Both Method 2 and Method 3, by contrast, recognize that changes in credit quality can drive a wedge between the issuer's current bullet spreads and its future spreads. Clearly, the assumptions of Method 1 are tenuous, given that investment-grade credit quality varies substantially over time. If a company's credit quality is more likely to follow the path predicted by the forward spread curve or by rating transition probabilities, then Method 1 gives too low an estimate for the future spread and too high an estimate for the value of the call option.

IMPLICATIONS FOR IMPLIED TREASURY YIELD VOLATILITY

It may be helpful to look at these three methods another way. For each method, we calculated the price of the embedded call option using the same assumption about Treasury volatility, but different assumptions about future spreads. We allowed Treasuries to be volatile, but we picked a predetermined level for the future spread. The different levels for the future spreads resulted in different option values. In essence, we changed one variable (the future spread) in the lattice model to solve for one unknown (the option price), but we held all other inputs in the model constant, including Treasury yield volatility.

---

[4] Bootstrapping is illustrated in the appendix to Chapter 5.

[5] See Arnold Shapiro, Eddy van de Wetering, Robin Brenner, Bin Li, and Gerald Lucas, "Merrill Lynch Exponential Spline Model," *Merrill Lynch Fixed Income Product Analysis* (August 8, 1994).

Alternatively, given the price of the option and a future spread, we can reverse engineer the option-pricing methodology to calculate the *implied* Treasury yield volatility. Under this alternative approach, we are again changing one variable (the option price) in the lattice model to solve for one unknown (the implied Treasury volatility), but we are holding all other inputs in the model constant, including the future spread.

For example, using an option value of 1.71% and a future spread of 109 basis points, the implied Treasury volatility is 10% (essentially, Method 3). Now, if we maintain the 109 basis point future spread assumption but raise the option value to 2.13%, the implied volatility rises to 11.49%. With all other factors held constant, the implied volatility must be higher because the option value is higher.

The purpose of these comparisons is to show that an estimate for implied volatility may embody an implicit assumption about future credit quality. Method 1 assumed static spreads and static ratings, which resulted in a high value for the call option (2.13%) and a high probability of exercise. If the future credit quality of the company is more likely to follow the path suggested by forward spreads that are modeled under Method 3, then the value of the option and the probability of exercise would be lower. Using the high option value under Method 1, but maintaining Method 3's more realistic assumption about forward spreads, we found that implied volatility increased. Therefore, the high option value can be traced to either an unrealistic assumption about future spreads or, alternatively, an unrealistic assumption about implied Treasury yield volatility. As with any measure of relative value, a model's estimate of implied volatility is a useful tool only to the extent that investors understand and agree with the model's assumptions.

OPTION VALUES FOR BONDS WITH DIFFERENT CREDIT RISKS

At first glance, intuition would suggest that call options in AAA bonds would have a low value because AAA companies can only get downgraded. The same argument would suggest that call options in BBB bonds would have a high value because the upgrade probability for a BBB company is about equal to the probability of a downgrade (see Exhibit 2). On closer examination, it is less clear whether options are more valuable in BBB or AAA bonds. Although the downgrade risk for BBBs is lower than that for AAAs, a downgrade from BBB to BB or below may widen spreads by 100 basis points or more, which would significantly reduce the chance that the issuer will exercise a call option. For AAA bonds, in contrast, the spread widening associated with a downgrade to AA, A, or even BBB may be relatively mild (e.g., 5 to 50 basis points). Reflecting this asymmetric risk, the term structure of credit spreads for BBB bonds is typically steeper than the spread curve for AAAs. Consequently, the forward spread derived from the bullet curve of BBB bonds is more than proportionately wider than the forward spread for AAAs.

Exhibit 6: Call Option Values for Bonds with Different Credit Ratings and Spread Curves

Issuer	AAA	AA	A	BBB
Yield on 10NC5 Par Bond	7.83	7.88	7.94	8.3
5-year bullet spread	40	45	50	85
10-year bullet spread	45	51	58	95
5-year forward spread	53	60	70	109
Difference between 5-year forward spread and current 5-year bullet	13	15	20	24
Option Value (% of par)	1.95	1.90	1.83	1.71
Treasury Yield Volatility	10.00%	10.00%	10.00%	10.00%
Implied Corporate Yield Volatility	9.32%	9.11%	9.00%	8.69%

Estimated option values are based on the forward spread implied from the bullet spread curve.
Each bond is priced at par with a 10-year final maturity and a European call option at par in the fifth year.
Option values are calculated assuming 10% Treasury yield volatility and forward rates implied by Treasury yields and corporate spreads.
Implied corporate yield volatilities are derived from the value of the options and forward rates implied by Treasury yields and corporate spreads.

Exhibit 6 shows the relationship between credit ratings and option values for 10NC5 bonds priced at par, where the option values are calculated under the forward spread method with 10% Treasury yield volatility. In this example, the spread curve for higher-quality, AAA bonds is relatively flat, with only a 5 basis point difference between 10-year and 5-year bullets (45 and 40 basis points, respectively). The spread curve for lower-quality, BBB bonds is relatively steep, with 10 basis points separating 10-year and 5-year bonds (95 and 85 basis points, respectively). Consequently, as shown in row 4, the 109 basis point forward spread for BBBs is much wider than the 53 basis point forward spread for AAAs. Moreover, the differential between the forward spread and the current bullet spread, shown in row 5, is also greater for issuers with steeper spread curves. Given these forward spreads, the call option value is highest in AAAs (1.95% of par) and lowest in BBBs (1.71% of par). Of course, the lower option value for lower-rated bonds is caused by the forward spread differential, and not by the credit rating, per se.

IMPLICATIONS FOR CORPORATE YIELD VOLATILITY

In the previous analysis, all the options are valued using the same assumption for Treasury yield volatility, 10%. Many investors are accustomed to using corporate yield volatility, rather than Treasury volatility, to evaluate embedded options in corporate bonds. The last row in Exhibit 6 gives the implied corporate yield volatilities for the bonds with different ratings. In estimating these implied volatilities, we are again using the lattice model to solve for one unknown (the implied corporate yield volatility), given a set of inputs (the Treasury yield curve, the corporate spread curve, and the value of the option originally estimated under the assumption of 10% Treasury yield volatility).

For each rating category, the estimates for the implied corporate yield volatility are less than the 10% Treasury yield volatility. In addition, bonds with lower ratings have a lower implied corporate yield volatility than do higher-rated bonds (e.g., the implied corporate yield volatility for the BBB bond is 8.69%, compared with 9.32% for the AAA bond).

These patterns in implied corporate yield volatility reflect two influences. First, because volatility is measured as the *percentage* change in yields, corporate bonds typically have lower yield volatility than Treasuries, simply because corporate yields are higher than Treasury yields.[6] Therefore, because BBB bonds trade at higher yields than AAA bonds, a parallel shift in the yield curve gives rise to a lower *percentage* change in BBB bonds compared with AAA bonds. Second, because the spread curve is steeper for lower-rated bonds than for higher-rated bonds, the probability of exercise is lower for BBBs than for AAAs. Other factors held equal, a steep spread curve gives rise to a relatively low option value and a low implied corporate yield volatility.

THE RELATIONSHIP BETWEEN FORWARD SPREADS AND TRANSITION PROBABILITIES

It is instructive to analyze why Method 2 and Method 3 give different values for embedded options. In our example of the 10NC5 BBB bond, the option value under Method 2 is 1.83% of par, compared with 1.71% under Method 3. Both of these methods assume that credit quality can change over time. Under Method 2, the company's future credit quality is characterized by a probability distribution that is based on historical data on rating transitions. Under Method 3, the rating transition probabilities are not given explicitly; rather, they are embodied in the forward spread. As noted, the forward spread is mainly determined by the slope of the bullet spread curve, which in turn reflects investors' expectations about the risk of a change in the company's credit quality. A steep spread curve, and, therefore, a high forward spread, indicates that investors expect a significant probability of spread widening, most likely accompanied by a high probability of a downgrade. Hence, one reason that Method 2 gives a higher option value than Method 3 is that the historical rating transition probabilities may imply a more favorable outlook for credit quality than the probabilities implied by the forward spread.

To illustrate this effect, Method 2 can be modified to give a more negative outlook for credit quality by simply modifying the transition matrix. Specifically,

---

[6] See Chapter 7.

instead of assuming a 22.66% historical probability of an upgrade from BBB to single A, we may believe the issuer has only a 17.66% chance of an upgrade (Exhibit 7, row 1). Likewise, the modified transition matrix assumes an 18.9% probability of transitioning from BBB to BB, compared with the 13.9% historical probability. Given this more negative outlook, the value of the call option is 1.71% of par, essentially the same as under Method 3, which used the forward spread implied by the bullet spread curve.

Besides the assumption about rating transition probabilities, Method 2 also makes an important assumption about spread levels in the future. In our example, we assumed that if the company remains BBB rated, then its future spread will be 85 basis points, the same as the spread on BBBs today, and we made a similar assumption for each of the rating categories. These assumptions are somewhat tenuous because bullet spreads vary over time. For example, a general widening of spreads over the next 5 years would decrease the value of the option, and spread narrowing would increase its value. If an investor expects spreads to be 5 basis points wider than the spreads in Exhibit 4, then the option value under Method 2 would be 1.72% of par, close to the value under Method 3.

A more fundamental difference between the second and third methods is in the way they treat default risk. Under Method 2, in which default risk is modeled explicitly in terms of the transition probability, the option has no value in the event of default. Under Method 3, default risk is embodied in the 109 basis point forward spread, which reflects a probability that the BBB company may default over the next 5 years. However, the exact probability of default implied by a forward spread is unknown. While a high forward spread may reflect a high expectation of default, it could also be interpreted as reflecting a high probability that spreads will widen, in general, over the next 5 years with only a moderate probability of default.

Exhibit 7: Call Option Value Estimation Using Modified Rating Transition Probabilities

Bond: 8.3% 10-year BBB rated, European call in 5 years.
Priced at par.
Treasury yield volatility: 10%

	Rating at 5-year Horizon								
	AAA	AA	A	BBB	BB	B	C	D	
5-year Modified Rating Transition Probability (%)	0.59	1.74	17.66	51.03	18.90	5.82	1.59	2.66	
5-year Bullet Spreads (bps)	40	45	50	85	250	350	NA*	NA*	Estimated
Option Value (% of par)	3.02	2.90	2.79	2.13	0.31	0.04	0	0	Option Value
Option Value × Probability	0.02	0.05	0.49	1.09	0.06	0.00	0.00	0.00	1.71

* If the company's rating falls to C or D, the option is assumed to have zero value.
Compared with the base-case rating transitions used in Exhibit 4, the modified transitions project a more negative outlook for credit quality. That is, the probability of an upgrade to single-A is 17.66% (versus 22.66% in Exhibit 4), and the probability of a downgrade to BB is 18.9% (versus 13.9% in Exhibit 4).

Exhibit 8: Put Option Value Estimation Based on Rating Transitions

Bond: 7.64% 10-year BBB rated, European put in 5 years.
Priced at par.
Treasury yield volatility: 10%

	Rating at 5-year Horizon								
	AAA	AA	A	BBB	BB	B	C	D	
5-year Rating Transition Probability (%)	0.59	1.74	22.66	51.03	13.90	5.82	1.59	2.66	
5-year Bullet Spreads (bps)	40	45	50	85	250	350	NA*	NA*	Estimated
Option Value	1.82	1.87	1.93	2.41	5.22	7.06	0	0	Option Value
Option Value X Probability	0.01	0.03	0.44	1.23	0.73	0.41	0.00	0.00	2.85

* If the company's rating falls to C or D, the option is assumed to have zero value.

THE EFFECT OF CREDIT RISK ON PUTABLE BONDS

The analysis of putable bonds differs slightly from that of callables. A key difference is that investors take short positions in call options but long positions in put options. From the point of view of the investor, both callable and putable bonds provide some protection against the risk of deteriorating credit quality. When the issuer of a callable bond is downgraded, the investor is harmed by the widening of spreads, but that widening would be partly offset by the fact that the investor's *short* position in the call option will decrease in value. Similarly, when the issuer of a putable bond is downgraded, an investor's loss that results from the widening of spreads will be mitigated by the increased value of the *long* position in the put. In the event of a downgrade of a putable bond, investors may be able to eliminate their exposure to the weakening credit by exercising the put. Because investors value this option, they should be willing to pay more for putable bonds in which the issuer has a moderate degree of credit risk. However, when the risk of default becomes high, the put option may have little value to investors.

Exhibit 8, which examines a 10-year, BBB-rated bond with a European put option in 5 years, illustrates the effect of credit risk on put option values. The analysis uses the rating transition methodology, which we applied earlier to price callable bonds. For example, in the scenario in which the issuer maintains its BBB rating in 5 years, the future spread is 85 basis points and the option value is 2.41% of par. The put has a relatively low value under scenarios when the issuer's credit quality improves, because the narrowing of spreads will reduce the likelihood that investors will want to exercise the put. In the example, if the issuer is upgraded to AA, its spreads would narrow and the put value is 1.87% of par. In contrast, the put becomes more valuable in scenarios when the issuer is downgraded to BB or B, because the option would allow investors to shorten their duration exposure to a company with eroding credit fundamentals. However, should the issuer default, the put would expire worthless. By calculating the value of the put under each rating scenario and weighting these values by the rating transition probabilities, the last row of Exhibit 8 shows that the put value is 2.85% of par.[7]

As in the case of embedded call options discussed earlier, the value of an embedded put option depends on the model's assumption about the issuer's credit risk. In the rating transition method, the future credit rating and future spread is represented by a probability distribution, giving the option value of 2.85% of par in our example. In contrast, had we assumed that the issuer would remain BBB rated, the option value would be 2.41% of par. Hence, failure to recognize the risk of credit migration can lead to mistakes in valuing put options. To look at it another way, failure to account for credit risk can give erroneous estimates of implied volatility.

In the analysis in Exhibit 8, the put bond is viewed as a 10-year bond in which the investor has the option to reduce the final maturity by 5 years. In practice, many investors view put bonds differently; that is, they are viewed as short-term bonds with the option to extend to a longer maturity. Thus, the put bond in the example could be viewed as a 5-year bond in which the investor has a call option on a 5-year bond, 5 years forward. Analytically, it makes no difference whether put bonds are viewed as long-term bonds with options to shorten or as short-term bonds with options to lengthen. Moreover, the three methods of valuing options with credit risk can be easily adapted to either point of view. Putable bond valuation and strategies are discussed in greater detail in Chapter 18.

Exhibit 9 gives the option values for 10PUT5 bonds with different credit ratings. For each bond, the options are priced under the forward spread method with the assumption of 10% Treasury yield volatility. In these calculations, the bullet spreads and implied forward spreads are the same as the spreads in the analysis of the callable bonds in Exhibit 6. In Exhibit 9, put options are most highly valued in the bonds with lower credit ratings (e.g., the put is worth 2.80% of par for the BBB bond compared with 2.71% for the AAA bond). This pattern in put option values contrasts with that of call options in Exhibit 6, where the bonds with lower ratings had lower option values. A steep spread curve and a high forward spread imply a significant risk of credit deterioration, which explains why the put options have a higher value in BBB bonds than in AAA bonds.

The last row of Exhibit 9 displays the implied corporate yield volatility. For each rating category, we solved for the implied corporate yield volatility, given a set of inputs (the Treasury yield curve, the corporate spread curve, and the value of the option originally estimated under the assumption of 10% Treasury yield volatility). Notice that the implied corporate yield volatilities are lower for bonds with lower credit ratings (e.g., 8.63% for BBBs compared with 9.33% for AAAs). Moreover, all of the implied corporate volatilities are lower than the 10% Treasury yield volatility. Thus, although a steep spread curve implies a high risk

---

[7] In Exhibit 8, the putable bond has a 10PUT5 European structure, which is the mirror image of the 10NC5 European structure for the callable bond in Exhibit 4. However, the value of the put option is 2.85%, which is much higher than the 1.83% call option value. The primary reason why the put option has a higher value than the call option is that the analysis assumes an upward-sloping yield curve.

of credit deterioration and higher put value, the effect of credit risk on implied corporate yield volatility is more than offset by the fact that yield volatility is measured in percentage terms.

CONCLUSIONS

Credit risk complicates the valuation of bonds with embedded options. For corporate bonds with call or put options, the probability of exercise depends both on the path of Treasury rates and on the path of the corporate issuer's credit quality and yield spreads. For example, if a company's yield spreads narrow in response to an improvement in credit quality, its call options will increase in value and its put options will decrease in value, other factors held constant. Thus, changes in credit quality will affect option values, even if Treasury rates move as expected.

We have shown that failure to account for credit risk can give rise to serious mistakes in option valuation. We have presented two approaches to modeling the effect of credit risk in embedded options: one that uses historical data on rating transition probabilities and another that uses forward spreads implied by a corporate issuer's bullet spreads. The two approaches will usually give different estimates for the value of an embedded option, as would be expected because one approach is backward-looking and based on aggregate historical data, while the other is forward-looking and based on information that is specific to the corporate issuer. However, to a first approximation, the two methods give similar estimates for the value of embedded options, and either is likely to be more accurate than the alternative of not modeling credit risk.

Exhibit 9: Put Option Values for Bonds with Different Credit Ratings and Spread Curves

Issuer	AAA	AA	A	BBB
Yield on 10NP5 Par Bond	7.16	7.22	7.28	7.64
5-year bullet spread	40	45	50	85
10-year bullet spread	45	51	58	95
5-year forward spread	53	60	70	109
Difference between 5-year forward spread and current 5-year bullet	13	15	20	24
Option Value (% of par)	2.71	2.73	2.79	2.80
Treasury Yield Volatility	10.00%	10.00%	10.00%	10.00%
Implied Corporate Yield Volatility	9.33%	9.13%	9.00%	8.63%

Each bond is priced at par with a 10-year final maturity and a put option at par in the fifth year.
Option values are calculated assuming 10% Treasury yield volatility and forward rates implied by Treasury yields and corporate spreads.
Implied corporate yield volatilities are derived from the value of the options and forward rates implied by Treasury yields and corporate spreads.

Chapter 18

Putable Bonds and Their Role in Corporate Bond Portfolios

I n Chapter 15, we discussed the basic features of putable bonds and how the spread for these structures is quoted in the market. In this chapter we discuss the performance of putable bonds when the Treasury yield curve changes and the strategies employing putable bonds. We begin by reviewing the relationship between putable bond volume and the slope of the yield curve.

PUTABLE BOND VOLUME AND THE SLOPE OF THE YIELD CURVE

Exhibit 1 shows the relationship between the volume of put bonds and the slope of the Treasury curve for the period 1986–1996. The graph reveals a strong negative correlation. Few corporations issued putable bonds when the yield curve steepened dramatically in 1992 and 1993. In fact, in 1993, only one putable bond came to market, the Associates Corporation 7.95% of 2010, putable in 1998. Conversely, putable bonds accounted for a double-digit share of the corporate bond volume in 1989, when the yield curve was very flat or slightly inverted.

Exhibit 2 gives correlation coefficients between the putable bond share of new issue volume and various spreads on the Treasury yield curve. For example, from 1986 to 1996, the correlation between the putable bond share and the spread between 10-year and 2-year Treasuries is −0.53. All of the correlations are reasonably high and statistically significant. They range from −0.54 to −0.24, with most of the correlations clustered around −0.5. This clustering is to be expected because movements along segments of the Treasury yield curve are highly correlated (e.g., a flattening of the 5-year to 2-year Treasury yield spread is usually accompanied by a flattening of the 30-year to 10-year spread).

These correlations should be interpreted as supporting evidence of a relation between putable bond volume and the slope of the curve, but not as a rigorous predictive model because the put bond share can never fall below 0% or rise above 100%, and because the relation may be nonlinear. Nevertheless, the correlation between putable bond issuance and the slope of the curve is high regardless of whether we measure putable bond financing as the dollar volume of issues, the number of issues, or the share of new issue volume.

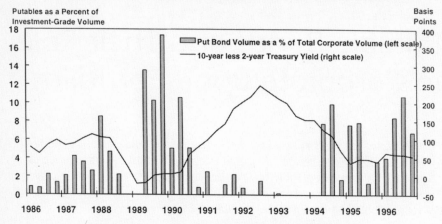

Exhibit 1: Put Bond Volume and the Yield Curve

Exhibit 2: Putable Bond Volume and Treasury Yield Curve Correlations

Treasury Yield Spread	Correlation Between Spread and Put Bond Share of the New Issue Market
30 year less 10 year	−0.424
30 year less 5 year	−0.496
30 year less 3 year	−0.518
30 year less 2 year	−0.520
30 year less 1 year	−0.522
30 year less 6 month	−0.502
30 year less 3 month	−0.486
10 year less 5 year	−0.534
10 year less 3 year	−0.541
10 year less 2 year	−0.535
10 year less 1 year	−0.524
10 year less 6 month	−0.494
10 year less 3 month	−0.468
5 year less 3 year	−0.530
5 year less 2 year	−0.522
5 year less 1 year	−0.505
5 year less 6 month	−0.460
5 year less 3 month	−0.422
3 year less 2 year	−0.497
3 year less 1 year	−0.465
3 year less 6 month	−0.385
3 year less 3 month	−0.326
2 year less 1 year	−0.426
2 year less 6 month	−0.314
2 year less 3 month	−0.245

Exhibit 3: The Relation between the Slope of the Treasury Yield Curve and Putable Bond Spreads

Bullet Spreads
10 year = 60 bps
30 year = 80 bps

Treasury Yields		Treasury Curve Slope	Coupon on a 30PUT10 Bond Issued at Par	Spread to 10-year Treasury	Savings vs. 10-year Bullet at 60 bps
10-year	30-year				
7.00%	7.00%	0 bps	7.32%	32 bps	28 bps
7.00%	7.25%	25 bps	7.42%	42 bps	18 bps
7.00%	7.50%	50 bps	7.42%	49 bps	11 bps
7.00%	7.75%	75 bps	7.54%	54 bps	6 bps
7.00%	8.00%	100 bps	7.57%	57 bps	3 bps

* Spreads are calculated from the Merrill Lynch OAM model, assuming 8% implied volatility.

One reason for the association between a flat curve and heavy putable bond volume is that many corporate issuers view putable bonds as a "cheap" alternative to financing with a shorter-term bullet. By this reasoning, a flat yield curve spurs putable bond issuance because the "savings" from issuing a putable bond is inversely related to the slope of the yield curve.

For example, consider the case of a 30-year bond putable in 10 years (denoted 30PUT10) issued by a high-rated company. Let's assume the company could sell a 10-year bullet at a 60 bps spread and a 30-year bullet at 80 bps. As shown in Exhibit 3, when the Treasury yield curve between 10s and 30s is completely flat, a 30PUT10 bond priced at par would trade at a 32 bps spread to the 10-year Treasury (assuming 7% Treasury yields and 8% implied volatility). Thus, the issuer would "save" 28 bps by issuing the putable bond. However, when the spread between 10-year and 30-year Treasuries is 50 bps, a 30PUT10 bond would be priced at a 49 bps spread to the 10-year Treasury, for a savings of only 11 bps. Accordingly, the savings from issuing a putable bond nearly disappeared in 1993, when the spread between 10s and 30s averaged more than 70 bps.

FORWARD RATES AND PUTABLE BOND VALUATION

Yields on putable bonds are quoted as a spread above a benchmark Treasury yield. As explained in Chapter 15, in practice the pricing of putable bonds can seem confusing because some bonds are quoted as a spread-to-put-date, while other bonds are quoted as a spread-to-maturity. While the price of a putable bond is the same regardless of whether its yield is quoted as a spread-to-put-date or a spread-to-maturity, the choice of quoting as a spread-to-put-date or a spread-to-maturity reveals how investors perceive the benefits of the embedded option. When a bond is quoted as a spread-to-put-date, the investor is viewing the bond as a short-term bond with an option to extend into a longer maturity bond. When a bond is quoted as a spread-to-maturity, then the investor is viewing the bond as a long-term bond with an option to shorten the maturity to the put date.

Putable bonds trade at tighter spreads than bullet bonds of the same issuing company. This is because investors are willing to give up some spread as compensation for the option to shorten the bond's maturity if interest rates rise.

In Chapter 16, we explained how to value a putable bond using the lattice model. The interest rate tree is simply a tree of forward rates. Thus, the value of an embedded put/extension option depends critically on the forward interest rate.

For example, for a 30PUT10 bond, the option value depends on the 20-year forward rate, 10 years forward. That forward rate will increase when interest rates rise in parallel or when the yield curve steepens between 10- and 30-year bonds. A higher forward rate implies that the put option is more valuable, or, equivalently, that the extension option is less valuable. Therefore, when the forward rate rises, the spread on a 30PUT10 will tighten relative to the 30-year Treasury, and the spread will widen relative to the 10-year Treasury.

In the following sections, we show how spreads on putable bonds vary under parallel and nonparallel shifts in the yield curve. The purpose of the analysis is to develop an intuition about how putable bond spreads change when Treasury rates change instantaneously. We analyze three bonds that have the same 30PUT10 structure but different coupon rates: 6.5%, 7.5%, and 8.5%. The analysis is based on the yield curve in March 1996 (10-year Treasury = 6.34%, 30-year Treasury = 6.73%), and it assumes an 8% yield volatility. We assume that the company issuing the putable bond could issue bullet bonds at the following spreads:

> 10-year bullet spread = 60 bps
> 30-year bullet spread = 80 bps

Given these levels for Treasury rates and spreads, the issuer's 20-year forward rate 10 years forward is 8.41%.

Parallel Shifts in the Yield Curve

Below we look at spreads of 30-year bonds putable in 10 years relative to both the 10-year Treasury and the 30-year Treasury.

30PUT10 Spreads to the 10-Year Treasury

Exhibit 4 shows the sensitivity of spreads on 30PUT10 bonds relative to the 10-year Treasury yield. In this case, the 30PUT10 option is viewed as an option to extend from a 10-year bond to a 30-year bond. The extension option becomes more valuable when rates fall. As a result, the spread to the 10-year Treasury will tighten when rates fall and widen when rates rise.

Notice that the spreads are much wider on the 6.5% bond than on the 7.5% and 8.5% bonds. This difference reflects that fact that the extension option for the 6.5% bond is nearly 200 bps out of the money, based on the 8.41% forward rate under the base case.

Exhibit 4: Spreads between 30PUT10 Bonds and 10-Year Treasuries

30PUT10 Coupon	Parallel Yield Curve Shifts				
	−100	−50	0	+50	+100
6.5%	38	48	55	58	59
7.5%	8	26	38	47	53
8.5%	−31	−7	12	27	39
20-Year Forward Rate, 10 years forward	7.30%	7.86%	8.41%	8.98%	9.54%

Exhibit 5: Spreads between 30PUT10 Bonds and 30-Year Treasuries

30PUT10 Coupon	Parallel Yield Curve Shifts				
	−100	−50	0	+50	+100
6.5%	33	17	−1	−19	−38
7.5%	54	44	30	16	0
8.5%	66	59	51	41	29
20-Year Forward Rate, 10 years forward	7.30%	7.86%	8.41%	8.98%	9.54%

High-coupon bonds have the most upside when rates rally (versus a 10-year bullet). Investors who believe that rates are poised to fall should buy put bonds with high coupons and sell 10-year bullet bonds. If rates fall by 50 bps, the spread on the 6.5% bond will tighten by only 7 bps (from 55 bps to 48 bps), while the spread on the 7.5% bond will tighten by 12 bps, and spread on the 8.5% bond will tighten by 19 bps.

If interest rates rise to a very high level, then the extension option will have a very low probability of being exercised. In these circumstances, the extension option will become almost worthless, and the spread on a 30PUT10 bond will converge to the 60 bps spread of a 10-year bullet.

Because of its low coupon, the 6.5% 30PUT10 bond is a defensive bond with limited downside. Even if rates rise by 100 bps, the spread would widen only 4 bps, from 55 to 59 bps. By contrast, the spread on the 7.5% would widen by 15 bps and the spread on the 8.5% would widen by 27 bps.

30PUT10 Spreads to the 30-Year Treasury

In the previous analysis, the 30PUT10 bonds were viewed as 10-year bonds with an option to extend. In Exhibit 5, these same put bonds are analyzed as 30-year bonds with an option to shorten to a 10-year bond. In this framework, the value of the put option increases when rates rise. Therefore, the spreads to the 30-year bond will tighten when rates rise and widen when rates fall. (Notice that the spread movements in Exhibit 4 are opposite to those in Exhibit 5.) As interest rates fall, the put option becomes less valuable, and the spreads will converge toward the 80 bps spread on a 30-year bullet.

Exhibit 6: The Yield Curve Shifts and Putable Bond Spreads
Spreads between 30PUT10 Bonds and 10-Year Treasuries

	Yield Curve Shifts						
	Flattening Rally	Parallel Rally	Steepening Rally	Unchanged	Flattening Rate Rise	Parallel Rate Rise	Steepening Rate Rise
10-Year Shift	−50	−50	−50	0	+50	+50	+50
30-Year Shift	−60	−50	−40	0	+40	+50	+60
30PUT10 Coupon	Spread to 10-Year Treasury						
6.5%	44	48	52	55	57	58	59
7.5%	17	26	32	38	43	47	51
8.5%	−17	−7	3	12	20	27	34
20-year Forward Rate, 10 years forward	7.30%	7.86%	8.12%	8.41%	8.70%	8.98%	9.26%

The spreads on the 8.5% bond are much wider than the spreads on the 6.5% and 7.5% bonds. This difference reflects the fact that the 8.5% coupon is slightly higher than the 20-year forward rate, 10 years forward (8.41%), indicating that the put option is just slightly out of the money. Because the 6.5% and 7.5% coupons are below the forward rate curve, the put options on these bonds are significantly in the money, and their spreads are tighter than the spreads on the 8.5% bond. If, over the next 10 years, market rates move to the level predicted by the forward curve, then investors would exercise the put option on the 6.5% and 7.5% bonds, but would not put the 8.5% bond back to the issuer.

Notice that the spreads on the 8.5% bond are less sensitive to interest rates than are spreads on the 6.5% and 7.5% bonds. For example, if rates rise by 50 bps, the spread on the 8.5% bond will tighten by 10 bps (from 51 to 41 bps), while the spread on the 7.5% bond will tighten by 14 bps, and the 6.5% bond will tighten by 18 bps. Investors who believe that rates are poised to rise should buy low-coupon put bonds and sell 30-year bullets.

Put Bond Spreads and the Slope of the Yield Curve

Exhibit 6 shows how spreads on putable bonds change under nonparallel shifts in the yield curve. For example, suppose that 10-year yields fall by 50 bps and that 30-year yields fall by 40 bps, a steepening rally. Under this scenario, the 8.5% 30PUT10 bond's spread to the 10-year yield would tighten by 9 bps, from 12 bps to 3 bps. By contrast, if yields fell in parallel by 50 bps, then the spread would tighten by 19 bps.

This difference can be traced to the fact that the extension option in a 30PUT10 bond depends on the 20-year forward rate, 10 years forward. Under our steepening rally scenario, the forward rate is falling by only 29 bps, 8.41% to 8.12%. This small change in the forward rate gives rise to a small change in the value of the extension option and only a modest tightening in the yield spread. Because of this dependence on forward rates, the spreads will tighten the most during a flattening rally, and they will widen the most during a steepening sell-off.

Exhibit 7: The Yield Curve Shifts and Putable Bond Spreads Spreads between 30PUT10 Bonds and 30-Year Treasuries

	Yield Curve Shifts						
	Flattening Rally	Parallel Rally	Steepening Rally	Unchanged	Flattening Rate Rise	Parallel Rate Rise	Steepening Rate Rise
10-Year Shift	−50	−50	−50	0	+50	+50	+50
30-Year Shift	−60	−50	−40	0	+40	+50	+60
30PUT10 Coupon	Spread to 10-Year Treasury						
6.5%	24	17	9	−1	−10	−19	−28
7.5%	49	44	37	30	23	16	8
8.5%	63	59	55	51	46	41	34
20-year Forward Rate, 10 years forward	7.30%	7.86%	8.12%	8.41%	8.70%	8.98%	9.26%

The spread could widen under some steepening rally scenarios. For example, if the 10-year yield fell by 50 bps and the 30-year yield decreased by 25 bps, then the forward rate would actually rise from 8.41% to 8.52%. Under this steepening rally scenario (not shown in Exhibit 6), the spread on the 8.5% 30PUT10 bond would widen from 12 bps to 16 bps.

Exhibit 7 shows how nonparallel shifts in the curve will affect the spread to the 30-year Treasury. As expected, these spread movements are opposite to those in Exhibit 6, which focused on the spread to the 10-year Treasury. When an investor sells a 30-year bullet and buys a 30PUT10 bond, the put bond performs best in a steepening sell-off and worse in a flattening rally.

For example, if the 10-year Treasury rate rises by 50 bps and the 30-year rate rises by 60 bps, then the spread on the 6.5% 30PUT10 bond would tighten by 29 bps (from −1 bp to −28 bps). By contrast, the spread would tighten by 20 bps under a 50 bps parallel sell-off, and by only 11 bps under a flattening sell-off. These differences can be traced to the fact that the value of the put option depends on the 20-year forward rate, which rises more under a steepening sell-off than under a flattening sell-off.

VOLATILITY

Up to this point, we have held implied volatility constant at 8%. In Exhibits 8 and 9, we show the sensitivity of putable bond spreads to changes in volatility. The analysis uses the base-case Treasury yield curve (10-year = 6.34%, 30-year = 6.73%) and base-case bullet spreads (10-year = 60 bps, 30-year = 80 bps).

Exhibit 8 shows how changes in implied volatility affect the spread to the 10-year Treasury. For low-coupon bonds, changes in volatility have a small affect on spreads. For example, for the 6.5% 30PUT10 bond, a 1% change in volatility (e.g., from 6% to 7%) will result in a 3 bps tightening of the spread to the 10-year Treasury (from 60 bps to 57 bps). For the high-coupon 8.5% bond, in contrast, a

1% increase in volatility would result in a 5 bps tightening. The spread on the high-coupon bond is more sensitive to volatility because the extension option is approximately at the money.

Exhibit 9 shows the relation between implied volatility and the spread to the 30-year Treasury. These spreads also tighten when volatility increases. Remember, an investor that owns a 30PUT10 bond is long an option. The bond can be viewed as a 30-year bond with an option to shorten (Exhibit 14) or as a 10-year bond with an extension option (Exhibit 8). In either case, the value of the option increases with implied volatility.

STRATEGIES WITH PUTABLE BONDS

In the remainder of this chapter we discuss two strategies employing putable bonds: market directional strategies and duration-neutral strategies.

Market Directional Strategies with Putable Bonds

Putable bonds can be used as part of a strategy to position a portfolio for changes in market rates. The most basic strategy is to swap into long-duration securities when rates are expected to fall and to move to shorter-duration securities when rates are expected to rise. For a putable bond with a 30PUT10 structure, its duration will lie in between that of a 10-year bullet and a 30-year bullet:

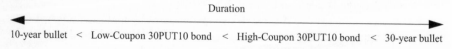

Duration

10-year bullet < Low-Coupon 30PUT10 bond < High-Coupon 30PUT10 bond < 30-year bullet

Exhibit 8: Implied Volatility and Putable Bond Spreads between 30PUT10 Bonds and 10-Year Treasuries

30PUT10 Coupon	Implied Volatility				
	6%	7%	8%	9%	10%
6.5%	60	57	55	51	48
7.5%	47	43	38	34	29
8.5%	23	18	12	7	2

Exhibit 9: Implied Volatility and Putable Bond Spreads between 30PUT10 Bonds and 30-Year Treasuries

30PUT10 Coupon	Implied Volatility				
	6%	7%	8%	9%	10%
6.5%	2	1	−1	−3	−4
7.5%	36	33	30	28	25
8.5%	58	54	51	48	45

Exhibit 10: Market Directional Putable Bond Strategies

Market View	Swap	Coupon
Lower Rates	Buy 30PUT10 Sell 10-Year Bullets	High-Coupon Putable
Lower Rates	Buy 10-Year Bullets Sell 30PUT10	Low-Coupon Putable
Lower Rates	Buy 30PUT10 Sell 30PUT10	High Coupon Low Coupon
Higher Rates	Buy 10-Year Bullets Sell 30PUT10	High-Coupon Putable
Higher Rates	Buy 30PUT10 Sell 10-Year Bullets	Low-Coupon Putable
Higher Rates	Buy 30PUT10 Sell 30PUT10	Low Coupon High Coupon

Exhibit 10 gives the recommended swaps under alternative assumptions about the direction of forward interest rates.

Duration-Neutral Putable Bond Strategies

The portfolio strategies in Exhibit 10 assume that investors have a strong view about the direction of interest rates. For example, when interest rates are expected to fall, an investor may swap from a 10-year bullet into a 30PUT10 bond. With those same expectations of falling rates, an investor might swap from a 30PUT10 bond into a 30-year bullet bond. We believe that it is more suitable to view portfolio strategies with putable bonds as strategies about interest rate volatility and convexity, rather than about the direction of rates.

Volatility and Convexity Analysis

The duration of putable bonds shortens when interest rates rise and lengthens when rates fall. By definition, these changes in duration indicate that putable bonds have positive convexity. Positive convexity is a good thing for a fixed-income portfolio, provided that it can be obtained at a reasonable cost. The implied volatility on a putable bond is a measure of that cost.

Implied volatilities on putables have typically ranged from 6% to 9%. Swaption implied vols can be used as a gauge for the fair value of putable implied vols. As shown in Exhibit 11, the swaption vol curve is downward sloping. For example, a 5-year/5-year swaption (comparable to a 10PUT5 bond) has an implied vol of 17%, while the implied vol on a 10-year/20-year swaption (30PUT10) is 12.2%. By contrast, the volatility curve for putable bonds has been relatively flat at around 8% or lower, regardless of structure. Given that flat vol curve, the best values in the putable market can be found in structures with short put dates and short maturities, such as 10PUT5 bonds.

Because they trade at low vols, many investors have overweighted putable bonds as a way to buy convexity cheaply and enhance returns. As the market becomes more efficient, implied volatilities on putable bonds should rise over time, but we do not expect putable vols will ever converge to swaption vols. First, a significant number of investors still do not buy putable bonds because they concentrate on the yield give-up relative to a bullet, rather than the return pickup if rates are volatile. Second, swaption vols should be higher than putable vols because volatility is measured as the *percentage* change in yields. Because corporate yields are higher than swap yields, a given percentage change in swap yields usually results in a smaller percentage change in corporate yields, even accounting for spread volatility and spread correlation (see Chapter 7).

High-Coupon/Low-Coupon Putable Bond Strategy

Low implied volatilities suggest that it is less costly to take a long position in convexity with putable bonds than it is with most alternative fixed-income securities. To capture the cheap convexity in putable bonds, we recommend that investors buy putables as part of a duration-neutral strategy. The cleanest way to capture the convexity advantage is with a strategy that combines high-coupon and low-coupon putable bonds.

For example, Exhibit 12 presents a portfolio with two putable bonds as of August 1996: Waste Management Inc. (WMX) 7.1% of 2026, putable in 2003, and Joseph Seagram & Sons (VO) 9.65% of 2018, also putable in 2003. The value of the embedded put options in these bonds depends on the volatility of forward rates. In the case of the WMX 7.1% bond, the value of its embedded put option depends on the 23-year rate, 7 years forward. Investors will put the bond if the 23-year bullet rate is above 7.1%, but investors will extend if the 23-year rate is below 7.1%. When the analysis was performed in August 1996, the 23-year forward rate for WMX was 8.38%, indicating that the WMX 7.1% bond will be put in 2003 unless that market rallies by at least 128 bps against forward rates.

The value of the put option in the VO 9.65% bond also depends on forward rates that begin in 2003. Because of its high coupon, the put option in the VO 9.65% is more than 100 basis points out of the money based on forward rates. Thus, if interest rates move to forwards, the VO 9.65% bond will extend to a 2018 maturity, while the WMX 7.1% bond will be put. At the time of the analysis, the implied volatilities on the WMX and VO put bonds were 7% and 6%, respectively. By contrast, 7-by-23 swaption vol was around 11%.

Exhibit 11: Mid-Market Swaption Implied Volatilties

	Swaption Expiry Date				
Swap into	2 yr	3 yr	5 yr	7 yr	10 yr
5 yr	18.5	18.0	17.0	16.2	15.0
10 yr	16.7	16.2	15.2	14.7	13.2
15 yr	15.7	15.2	14.2	13.7	12.5
20 yr	15.0	14.5	13.5	13.2	12.2

Data as of December 5, 1996

Exhibit 12: Return Difference between a Putable Portfolio and a Bullet Portfolio (1-Year Horizon)

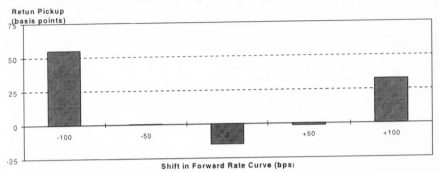

Putable Portfolio	Dollar Duration Weight	Bullet Portfolio	Dollar Duration Weight
WMX 7.1% 2026PUT2003	0.5	WMX 6⅜% 2003	0.65
VO 9.65% 2018PUT2003	0.5	VO 8.35% 2022	0.35

In Exhibit 12, we show the 1-year total returns of a portfolio that contains the WMX and VO put bonds and a portfolio of two bullet bonds: the WMX 6⅜% of 2003 and the VO 8.35% of 2022. The portfolios are constructed such that they will have the same expected option-adjusted durations at the 1-year horizon (6.9), and both portfolios have roughly equivalent exposure to WMX and VO credit risk. If interest rates move to levels predicted by the forward curve, the return on the putable portfolio is 6.32%, compared with 6.47% for the bullet portfolio. Thus, with no volatility in forward rates, putables will underperform bullets by 15 bps over the 1-year horizon.

However, because the portfolio of putable bonds has greater convexity, the return difference will favor the putables in a volatile rate environment, regardless of whether rates move higher or lower. For example, if rates rise or fall by 100 bps over the next year, the portfolio of putable bonds will outperform the bullet portfolio by 33 to 55 bps, respectively. For a 50 bps change in yields, the portfolios will have roughly equal returns. Therefore, investors should prefer the putable portfolio over the bullet portfolio if they expect that yields will continue to be volatile, but are uncertain about the direction of rates.

The convexity difference between the putable portfolio and the bullet portfolio can be demonstrated with an analysis of duration drift. Effectively, convexity measures the drift in duration as interest rates change. As shown in Exhibit 13, if rates rise by 100 bps over the 1-year horizon, then the duration of all four bonds will shorten. All four bonds have positive convexity. However, the rise in rates would cause the option-adjusted duration of the VO 9.65% putable bond to shorten markedly, from 8.64 to 6.37 over a 1-year horizon. As a result, in the rising rate scenario, the putable portfolio will shorten to 5.6, while the bullet portfolio will shorten to 6.52, a difference in duration drift of 0.93.

Exhibit 13: Duration Drift Analysis (1-Year Horizon)

Horizon	Putable Bond Durations at Horizon		Bullet Bond Durations at Horizon		Portfolio Durations		
Change in Yields	VO 9.65% of 2018PUT03	WMX 7.1% of 2026PUT03	VO 8.35% of 2022	WMX 6⅜% of 2003	Put Portfolio	Bullet Portfolio	Difference
−100	9.84	8.01	11.17	5.09	8.93	7.22	1.71
−50	9.25	6.01	10.82	5.06	7.63	7.08	0.55
0	8.21	5.47	10.48	5.03	6.84	6.94	−0.10
+50	7.26	4.99	10.15	5.01	6.13	6.81	−0.68
+100	6.37	4.82	9.38	4.98	5.60	6.52	−0.93
Option-Adjusted Duration (in August 1996)	8.64	6.08	10.76	5.66	7.36	7.45	−0.09
Portfolio Weight	0.5	0.5	0.35	0.65			

All durations are option-adjusted.

By contrast, if rates fall by 100 bps over the 1-year horizon, the durations of all four bonds will lengthen relative to the base case that rates move to forwards. However, a 100 bps decline in rates would cause the duration of the WMX 7.1% putable bond to lengthen dramatically, from 6.08 to 8.01 over the investment horizon. In the falling rate scenario, the duration of the putable portfolio will extend to 8.93, compared with 7.22 for the bullet portfolio, a difference of 1.71.

This example highlights why investors have become eager to buy putable bonds. Many investors are uncertain about the direction of interest rates, but most investors believe that interest rates will be volatile. As long as interest rates remain volatile, portfolios that contain putable bonds will earn higher returns than portfolios that contain bullet bonds with the same duration, but less convexity.

Index

Index

322   Index